SELF-EFFICACY, ADAPTATION, AND ADJUSTMENT

THEORY, RESEARCH, AND APPLICATION

THE PLENUM SERIES IN
SOCIAL/CLINICAL PSYCHOLOGY
Series Editor: C. R. Snyder
University of Kansas
Lawrence, Kansas

SELF-EFFICACY, ADAPTATION, AND ADJUSTMENT

THEORY, RESEARCH, AND APPLICATION

EDITED BY

JAMES E. MADDUX

George Mason University
Fairfax, Virginia

PLENUM PRESS • NEW YORK AND LONDON

Library of Congress Cataloging-in-Publication Data

Self-efficacy, adaptation, and adjustment : theory, research, and
application / edited by James E. Maddux.
      p.   cm. -- (The Plenum series in social/clinical psychology)
   Includes bibliographical references and index.
   ISBN 0-306-44875-0
   1. Adjustment disorders. 2. Self-efficacy. 3. Adaptability
(Psychology) 4. Adjustment (Psychology)   I. Series.
   [DNLM: 1. Adaptation, Psychological. 2. Volition. 3. Self
Concept. 4. Internal-External Control. 5. Mental Disorders-
-therapy. 6. Health Behavior.   BF 637.S38 S465 1995]
   RC455.4.S87S45 1995
   155.2'4--dc20
   DNLM/DLC
   for Library of Congress   95-3668
                                                           CIP

ISBN 0-306-44875-0

©1995 Plenum Press, New York
A Division of Plenum Publishing Corporation
233 Spring Street, New York, N.Y. 10013

10 9 8 7 6 5 4 3 2 1

CONTRIBUTORS

ALBERT BANDURA, Department of Psychology, Stanford University, Stanford, California 94305

NANCY BETZ, Department of Psychology, Ohio State University, Columbus, Ohio 43210

VIRGINIA BLAIR, Department of Psychology, George Mason University, Fairfax, Virginia 22030

ANGELA BOYKIN, Department of Psychology, George Mason University, Fairfax, Virginia 22030

LAWRENCE BRAWLEY, Department of Kinesiology, University of Waterloo, Waterloo, Ontario, Canada N2L 3G1

SHIRLEY BROWN, Department of Psychology, Rutgers University, New Brunswick, New Jersey 08903

CARLO C. DICLEMENTE, Department of Psychology, University of Houston, Houston, Texas 77204

CRAIG K. EWART, School of Public Health, Johns Hopkins University, Baltimore, Maryland 21205

SCOTT FAIRHURST, Department of Psychology, University of Houston, Houston, Texas 77204

GAIL HACKETT, Division of Psychology in Education, Arizona State University, Tempe, Arizona 85287

IRVING KIRSCH, Department of Psychology, University of Connecticut, Storrs, Connecticut 06269

JOHN LEWIS, Department of Psychology, George Mason University, Fairfax, Virginia 22030

JAMES E. MADDUX, Department of Psychology, George Mason University, Fairfax, Virginia 22030

LISA J. MEIER, Department of Psychology, George Mason University, Fairfax, Virginia 22030

ANN O'LEARY, Department of Psychology, Rutgers University, New Brunswick, New Jersey 08903

CHRISTOPHER PETERSON, Department of Psychology, University of Michigan, Ann Arbor, Michigan 48109

NANCY PIOTROWSKI, Department of Psychology, University of Houston, Houston, Texas 77204

DALE M. SCHUNK, Department of Educational Studies, Purdue University, West Lafayette, Indiana 47907

S. LLOYD WILLIAMS, Department of Psychology, Lehigh University, Bethlehem, Pennsylvania 18105

STEVEN ZACCARO, Department of Psychology, George Mason University, Fairfax, Virginia 22030

MICHELLE ZAZANIS, Department of Psychology, George Mason University, Fairfax, Virginia 22030

PREFACE

Since the publication of Albert Bandura's landmark 1977 *Psychological Review* article "Self-Efficacy: Toward a Unifying Theory of Behavior Change," the term "self-efficacy" has become ubiquitous in psychology and related fields. Hundreds of articles on self-efficacy have been published in journals devoted to the subfields of psychology—including social, personality, clinical, health, and industrial/organizational—and in the related fields of public health, medicine, nursing, and business administration. Some of these articles have tested various aspects of self-efficacy theory, while others have examined the application of self-efficacy theory to various practical problems, and others have simply mentioned self-efficacy somewhere in the introduction or discussion, as if trying to hitch a ride on a passing bandwagon. Keeping up with this growing body of literature—not to mention the literature on other topics relevant to perceived competence and control—can be a full-time job. This volume offers some relief to overwhelmed researchers and scientifically oriented practitioners (clinical and otherwise) by providing reviews of the research on most of the most important topics concerned with the relationship between self-efficacy and adaptation and adjustment.

Although more than a sampler of self-efficacy research, this volume is not a handbook on self-efficacy. The list of topics is selective, not exhaustive. The initial chapter list included about two dozen topics. My familiarity with the research on self-efficacy suggested at that time that there were a number of topics that would be of interest to researchers and practitioners, but that simply had not been the subject of a sufficient number of empirical studies to warrant chapter-length treatment. In the intervening years, several of the topics on the initial list have been given sufficient attention to warrant their inclusion were I drawing up the list today. Perhaps a second edition some time in the future will fill the gaps left by this volume. Also, as is always the case with edited volumes, several topics included in the final plan for the book were, for various reasons, later withdrawn. I especially regret the omission of chapters on pain control and organizational and management issues. Unforeseeable circumstances in their lives made it necessary for the authors of these chapters to withdraw reluctantly from the project. Their contributions are missed, and I hope all is well with them now.

The title of this volume reflects the two major assumptions that guided its development and the writing of the individual chapters. The first is that beliefs about personal control and mastery are essential for psychological adaptation and adjustment. In this volume, psychological adaptation and adjustment are defined broadly and go beyond the traditional clinical notion of the absence of mental disorder or dysfunction. Effective adaptation and sound psychological adjustment also require good physical health and effective functioning in the major life domains of work (for adults) and school (for children). Chapter 2 discusses this first assumption in detail, and the other chapters deal with specific aspects of adaptation and adjustment.

The second and more general assumption is that theory, research, and application (clinical and otherwise) are inextricably linked, an assumption that also guides the series in which this volume appears. Thus, this book is intended for both the researcher concerned with basic issues in social cognition (especially the self and self-regulation) and for the practitioner interested in remaining informed about the empirical foundations of psychological interventions. Although surveys suggest that the scientific practitioner is a breed rarer than most of us wish (Cohen, Sargent, & Sechrest, 1986; Morrow-Bradley & Elliot, 1986), I hope this volume will convince a few skeptical practitioners that a theory well-grounded in research can provide useful guidelines for designing effective interventions for the clinic, the classroom, and daily life.

This volume is organized into five sections. Part I offers an introduction to self-efficacy theory and research and discusses some important conceptual issues. Part II describes applications in clinical psychology; Part III, applications in health psychology; and Part IV, various other applications. Part V consists of commentary chapters by Irving Kirsch, Albert Bandura, and me.

The introductory chapter in Part I provides an overview of self-efficacy theory and a review of research on several important general theoretical issues. The chapter also attempts to make some connections between self-efficacy theory and related constructs concerned with personal control and mastery. To avoid unnecessary redundancy, I asked the other contributors to *not* include in their chapters lengthy introductions to self-efficacy theory. These chapters, therefore, do not provide overviews of self-efficacy theory that would be found at the beginning of journal articles or chapters on self-efficacy that have appeared in other volumes not devoted specifically to self-efficacy theory. For this reason, readers not familiar with self-efficacy theory should read the introductory chapter before the chapters on specific applications. I also hope that readers familiar with self-efficacy will find the introductory chapter to be a useful review of general conceptual issues.

Parts II and III reflect the fact that most of the research conducted by psychologists on the application of self-efficacy theory to problems of adjustment has been concerned with either traditional "clinical" disorders or "mental health" (e.g., anxiety, depression) or topics from health psychology (e.g., prevention, stress). However, the field called "clinical psychology" has become increasingly difficult to define over the past two decades. As we have learned more about the generality of psychological change processes, the relationship between normal development and maladaptation, and the biological basis of behavioral and emotional problems, the boundaries between clinical psychology and other subfields have become more and more blurred. In particular, because psychological and medical theorists, researchers, and practitioners have come to acknowledge the close relationship between physical health and psychological well-being, the line between clinical and health psychology has become fuzzy at best. Thus, this division is made in this volume merely to provide an organizational scheme and is not an endorsement of the traditional dichotomy between mental health/illness and physical health/illness.

In fact, the partitioning of this book into sections called "clinical" and otherwise is done largely for convenience and is not an endorsement of the traditional and rigid boundaries between subfields of psychology or the traditional distinction between so-called "clinical" and "nonclinical" problems and populations. As discussed in Chapter 2, the social cognitive approach that provides the conceptual foundation for this volume rejects the partitioning of human behavior into "healthy" and "dysfunctional" categories. Nonetheless, the problems of adaptation and adjustment discussed in Part II—anxiety, depression, and various addictive behavior problems (smoking, alcoholism, drug abuse, and eating disorders)—fall within the realm of traditional "clinical" problems and are among the most commonly encountered in traditional clinical settings. In fact, Bandura's initial studies of self-efficacy were conducted with individuals complaining of fear and avoidance behavior that would probably meet the criteria for clinical phobic disorders.

In Part II, Chapter 2 presents a general social cognitive approach to understanding adjustment and problems of adjustment and a more specific approach based on self-efficacy theory and research. Thus, the reader is encouraged to begin with Chapter 2. Chapters 3, 4, and 5 then present theory and research on the use of self-efficacy in understanding anxiety and phobic disorders, depression, and addictive behaviors, respectively.

Several topics that do not fit into either of these two major categories—career and vocational choice, education and instruction, and collective efficacy—have been placed together in a section of "other applications." This appellation is not intended to imply that these topics are more peripheral or less important than those included in the clinical and health sections. Few decisions have as great an impact on psychological adjustment and well-being as one's choice of vocation or career. Few experiences have as great an impact on the development of a child's personal competence and control beliefs as his or her academic successes and failures. And few issues are more important to the development of a healthy and effective society than our shared beliefs about our ability to get things done collectively, whether in businesses, charitable organizations, or governments.

Part V contains three commentary chapters. In the first, Irving Kirsch, rather than commenting on each individual chapter, addresses an important conceptual issue—the relationship between self-efficacy beliefs and outcome expectancies. Albert Bandura responds with a commentary addressing the conceptual issues raised by Kirsch. My closing brief commentary is an attempt to find common ground on the major issues on which Kirsch and Bandura seem to be in strong disagreement.

I asked the contributing authors to use the writing of their chapters as an opportunity for not only presenting reviews of their work and the relevant work of other people, but also for helping to set an agenda for future research on their specific topics. I think they have succeeded well in this regard. I think they also have succeeded in presenting their material in a clear, succinct, and lively manner. I am especially pleased with the attention they devoted to practical applications. They made my job as editor easier than I expected. I am grateful for their efforts, their cooperation, and their willingness to conform to some of my editorial idiosyncrasies. I am also grateful to Irving Kirsch and Albert Bandura for taking time from their other many projects to prepare their commentary chapters.

I am also grateful to my friend and colleague Lawrence Brawley at the University of Waterloo, Angela Boykin and John Lewis of George Mason University's clinical program, and one former student, Dr. Lisa Meier—one of the finest scientist-practitioners with whom I have worked in almost 15 years in clinical training programs. Without their help, I would never have been able to complete my own chapters in addition to serving as editor. I am especially grateful to Larry for agreeing to join me as coauthor of the "self-efficacy and healthy behavior" chapter halfway through the writing of it, after I had been struggling with it for many months. Rick Snyder, the editor of this series, has been a helpful guide throughout this project and gave me the encouragement I needed to turn a brief "idea" letter into a full prospectus.

Four people in the Department of Psychology at George Mason University deserve special mention for the support they gave largely just by being my friends: Susanne Denham, John Riskind, June Tangney, and Steve Zaccaro. I'm lucky to have colleagues who are both fine scholars and terrific people.

Finally, I owe a special "thanks" to Albert Bandura, the intellectual "godfather" of this project. His work serves as the foundation for almost every sentence of every chapter. In addition, a number of the contributors have worked with him personally. I wish I could say I was among them, for I have admired the man's work since I took my first psychology course in 1973. Largely because of the Bandura and Walters "Bobo doll" studies, I became a social learning theorist at age 19. My second epiphany came in the summer of 1977, at the end of my first year of clinical training, when I read the 1977 *Psychological Review* article. Thoreau once said, "How many a man has dated a new era in his life from the reading of a book!" My new era began with the reading of that article. That in our occasional correspondence we are "Al" and "Jim" is something the 19-year-old that remains in me still finds a little hard to believe.

JAMES E. MADDUX

Washington, D.C.

REFERENCES

Bandura, A. (1977). Self-efficacy: Toward a unifying theory of behavioral change. *Psychological Review, 84*, 191–215.

Cohen, H., Sargent, M. M., & Sechrest, L. B. (1986). Use of psychotherapy research by professional psychologists. *American Psychologist, 41*, 198–206.

Morrow-Bradley, C., & Elliot, R. (1986). Utilization of psychotherapy research by practicing psychotherapists. *American Psychologist, 34*, 17–34.

CONTENTS

Chapter 3

Self-Efficacy and Anxiety and Phobic Disorders 69

S. Lloyd Williams

Chapter 4

Self-Efficacy and Addictive Behaviors 109

Carlo C. DiClemente, Scott K. Fairhurst,
   and Nancy A. Piotrowski

Chapter 5

Self-Efficacy and Depression 143

James E. Maddux and Lisa J. Meier

PART III. APPLICATIONS IN HEALTH PSYCHOLOGY

Chapter 6

Self-Efficacy and Healthy Behavior: Prevention, Promotion,
and Detection 173

James E. Maddux, Lawrence Brawley, and Angela Boykin

Chapter 7

Self-Efficacy and Recovery from Heart Attack: Implications for a
Social-Cognitive Analysis of Exercise and Emotion 203

Craig K. Ewart

Chapter 8

Self-Efficacy and the Physiological Stress Response 227

Ann O'Leary and Shirley Brown

PART IV.   OTHER APPLICATIONS

Chapter 9

Self-Efficacy and Career Choice and Development 249

Gail Hackett and Nancy Betz

Chapter 10

Self-Efficacy and Education and Instruction 281

Dale M. Schunk

Chapter 11

Collective Efficacy 305

Steven Zaccaro, Virginia Blair, Christopher Peterson,
and Michelle Zazanis

PART V. COMMENTARY

PART I

INTRODUCTION

CHAPTER 1

SELF-EFFICACY THEORY
AN INTRODUCTION

James E. Maddux

In the course of even the most ordinary lives, people face an infinite number of decisions, problems, and challenges. Despite the statistics on the prevalence of emotional and behavioral dysfunction, most people most of the time are able to effectively make decisions, solve problems, and overcome challenges. Understanding how people adapt and adjust to life's infinite challenges is, perhaps, the most important problem for scientific psychology. Not surprisingly, most of the important models of human learning, cognition, emotion, personality, and social interaction have tried to account for the individual's capacity for adaptively responding to environmental changes, often referred to as *competence* (e.g., Sternberg & Kolligan, 1990; White, 1959). The study of beliefs about personal competence and the role of such beliefs in human adaptation and adjustment have a long history in clinical, personality, and social psychology. The theories of effectance motivation (White, 1959), achievement motivation (McClelland, Atkinson, Clark, & Lowell, 1953), social learning (Rotter, 1966), and helplessness (Abramson, Seligman, & Teasdale, 1978) are just a few of the many theories that have sought to explore and explain the relationship between perceptions of personal competence and adaptation, adjustment, and psychological well-being.

JAMES E. MADDUX • Department of Psychology, George Mason University, Fairfax, Virginia 22030.

Self-Efficacy, Adaptation, and Adjustment: Theory, Research, and Application, edited by James E. Maddux. Plenum Press, New York, 1995.

Self-efficacy theory (Bandura, 1977, 1982b, 1986) is one of the more recent in a long tradition of personal competence or efficacy theories and has generated more research in clinical, social, and personality psychology in the past decade and a half than other such models and theories. The crux of self-efficacy theory is that the initiation of and persistence at behaviors and courses of action are determined primarily by judgments and expectations concerning behavioral skills and capabilities and the likelihood of being able to successfully cope with environmental demands and challenges. Self-efficacy theory also maintains that these same factors play an important role in psychological adjustment and dysfunction and in effective therapeutic interventions for emotional and behavioral problems.

This volume examines the role of self-efficacy beliefs and related influences in human adaptation and adjustment. Because human beings face varied challenges to their adaptation, this volume defines adaptation broadly and does not limit the term to traditional pathology-based categories or to problems of traditional "clinical" concern, although such problems are addressed. This first chapter describes self-efficacy theory and its place in a more general social cognitive theory. The second chapter offers a more detailed discussion of the role of self-efficacy in human adaptation and adjustment and some general guidelines for enhancing adaptation and adjustment using self-efficacy theory. The remaining chapters discuss in detail theory and research on the application of self-efficacy theory to specific spheres of adjustment, including topics from clinical psychology, health psychology, educational psychology, and organizational psychology. Because self-efficacy theory is an aspect of a more general *social cognitive theory*, this more general framework will be described before presenting self-efficacy theory in detail.

SOCIAL COGNITIVE THEORY

Social cognitive theory is an approach to understanding human cognition, action, motivation, and emotion that assumes that people are capable of self-reflection and self-regulation and that they are active shapers of their environments rather than simply passive reactors to them. Although the notions of volition and freedom in human behavior have generated some controversy (e.g., Howard & Conway, 1986; Williams, 1992), they are essential ideas in social cognitive theory, which makes the following specific assumptions (Bandura, 1986, 1989).

1. People have powerful *symbolizing* capabilities that allow for creation of internal models of experience, the development of innovative

courses of action, the hypothetical testing of such courses of action through the prediction of outcomes, and the communication of complex ideas and experiences to others.

2. Most behavior is *purposive* or *goal-directed* and is guided by *forethought* (anticipating, predicting, etc.). This capacity for intentional behavior is dependent on the capacity for symbolizing.

3. People are *self-reflective* and capable of analyzing and evaluating their own thoughts and experiences. These metacognitive, self-reflective activities set the stage for self-control of thought and behavior.

4. People are capable of *self-regulation* by influencing direct control over their own behavior and by selecting or altering environmental conditions that, in turn, influence their behavior. People adopt personal standards for their behavior, evaluate their behavior against these standards, and thus create their own incentives that motivate and guide behavior.

5. People learn *vicariously* by *observing* other people's behavior and its consequences. Vicarious learning through observation greatly reduces people's dependency on trial-and-error learning and allows for the rapid learning of complex skills that would not be possible if people learned only by taking action and directly experiencing the consequences of their own behavior.

6. The previously mentioned capacities for symbolization, self-reflection, self-regulation, and vicarious learning are the result of the evolution of complex neurophysiological mechanisms and structures. Physiological and experiential forces interact to determine behavior and provide it with tremendous plasticity.

7. Environmental events, inner personal factors (cognition, emotion, and biological events), and behavior are mutually interacting influences. Thus, people respond cognitively, affectively, and behaviorally to environmental events; but, more important, through cognition they also exercise control over their own behavior, which then influences not only the environment but also cognitive, affective, and biological states. This principle of *triadic reciprocal causation* or *triadic reciprocality* is, perhaps, the most important assumption of social cognitive theory. Although these influences are reciprocal, they are not necessarily simultaneous or of equal strength. In other words, everything is not influencing everything else equally and at the same time. However, a complete understanding of human behavior in any situation requires an understanding of all three sources of influence—cognition, behavior, and environmental events. Bandura (1989) also has referred to this framework as a model of *emergent interactive agency*.

SOCIAL COGNITIVE THEORY AND
SUBFIELDS OF PSYCHOLOGY

The different subfields of psychology are concerned with different aspects of these reciprocal relationships (Bandura, 1990; Kihlstrom & Harackiewicz, 1990). Personality researchers, for example, have conducted countless studies using measures of general traits and motives ("inner" factors) to predict behavior (Kihlstrom & Harackiewicz, 1990). Social psychologists have examined extensively the relationships between specific attitudes (also properties of the person) on behavior and the influence of behavior on attitudes (e.g., self-perception theory). The influence of the environment on the person has been the concern of experimental social psychologists (e.g., modeling, persuasion) and applied behavior analysts (e.g., schedules of reinforcement). Cognitive psychology is concerned largely with cognition–action influences, in particular, how people attend to, acquire, and process information about their environments and themselves (Bandura, 1990; Kihlstrom & Harackiewicz, 1990). In addition, the neurosciences in psychology and medicine are concerned with the physiological and biochemical correlates and substrates of cognition and emotion. Thus, social cognitive theory offers linkages to and among all the major subfields of psychology and to other disciplines concerned with understanding the complexity of human thought and action.

COMPARISONS WITH OTHER THEORIES

Social cognitive theory views the three major alternative approaches to explaining personality and behavior—psychodynamic theories, trait theories, and radical behaviorism—as unable to account satisfactorily for the complexity and plasticity of human behavior (Bandura, 1986). Psychodynamic theories are difficult to test empirically, cannot account adequately for the tremendous situational variation in individual behavior, are deficient in predicting future behavior, and have not led to the development of efficient and effective methods for changing psychosocial functioning. Trait theories do not have good predictive utility and do not sufficiently consider the documented impact of situational influences. Radical behaviorism makes assumptions about behavior that have been disputed by empirical findings. For example, research has demonstrated that environmental events (antecedents and consequences) do not control behavior automatically, that anticipated consequences predict behavior better than actual consequences, that complex patterns of behavior can be learned through observation alone in the absence of reinforcement, and that operant explanations alone cannot account for the complexity of human learning and behavior. Because social cognitive theory assumes that people process and use information in symbolic form, evaluate their own thoughts and behaviors, predict and anticipate events and consequences, set goals and strive toward them, and regulate their own behavior, it surpasses the previously mentioned approaches in its ability to account for situational influences and differences, to explain the effects of belief and expectancies, to predict behavior accurately, and to provide models and strategies for effective behavior change. (See Bandura, 1986, for a full account of the social cognitive theory and the problems of other approaches.)

SELF-EFFICACY THEORY

Self-efficacy theory is concerned primarily with the role of personal cognitive factors in the triadic reciprocality model of social cognitive theory—with both the effect of cognition on affect and behavior and the effect of behavior, affect, and environmental events on cognition. Self-efficacy theory maintains that all processes of psychological and behavioral change operate through the alteration of the individual's sense of personal mastery or self-efficacy (Bandura, 1977, 1982b, 1986). *Self-efficacy* was originally defined as a rather specific type of expectancy concerned with one's beliefs in one's ability to perform a specific behavior or set of behaviors required to produce an outcome (Bandura, 1977). The definition of *self-efficacy* has been expanded, however, to refer to "people's beliefs about their capabilities to exercise control over events that affect their lives" (Bandura, 1989, p. 1175) and their "beliefs in their capabilities to mobilize the motivation, cognitive resources, and courses of action needed to exercise control over task demands" (Bandura, 1990, p. 316). Thus, self-efficacy judgments are concerned "not with the skills one has but with judgments of what one can do with whatever skills one possesses" (Bandura, 1986, p. 391). According to Bandura (1977), "people process, weigh, and integrate diverse sources of information concerning their capability, and they regulate their choice behavior and effort expenditure accordingly" (p. 212). Thus, expectations concerning mastery or efficacy have generative capability and determine choice of goals and goal-directed actions, expenditure of effort in the pursuit of goals, persistence in the face of adversity, and emotional or affective experiences (Bandura, 1986; Locke & Latham, 1990).

GENERALITY AND SPECIFICITY OF SELF-EFFICACY BELIEFS

Most conceptions of self-belief or self-evaluation have been global or trait constructs, such as *self-concept*—the sum total of beliefs about the self, or *self-esteem*—the sum total of the evaluation of these beliefs, how one feels about these beliefs and about oneself, or one's assessment of one's worth or value as a person (e.g., Wylie, 1979). However, general measures of self-concept and self-esteem have not provided much understanding of psychosocial functioning in specific behavioral or situational domains (Bandura, 1986, 1990). As the vast majority of research on attitude–behavior relationships has demonstrated, specific cognitive measures predict specific behaviors more accurately than do omnibus or global measures of traits or motives (e.g., Ajzen & Fishbein, 1980). For this reason, self-efficacy is conceptualized and measured not as a personality trait, but, instead, is defined and measured in the context of relatively specific behaviors in specific situations or contexts. However, the level of specificity at which self-efficacy is measured will be determined by the nature of the task and situation at hand, and by the nature of the task and situation to which one wishes to generalize, or in which one wishes to predict (Bandura, 1992). For example, an assessment of self-efficacy for the generic skill of driving an automobile needs to include at least specification of the general conditions under which one will be driving (urban traffic vs. rural freeways), although assessment that is too highly specified (e.g., driving in Manhattan during rush hour in a snow storm) will have limited applicability (Bandura, 1992).

Although *self-efficacy* sometimes is used to refer to one's general sense of competence and effectiveness (e.g., Smith, 1989), the term is most useful when defined, operationalized, and measured specific to a behavior or set of behaviors in a specific context (e.g., Kaplan, Atkins, & Reinsch, 1984; Manning & Wright, 1983). General self-efficacy scales have been developed (Sherer et al., 1982; Tipton & Worthington, 1984), but these scales have not resulted in much useful research on specific types of behavior change. For example, research indicates that the best way to predict a smoker's attempt and success at giving up cigarettes is to measure his self-efficacy expectancy for quitting, not his general self-confidence or self-esteem. In addition, measuring self-efficacy expectancies for quitting smoking will be more successful if we measure the smoker's expectations for being able to refrain from smoking under specific situations (e.g., while at a party, after eating, when around other smokers; DiClemente, 1986).

Rejecting the notion of perceived efficacy as a personality trait does not entail rejecting the possible generality of self-efficacy. Perceived efficacy in one behavioral–situational domain will generalize to other behaviors and situations depending on the extent to which the behaviors and situations share crucial features and require similar skills and functions (Bandura, 1990). In addition, beliefs about mastery and personal effectiveness are, of course, important aspects of self-concept and self-esteem. If one's sense of competence is high for an ability one values, then this will contribute to high self-esteem (or low self-esteem if perceived competence for the valued skill is low). Judgments of inefficacy in unvalued areas of competence are unlikely to influence significantly self-concept and self-esteem.

DIMENSIONS OF SELF-EFFICACY

Self-efficacy expectancies are viewed as varying along three dimensions: magnitude, strength, and generality (Bandura, 1977, 1982b, 1986).

Magnitude of self-efficacy, in a hierarchy of behaviors, refers to the number of "steps" of increasing difficulty or threat a person believes himself capable of performing. For example, a person who is trying to abstain from smoking may believe that he can maintain abstinence under conditions in which he feels relaxed and in which no others present are smoking. He may doubt, however, his ability to abstain under conditions of higher stress and/or when in the presence of other smokers (DiClemente, 1986).

Strength of self-efficacy expectancy refers to the resoluteness of a person's convictions that he or she can perform a behavior in question. For example, two smokers may believe themselves capable of abstaining from smoking at a party, but one may hold this belief with more conviction or confidence than the other. Strength of self-efficacy expectancy has been related repeatedly to persistence in the face of frustration, pain, and other barriers to performance (Bandura, 1986).

Generality of self-efficacy expectancies refers to the extent to which success or failure experiences influence self-efficacy expectancies in a limited, behaviorally specific manner, or whether changes in self-efficacy expectancy extend to other similar behaviors and contexts (e.g., Smith, 1989). For example, the smoker whose self-efficacy expectancy for abstinence has been raised by successful abstinence in a difficult or high-risk situation (e.g., in a bar around other smokers) may extend his feelings of self-efficacy to other contexts in which he has not yet experienced success or mastery. In addition, successful abstinence might generalize to other contexts of self-control, such as eating or maintaining an exercise regimen.

Although a thorough analysis of self-efficacy expectancy requires a detailed assessment of magnitude, strength, and generality (Bandura, 1977), most studies rely on unidimensional measures of self-efficacy expectancy that most resemble the strength dimension (e.g., confidence in one's ability to perform a behavior under certain conditions).

DETERMINANTS OF SELF-EFFICACY BELIEFS

In self-efficacy theory, beliefs about personal resources and abilities are the product of the interaction of information from six primary sources: (a) performance or enactment experiences; (b) vicarious experiences; (c) imaginal experiences; (d) verbal persuasion; (e) physiological arousal; and (f) emotional states (Bandura, 1977, 1986; Williams, Chap. 3, this volume). These six sources differ in their power to influence self-efficacy beliefs.

Performance Experiences

Performance experiences, in particular, clear success or failure, are the most powerful sources of self-efficacy information (Bandura, 1977). Success at a task, behavior, or skill strengthens self-efficacy expectancies for that task, behavior, or skill, whereas perceptions of failure diminish self-efficacy expectancy. Persons who once tried to quit smoking for a day but failed probably will doubt their ability to quit for a day in the future. On the other hand, a person who is able to go a full day without smoking may hold strong self-efficacy expectancies for abstaining for another day.

Vicarious Experiences

Vicarious experiences (observational learning, modeling, imitation) influence self-efficacy expectancy when people observe the behavior of others, see what they are able to do, note the consequences of their behavior, and then use this information to form expectancies about their own behavior and its consequences. The effects of vicarious experiences depend on such factors as the observer's perception of the similarity between himself and the model, the number and variety of models, the perceived power of the models, and the similarity between the problems faced by the observer and the model (Bandura, 1986; Schunk, 1986). Vicarious experiences generally have weaker effects on self-efficacy expectancy than do direct personal experiences (e.g., Bandura, Adams, & Beyer, 1977).

Imaginal Experiences

Social cognitive theory posits that people have tremendous capacity for symbolic cognitive activity. Thus, people are capable of the anticipatory visualization of possible situations and events, their own behavioral and emotional reactions to these situations and events, and the possible consequences of their behavior. People can generate beliefs about personal efficacy or inefficacy by imagining themselves or others behaving effectively or ineffectively in future situations (Cervone, 1989; Williams, Chap. 3, this volume). Such images may be derived from actual or vicarious experiences with situations similar to the one anticipated, or they may be induced by verbal persuasion, as when a psychotherapist guides a client through imaginal interventions, such as systematic desensitization and covert modeling (Williams, Chap. 3, this volume). Imagining oneself performing successfully or unsuccessfully, however, is not likely to have as strong an influence on self-efficacy as an actual success or failure experience (Williams, Chap. 3, this volume).

Verbal Persuasion

Verbal persuasion (or social persuasion) is a less potent source of enduring change in self-efficacy expectancy than performance experiences and vicarious experiences. The potency of verbal persuasion as a source of self-efficacy expectancies should be influenced by such factors as the expertness, trustworthiness, and attractiveness of the source, as suggested by decades of research on verbal persuasion and attitude change (e.g., Petty & Cacioppo, 1981). Experimental studies have shown that verbal persuasion is a moderately effective means for changing self-efficacy beliefs (e.g., Maddux, Norton, & Stoltenberg, 1986; Maddux & Rogers, 1983; Newman & Goldfried, 1987).

Physiological States

Physiological states influence self-efficacy when people associate aversive physiological arousal with poor behavioral performance, perceived incompetence, and perceived failure. Thus, when persons become aware of unpleasant physiological arousal, they are more likely to doubt their behavioral competence than if the physiological state were pleasant or neutral. Likewise, comfortable physiological sensations are likely to lead one to feel confident in one's ability in the situation at hand. Physiological indicants of self-efficacy expectancy, however, extend beyond autonomic arousal because, in activities involving strength and stamina, perceived efficacy is influenced by such experiences as fatigue and pain, or the absence thereof (e.g., Bandura, 1986).

Emotional States

Although physiological cues are important components of emotions, emotional experiences are not simply the product of physiological arousal

(Ortony, Clore, & Collins, 1988; Williams, Chap. 3, this volume). Thus, emotions or moods can be an additional source of information about self-efficacy. People are more likely to have self-efficacious beliefs about performance when their affect is positive than when it is negative. For example, both anxiety and depression may have a deleterious impact on self-efficacy (Maddux & Meier, Chap. 5, this volume; Williams, Chap. 3, this volume).

Distal and Proximal Sources

Determinants of current self-efficacy beliefs may be either *distal* (past) or *proximal* (current or immediate), and self-efficacy for a specific performance in a specific situation measured at a specific time will be the result of the confluence of distal and proximal information from all six sources. For example, one's self-efficacy in a current important social interaction, such as a job interview or a date with someone to whom one is strongly attracted, will be determined by a variety of distal sources of self-efficacy information, including past successes and failures in similar situations with similar persons, evaluations of one's social skills made by other people, observations of others similar to oneself under similar circumstances, and recollections of one's physiological and emotional state in similar situations. In addition, proximal sources of information will include one's current physiological and affective state (e.g., anxious vs. relaxed; sad vs. happy; tired vs. energetic), one's own evaluation of one's ongoing performance via self-observation and self-monitoring, and interpretations of the reactions of the other person that may indicate on a moment-to-moment basis the success or failure of one's attempts at winning the other's favor. Just as proximal (immediate) consequences usually exert greater control over behavior than distal (future) consequences, proximal (current) information about self-efficacy is likely to have a more powerful immediate effect on current self-efficacy than distal (past) information.

MEDIATING MECHANISMS

Self-efficacy beliefs influence behavior through four mediating processes: (a) goal-setting and persistence; (b) affect; (c) cognition; and (d) selection of environments and activities (Bandura, 1990, 1986, 1989).

Goal-Setting and Persistence

Self-efficacy beliefs influence people's choice of goals and goal-directed activities, expenditure of effort, and persistence in the face of challenge and obstacles (Bandura, 1986; Locke & Latham, 1990). In the face of difficulties, people with a weak sense of personal efficacy develop doubts about their ability to accomplish the task at hand and give up easily, whereas those with a strong sense of self-efficacy increase their efforts to master a challenge when obstacles arise. Perseverance usually produces the desired results, and this success then increases the individual's sense of efficacy. Motivation toward difficult goals is enhanced by overestimates of personal capabilities (i.e., positive illusions, Taylor & Brown, 1988), which then become self-fulfilling prophecies when people set their sights high, persevere, and then surpass their usual level of accomplishment.

Through the monitoring of self and situation, people develop beliefs not only about their current *level* of competence, but also beliefs (expectations) about *rate* of improvement in competence. Thus, at any given time, initiation and persistence may be influenced not only by beliefs about current level of competence, but also by expected rate of change in competence and the rate at which one expects to attain a goal. For example, an individual about to embark on the learning of a new skill or the mastery of a body of knowledge will base his decision to attempt and persist not only on his beliefs about his current abilities and whether or not he thinks he will become more skillful or more knowledgeable, but also on how quickly he expects to become more skillful or knowledgeable. People are more likely to attempt new behaviors and persist in the face of difficulties if they expect improvement in ability to come quickly rather than slowly. Although contemporaneous self-efficacy beliefs will remain the major determinant of persistence and affective reactions (e.g., anxiety, despondency), expected and perceived rate of improvement should also be influential.

Cognition

Self-efficacy beliefs influence cognition in four ways. First, they influence the goals people set for themselves. People with stronger self-efficacy beliefs for their performance set higher goals and commit to goals more strongly than do people with weaker beliefs about their abilities. Second, self-efficacy beliefs influence the plans or strategies people envision for attaining these goals. Third, they influence the development of rules for predicting and influencing events. Finally, self-efficacy for problem solving influences the efficiency and effectiveness of problem solving. When faced with complex decision-making tasks, people who believe strongly in their problem-solving abilities remain highly efficient and highly effective problem solvers and decision makers; those who doubt their abilities become erratic, inefficient, and ineffective (e.g., Bandura & Jourden, 1991; Bandura & Wood, 1989; Wood & Bandura, 1989).

Affect

Self-efficacy beliefs are powerful determinants of affective or emotional responses to life events, responses that can then influence cognition and action. Two domains of self-efficacy are important in the realm of emotion. First, self-efficacy beliefs about behavioral performance influence the type and intensity of affect. For example, low self-efficacy beliefs for the prevention of aversive or harmful events lead to agitation or anxiety (Bandura, 1988; Maddux & Lewis, Chap. 2, this volume; Williams, Chap. 3, this volume). Low self-efficacy beliefs for attaining highly desired goals or outcomes lead to despondency or depression (Bandura, 1986; Maddux & Meier, Chap. 5, this volume). These emotional responses then influence subsequent coping attempts. Because emotional responses such as stress have important biological components, self-efficacy beliefs can affect physiological processes, such as those that influence the immune system (see O'Leary & Brown, Chap. 8, this volume).

Second, self-efficacy for controlling the *cognitions* that influence emotion can, in part, determine emotional responses. People can become distressed about their apparent inability to control or terminate disturbing thoughts and aversive cognitions, such as those related to anxiety (Kent & Gibbons, 1987; Wegner, 1989). Both anxiety and depression are, in part, caused and maintained by expectations that the aversive emotion is highly likely to continue or to be experienced again (Kirsch, 1990). Thus, low self-efficacy for controlling ruminations related to anxiety, despondency, or other emotions, such as anger, can become self-perpetuating because one's expectations for poor control produce the very emotions one wishes to prevent.

Selection of Environments

People usually choose to enter situations in which they expect to perform successfully, and avoid situations in which they anticipate that the demands placed on them will exceed their abilities. Therefore, self-efficacy beliefs determine people's selections of situations and activities, selections that greatly influence the continued development of these same beliefs (e.g., Taylor & Brown, 1988). For this reason, beliefs about self-efficacy "create their own validation" (Bandura, 1989). People enter those situations in which they expect success and for which they believe they possess the necessary level of skill, and their subsequent success enhances their sense of efficacy. However, because people often avoid situations and activities in which they expect not to perform skillfully (although they may indeed possess the requisite skills), they deprive themselves of potential success experiences that would counteract their low sense of efficacy. As noted in the principle of triadic reciprocality, cognitions influence choices of environments and behaviors, which then influence behavioral performance and, ultimately, beliefs concerning those environments and behaviors. One of the most important of these choices is selection of vocation or career, which is better predicted by measures of self-efficacy than by measures of actual ability (Hackett & Betz, Chap. 9, this volume).

OUTCOME EXPECTANCY

An outcome expectancy is the belief that a behavior will produce an outcome or result, as opposed to a self-efficacy expectancy, which is a belief that one can perform the behavior that might produce the outcome. In self-efficacy theory, outcome expectancies are determined primarily by self-efficacy expectancies. The outcomes people expect depend largely on how well they expect to perform (Bandura, 1986). Thus, under most conditions, measures of outcome expectancies do not add much to the prediction of behaviors or intentions beyond the contributions of self-efficacy beliefs.

The relationship between self-efficacy and outcome expectancy has been a source of confusion and controversy (e.g., Borkovec, 1978; Corcoran, 1991; Kazdin, 1978; Kirsch, 1986; Teasdale, 1978), and good studies of their relationship and relative predictive utility are few. Eastman and Marzillier (1984), for example, have argued that Bandura does not provide a clear conceptual distinction between the two expectancies, and does not sufficiently emphasize the importance of outcome expectations. Bandura's (1984, 1986) response to these criticisms was that self-efficacy expectancies and outcome expectancies are conceptually distinct, but that the types of outcomes people anticipate are determined primarily by their expected performance proficiency—that self-efficacy beliefs account for most of the variance in expected outcomes. In other words, self-efficacy expectancies usually determine and predict outcome expectancies; consequently, outcome expectancies usually are not useful in predicting behavior beyond what can be predicted from measures of self-efficacy. However, when outcomes are not determined entirely by quality of performance (e.g., when environmental constraints limit the relationship between performance competence and size of reward), self-efficacy expectancies are not so closely related to outcome expectancies. In such cases, outcome expectancies may also be important independent predictors of behavior.

Measurement Issues

Most studies that have examined both self-efficacy and outcome expectancy seem to suggest that self-efficacy determines outcome expectancy and that outcome expectancy does not add significant predictive utility beyond that offered by self-efficacy. Most of these studies, however, have employed questionable measures of self-efficacy and outcome expectancy. For example, in some studies, dependent measures of self-efficacy expectancy and outcome expectancy have failed to make a clear distinction between perceived ability to perform a behavior and the perceived probability that the behavior will lead to certain outcomes (e.g., Davis & Yates, 1982; Manning & Wright, 1983; Taylor, 1989). In other studies, outcome expectancy has been measured as outcome value by items that assess the positive or negative valence of consequences instead of the probability of the occurrence of the consequences (e.g., Cooney, Kopel, & McKeon, 1982; Lee, 1984a, 1984b). Traitlike measures of outcome expectancy, such as locus of control, have been used rather than situation-specific and behavior-specific measures (Devins et al., 1982; Meier, McCarthy, & Schmeck, 1984).

Other studies have found that self-efficacy is a better predictor of actual level of skill than is outcome expectancy (e.g., Barling & Abel 1983; Shell, Murphy, & Bruning, 1989); it is not surprising, however, that a measure of perceived ability would be a better predictor of actual ability than would be a measure of expected consequences of performance. Finally, in some studies, self-efficacy has been measured as an expectancy for goal attainment rather than a belief that one is capable of performing the behaviors that might lead to goal attainment (e.g., Sexton, Tuckman, & Crehan, 1992). When studies employ measures of constructs that are consistent with neither conceptual definitions nor with measures in other studies, conclusions are difficult to draw. Some research, however, indicates that when defined and measured carefully and in a manner consistent with the conceptual distinction, self-efficacy expectancy and outcome expectancy can each be important in the prediction of intentions and behavior (e.g., Litt, 1988; Maddux et al., 1986; Sanna, 1992; Shell, Murphy, & Bruning, 1989; Stanley & Maddux, 1986a).

Response Expectancies, Self-Efficacy, and Intentions

Some researchers have raised questions about the relationships among self-efficacy, outcome expectancy, and intentions in situations in which performing a behavior may lead to involuntary aversive reactions such as fear, pain, or discomfort (Baker & Kirsch, 1991; Corcoran & Rutledge, 1989; Kirsch, 1982, 1985a). Kirsch has argued that if self-efficacy ratings are ratings of perceived ability to successfully accomplish a task, then they should not be influenced by expected rewards or expected aversive consequences, two types of outcome expectancies. Research has demonstrated, however, that self-efficacy expectancies in situations involving potential fear and pain *can* be enhanced by providing financial incentives and diminished by strong fear and pain expectancies (Corcoran & Rutledge, 1989; Baker & Kirsch, 1991; Kirsch, 1982). Fear and pain expectancies are *response expectancies*—beliefs about one's own nonvolitional reactions to events—which are a type of outcome expectancy (Kirsch, 1985b). Thus, in situations that involve pain or fear, self-efficacy appears to be determined partly by outcome expectancies (e.g., Baker & Kirsch, 1991).

When people anticipate aversive outcomes (e.g., fear or pain) and are not *willing* to engage in behavior that may produce those outcomes, their linguistic habit is to say that they *cannot* perform the behavior (low self-efficacy) rather than they *will not* perform it. Measures of willingness may simply be measures of *intention* (Baker & Kirsch, 1991), as employed in the theory of reasoned action (Ajzen & Fishbein, 1980). Therefore, in situations in which fear or pain is anticipated, measures of perceived ability to perform the behavior (self-efficacy) may be measures of intention to perform the behavior. In other words, in pain and fear situations, "I can" means "I will," which means "I intend to." This intention is determined primarily by the strength of the person's pain or fear expectancies. The mislabeling of intention and perceived ability may occur in other important domains in which people are asked to engage in behaviors that may lead to immediate discomfort, such as dieting, exercising, or violating personal norms (Baker & Kirsch, 1991). In each of these situations, "self-efficacy"—what people say they can and cannot do—may be determined largely by outcome expectancies—the anticipation of both positive and aversive consequences (Baker & Kirsch, 1991).

On the other hand, there is compelling evidence that avoidance behavior is determined by self-efficacy, not by anticipated anxiety, and that anticipated anxiety is determined by perceived self-efficacy (Bandura, 1992; see also Williams, Chap. 3, this volume). As a way to resolve these seemingly contradictory findings, Kirsch (Chap. 12, this volume) offers a distinction between *task self-efficacy* (Can I perform the behavior?) and *coping self-efficacy* (Can I prevent, manage, or control the potential aversive consequences of this behavior? See Williams, Chap. 3, this volume). Kirsch suggests that it is *task* self-efficacy in potentially aversive situations, not *coping* self-efficacy, that is largely equivalent to willingness and intention and is influenced by outcome expectancies. The distinction between task self-efficacy and coping self-efficacy closely resembles Bandura's (1986) distinction between perceived skill (such as performing a simple motor act) and perceived *generative* or *operative capability* in the face of changing and unpredictable circumstances, including inconveniences and impediments, only the latter of which he defines as self-efficacy. Thus, Kirsch and Bandura seem to disagree primarily on whether perceived ability at a motor task should be considered a type of self-efficacy, or whether to restrict the term self-efficacy to generative/operative capability. The meaning that people attach to a self-efficacy measure seems to depend partly on the situation at hand. In situations in which the possibility of immediate aversive outcomes is high, people may interpret self-efficacy ("Can you . . .?") questions not as questions about ability or skill, but as questions about willingness. In addition, the relationship between measures of self-efficacy and outcome expectancy depends on how clearly they are defined and measured. If outcome expectancy is defined and measured as simply an expectancy for goal achievement ("Do you expect to lose 5 pounds?") rather than the expectancy that a certain behavior is likely to lead to that goal ("Do you believe that running 3 miles a day will help you lose 5 pounds?"), then a strong correlation between outcome expectancy and self-efficacy is inevitable, because one has not distinguished between performance beliefs and behavior–outcome beliefs. However, if outcome expectancy is defined and measured as the perceived contingency between a behavior and a consequence ("Do you believe that running 5 miles a day will help you lose 5 pounds?"), then its correlation with self-efficacy ("Do you believe you can run 3 miles a day?") probably will be lower, and outcome expectancy may add to self-efficacy in predicting intentions and behaviors.

A strong correlation between self-efficacy and outcome expectancy is also guaranteed if self-efficacy is defined as perceived likelihood of goal attainment ("Do you think you will be able to lose 5 pounds?"), because goal attainment depends on the ability to perform certain behaviors and on the consequences of those behaviors. Self-efficacy measures should be concerned, as much as possible, with behavioral performance beliefs, and outcome expectancy measures with behavior–outcome beliefs, as Bandura has repeatedly indicated (e.g, 1977, 1991).

Interactions over Time

Social cognitive theory assumes that the relationships among cognition, behavior, and situational events will change as the reciprocal influences play themselves out over time (Bandura, 1986). However, most studies that have employed both self-efficacy and outcome expectancy have examined these variables and their relation to behavior at a single point in time (Sexton et al., 1992; Sexton & Tuckman, 1991). Recent research suggests that multiple trials over time are necessary to understand fully the relationship between self-efficacy, outcome expectancy, and behavior, although the nature of the changes in these relationships is not quite clear (Sexton et al., 1992; Sexton & Tuckman, 1991).

OUTCOME VALUE

Outcome value or importance has been proposed as an additional component of the self-efficacy model (Maddux et al., 1986; Maddux & Rogers, 1983; Teasdale, 1978), but has not been studied extensively in self-efficacy research. Most researchers seem to assume, logically, that outcome value needs to be high for self-efficacy expectancy and outcome expectancy to influence behavior. Considerable research in expectancy-value theory has shown that outcome value (reinforcement value, incentive value) is an important predictor of response strength and response probability (e.g., Kirsch, 1986; McClelland, 1985). Only a few studies, however, have investigated the role of outcome value in conjunction with self-efficacy expectancy and outcome expectancy (Barnes, 1984; Maddux et al., 1986; Maddux & Stanley, 1986; Manning & Wright, 1983). The findings have been mixed. Maddux et al. (1986) found that outcome value did not add significantly to the prediction of behavioral intentions when examined in conjunction with self-efficacy expectancy and outcome expectancy. Barnes (1984), however, corrected a problem in the measurement of outcome value found in Maddux et al. (1986) and found that outcome value did serve as a significant predictor variable independent of self-efficacy expectancy and outcome expectancy.

Value and Velocity

Recent research indicates that the notion of outcome value and its relationship to satisfaction with outcomes is not as simple as once was believed. Hsee and Abelson (1991) proposed that actual value or *position relation*—how positive or negative an outcome is rated on a satisfaction/dissatisfaction scale—is only one aspect of outcome value and probably not the most important aspect. Hsee and Abelson (1991) also proposed that *displacement relation* and *velocity relation* are important determinants of satisfaction with outcomes. *Displacement relation* is "the directional distance (i.e., displacement) between the original (reference) outcome position and the position after a change" (p. 341). Satisfaction (dissatisfaction) depends on how much more (less) an outcome departs from its original position in a positive direction. *Velocity relation* is the "rate (i.e., velocity) at which the outcome is changing" (p. 342). Satisfaction is greater (less) when the velocity is more (less) positive. They concluded from their research that "[p]eople engage in a behavior not just to seek its actual outcome, but to seek a positive velocity of outcomes that the behavior creates over time" (p. 342). Research on self-efficacy examining outcome value has examined only actual value or the position relation. Clearly, displacement relation and, more important, velocity relation of outcome value need further examination.

Positive and Negative Dimensions of Value

The apparent simplicity of the notion of outcome value is further belied by research on the asymmetrical effect of positive and negative events on emotion or mood (Taylor, 1991). First, people respond to negative events with greater physiological, affective, cognitive, and behavioral activity than to neutral or positive events (Taylor, 1991). In addition, positive and negative affect seem to be qualitatively distinct experiences rather than endpoints of a single continuum. Thus, outcome value may not be a single continuum but rather two relatively independent dimensions—positive and negative value. This does not mean that there are two different types of events or outcomes—positive and negative events; it does mean, however, that any event can be assessed on both positive and negative dimensions.

One implication of these findings is that "outcome importance" may be preferable to "outcome value" because "importance" allows for the consideration of positive or desired outcomes and negative or undesired outcomes, while "value" more easily suggests only the positive dimension of evaluation.

Interaction of Relations and Dimensions

The richness and complexity of the outcome value construct (and its measurement) increases when differences in *relations* (Hsee & Abelson, 1991) are considered along with differences in positive and negative *dimensions* of evaluation (Taylor, 1991). Not only events (actual or anticipated) can be evaluated along both positive and negative dimensions, but each dimension can be evaluated as a position relation, a displacement relation, and a velocity relation. Not only can satisfaction with the positivity of events be determined more by the rate of change (velocity relation) than by the fixed value (position relation), but dissatisfaction with an event should be influenced more by the rate or velocity with which it seems to be getting worse, rather than with its actual or anticipated position. The notion of negative event or outcome velocity has been incorporated in the "harm-looming" model of fear and anxiety (Riskind, Kelly, Moore, Harmon, & Gaines, 1992; Riskind & Maddux, 1993), which proposes that fear or anxiety are largely the result of the perception that a potential harm from event or object is moving toward one (either literally or symbolically) at an accelerated pace.

RELATED CONCEPTS OF MASTERY, CONTROL, AND COMPETENCE

Although the term self-efficacy is of rather recent origin, interest in perceived competence is not. A number of theorists have explored the nature of beliefs about personal mastery and competence and the effects of these feelings and beliefs on behavior and psychological adjustment. An understanding and appreciation of self-efficacy theory and the research bearing on it are enhanced by understanding the relationships between self-efficacy and other concepts concerned with mastery and efficacy, a few of which are described below. Each of these can be viewed as *social cognitive* concepts because each deals with people's thoughts, beliefs, motives, explanations, and predictions about themselves and other people. The following discussion does not exhaust the vocabulary of terms and concepts in the psychological literature related to personal efficacy, mastery, and control (e.g., Maddux, 1991). Others include hopelessness (Alloy, Kelly, Mineka, & Clements, 1990), hope (Snyder et al., 1991), mastery orientation (Dweck & Leggett, 1988), autonomy orientation (Deci & Ryan, 1985), transactional theory of stress and coping (Lazarus & Folkman, 1984), cognitive adaptation theory (Taylor, 1983), self-guides (Higgins, 1987), achievement motivation (e.g., McClelland, 1985), personal strivings (Emmons, 1986), and desire for control (Burger, 1985). Although discussion of the relationships among all of these concepts and theories and their relationship to self-efficacy is beyond the scope of this chapter, close examination reveals that the numerous notions and terms can be reduced to a fairly small number of basic social-cognitive building blocks, including causal attributions/explanations, agency/self-efficacy beliefs, means–end beliefs/outcome expectancies, goals or desired outcomes (including feelings of mastery or effectance), and goal/outcome value.

EXPECTANCY

Expectancy theories or expectancy-value theories deal with the expectations that specific means (behaviors) will be effective in obtaining specific rewards, goals, or outcomes, and with the value placed on these rewards, goals, or outcomes (e.g., Edwards, 1954; Lewin, 1938; Mitchell, 1974; Rotter, 1954; Tolman, 1932). Recent models in the expectancy-value tradition include protection motivation theory (Maddux & Rogers, 1983; Rogers, 1975), the theory of reasoned action (Fishbein & Ajzen, 1975), and control theory (Carver & Scheier, 1981). The expectancy in expectancy-value theories traditionally has been outcome expectancies. Until recently, few expectancy-value models made clear the distinction between expectations that specific behaviors will lead to desired outcomes, an outcome expectancy, and the expectation that one will be able to perform successfully the behaviors in question, a self-efficacy expectancy.

RESPONSE EXPECTANCY

Response expectancy theory (Kirsch, 1985b, 1990) is concerned with the role of expectancies for subjective experiences rather than for objective outcomes. Kirsch (1985b) defined *response expectancies* as expectancies regarding "the occurrence of nonvolitional responses . . . responses that are experienced as occurring automatically, that is, without volitional effort [and] include emotional reactions (e.g., fear, sadness, elation), sexual arousal, conversion symptoms, pain, and so forth." (p. 1189). Such nonvolitional responses have reinforcement value and thus are among the determinants of volitional behavior. Response expectancies influence subjective experience, physiological functioning, and overt behavior (Kirsch, 1990). Because a nonvolitional response (e.g., fear, pain) is one of many possible expected outcomes of engaging in a behavior, a response expectancy is a special kind of outcome expectancy. The reinforcement (and punishment) value of the nonvolitional response is an outcome value.

LOCUS OF CONTROL

Locus of control of reinforcement (Rotter, 1966, 1990) is "the degree to which persons expect that a reinforcement or an outcome of their behavior is contingent on their own behavior or personal characteristics versus the degree to which persons expect that the reinforcement of outcome is a function of chance, luck, or fate, is under the control of powerful others, or is simply unpredictable" (Rotter, 1990, p. 489). Thus, locus of control is the general belief that one's behavior can have an impact on the environment and that one is capable of controlling outcomes through one's own behavior. Although it sounds similar to self-efficacy expectancy, locus of control is a generalized outcome expectancy because it is concerned with the extent to which one believes one's behavior controls outcomes, not confidence in one's ability to perform certain behaviors (Bandura, 1986). Empirical evidence supports making this distinction between self-efficacy and locus of control (Smith, 1989; Taylor & Popma, 1990).

PERCEIVED CONTROL

Perceived control is usually defined as the belief that one is capable of achieving a particular goal (e.g., Ajzen, 1985; Langer, 1983; Thompson, 1991). Defined in this way, a belief about perceived control involves both beliefs about the contingency between certain behaviors or strategies and desired goals or outcomes and beliefs about one's ability to execute the behaviors or strategies—outcome expectancies and self-efficacy expectancies (e.g., Thompson, 1991). However, recent research suggests that perceived control beliefs may not be simply the combination of self-efficacy beliefs and outcome expectancy. Skinner, Chapman, and Baltes (1988) factor analyzed an extensive children's questionnaire concerning perceptions of control and found separate factors for (using their terms) *means–end beliefs* ("beliefs about an individual's expectancies about the extent to which certain classes of potential causes are effective in producing desired outcomes"—i.e., outcome expectancies), *agency beliefs* ("beliefs about the relation between the agent and certain means . . . an individual's expectancies about the extent to which he or she possesses these means"—i.e., self-efficacy expectancies), *control beliefs* ("beliefs about the relation between the agent and a desired outcome or class of outcomes . . . expectancies about the extent to which he or she can obtain desired outcomes, with no explicit reference to the means used"—i.e., perceived control). Thus, the research of Skinner et al. (1988) suggested that perceptions of control may be more than just the sum of self-efficacy beliefs and outcome expectancies. Bandura (in press), however, has challenged the logic of this tripartite conceptualization of control by noting that when people are asked about their beliefs about producing ends (control beliefs) without any mention of ends, they undoubtedly consider the means they believe they have at their disposal, even if means are not mentioned in the assessment of control beliefs.

PROBABILITY OF SUCCESS

McClelland (1985) has proposed a general behavior theory that considers motivation, incentive value, and probability of success to be the major determinants of achievement-related behavior and affiliative acts. Probability of success "is determined not only by actual skill but also by the individual's beliefs about the efficacy of making a response that may be somewhat independent of the individual's skill in making it." (p. 814). McClelland makes a distinction between beliefs about "efficacy of effort in bringing about a consequence through a particular response in a given situation" and "generalized confidence . . . a person has that he or she can bring about outcomes through instrumental activities of any kind." (p. 814). A belief about "efficacy of effort" seems similar to an outcome expectancy. Although McClelland suggested that "generalized confidence" is nearly the same as a self-efficacy expectancy, his definition of generalized confidence is more similar to Rotter's definition of locus of control, which is a kind of generalized outcome expectancy, than to Bandura's definition of self-efficacy expectancy, which is a belief about one's ability to perform behaviors or execute behavioral strategies.

EFFECTANCE MOTIVATION

In attempting to explain human behavior that is not directed toward the satisfaction of biological needs such as hunger, thirst, and sexual desire, White (1959) proposed that humans must be motivated by a different kind of goal, the goal of exploring, manipulating, and mastering the environment. White called this motivation *effectance motivation* and said that its satisfaction leads to a "feeling of efficacy." According to White, we are biologically driven to explore and master our environment, and we feel good when we explore new situations, learn about them, and deal with them effectively. White also proposed that this feeling of efficacy is an aim in itself, apart from the practical value of the things we learn about the environment. Effectance motivation is concerned with a basic, biologically based drive to master the environment, but does not deal directly with the role of beliefs or expectations concerning mastery.

LEVEL OF ASPIRATION

Theory and research on *level of aspiration* (e.g., Festinger, 1942) are concerned with what people would like to achieve or what they "aspire to" and how their aspirations influence their behavior. Level of aspiration is concerned with the *goals* that people set for themselves in situations relevant to achievement or mastery, not the levels of performance people *expect* to attain (Kirsch, 1986). In much of the early research on level of aspiration, however, investigators did not make this distinction clearly. Sometimes they asked people about what they would like to be able to do or achieve; other times they asked people what they expected to be able to achieve. The studies that made this important distinction found that peoples' levels of aspiration were usually greater than their expectancies for success (Kirsch, 1986). These older studies also found that expectancies concerning performance levels were more strongly correlated with past performance than was level of aspiration.

CAUSAL ATTRIBUTIONS AND EXPLANATORY STYLE

Theory and research on *explanatory style* or *attributional style* also are concerned with beliefs about personal control and effectiveness (e.g., Peterson & Stunkard, 1992). Most of this work has been directed toward understanding the effect of explanations for negative life events on perceived helplessness and depression (see Brewin, 1985; Robins, 1988; and Sweeney,

Anderson, & Bailey, 1986 for reviews). Helplessness beliefs are closely related to self-efficacy beliefs and outcome expectancies (see Maddux & Meier, Chap. 5, this volume). Explanations or attributions, however, are beliefs about the causes of events that have already occurred; self-efficacy and outcome expectancy are beliefs about possible future events. The relationship between causal attributions or explanations and self-efficacy and outcome expectancies is unclear, as are the ways attributions, self-efficacy, and outcome expectancies interact to influence behavior and affect. For example, some theories propose the attributions influence affect and behavior indirectly via their influence on expectancies (e.g., the helplessness/hopelessness model of depression, Peterson & Stunkard, 1992; the Scheier & Carver (1988) model of behavioral self-regulation). Because self-efficacy is influenced by past success or failure and observations of the behavior of others, attributions made about these actual and vicarious experiences probably influence self-efficacy (Schunk, this volume). In addition, self-efficacy may mediate the relationship between attributions and performance (Forsterling, 1986). Conversely, self-efficacy may influence attributions (e.g., Alden, 1986; Bandura, 1992; McAuley, Duncan, & McElroy, 1989). A person with low self-efficacy for a performance domain may be more likely to attribute failure in that domain to lack of ability than to lack of effort; the opposite pattern may hold for those with high self-efficacy (Bandura, 1992; see also Maddux & Meier, Chap. 5, this volume.)

Schiaffino and Revenson (1992) have provided the most complete analysis of the relationships among attributions, self-efficacy, and outcome expectancy, although the complexity of their findings raises as many questions as it answers. In a study of coping with a chronic illness, rheumatoid arthritis (RA), Schiaffino and Revenson (1992) provided evidence that causal attributions and self-efficacy interact in influencing depression and physical disability. Self-efficacy was negatively related to depression for subjects who made internal, stable, global attributions for RA flare-ups; however, self-efficacy had little relationship to depression for subjects who made external, unstable, specific attributions for flare-ups. The pattern of relationships was different for physical disability. For subjects who made internal, stable, global attributions, self-efficacy was (surprisingly) positively related to disability; but, for subjects who made external, unstable, specific attributions, self-efficacy and disability were negatively related. Clearly, these relationships require further exploration.

SUMMARY

Self-efficacy theory focuses on the cognitive aspects of mastery and effectiveness rather than on more affective constructs such as needs, motives, values, and feelings of efficacy. Yet, to focus on cognitions and expectations is not to diminish the importance of the affective and evaluative aspects of perceived control and mastery. A comprehensive explanation of human behavior and adjustment needs to consider the individual's inherent motivation toward mastery and achievement, the feelings of satisfaction one derives from meeting challenges and overcoming obstacles, the value attached to the specific goal or outcome sought at a given time and place, and the individual's assessment of the likelihood of attaining the goal or goals—an assessment that includes beliefs about behavior–outcome contingencies and beliefs about personal ability. Because of the practical problems inherent in constructing studies that consider every possible influence on behavior, a researcher's choice of factors to investigate will depend partly on what he or she wishes to predict. Assessment of motives or needs may be more useful in predicting general trends in mastery-oriented behavior over relatively long periods of time. Predicting relatively specific behaviors in specific situations over relatively brief time frames is likely to be more successful when specific expectancies and values are assessed (Ajzen & Fishbein, 1980).

CONCLUDING COMMENTS

All theories should be subjected to critical evaluation, and self-efficacy theory has had its share of critics. Some, for example, have addressed the seeming ambiguity of the definitions of self-efficacy and outcome expectancy (e.g., Corcoran, 1991; Eastman & Marzillier, 1984; Lee, 1989), or the similarity between self-efficacy and intentions in situations involving anticipated aversive consequences (e.g., Kirsch, 1982, 1985a). These two issues are discussed in earlier sections of this chapter. Lee (1989) used self-efficacy theory to exemplify the problems in all theories of behavior that rely on cognitive constructs and explanations: that they confuse description of behavior change with explanation of behavior change; that they rely on poorly defined and unobservable interactions among poorly defined variables; and that they are unable to make precise predictions about behavior. She concluded that social cognitive models are not testable and therefore are not useful. Granted, constructs such as self-efficacy and outcome expectancy present definitional and measurement difficulties (as discussed in this chapter and in greater detail in Kirsch, Chap. 12, this volume), but refinement and consistency in definition and measurement are likely to develop as theorists and researchers become aware of these difficulties and address them. The pros and cons of employing cognitive constructs in explanations of human behavior have been discussed repeatedly since the days of Watson and Pavlov and cannot be given full treatment here. However, Lee's wholesale dismissal of human thought is at odds with hundreds of studies that demonstrate the centrality of cognition in human social behavior (e.g., Fiske & Taylor, 1991). The chapters in this volume and the decades of research on such social cognitive constructs as schemas, attributions, expectancies, and goals amply demonstrate the measurability of covert variables and their utility in explaining and predicting behavior (e.g., Bandura, 1986; Fiske & Taylor, 1991; Locke & Latham, 1990).

The chapters to follow provide compelling support for the utility of self-efficacy theory in predicting behavior and guiding the development of effective interventions for problems of adjustment. Self-efficacy theory's most important contribution to the body of research on perceived competence/control and psychological adaptation and adjustment—as this volume will attempt to demonstrate—is not made by offering an opposing alternative framework to other models of personal efficacy, but rather by offering a perspective that is compatible with other approaches. Self-efficacy theory and research have contributed to the study of perceived control and competence in at least three ways. First, self-efficacy theory emphasizes the distinction between three important variables concerned with personal control and motivation—self-efficacy expectancy, outcome expectancy, and outcome value. Second, self-efficacy theory emphasizes the measurement of these variables, especially self-efficacy, with a greater degree of behavioral and situational specificity than has been the case in other theories and bodies of research. Third, and most important, self-efficacy theory provides a model to explain the origin and effects of perceptions of perceived control and guidelines for changing human behavior and enhancing adjustment and adaptation. For this reason, self-efficacy theory has stimulated a tremendous body of research that has greatly enhanced our understanding of the determinants of mastery and control beliefs and the role of these beliefs in psychological adaptation and adjustment, as the rest of this volume demonstrates.

ACKNOWLEDGMENT: I am grateful to Albert Bandura for numerous helpful comments and suggestions on an earlier version of this chapter. He corrected a number of errors and helped me clarify some confusing passages. I retain sole responsibility for whatever error and confusion remain.

REFERENCES

Abramson, L. Y., Seligman, M. E. P., & Teasdale, J. D. (1978). Learned helplessness in humans: Critique and reformulation. *Journal of Abnormal Psychology, 87*, 49–74.
Ajzen, I. (1985). From intentions to actions: A theory of planned behavior. In J. Kuhl & J.

Beckman (Eds.), *Action control: From cognition to behavior* (pp. 11–39). New York: Springer-Verlag.

Ajzen, I., & Fishbein, M. (1980). *Understanding attitudes and predicting social behavior*. New York: Prentice-Hall.

Alden, L. (1986). Self-efficacy and causal attributions for social feedback. *Journal of Research in Personality, 20,* 460–473.

Alloy, L. B., Kelly, K. A., Mineka, S., & Clements, C. M. (1990). Comorbidity in anxiety and depressive disorders: A helplessness/hopelessness perspective. In J. D. Masur & C. R. Cloniger (Eds.), *Comorbidity in anxiety and mood disorders* (pp. 499–553). Washington, DC: American Psychiatric Press.

Baker, S. L., & Kirsch, I. (1991). Cognitive mediators of pain perception and tolerance. *Journal of Personality and Social Psychology, 61,* 504–510.

Bandura, A. (1974). Behavior theory and the models of man. *American Psychologist, 29,* 859–869.

Bandura, A. (1977). Self-efficacy: Toward a unifying theory of behavioral change. *Psychological Review, 84,* 191–215.

Bandura, A. (1982a). The assessment and predictive generality of self-percepts of efficacy. *Journal of Behavioral and Experimental Psychiatry, 13,* 195–199.

Bandura, A. (1982b). Self-efficacy mechanism in human agency. *American Psychologist, 37,* 122–147.

Bandura, A. (1983). Self-efficacy determinants of anticipated fears and calamities. *Journal of Personality and Social Psychology, 45,* 464–469.

Bandura, A. (1984). Recycling misconceptions of perceived self-efficacy. *Cognitive Therapy and Research, 8,* 231–255.

Bandura, A. (1986). *Social foundations of thought and action*. New York: Prentice-Hall.

Bandura, A. (1988). Self-efficacy conception of anxiety. *Anxiety Research, 1,* 77–98.

Bandura, A. (1989). Human agency in social cognitive theory. *American Psychologist, 44,* 1175–1184.

Bandura, A. (1990). Some reflections on reflections. *Psychological Inquiry, 1,* 101–105.

Bandura, A. (1991). Human agency: The rhetoric and the reality. *American Psychologist, 46,* 157–162.

Bandura, A. (1992). On rectifying the comparative anatomy of perceived control: Comments on "Cognates of Personal Control." *Applied & Preventive Psychology, 1,* 121–126.

Bandura, A. (in press). *Self-efficacy: The exercise of control*. New York: Freeman.

Bandura, A., Adams, N. E., & Beyer, A. (1977). Cognitive processes mediating behavior change. *Journal of Personality and Social Psychology, 35,* 125–139.

Bandura, A., Adams, N. E., Hardy, A. B., & Howells, G. N. (1980). Tests of the generality of self-efficacy theory. *Cognitive Therapy and Research, 4,* 39–66.

Bandura, A., & Jourden, F. J. (1991). Self-regulatory mechanisms governing the impact of social comparison on complex decision making. *Journal of Personality and Social Psychology, 60,* 941–951.

Bandura, A., & Wood, R. E. (1989). Effect of perceived controllability and performance standards on self-regulation of complex decision-making. *Journal of Personality and Social Psychology, 56,* 805–814.

Barling, J., & Abel, M. (1983). Self-efficacy beliefs and tennis performance. *Cognitive Therapy and Research, 7,* 265–272.

Barnes, J. (1985). The relative utility of self-efficacy expectancy, outcome value, and behavioral intentions in explaining and predicting behavior. Unpublished doctoral dissertation, Texas Tech University, Lubbock, Texas.

Borkovec, T. D. (1978). Self-efficacy: Cause or reflection of behavioural change? In S. Rachman

(Ed.), *Advances in behaviour therapy and research* (Vol. 1, pp. 163–170). Oxford: Pergamon Press.

Brewin, C. R. (1985). Depression and causal attribution: What is their relation? *Psychological Bulletin, 98,* 297–309.

Burger, J. M. (1985). Desire for control and achievement-related behaviors. *Journal of Personality and Social Psychology, 35,* 351–363.

Carver, C. S., & Scheier, M. F. (1981). *Attention and regulation: A control theory approach to human behavior.* New York: Springer-Verlag.

Cervone, D. (1989). Effects of envisioning future activities on self-efficacy judgments and motivation: An availability heuristic interpretation. *Cognitive Therapy and Research, 13,* 246–261.

Cooney, N. L., Kopel, S. A., & McKeon, P. (1982, August). *Controlled relapse training and self-efficacy in ex-smokers.* Paper presented at the 90th Annual Meeting of the American Psychological Association, Washington, DC.

Corcoran, K. J. (1991). Efficacy, "skills," reinforcement, and choice behavior. *American Psychologist, 46,* 155–157.

Corcoran, K. J., & Rutledge, M. W. (1989). Efficacy expectation changes as a function of hypothetical incentives in smokers. *Psychology of Addictive Behaviors, 3,* 22–28.

Davis, F. W., & Yates, B. T. (1982). Self-efficacy expectancies versus outcome expectancies as determinants of performance deficits and depressive affect. *Cognitive Therapy and Research, 6,* 23–36.

Davison, G. C., Haaga, D. A. F., Rosenbaum, J., Dolexal, S. L., & Weinstein, K. A. (1991). Assessment of self-efficacy in articulated thoughts: "States of mind" analysis and association with speech-anxious behavior. *Journal of Cognitive Psychotherapy: An International Quarterly, 5,* 83–92.

Deci, E. L., & Ryan, R. M. (1985). *Intrinsic motivation and self-determination in human behavior.* New York: Plenum Press.

Devins, G. M., Binik, Y. M., Gorman, P., Dattell, M., McClosky, B., Oscar, G., & Briggs, J. (1982). Perceived self-efficacy, outcome expectancies, and negative mood states in end-stage renal disease. *Journal of Abnormal Psychology, 91,* 241–244.

DiClemente, C. C. (1986). Self-efficacy and the addictive behaviors. *Journal of Social and Clinical Psychology, 4,* 302–315.

Dweck, C. S., & Leggett, E. L. (1988). A social-cognitive approach to motivation and personality. *Psychological Review, 95,* 256–273.

Eastman, C., & Marzillier, J. S. (1984). Theoretical difficulties in Bandura's self-efficacy theory. *Cognitive Therapy and Research, 8,* 213–229.

Edwards, W. (1954). The theory of decision making. *Psychological Bulletin, 51,* 380–417.

Emmons, R. A. (1986). Personal strivings: An approach to personality and subjective well-being. *Journal of Personality and Social Psychology, 51,* 1058–1068.

Festinger, L. (1942). A theoretical interpretation of shifts in level of aspiration. *Psychological Review, 49,* 235–250.

Fishbein, M., & Ajzen, I. (1975). *Belief, attitude, intention, and behavior: An introduction to theory and research.* Reading, MA: Addison-Wesley.

Fiske, S. T., & Taylor, S. E. (1991). *Social cognition.* New York: McGraw-Hill.

Forsterling, F. (1986). Attributional conceptions in clinical psychology. *American Psychologist, 41,* 275–285.

Harvey, J. H., Ickes, W., & Kidd, R. F. (1978). *New directions in attribution research* (Vol. 2). Hillsdale, NJ: Erlbaum.

Higgins, T. E. (1987). Self-Discrepancy: A theory relating self and affect. *Psychological Review, 94,* 319–340.

Howard, G. S., & Conway, C. G. (1986). Can there be an empirical science of volitional action? *American Psychologist*, *41*, 1241–1251.

Hsee, C. K., & Ableson, R. P. (1991). Velocity relation: Satisfaction as a function of the first derivative of outcome over time. *Journal of Personality and Social Psychology*, *60*, 341–347.

Hyland, M. E. (1988). Motivational control theory: An integrative framework. *Journal of Personality and Social Psychology*, *55*, 642–651.

Kaplan, R. M., Atkins, C. J., & Reinsch, S. (1984). Specific efficacy expectations mediate exercise compliance in patients with COPD. *Health Psychology*, *3*, 223–242.

Kazdin, A. E. (1978). Conceptual and assessment issues raised by self-efficacy theory. In S. Rachman (Ed.), *Advances in behaviour research and therapy* (Vol. 1, pp. 177–185). Oxford: Pergamon Press.

Kent, G., & Gibbons, R. (1987). Self-efficacy and the control of anxious cognitions. *Journal of Behavior Therapy and Experimental Psychiatry*, *18*, 33–40.

Kihlstrom, J. F., & Harackiewicz, J. M. (1990). An evolutionary milestone in the psychology of personality. [Review of A. Bandura, *Social foundations of thought and action*]. *Psychological Inquiry*, *1*, 86–100.

Kirsch, I. (1980). "Microanalytic" analyses of efficacy expectations as predictors of performance. *Cognitive Therapy and Research*, *4*, 259–262.

Kirsch, I. (1982). Efficacy expectations or response predictions: The meaning of efficacy ratings as a function of task characteristics. *Journal of Personality and Social Psychology*, *42*, 132–136.

Kirsch, I. (1985a). Self-efficacy and expectancy: Old wine with new labels. *Journal of Personality and Social Psychology*, *49*, 824–830.

Kirsch, I. (1985b). Response expectancy as a determinant of experience and behavior. *American Psychologist*, *40*, 1189–1202.

Kirsch, I. (1986). Early research on self-efficacy: What we already know without knowing we knew. *Journal of Social and Clinical Psychology*, *4*, 339–358.

Kirsch, I. (1990). *Changing expectations: A key to effective psychotherapy*. Belmont, CA: Brooks/Cole.

Langer, E. J. (1983). *The psychology of control*. Beverly Hills, CA: Sage.

Lazarus, R. S., & Folkman, S. (1984). *Stress, appraisal, and coping*. New York: Springer.

Lee, C. (1984a). Accuracy of efficacy and outcome expectations in predicting performance in a simulated assertiveness task. *Cognitive Therapy and Research*, *8*, 37–48.

Lee, C. (1984b). Efficacy expectations and outcome expectations as predictors of performance in a snake-handling task. *Cognitive Therapy and Research*, *8*, 509–516.

Lee, C. (1989). Theoretical weaknesses lead to practical problems: The example of self-efficacy theory. *Journal of Behaviour Therapy and Experimental Psychiatry*, *20*, 115–123.

Lewin, K. (1938). *The conceptual representation and the measurement of psychological forces*. Durham, NC: Duke University Press.

Litt, M. D. (1988). Self-efficacy and perceived control: Cognitive mediators of pain tolerance. *Journal of Personality and Social Psychology*, *54*, 149–160.

Locke, E. A. (1991). Goal theory vs. control theory: Contrasting approaches to understanding work motivation. *Motivation and Emotion*.

Locke, E. A., Frederick, E., Lee, C., & Bobko, P. (1984). Effect of self-efficacy, goals, and task strategies on task performance. *Journal of Applied Psychology*, *69*, 241–251.

Locke, E. A., & Latham, G. P. (1990). *A theory of goal setting and task performance*. Englewood Cliffs, NJ: Prentice-Hall.

Madden, T. J., Ellen, P. S., & Ajzen, I. (1992). A comparison of the theory of planned behavior and the theory of reasoned action. *Personality and Social Psychology Bulletin*, *1*, 3–9.

Maddux, J. E. (1991). Self-efficacy. In C. R. Snyder & D. R. Forsyth (Eds.), *Handbook of social and clinical psychology* (pp. 57–78). New York: Pergamon.

Maddux, J. E., & Barnes, J. (1985). *The orthogonality and relative predictive utility of self-efficacy expectancy, outcome expectancy, and outcome value: A review of empirical studies.* Unpublished manuscript. George Mason University. Fairfax, VA.

Maddux, J. E., Norton, L. W., & Stoltenberg, C. D. (1986). Self-efficacy expectancy, outcome expectancy, and outcome value: Relative effects on behavioral intentions. *Journal of Personality and Social Psychology, 51,* 783–789.

Maddux, J. E., & Rogers, R. W. (1983). Protection motivation and self-efficacy: A revised theory of fear appeals and attitude change. *Journal of Experimental Social Psychology, 19,* 469–479.

Maddux, J. E., Sherer, M., & Rogers, R. W. (1982). Self-efficacy expectancy and outcome expectancy: Their relationships and their effects on behavioral intentions. *Cognitive Therapy and Research, 6,* 207–211.

Maddux, J. E., & Stanley, M. A. (1986). Self-efficacy theory in contemporary psychology: An overview. *Journal of Social and Clinical Psychology, 4,* 249–255.

Manning, M. M., & Wright, T. L. (1983). Self-efficacy expectancies, outcome expectancies, and the persistence of pain control in childbirth. *Journal of Personality and Social Psychology, 45,* 421–431.

McAuley, E., Duncan, T. E., & McElroy, M. (1989). Self-efficacy cognitions and causal attributions for children's motor performance: An exploratory investigation. *Journal of Genetic Psychology, 150,* 65–73.

McClelland, D. C. (1985). How motives, skills, and values determine what people do. *American Psychologist, 40,* 812–825.

McClelland, D. C., Atkinson, J. W., Clark, R. W., & Lowell, E. L. (1953). *The achievement motive.* New York: Appleton-Century-Crofts.

Meier, S., McCarthy, P. R., & Schmeck, R. R. (1984). Validity of self-efficacy as a predictor of writing performance. *Cognitive Therapy and Research, 8,* 107–120.

Mitchell, T. R. (1974). Expectancy models of job satisfaction, occupational preference, and effort: A theoretical, methodological, and empirical appraisal. *Psychological Bulletin, 81,* 1053–1077.

Newman, C., & Goldfried, M. R. (1987). Disabusing negative self-efficacy expectations via experience, feedback, and discrediting. *Cognitive Therapy and Research, 11,* 401–417.

Nicholls, J. G. (1984). Achievement motivation: Conceptions of ability, subjective experience, task choice, and performance. *Psychological Review, 91,* 328–346.

Ortony, A., Clore, G. L., & Collins, A. (1988). *The cognitive structure of emotions.* Cambridge: Cambridge University Press.

Peterson, C., & Stunkard, A. J. (1992). Cognates of personal control: Locus of control, self-efficacy, and explanatory style. *Applied and Preventive Psychology, 1,* 111–117.

Petty, R. E., & Cacioppo, J. T. (1981). *Attitudes and persuasion: Classic and contemporary approaches.* Dubuque, IA: Brown.

Powers, W. T. (1991). Commentary on Bandura's "Human Agency." *American Psychologist, 46,* 151–153.

Riskind, J. R., Kelly, K., Moore, R., Harmon, W., & Gaines, H. (1992). The loomingness of danger: Does it discriminate focal phobias and general anxiety from depression? *Cognitive Therapy and Research, 16,* 603–622.

Riskind, J. R., & Maddux, J. E. (1993). Loomingness, helplessness, and fearfulness: An integration of harm-looming and self-efficacy models of fear. *Journal of Social and Clinical Psychology, 12,* 73–89.

Robins, C. J. (1988). Attributions and depression: Why is the literature so inconsistent? *Journal of Personality and Social Psychology, 54,* 880–889.

Rogers, R. W. (1975). A protection motivation theory of fear appeals and attitude change. *Journal of Psychology, 91,* 93–114.

Rogers, R. W. (1984). Changing health-related attitudes and behavior: The role of preventive health psychology. In R. P. McGlynn, J. E. Maddux, C. D. Stoltenberg, & J. H. Harvey (Eds.), *Social perception in clinical and counseling psychology* (pp. 91–112). Lubbock, TX: Texas Tech Press.

Rotter, J. B. (1954). *Social learning and clinical psychology.* Englewood Cliffs, NJ: Prentice-Hall.

Rotter, J. B. (1966). Generalized expectancies for internal versus external control of reinforcement. *Psychological Monographs, 80* (1, Whole No. 609), 1–28.

Rotter, J. B. (1990). Internal versus external control of reinforcement: A case history of a variable. *American Psychologist, 45,* 489–493.

Rotter, J. B. (1992). Some comments on the "Cognates of Personal Control." *Applied and Preventive Psychology, 1,* 127–129.

Sanna, L. J. (1992). Self-efficacy theory: Implications for social facilitation and social loafing. *Journal of Personality and Social Psychology, 62,* 774–786.

Schiaffino, K. M., & Revenson, T. A. (1992). The role of perceived self-efficacy, perceived control, and causal attributions in adaptation to rheumatoid arthritis: Distinguishing mediator from moderator effects. *Personality and Social Psychology Bulletin, 18,* 709–718.

Schunk, D. H. (1986). Vicarious influences on self-efficacy for cognitive skill learning. *Journal of Social and Clinical Psychology, 4,* 316–327.

Schwartz, R. M., & Garamoni, G. L. (1989). Cognitive balance and psychopathology: Evaluation of a information processing model of positive and negative states of mind. *Clinical Psychology Review, 9,* 271–294.

Sexton, T. L., & Tuckman, B. W. (1991). Self-beliefs and behavior: The role of self-efficacy and outcome expectation over time. *Personality and Individual Differences 12,* 725–736.

Sexton, T. L., Tuckman, B. W., & Crehan, K. (1992). An investigation of the patterns of self-efficacy, outcome expectation, outcome value, and performance across trials. *Cognitive Therapy and Research, 16,* 329–348.

Shell, D. F., Murphy, C. C., & Bruning, R. H. (1989). Self-efficacy and outcome expectancy mechanisms in reading and writing achievement. *Journal of Educational Psychology, 81,* 91–100.

Sherer, M., Maddux, J. E., Mercandante, B., Prentice-Dunn, S., Jacobs, B., & Rogers, R. W. (1982). The self-efficacy scale: Construction and validation. *Psychological Reports, 51,* 663–671.

Simon, K. M. (1979). Effects of self-comparison, social comparison, and depression on goal-setting and self-evaluative reactions. Unpublished doctoral dissertation. Stanford University.

Skinner, E. A., Chapman, M., & Baltes, P. B. (1988). Beliefs about control, means–ends, and agency: A new conceptualization and its measurement during childhood. *Journal of Personality and Social Psychology, 54,* 117–133.

Smith, R. E. (1989). Effects of coping skills training on generalized self-efficacy and locus of control. *Journal of Personality and Social Psychology, 56,* 228–233.

Snyder, C. R., Harris, C., Anderson, J. R., Holleran, S. A., Irving, L. M., Sigmon, S. T., Yoshinobo, L., Gibb, J., Langelle, C., & Narney, P. (1991). The will and the ways: Development and validation of an individual-differences measure of hope. *Journal of Personality and Social Psychology, 60,* 570–585.

Staats, A. W. (1991). Unified positivism and unification psychology: Fad or new field? *American Psychologist, 46,* 899–912.

Stanley, M. A., & Maddux, J. E. (1986a). Cognitive processes in health enhancement: Investigation of a combined protection motivation and self-efficacy model. *Basic and Applied Social Psychology, 7,* 101–113.

Stanley, M. A., & Maddux, J. E. (1986b). Self-efficacy expectancy and depressed mood: An investigation of causal relationships. *Journal of Social Behavior and Personality, 4,* 575–586.

Stanley, M. A., & Maddux, J. E. (1986c). Self-efficacy theory: Potential contributions to understanding cognitions in depression. *Journal of Social and Clinical Psychology, 4,* 268–278.

Sternberg, R. J., & Kolligan, J., Jr. (Eds.). (1990). *Competence considered.* New Haven, CT: Yale University Press.

Sweeney, P. D., Anderson, K., & Bailey, S. (1986). Attributional style in depression: A meta-analytic review. *Journal of Personality and Social Psychology, 50,* 974–991.

Taylor, S. E. (1983). Adjustment to threatening events. *American Psychologist, 38,* 1161–1173.

Taylor, S. E. (1989). *Positive illusions: Creative self-deception and the healthy mind.* New York: Basic Books.

Taylor, S. E. (1991). Asymmetrical effects of positive and negative events: The mobilization–minimization hypothesis. *Psychological Bulletin, 110,* 67–85.

Taylor, S. E., & Brown, J. (1988). Illusion and well-being: A social psychological perspective on mental health. *Psychological Bulletin, 103,* 193–210.

Taylor, K. M., & Popma, J. (1990). An examination of the relationships among career decision-making self-efficacy, career salience, locus of control, and vocational indecision. *Journal of Vocational Behavior, 37,* 17–31.

Teasdale, J. D. (1978). Self-efficacy: Toward a unifying theory of behavioural change? In S. Rachman (Ed.), *Advances in behaviour research and therapy* (Vol. 1, pp. 211–215). Oxford: Pergamon.

Thompson, S. C. (1991). Intervening to enhance perceptions of control. In C. R. Snyder & D. R. Forsyth (Eds.), *Handbook of social and clinical psychology* (pp. 607–623). New York: Pergamon.

Tipton, R. M., & Worthington, E. L. (1984). The measurement of generalized self-efficacy: A study of construct validity. *Journal of Personality Assessment, 48,* 545–548.

Tolman, E. C. (1932). *Purposive behavior in animals and men.* New York: Century-Appleton-Crofts.

Watson, D., Clark, A. L., & Tellegen, A. (1988). Development and validation of brief measures of positive and negative affect: The PANAS scales. *Journal of Personality and Social Psychology, 54,* 1063–1070.

Wegner, D. M. (1989). *White bears and other unwanted thoughts: Suppression, obsession, and the psychology of mental control.* New York: Viking Penguin.

White, R. W. (1959). Motivation reconsidered: The concept of competence. *Psychological Review, 66,* 297–333.

Williams, R. N. (1992). The human context of agency. *American Psychologist, 47,* 752–760.

Wood, R., & Bandura, A. (1989a). Impact of conceptions of ability on self-regulatory mechanisms and complex decision making. *Journal of Personality and Social Psychology, 56,* 407–415.

Wood, R., & Bandura, A. (1989b). Social cognitive theory of organizational management. *Academy of Management Review, 14,* 361–384.

Wurtele, S. K. (1986). Self-efficacy and athletic performance: A review. *Journal of Social and Clinical Psychology, 4,* 290–301.

Wurtele, S. K., & Maddux, J. E. (1987). Relative contributions of protection motivation theory components in predicting exercise intentions and behavior. *Health Psychology, 6,* 453–466.

Wylie, R. (1979). *The self concept.* Lincoln: University of Nebraska Press.

Part II

APPLICATIONS IN CLINICAL PSYCHOLOGY

CHAPTER 2

SELF-EFFICACY AND ADJUSTMENT

BASIC PRINCIPLES AND ISSUES

JAMES E. MADDUX and JOHN LEWIS

Despite the continuing controversy over what psychological health is and how one might best achieve it, psychologists seem to agree on at least one principle—that a sense of control over our behavior, our environment, and our own thoughts and feelings is essential for good psychological adjustment (e.g., Korchin, 1976). When the world seems predictable and controllable and when behavior, thoughts, and emotions seem within their control, people are better able to meet life's challenges, deal with stress, build healthy relationships, and achieve personal satisfaction and peace of mind (e.g., Kobasa, 1979; Taylor, 1983; Thompson, 1981, 1991). Although a sense of control, competence, or mastery does not ensure good psychological adjustment, good adjustment is difficult, if not impossible, without such beliefs. The most common complaints of emotional distress that lead people to seek professional help—anxiety and depression (Smith, Glass, & Miller, 1980)—are both characterized by the belief that the good things in life cannot be obtained and that the bad things in life cannot be avoided through one's own efforts. Sometimes perceptions of lack of control are

JAMES E. MADDUX and JOHN LEWIS • Department of Psychology, George Mason University, Fairfax, Virginia 22030.

Self-Efficacy, Adaptation, and Adjustment: Theory, Research, and Application, edited by James E. Maddux. Plenum Press, New York, 1995.

the direct result of ineffective behavior; but such perceptions also can produce ineffective behavior, as well as inaction and inertia. A sense of personal control, mastery, or efficacy is at the heart of self-efficacy theory. A self-efficacy approach to psychological adjustment proposes that a sense of personal efficacy or control is essential for psychological adjustment and behavioral effectiveness. Research has shown, for example, that low self-efficacy expectancies are an important feature of depression (Maddux & Meier, Chap. 5, this volume), anxiety problems and specific fears (Bandura, 1986a; Williams, Chap. 3, this volume), social or interpersonal anxiety (Leary & Atherton, 1986; Maddux, Norton, & Leary, 1988), and substance abuse and addictions (DiClemente, Fairhurst, & Piotrowski, Chap. 4, this volume).

Self-efficacy theory has inspired a tremendous body of research on the etiology, assessment, and treatment of emotional and behavioral problems. Much work also has been conducted on several other topics that may be of interest to clinical researchers and practitioners, such as pain control (Dolce, 1987), academic achievement (Schunk, Chap. 10, this volume), career choice (Betz & Hackett, this volume), athletic performance (Wurtele, 1986), and a variety of health-related behaviors (Bandura, 1986a; O'Leary & Brown, Chap. 8, this volume; Maddux, Brawley, & Boykin, Chap. 6, this volume). This chapter does not attempt to review all of this work; instead, it presents a general discussion of the relationship between self-efficacy and psychological adjustment, and presents guidelines for psychological interventions based on self-efficacy theory. Because self-efficacy theory is subsumed within the larger social-cognitive theoretical framework, understanding the role of self-efficacy in adaptation and adjustment first requires explication of a broader *social cognitive* model of psychological adjustment, dysfunction, and change (see also Maddux, Chap. 1, this volume).

SOCIAL COGNITIVE VIEW OF PSYCHOLOGICAL ADJUSTMENT

As noted in greater detail in the first chapter of this volume, social cognitive theory makes two major assumptions: (a) that human behavior is best understood in the context of the reciprocal interaction of person, behavior, and environment; and (b) that human beings have tremendous cognitive capacities, including the ability to self-reflect, self-motivate, and self-regulate (Bandura, 1986a; Cervone & Williams, 1992). The following ideas concerning psychological adjustment are based on the principles of social cognitive theory described in the first chapter of this volume.

INTERACTIVE DOMAINS OF ADJUSTMENT

The social cognitive view assumes three related but relatively independent domains of personal adjustment: *behavior, cognition,* and *emotion.* Cognition and emotion are *personal* factors in social cognitive theory's triadic reciprocality model; behavior is viewed as a separate factor. Most common problems of adjustment can be viewed as consisting of difficulties in thinking, feeling, and doing (Mahoney, 1991; Persons, 1989; Yeates, Schultz, & Selman, 1990). Depressed people feel despondent, think pessimistic thoughts, and engage in fewer effective and pleasurable activities. In dysfunctional intimate relationships, partners feel angry and hurt, think critical thoughts about the other person, and behave in ways that damage the relationship. People with anxiety or fear problems feel apprehensive, think catastrophic thoughts, and avoid feared activities. Although anxiety itself is best conceived as an emotion rather than a composite of emotion, cognition, and behavior (Bandura, 1988), the difficulties associated with problematic anxiety include disturbing thoughts and disruptive avoidant behavior. The personal factors of emotion and cognition influence behavior and vice versa, and cognition and emotion influence each other. Change in one usually leads to change in the other two.

COGNITIVE MECHANISMS OF CHANGE

Social cognitive theory distinguishes between *mechanisms* of change and *procedures* for change (Bandura, 1986a). Mechanisms of change are mediating explanatory processes and are primarily cognitive (Maddux, Chap. 1, this volume). The most effective procedures of change, however, are behavioral or enactive; psychological change is best induced by procedures that provide opportunities for people to engage in new and more effective behavior. These behavioral changes initiate cognitive and affective changes that support the behavioral change and encourage its durability.

SELF-REGULATION

Perhaps the cognitive capacity most important in human adaptation and adjustment is self-regulation. Psychologically adjusted and adaptive people are capable of setting personal goals and using self-reflection, planning, and self-regulation in the pursuit of their goals. Conversely, psychological dysfunction can be viewed as ineffective or maladaptive self-regulation in the pursuit of goals (e.g., Emmons, 1992; Scheier & Carver, 1988). Therefore, understanding and facilitating psychological adaptation depends on understanding the importance of cognitive mediation in human behavior, including symbolizing, self-reflection, forethought, and self-regulation. (See also Maddux, Chap. 1, this volume.)

SITUATIONAL AND BEHAVIORAL SPECIFICITY

According to the social cognitive principle of *reciprocal determinism* (Bandura, 1986a; Maddux, Chap. 1, this volume), understanding the specific aspects of behaviors and the situations in which they occur is crucial to understanding adjustment difficulties and designing successful change procedures. The adaptiveness or maladaptiveness of behavior, cognition, and affect can be understood and assessed only in the context of situational demands and situational or social norms that were derived in social settings and are applied in social settings (e.g., Wakefield, 1992). Therefore, "normal" and "abnormal" are properties not of persons, behaviors, thoughts, emotions, or situations but of the complex interaction of all of these factors. Adjustment problems can be understood only through an examination of specific examples of specific problem behaviors, cognitions, and emotions in specific situations—both actual (past) examples and hypothetical or anticipated (future) examples. Discussions of adjustment difficulties limited to generic problems in generic types of situations are likely to lead only to vague and ineffective generic suggestions for behaving, thinking, and feeling more adaptively (e.g., "positive thinking") rather than specific ways to think, feel, and act more adaptively.

MALADAPTIVENESS AS INEFFECTIVENESS—NOT ILLNESS

Psychological dysfunction is best viewed as behavioral, cognitive, and affective responses that are inefficient and ineffective, rather than as symptoms of psychic "illness." In some cases, of course, psychological dysfunction may be the result of identified physiological dysfunction (e.g., schizophrenic disorders, bipolar affective disorders) and may be alleviated by biological interventions. In these relatively uncommon cases, "illness" can be said to exist in its literal rather than its metaphorical sense. In most examples of human problems in adjustment and adaptation, however, when the term *illness* is used, it refers to an "underlying" psychological pathology that by nature cannot be isolated and identified. Such explanations are unscientific and serve no useful practical purpose. In attempting to understand psychological dysfunction, efforts are better expended identifying patterns of effective and ineffective behavioral, cognitive, and emotional responding rather than searching for "mental illnesses."

Nonutility of Diagnostic Classification

Because they are not "diseases," patterns of maladaptive psychological response do not lend themselves to classification into discrete categories of "disorders" having discrete "symptoms." Not only do behavioral, cognitive, and affective problems defy easy categorization, but such categorization, even when done reliably, is usually not conducive to understanding an individual's difficulties in a manner that leads to practical interventions for their resolution (Persons, 1989; Williams, Chap. 3, this volume). Rigid diagnostic categories can obscure important individual differences in adaptation and maladaptation and may lead to error and bias in the clinician's attention, information-gathering, and judgment (e.g., Maddux, 1993; Turk & Salovey, 1988). Specific aspects of behavioral, cognitive, and affective adaptiveness and maladaptiveness and the situations in which they occur are better targets of change than are diagnostic categories or underlying psychic diseases. Therefore, agents interested in facilitating an individual's adaptation can better invest their energy in identifying and assessing such individualized targets of change, rather than in formal diagnostic activities.

In addition, designing effective interventions requires a conceptualization of human functioning and behavior change that is firmly grounded in theory. Therefore, a classification scheme that is by design atheoretical (i.e., the DSM-III-R; American Psychiatric Association, 1987) will not provide information essential for facilitating psychological change. Such a system may suggest in general terms *what* to change but not *how* to change it.

Continuity between "Normal" and "Abnormal"

Because psychological dysfunction is identified by its maladaptiveness, because adaptiveness is highly situation-dependent and norm-dependent (Wakefield, 1992), and because human adaptation and dysfunction cannot easily be compartmentalized into discrete illness categories, the distinction between normal and abnormal or between adaptive and maladaptive is elusive, if not illusory, and essentially arbitrary. Virtually every major theory of personality and "psychopathology" assumes that adaptive and maladaptive psychological phenomena differ not in kind but in degree—that continuity exists between normal and abnormal and between adaptive and maladaptive.

In addition, no one has yet presented compelling reasons to believe that maladaptive behaviors, cognitions, and emotions, or those persons labeled "abnormal" because they deviate from accepted standards of conduct are governed by processes that are different from the processes that explain adaptive or socially acceptable behavior (e.g., Bandura, 1978). Nor has anyone presented compelling evidence that the explanations for the problems of people who present themselves to mental health professionals ("clinical" populations) differ from the explanations for the problems of those whose problems may not be severe enough to warrant consultation with a professional, and those who simply suffer alone or seek the assistance of friends, family, or clergy ("nonclinical" populations; e.g., Bandura, 1978). Research documenting the continuities between the characteristics of so-called "clinical" (i.e., abnormal) and "nonclinical" (i.e., normal) populations undermines the validity and utility of these distinctions (e.g., Livesley, Jackson, & Schroeder, 1992; Persons, 1986; Shaywitz, Escobar, Shaywitz, Fletcher, & Makuck, 1992; Trull, 1992; Watson, Sawrie, & Biderman, 1991). The assessment of the severity of maladaptive patterns is of much concern, but assessment of severity need not lead to arbitrary distinctions between normal and abnormal or clinical and nonclinical.

CONTINUITY OF FORMAL AND INFORMAL CHANGE PROCESSES

Because of the continuity between adaptive and maladaptive psychological functioning and between "clinical" and "nonclinical" problems and populations, the basic processes that explain change facilitated by professional assistance and formal interventions also explain change that occurs without the benefit of professional assistance. "Clinical" change is not fundamentally different from "nonclinical" change simply because it occurs in a clinical setting and is assisted by a clinician or professional (Leary & Maddux, 1987; Prochaska, DiClemente, & Norcross, 1992). Formal, professionally assisted interventions are often more effective and efficient than the intentional and unintentional interventions that occur in everyday life, not because the basic mechanisms or processes of formal change are different or superior, but because formal change *techniques* are often more focused, structured, and specific.

ACTIVE NATURE OF INTERVENTIONS

Because they target specific aspects of behavioral, cognitive, and affective functioning and not "diseases," change procedures based on psychological principles are *interventions* and not "treatments." To ensure success, such interventions must be active rather than passive and must provide opportunities for learning new skills, adopting new attitudes and beliefs about self and world, and reducing emotional states that interfere with effective cognitive and behavioral responses to problems and challenges. Interventions should rely more on action than simple insight, but also should ensure that adaptive cognitive and affective change occurs along with behavioral change. Cognitive change can be facilitated by discussion and persuasion, but, to be made firm and enduring, requires action consistent with the cognitive change.

SELF-EFFICACY, ADAPTATION, AND ADJUSTMENT

In addition to the previously mentioned principles, an approach to adaptation and adjustment based on self-efficacy theory includes the following principles.

THREE PATHWAYS OF INFLUENCE

Self-efficacy beliefs influence psychological adjustment through their impact on goal-setting and persistence, cognitive efficiency, and emotional adaptiveness. These pathways operate at times with relative independence but, as do all social cognitive processes and variables, usually influence adjustment in an interactive fashion.

Goal-Setting and Persistence

A strong sense of self-efficacy leads people to set challenging personal goals and to persist toward those goals in the face of obstacles (e.g., Bandura, 1986a). People who have confidence in their abilities set their sights high; those plagued by self-doubt settle for less. Challenging and clear goals usually lead to greater achievement (e.g., Locke & Latham, 1990). In addition, a strong sense of personal efficacy leads to greater persistence when encountering difficulties in pursuit of a goal. Therefore, those with strong self-efficacy beliefs not only strive for more, but because they persist, they also accomplish more.

Cognitive Efficiency

Strong efficacy beliefs produce greater cognitive efficiency. People who have confidence in their ability to solve problems use their cognitive resources more effectively than people who doubt their cognitive and intellectual skills (Bandura & Wood, 1989; Wood & Bandura, 1989). Such efficiency usually leads to better solutions and greater achievement. For example, people with high self-efficacy are more likely to remain *task diagnostic* and continue to search for solutions to problems in the face of obstacles; under such conditions, however, those with low self-efficacy are more likely to become *self-diagnostic* and reflect on their inadequacies rather than devote their efforts toward assessing the obstacle or problem (Bandura & Wood, 1989; Wood & Bandura, 1989). Because effective negotiation of the events of daily life often requires making good decisions and making them quickly, people who are more confident and efficient decision makers are clearly at an advantage over those who are less so.

Emotional Adaptiveness

Strong beliefs about personal competence and ability produce adaptive emotional states, whereas beliefs about personal inefficacy produce distressing emotional states that not only are painful but also lead to further cognitive and behavioral ineffectiveness. People with a strong sense of self-efficacy approach challenging or threatening situations without debilitating anxiety or despondency, and they are less likely than people with weak efficacy beliefs to explain negative life events in ways that lead to despondency and inaction (Maddux & Meier, Chap. 5, this volume; Williams, Chap. 3, this volume). Excessive apprehension and despondency can produce cognitive confusion, inefficiency, behavioral inertia, and disorganization.

SELF-CONFIRMING ASPECTS OF SELF-EFFICACY BELIEFS

The powerful impact of self-efficacy beliefs on psychological adjustment and behavioral effectiveness derive in large part from their self-confirming properties. Once beliefs about strong or weak personal efficacy are firmly established, they resist change and become self-perpetuating. People with a strong sense of efficacy set higher goals and display greater persistence; they choose environments in which success is likely, and they attend to efficacy-enhancing information and distort information to render it consistent with their current beliefs.

Self-Fulfilling Nature of Expectancies

The predictions people make about their behavior, their affective reactions, and the responses of others often become self-fulfilling prophecies (e.g., Darley & Fazio, 1980; Jones, 1986; Kirsch, 1990). Expectancies and hypotheses about self, others, and events often lead people to behave in ways that bring about the events they predict and to perceive events in ways that confirm their hypotheses. A strong sense of personal efficacy leads people to strive for higher goals, persist more adamantly in the face of obstacles, and delay gratification, all of which increase the likelihood of eventual success (e.g. Wood & Bandura, 1989). Thus, perceptions of control can result in the kind of behavioral persistence and effectiveness that then becomes evidence for the initial belief about one's efficacy.

Construction and Selection of Environments

People often construct their social worlds in order to maximize the receipt of positive information about themselves and minimize or avoid negative information (Taylor, 1989; Swann, 1983, 1984). For example, people are more likely to associate with those whom they perceive are less capable in personally important areas of competence (Taylor, 1989; Tesser & Paulhus, 1983). People also select situations that allow them to display their talents and hide their deficiencies (Taylor, 1989; Swann, 1983, 1984). A strong sense of personal efficacy becomes self-perpetuating, because people associate with others who help them feel competent by comparison and put themselves in situations that both increase opportunities for displays of competence and obscure areas of ineffectiveness (Bandura, 1992).

Attention, Information Processing, and Memory

People selectively attend to and process information about themselves and their world (Fiske & Taylor, 1991). More important, well-adjusted people are likely to seek out and attend to positive rather than negative information about themselves (Taylor & Brown, 1988). In addition, people often desire certain outcomes and goals so strongly that, when the desired events occur, they are likely to conclude that they produced them, despite lack of evidence for this conclusion (Taylor, 1989). Finally, people selectively remember and forget. Information that is consistent with the self-image is more likely to be recalled than is inconsistent information (Taylor, 1989; Greenwald, 1980). Therefore, those with a fairly strong sense of self-efficacy are more likely to remember success information than failure information. If negative information about self-efficacy manages to survive these filters, it may have only a temporary effect, rather than an enduring impact on self-conceptions (Taylor & Brown, 1988; Swann, 1983). Therefore, a strong sense of efficacy is self-confirming because people with high self-efficacy attend to, process, and remember information consistent with their positive self-concepts and may even distort information to make it consistent with their efficacy beliefs (Fiske & Taylor, 1991; Taylor & Brown, 1988).

ACCURACY OF SELF-EFFICACY BELIEFS AND ADJUSTMENT

The impact of self-efficacy beliefs on emotional and behavioral adaptation and adjustment is not highly dependent on the accuracy of these beliefs. Competent people who strongly doubt their abilities will experience distress and performance difficulties, whereas less able but more confident others will perform with greater ease and facility. Although a clear and accurate view of self and world traditionally has been considered a hallmark of psychological health (e.g., Korchin, 1976), recent theory and research suggest that good psychological health and adjustment are characterized by "positive illusions" of personal ability and control over important life events (Seligman, 1990; Taylor & Brown, 1988). Healthy, well-adjusted people have an inflated sense of competence and of their ability to affect events in a positive way (Fiske & Taylor, 1991; Taylor, 1989). Research on "positive illusions" suggests that people may become distressed and seek professional help when they have lost the illusions that have heretofore facilitated their adjustment (Taylor, 1989; Taylor & Brown, 1988); Stressful events are less stressful and more tolerable when we believe we can control them—even when this belief is a fiction (Taylor, 1983; Williams, Chap. 3, this volume). Thus, self-efficacy beliefs need not be accurate to be adaptive. Not only is positive and optimistic distortion the norm, it also is healthy and adjustment-enhancing—within limits. Beliefs about personal abilities or response-outcome contingencies that are overly optimistic can be maladaptive if they lead people to set unreasonable goals that ensure failure and disappointment, or persist to the point at which persistence becomes counterproductive and self-defeating (Baumeister & Scher, 1988).

SELF-EFFICACY AND PROCESSES OF CHANGE

Because a sense of control or mastery is essential for sound emotional and psychological functioning, the sense that one has lost control over one's life and environment often leads people to seek the help of psychotherapists and counselors. Although emotional distress (e.g., depression, anxiety, anger, fear) is, in most cases, the immediate precipitant of help-seeking, this distress is always accompanied by, if not directly caused by, beliefs of helplessness, hopelessness, pessimism, and personal incompetence. Alleviation of this state of "demoralization" is a major goal of all psychological interventions (J. D. Frank & J. B. Frank, 1991).

From the perspective of self-efficacy theory, this demoralization is the result of the belief that one can do little or nothing to control important life events and achieve valued life goals. A self-efficacy perspective also suggests that people are motivated to seek professional help following failure or perceived failures in one or more important areas of life. Because of these perceived failures, people may come to hold a number of specific low self-efficacy expectancies about specific competencies. These low self-efficacy expectancies may lead them to give up or stop trying to be effective in their lives and then, after repeated failure, come to believe that they will continue to be ineffective in coping with difficulties in life. For these reasons, most psychological interventions set as an important goal not only helping people *get* back in control of their lives but also *feel* in control of their lives—to regain or develop for the first time a sense of personal mastery or efficacy over important aspects of life (J. D. Frank & J. B. Frank, 1991). Self-efficacy theory proposes that the enhancement of the individuals sense of mastery or personal efficacy—in specific situations and across a range of situations—is an essential mechanism of change in effective strategies for facilitating adaptation and adjustment. Once a client begins to experience some success in one or two aspects of his or her life, the client may develop stronger self-efficacy expectancies for behaviors in other areas of life. For example, an extremely shy client may be helped with calling a friend to arrange a lunch date, or a severely depressed person may be encouraged to simply get up and get dressed in the morning. According to self-efficacy theory, these small successes will strengthen the client's sense of self-efficacy and his or her expectations for additional, more important successes. Different interventions, or different components of an intervention, may be equally effective because they exert equal influence on self-efficacy for the crucial behavioral and cognitive skills imparted by the interventions (Bandura, 1986).

Most of the clinical research on self-efficacy theory has been applied toward understanding and predicting behavior in a wide range of areas, such as fears and phobias, anxiety and panic, depression, and addictive behaviors. Fewer studies have examined the application of self-efficacy theory to the development of clinical interventions, and few researchers have designed interventions specifically to enhance the client's self-efficacy. The exception to this generalization is the research on interventions for fear disorders (Williams, Chap. 3, this volume). Few theories or models provide explicit step-by-step guidelines for developing interventions, but a good theory should provide the clinician with a conceptual framework that serves as a general guide to understanding and conducting clinical interactions (Kanfer, 1984). Therefore, self-efficacy theory may be most useful not by suggesting specific new techniques for engineering behavior change, but by emphasizing the importance of arranging experiences designed to increase the client's sense of efficacy or mastery in the specific domains that have resulted in distress and demoralization (e.g.,

Riskind, 1982). Self-efficacy theory can provide clinicians with some general principles for designing and structuring interventions for a variety of problems. An emphasis on self-efficacy also provides an index of the way clients cognitively process behavior changes and experiences that occur in psychotherapy (Goldfried & Robins, 1982).

SELF-EFFICACY AND STAGES OF CHANGE

Beliefs about personal efficacy play a major role in the process of behavior change from beginning to end. A recent Stages of Change model proposed that self-initiated and professionally facilitated change consists of five stages: *Precontemplation, Contemplation, Preparation, Action,* and *Maintenance* (Prochaska et al., 1992). Each of these stages can be partially defined and differentiated by the role played by self-efficacy beliefs. In the Precontemplation stage, people have no intention of changing because they see no need to change. Because they have not seriously thought about changing, they probably have not developed firm beliefs about their self-efficacy for changing. People in the Contemplation stage are aware of their problems and are thinking seriously about the possibility of change, but have not committed to change. In this stage, people consider the pros and cons of changing. Certainly among the most important considerations at this point will be the possibility of change, including questions about what strategies might be effective (outcome expectancies) and what strategies the person might be able to personally implement (self-efficacy expectancies).

In the Preparation stage, people have taken recent unsuccessful action and strongly intend to take action again in the near future. They are still undergoing serious contemplation about the pros and cons and possibilities of change, but also have made some effort to change. In this stage, beliefs about personal efficacy will be stronger than in the Contemplation stage and will be greatly influenced by the individual's interpretations of his or her past change attempts. People at this stage are also likely to have strongly optimistic beliefs about the possible benefits of change (outcome expectancies). At this stage, self-efficacy will probably be moderately high, but fairly fragile, because the person has not experienced sufficient success in his or her change attempts.

In the Action stage, people have made a commitment to change and are making deliberate attempts to overcome their problems by changing their behavior, experiences, or environment. People at this stage see themselves as working hard to change. Self-efficacy beliefs will be especially critical during this stage, because people will be monitoring their change attempts and evaluating their successes and failures. Those able to view their attempts in a way that facilitates their sense of efficacy are likely to persist in the face of obstacles and setbacks. In the final Maintenance stage, people work to consolidate and solidify their successes and work to prevent relapse. Beliefs about personal efficacy will also be crucial during this stage as people continue to experience difficulties and obstacles; their interpretations of these setbacks or relapses can either facilitate or undermine their self-efficacy, which will then determine the strength of their persistence and resilience.

The Stages of Change model also proposes that people do not change in a linear pattern, but, instead, "spiral" in and out of these stages as they encounter both success and relapse. Thus, change is upward in direction, but at the same time is circular. This spiraling change pattern, rather than a linear one, is consistent with the assumption that self-efficacy beliefs are fluid rather than static and can ebb and flow as people encounter and interpret success and difficulties. Fluctuations in the strength of self-efficacy beliefs may be the major factor that accounts for the movement of an individual in and out of these stages of change. For example, people in the Preparation stage who have made some previous but unsuccessful attempt at changing and who interpret this lack of success as an indication of an inability to change are likely to fall back into the Contemplation stage; however, those who focus on past successes rather than failures and who view these successes as indicative of their ability to change (e.g., Dweck & Liggett, 1988) will probably persist and move into the Action stage.

ASSESSMENT OF SELF-EFFICACY AND ADJUSTMENT DIFFICULTIES

A social cognitive approach to understanding human adaptation and adjustment stresses the importance of situational, behavioral, cognitive, and affective specificity in the assessment of problems in adaptation. Toward this end, the self-efficacy model and the considerable research on measurement of self-efficacy expectancies may be useful by specifying targets of intervention and evaluating intervention effectiveness.

Specifying Targets for Intervention

The assessment of self-efficacy can assist in targeting specific competency-related beliefs and situations, predicting areas of potential difficulty, and tailoring interventions to meet an individual's special needs. For example, a self-efficacy inventory that provides detailed information about "at risk" situations for people with eating problems or substance abuse problems (e.g., DiClemente, Fairhurst, & Piotrowski, Chap. 4, this volume; Schneider, O'Leary, & Bandura, 1985) can help the clinician clarify, anticipate, and prevent problems that clients typically encounter when attempting new or anxiety-provoking behaviors (e.g., behaving assertively with a teacher or employer, asking an attractive person for a date, controlling food intake in the face of temptation, or refusing a drink or cigarette when offered one at a party). Such information can also assist in the timing of specific interventions, because the clinician and the client are better able to anticipate situations in which difficulties are likely to occur and then plan strategies for coping with these situations.

Evaluating Intervention Effectiveness

The assessment of self-efficacy before, during, and following an intervention may be useful in the evaluation of the intervention's effectiveness. As noted earlier, most theories and models of psychotherapy emphasize the importance of helping the client attain a greater sense of personal mastery or competence (J. D. Frank & J. B. Frank, 1991; Goldfried & Robins, 1982; Korchin, 1976). However, perceptions of personal mastery, if measured at all as a part of treatment evaluation, usually have been measured as global traitlike constructs (e.g., locus of control, self-esteem). In understanding adaptation and adjustment, evaluating specific self-efficacy expectancies about specific behaviors and specific life goals is usually more useful than simply examining a person's general sense of competence or effectiveness. Specificity helps a clinician determine exactly what beliefs and behaviors need to be changed in what situations to help the person experience success and begin to feel and be more effective and productive. According to Bandura (1986), "a global self-conception does not do justice to the complexity of self-efficacy percepts, which vary across different activities, different levels of the same activity, and different circumstances" (1986a, p. 410).

Self-efficacy theory has encouraged research on the development of assessment instruments that are problem-specific and therefore more useful clinically than omnibus measures of self-esteem or self-concept or instruments designed to assess "personality." Such measures should be of particular interest to behavioral and cognitive–behavioral clinicians because of their emphasis on careful specification of targets of change and techniques for facilitating change.

Most measures of self-efficacy expectancies have been developed for research rather than for direct clinical use, but many of them share a number of characteristics that make them suitable for use in clinical settings: face validity, brevity, and specificity. In addition, research suggests that self-efficacy measures are largely nonreactive in that the act of assessing self-efficacy does not influence self-efficacy (Bandura, 1992). For these reasons, measures of self-efficacy can be used at frequent intervals to efficiently monitor client progress.

Outcome Expectancy and Outcome Value

Although a number of measures of self-efficacy expectancies have been developed that are suitable for clinical use, the measurement of outcome expectancy and outcome value has been largely ignored. The major exception to this observation is the work on mood regulation expectancies described later in this chapter (see also Maddux & Meier, Chap. 5, this volume). Research suggests that outcome expectancy and outcome value can be useful predictors of emotions and behaviors (Goozh & Maddux, 1993; Kirsch, Mearns, & Catanzaro, 1990; Mearns, 1991). Thus, the development of measures of these constructs deserves attention. For example, an outcome expectancy measure might consist of a list of possible coping strategies for a specific problem and allow for ratings of the client's perception of the potential effectiveness of these strategies (e.g., the Negative Mood Regulation Scale; Mearns, 1991). An outcome value measure might consist of a list of the anticipated consequences (both positive and negative) that might result from being more assertive or losing weight and the extent to which these consequences are desired or feared (e.g., Saltzer, 1981). Both kinds of measures might assist the therapist in assessing a client's motivation for treatment in general, the value placed on attaining certain treatment goals, and expectations about the effectiveness of specific intervention strategies.

DISTINGUISHING THREE DOMAINS OF SELF-EFFICACY

The distinction among three domains of adjustment—behavioral, cognitive, and emotional—suggests a strategy for organizing and understanding self-efficacy beliefs. Self-efficacy can be assessed for *behaviors* (e.g., social skills, assertiveness skills, smoking and drinking behavior), *cognitions* (e.g., the ability to control intrusive or depressive thoughts), and *emotions* (e.g., the ability to control one's mood in general, or in specific problematic situations, such as being assertive with one's employer or managing one's anxiety when asking someone for a date). These distinctions also may be useful in designing intervention strategies. Effective psychological interventions lead to significant change in all three domains, although different theories and approaches to psychotherapy differ in their emphasis of one type of change over the others. Thus, to be most effective, interventions should be directed toward enhancing self-efficacy for behavioral control, cognitive control, and affective or emotional control.

Behavioral Self-Efficacy

Behavioral self-efficacy refers to the belief in one's ability to perform the specific actions needed to gain mastery over a problem situation. *Self-efficacy* was originally defined as a belief about behavior, and the vast majority of research on self-efficacy has been concerned with self-efficacy for the performance of behaviors and behavioral strategies. In fact, a number of studies have demonstrated that measures of self-efficacy are better predictors of behavior than is past performance (Bandura, 1986a; Williams, Chap. 3, this volume). The research concerning behavioral self-efficacy comprises the vast majority of the chapters in this volume.

Behavioral self-efficacy is important in adjustment in innumerable ways. Because most successful interventions for problems of adjustment involve teaching new behaviors or skills, altering and measuring changes in self-efficacy for these skills are essential for arranging and measuring treatment efficacy. Not only must people be taught new skills (e.g., how to behave more assertively), they must also be taught to believe that they can do what they have been instructed to do in those situations in which it matters the most—when the psychotherapist or counselor is not present. In self-efficacy theory, behavioral self-efficacy is best changed through the exercise of the behaviors of interest. The successful exercise of a new skill (or an old skill in a new situation) leads to the enhancement of behavioral self-efficacy, which then encourages the client to initiate the behavior in other situations and to persist in the face of obstacles.

Cognitive Self-Efficacy

Cognitive self-efficacy refers to perceptions of the ability to exercise control over one's thoughts. Because a self-efficacy belief is itself a cognition, cognitive self-efficacy is a cognition concerning one's cognitions. For the client and the clinician, the cognitions of interest usually are those that influence the performance of desired new behaviors or the experience of emotional states. However, the perception of lack of control over thoughts is sometimes a major problem itself, as in obsessive–compulsive problems (see also Wegner, 1989). Because social cognitive theory assumes that behavior is largely guided by forethought and the anticipation of consequences, facilitating control over thoughts and a sense of control over thoughts is important in social cognitive interventions.

In addition, facilitating self-efficacy for control of cognitions can help clients set more realistic and attainable goals when dealing with stressful situations, especially situations that may not be affected by a client's behavioral changes. For example, Rothbaum, Weisz, and Snyder (1982) have made a distinction between *primary control*—changing the external world to meet one's needs through the exercise of behavior—and *secondary control*—adjusting "internally" by changing one's thoughts and feelings about an otherwise uncontrollable situation. Cognitive self-efficacy is concerned with secondary control, with the ability to control and adapt one's thoughts to a situation that cannot be changed directly.

Several common problems presented to mental health practitioners include as a major feature the perception of loss of control over one's own cognitive processes. The most obvious of these is obsessive–compulsive disorder, in which the individual is troubled by recurring thoughts of a disturbing nature and by repetitive behaviors that serve to help the individual control these thoughts. In addition, both depression and anxiety are characterized by the inability, or the perception of inability, to control the thoughts that influence mood (e.g., Kirsch, 1990). The socially anxious person expects to be anxious in social situations and has difficulty controlling these anxiety-producing expectancies. The depressed person feels unable to control his or her depressive ruminations and therefore expects to remain depressed.

Little research has been conducted on assessing self-efficacy for controlling cognitions, but what has been done is promising (e.g., Ozer & Bandura, 1990). For example, a recent study of dental anxiety (Kent & Gibbons, 1987) found that persons low in dental anxiety had fewer negative thoughts about dental appointments than persons high in dental anxiety, and, more important, that low anxiety persons expressed having more control over their negative thoughts than high anxiety persons. If self-efficacy can be applied to the control of anxiety-related cognitions, then it also might be applied effectively to the control of anxiety and other emotions.

Emotional Self-Efficacy

Emotional self-efficacy refers to beliefs in the ability to perform actions that influence one's moods or emotional states. A sense of emotional self-efficacy is important because people who seek psychotherapy do so not only because they are in distress *now*, but also because they expect their distress to continue—because they believe their feelings are beyond their own control. Psychotherapy clients usually have already tried a number of strategies to improve their distressing mood, and these attempts usually have been unsuccessful or only temporarily successful. Thus, clients usually have low expectations for being able to alleviate their emotional distress (depression, anxiety, anger). Response expectancy theory (Kirsch, 1985, 1990) proposes that negative emotional states such as anxiety and depression are in part created by, and can be exacerbated and maintained by expectations that the aversive state will continue and cannot be controlled. In addition, research has indicated that expectancies can directly influence mood, including dysphoric mood. For example, fear of anxiety is an important component of maladaptive anxiety states (Reiss, 1991), and the belief that one will remain depressed is an important aspect of depressive hopelessness (Beck, Rush, Shaw, & Emery, 1979).

Emotions are controlled not directly but through changes in cognition or behavior (e.g., thought-stopping, cognitive rehearsal, exercise, relaxation techniques). In fact, people care about controlling their thoughts and behaviors largely because they want to control their feelings. Thus, emotional self-efficacy may be measurable only indirectly through the measurement of self-efficacy for cognitive and behavioral strategies for controlling mood, such as thought-stopping, cognitive self-regulation, relaxation procedures, exercise, and engaging in pleasant or mastery-related behaviors.

The measurement of emotional self-efficacy remains an unexplored topic. However, emotional *outcome expectancies* have been the subject of research in studies of mood regulation expectancies. A *mood-regulation expectancy* has been defined as a belief about the effectiveness of specific cognitive and behavioral strategies in alleviating negative mood states (Catanzaro & Mearns, 1990; Kirsch et al., 1990; Mearns, 1991). Mood-regulation expectancies have been found to be good predictors of depression following the end of romantic relationship (Mearns, 1991) and better predictors of active coping responses and dysphoria than degree of stress or family support (Kirsch, et al., 1990; see also Maddux & Meier, Chap. 5, this volume). Although useful, a focus on outcome expectancies or response expectancies may be somewhat limited. For example, clients who believe their moods are uncontrollable and their distress unrelieveable may believe either that there are no additional strategies left untried that might make them feel better (low outcome expectancies) or that they are incapable of doing what others seem capable of doing to relieve their distress (low self-efficacy), or both. Thus, mood-regulation expectancies can be viewed as consisting of mood-regulation outcome expectancies— the belief that the coping strategy will alleviate one's dysphoria—and mood-regulation self-efficacy expectancies—the belief that one can execute the strategies that might alleviate the negative mood. A measure that assesses beliefs in one's ability to implement mood-regulation strategies might also prove useful.

STRATEGIES FOR ENHANCING SELF-EFFICACY

A self-efficacy approach to psychological interventions is based on the assumption that the individual seeking assistance is experiencing a low and ineffective sense of personal control and that one of the major goals of the intervention is its restoration. There are a number of strategies for restoring self-efficacy.

INTEGRATING SOURCES OF SELF-EFFICACY INFORMATION

The major sources of self-efficacy information (See Maddux, Chap. 1, this volume)—verbal persuasion, vicarious experience, imaginal experience, physiological and emotional arousal, and performance experience—suggest strategies for constructing effective interventions. Most effective psychological interventions involve combinations of more than one source of self-efficacy information. For example, successful treatment with agoraphobic clients may require intervention using all sources of efficacy information.

1. *Emotional and Physiological Arousal*—teaching the client to relax and feel less anxious when out in public
2. *Verbal Persuasion*—encouraging the client to attempt feared behaviors and challenging the client's expectations of catastrophe
3. *Vicarious Experiences*—observation of filmed or live models (such as the therapist) engaging in feared behaviors or participation in an agoraphobic group
4. *Imaginal Experience*—imagining oneself engaging in feared behaviors (e.g., systematic desensitization)
5. *Performance Experiences*—actual practice in engaging in feared behaviors, such as leaving one's home and approaching a feared situation or setting such as a supermarket (see also Williams, Chap. 3, this volume).

Verbal Persuasion

All effective psychological interventions begin and end with communication, regardless of the techniques employed in between. Thus, most interventions rely strongly on verbal persuasion as a means of enhancing a client's sense of self-efficacy and encouraging clients to take small risks that may lead to small successes (J. D. Frank & J. B. Frank, 1991; Harvey, Weary, Maddux, Jordan, & Galvin, 1985). In addition, therapists influence outcome expectancies and outcome values through persuasion by discussing with clients alternative plans for achieving desired goals, the anticipated reactions of others to changes in the client's behavior, the client's own reactions (behavioral, cognitive, and emotional) to life events, and ways of diminishing the importance the client places on certain goals. In cognitive and cognitive–behavioral therapies, the therapist engages the client in a discussion of the client's dysfunctional beliefs, attitudes, and expectancies, and helps the client see the irrationality and self-defeating nature of such beliefs. The therapist encourages the client to adopt new, more adaptive beliefs, and the client is then encouraged to act on these new beliefs and expectancies and to encounter the success that will lead to more enduring alterations in self-efficacy expectancies and adaptive behavior. (See Hollon & Beck, 1986, and Ingram, Kendall, & Chen, 1991, for reviews of cognitive and cognitive–behavioral psychotherapy.)

Vicarious Experience

Some interventions use vicarious and imaginal means to teach new skills and enhance self-efficacy. For example, modeling films and videotapes have been used successfully to encourage socially withdrawn children to interact with other children. In such films, the socially withdrawn child observes another child similar to himself encounter and then master problems similar to his own. The child model initially expresses some fear about approaching another group of children, but then takes a chance and starts talking to the children and joins in their play. The children viewing the film see the model child, someone much like themselves, experience success and come to believe that they too can do the same thing (see Conger & Keane, 1981, for a review). *In vivo* modeling has been used successfully in the treatment of phobic individuals; this research has shown that changes in self-efficacy expectancies for approach behaviors mediate adaptive behavioral changes (Bandura, 1986a).

Imaginal Experience

When models are unavailable or impractical, imagining oneself or others engaging in feared behaviors or overcoming difficulties can be used to enhance self-efficacy and motivation (e.g., Cervone, 1989) and facilitate effective coping. For example, cognitive therapy for anxiety and fear problems often involves modifying visual images of danger and anxiety, including images of oneself coping effectively with the feared situation (Beck & Emery, 1985). Imaginal or covert modeling has also been used successfully in interventions to increase assertive behavior and self-efficacy for assertiveness (Kazdin, 1979). Live or filmed models may be difficult to obtain, but the client's imagination and ability to symbolize is a more easily harnessed resource. Systematic desensitization (Wolpe, 1958) and implosion (Stamfl & Levis, 1967) are traditional behavioral therapy techniques that rely on imaginal abilities.

Physiological and Emotional States

People feel more self-efficacious when emotionally calm than when aroused and distressed. Thus, strategies for controlling and reducing emotional arousal, specifically anxiety, during attempts to implement new behaviors should increase self-efficacy and increase the likelihood of successful implementation. Among the more common strategies for reducing emotional or physiological arousal and the association between this arousal and low self-efficacy are hypnosis, biofeedback, relaxation training, meditation, and medication.

Enactive Experience

Actual performance of behaviors that lead to success is the most powerful way to enhance personal efficacy. For example, the most effective interventions for phobias and fears involve *guided mastery—in vivo* experience with the feared object or situation during therapy sessions and between sessions as "homework" assignments (see Williams, Chap. 3, this volume). In cognitively based treatments of depression, depressed clients are provided structured guidance in the arrangement of success experiences that will counteract low self-efficacy expectancies (Beck et al., 1979). Research is needed that provides a systematic analysis of how people interpret their performances to provide guidelines for structuring performance experiences to best enhance their impact on maladaptive, low self-efficacy beliefs (Bandura, 1986a).

Enhancing the Impact of Success Experiences

Because people often discount the credibility of information about themselves that is inconsistent with their current views of themselves (see Fiske & Taylor, 1991), clients who feel distressed and believe they are incompetent and helpless are likely to ignore or discount information from their therapists and from their own behavioral successes that is not consistent with both their mood and their negative self-schema (Fiske & Taylor, 1991). Clients may encounter success experiences in certain areas of their lives yet fail to benefit fully from these experiences because they interpret these experiences in ineffective ways, such as by overlooking or ignoring them, or discounting their importance (Goldfried & Robins, 1982). Therefore, therapists need to make concerted efforts to increase the probability that their clients will not only experience success but also interpret that success *as success* and as their own doing. A self-efficacy framework in psychotherapy can be useful in helping clients cognitively process success experiences more beneficially in four specific ways (Goldfried & Robins, 1982).

Discriminating between Past and Present Behaviors

Helping people discriminate between past and present behavior can help them more accurately gauge their progress in psychological interventions. People are more likely to feel more self-efficacious when they contrast recent successful coping strategies with past ineffective behaviors, and view competence not as a trait but as a set of specific behaviors performed in specific situations, and by being discouraged from comparing their behavior with others who may seem more competent. People who view competence as acquirable through effort and experience are more likely to persist in the face of obstacles to success than those who view competence as a fixed entity or trait (Dweck & Liggett, 1988; Wood & Bandura, 1989). Therefore, clinicians need to continually remind clients that competence in a particular skill is not immutable, but can be increased through effort.

Retrieving Past Success Experiences More Effectively

People are more likely to attend to and recall experiences that are consistent rather than discrepant with their current self-perceptions. In addition, memory is sometimes mood-dependent. For example, non-depressed people access positive self-beliefs more easily than negative self-beliefs, but depressed people process negative self-beliefs more easily than positive ones (Bargh & Tota, 1988). Thus, mood-dependent memories can be mood-reinforcing (see also Fiske & Taylor, 1991). Therefore, clinicians need to encourage clients to become more vigilant for success experiences and more actively selective in recalling past successes, which then can become a guide to future behavior. In other words, "clients must not only behave in competent ways but must also view these behavior patterns as being part of their personal history" (Goldfried & Robins, 1982, p. 371).

Increasing Cognitive, Behavioral, and Affective Congruence

Therapists can assist clients in aligning or attaining greater consonance among expectancies, anticipatory feelings, behaviors, objective consequences of behaviors, and their self-evaluation. For example, clients may perform adequately in threatening situations, yet feel unpleasant emotional arousal and thus face two conflicting sources of self-efficacy information. In such situations, the therapist needs to emphasize that the emotional arousal did not predict the outcome of the situation and thereby discount a source of efficacy information that previously had great importance for the client but was maladaptive (Goldfried & Robins, 1982).

Changing Causal Attributions

Although the relationship between causal attributions and self-efficacy has not been explored extensively, changing causal attributions is likely to influence self-efficacy and vice versa. For this reason, clinicians should encourage clients to attribute success to their own effort and competence rather than to environmental circumstances or to the expertise and insights of the clinician (Forsterling, 1986; Thompson, 1991). Success experiences should be attributed to one's own efforts (internal cause) and should be used as evidence for the acquisition of an enduring skill or ability (stable cause) and the enhancement of general competence (global cause).

INCREASING CLIENT INVOLVEMENT IN PLANNING INTERVENTIONS

To become fully invested in interventions, people must have a clear sense of what the intervention entails. When clients know what is expected of them, are aware of what is going to happen to them, and are given explicit choices among intervention strategies, their perceptions of efficacy are more likely to be enhanced than if they are kept in the dark and not provided with options (Thompson, 1991). Understanding the clinician's conceptualization of their problem and the rationale and components of interventions can help provide clients with a greater sense of control over treatment. The clinician can further enhance the client's sense of efficacy by eliciting the client's input and feedback in the treatment process and by letting the client assume an active part in making decisions about aspects of the intervention, such as between-session assignments. Making explicit the rationale and details of the intervention may help clients learn to use strategies learned in therapy on their own, thus facilitating independence from the therapist and enhancing internal attributions of control (Thompson, 1991).

SETTING CONCRETE GOALS

The phrase "seeing is believing" underscores the importance of providing clients with tangible evidence of their success in interventions. According to self-efficacy theory, enactive experiences are the most powerful sources of efficacy information. When clients are able to actually see themselves cope effectively with difficult situations, their sense of mastery is heightened. Performance goals that are concrete, specific, and proximal (short-range) provide greater incentive and motivation and greater evidence of efficacy than goals that are abstract, vague, and set in the distant future (Locke & Latham, 1990; Williams, 1990). Concrete goals allow the client to identify the specific behaviors needed for successful achievement and to know when they have succeeded (Locke & Latham, 1990; Riskind, 1982; Thompson, 1991).

The most concrete performance goals are those based on behavioral accomplishments, such as increasing the snake phobic person's approach behavior, having the socially anxious person initiate conversations with others, or having depressed clients construct daily schedules. Providing clients with regular feedback on their progress via brief measures of cognitions or mood can also help clients quantify treatment gains that otherwise may seem elusive.

MODIFYING IMAGERY

When situations present difficult challenges to their coping abilities, people often produce imagery congruent with their perceptions of low self-efficacy. For example, maladaptive, distorted imagery has been identified as an important component of anxiety and depression (Beck & Emery, 1985; Beck et al., 1979). Various techniques have been suggested to help clients modify distortions and maladaptive assumptions contained in their visual images of danger and anxiety (e.g., Beck & Emery, 1985). For example, frequent repetition of images in which the client perceives himself or herself as completely unable to cope with a difficult situation may help reduce distortions and bring fantasy more in line with reality. Therapists can also help clients "decatastrophize" fearful outcomes inherent in their imagery regarding low self-efficacy expectancies. Images of low coping abilities in various situations can also be replaced with more positive images, depicting the client competently overcoming challenges to his or her coping abilities. Finally, when unsure of their abilities to cope with a particular situation, clients can gain "cognitive control" over the situation by imagining a future "possible self" (Markus & Nurius, 1986) that can deal effectively with the situation (Fiske & Taylor, 1991).

ENCOURAGING DISTORTIONS

As noted previously, beliefs about self and world need not be accurate to be adaptive. Psychological adjustment is enhanced by minor distortions in the perception of control over important life events. In addition, strong beliefs about control and self-efficacy are self-confirming because such beliefs encourage the setting of challenging goals, persistence in the face of obstacles, attention to efficacy-enhancing information, and the selection of efficacy-enhancing environments. For these reasons, clinicians should be concerned less with encouraging accuracy in a client's self-efficacy beliefs (i.e., the degree to which these beliefs are congruent with objective evidence of competence and skill) and more with encouraging self-confirming and self-enhancing inaccuracies or distortions. Encouraging discouraged people to believe that they are more competent than objective evidence suggests will prompt them into action and toward improvement and success more readily than will getting them to face the harsh reality of their current low level of skill.

PROVIDING A VARIETY OF STRATEGIES

Clients are likely to experience a greater sense of control over their problems when they have several options for coping. People base their efficacy perceptions not only on their level of performance and proficiency, but also on the flexibility of their coping strategies (Williams, 1990). Having several strategies for coping with problems allows clients to fall back on alternative methods of obtaining goals when one strategy fails. Knowing that an alternative strategy is available may reduce clients' anxiety, increase their self-efficacy, and thus increase the probability that the chosen strategy will be implemented correctly and successfully.

SUMMARY

A strong sense of personal control or self-efficacy is important in psychological adaptation and adjustment. People often seek professional assistance when recent difficult life experiences have led to a reduction of their sense of personal control or efficacy. Thus, one of the major goals of psychological interventions is the restoration or elevation of this sense of efficacy or competence. A self-efficacy approach to understanding psychological adjustment and designing effective interventions to enhance adjustment begins with a set of principles from a broader social cognitive theory.

1. Human functioning is best understood in terms of the interaction of person, behavior, and environment.
2. Human beings have tremendous cognitive capacities, including the ability to self-reflect, self-motivate, and self-regulate; effective self-regulation is essential for effective adjustment.

3. Adjustment should be viewed in terms of interacting behavioral, cognitive, and emotional domains.
4. Maladaptiveness is cognitive, emotional, and behavioral ineffectiveness, not illness.
5. Effectiveness in human functioning is continuous, not dichotomous. Thus, the distinction between normal (clinical) and abnormal (nonclinical) problems and populations is an artifact of language and not a reflection of reality.
6. Adjustment and maladjustment can only be understood by understanding specific behaviors, cognitions, and emotions in specific situations.
7. Formal diagnostic categories do not provide useful conceptualizations of problems of adjustment.
8. Formal or "clinical" change and informal or "nonclinical" change share the same basic processes and mechanisms.
9. The mediators and mechanisms of change are primarily cognitive, but effective change procedures are usually behavioral.
10. Interventions for enhancing adjustment should facilitate action and behavior change.

Several additional principles of change are suggested by self-efficacy theory.

1. Self-efficacy influences adjustment through its impact on goal-setting and persistence toward goals, cognitive efficiency, and emotional adaptiveness (which, in turn, influence self-efficacy).
2. Self-efficacy beliefs are self-confirming because of the self-fulfilling nature of expectancies, because people construct and select environments to maximize receipt of positive information about themselves, and because people selectively attend to and process information about themselves in a manner that enhances their sense of control and competence.
3. The importance of self-efficacy in adaptation and adjustment is not completely dependent on the accuracy of efficacy beliefs. Positive illusions about personal control and efficacy are adaptive, because they serve to maintain a positive self-image and lead one to strive for goals that may appear beyond one's reach.
4. Self-efficacy theory can provide guidelines for designing useful methods for assessing problems of adjustment through the specification of targets for interventions and the evaluation of the effectiveness of interventions.
5. Such assessments can be facilitated by understanding the distinction between behavioral, cognitive, and emotional self-efficacy.

6. Interventions can be better directed toward increasing self-efficacy by helping clients view success experiences more constructively, by increasing client involvement in planning interventions, by setting concrete goals, by encouraging adaptive distortions of self and world, and by providing clients with a variety of coping and control strategies.

Acknowledgments: The authors thank John Riskind, Irving Kirsch, Carlo DiClemente, and Lloyd Williams for their constructive comments on an earlier version of this chapter.

REFERENCES

Abramson, L. Y., Seligman, M. E. P., & Teasdale, J. D. (1978). Learned helplessness in humans: Critique and reformulation. *Journal of Abnormal Psychology, 87,* 49–74.

American Psychiatric Association. (1987). *Diagnostic and statistical manual of mental disorders* (3rd ed. rev.). Washington, DC: Author.

Anderson, C. A., & Arnoult, L. H. (1985). Attributional style and everyday problems in living: Depression, shyness, and loneliness. *Social Cognition, 3,* 16–35.

Anderson, C. A., Horowitz, L. M., & French, R. (1983). Attributional style of lonely and depressed people. *Journal of Personality and Social Psychology, 45,* 127–136.

Annis, H. M. (1982). *Situational Confidence Questionnaire.* Toronto: Addiction Research Foundation.

Bandura, A. (1977). Self-efficacy: Toward a unifying theory of behavioral change. *Psychological Review, 84,* 191–215.

Bandura, A. (1978). On paradigms and recycled ideologies. *Cognitive Therapy and Research, 2,* 79–103.

Bandura, A. (1982). Self-efficacy mechanism in human agency. *American Psychologist, 37,* 122–147.

Bandura, A. (1984). Recycling misconceptions of perceived self-efficacy. *Cognitive Therapy and Research, 8,* 231–255.

Bandura, A. (1986). *Social foundations of thought and action.* New York: Prentice-Hall.

Bandura, A. (1988). Self-efficacy conception of anxiety. *Anxiety Research, 1,* 77–98.

Bandura, A. (1991). Self-efficacy mechanism in physiological activation and health-promoting behavior. In J. Madden IV (Ed.), *Neurobiology of learning, emotion, and affect.* New York: Raven Press.

Bandura, A. (1992). Exercise of personal agency through the self-efficacy mechanism. In R. Schwarzer (Ed.), *Self-efficacy: Thought control of action* (pp. 3–38). Washington, DC: Hemisphere.

Bandura, A., Adams, N. E., Hardy, A. B., & Howells, G. N. (1980). Tests of the generality of self-efficacy theory. *Cognitive Therapy and Research, 4,* 39–66.

Bandura, A., Reese, L., & Adams, N. E. (1982). Microanalysis of action and fear arousal as a function of differential levels of perceived coping self-efficacy. *Journal of Personality and Social Psychology, 43,* 5–21.

Bandura, A., & Wood, R. E. (1989). Effect of perceived controllability and performance standards on self-regulation of complex decision making. *Journal of Personality and Social Psychology, 56,* 805–814.

Bargh, J. A., & Tota, M. E. (1988). Context-dependent automatic processing in depression: Accessibility of negative constructs with regard to self but not to others. *Journal of Personality and Social Psychology, 54,* 925–939.

Barlow, D. H. (1988). *Anxiety and its disorders: The nature and treatment of anxiety and panic.* New York: Guilford.

Baumeister, R. F., & Scher, S. J. (1988). Self-defeating behavior patterns among normal individuals: Review and analysis of common self-destructive tendencies. *Psychological Bulletin, 104,* 3–22.

Beck, A. T. (1976). *Cognitive therapy and the emotional disorders.* New York: International Universities Press.

Beck, A. T., & Emery, G. (1985). *Anxiety disorders and phobias: A cognitive perspective.* New York: Basic Books.

Beck, A. T., Rush, A. J., Shaw, B. F., & Emery, G. (1979). *Cognitive therapy for depression.* New York: Guilford.

Betz, N. E., & Hackett, G. (1981). The relationship of career-related self-efficacy expectations to perceived career options in college women and men. *Journal of Counseling Psychology, 28,* 399–410.

Betz, N. E., & Hackett, G. (1986). Applications of self-efficacy theory to understanding career choice behavior. *Journal of Social and Clinical Psychology, 4,* 279–289.

Biran, M., & Wilson, G. T. (1981). Treatment of phobic disorders using cognitive and exposure methods: A self-efficacy analysis. *Journal of Consulting and Clinical Psychology, 49,* 886–899.

Buss, A. H. (1980). *Self-consciousness and social anxiety.* San Francisco: Freeman.

Cantanzaro, S. J., & Mearns, J. (1990). Measuring generalized expectancies for negative mood regulation: Initial scale development and implications. *Journal of Personality Assessment, 54,* 546–563.

Cervone, D. (1989). Effect of envisioning future activities on self-efficacy judgments and motivation: An availability heuristic interpretation. *Cognitive Therapy and Research, 13,* 247–261.

Cervone, D., & Williams, S. L. (1992). Social cognitive theory and personality. In G. V. Caprara & G. L. Van Heck (Eds.), *Modern personality psychology: Critical reviews and new directions* (pp. 200–252). New York: Harvester-Wheatsheaf.

Coelho, R. J. (1984). Self-efficacy and cessation of smoking. *Psychological Reports, 54,* 309–310.

Colletti, G., Supnick, J. A., & Rizzo, A. A. (1981, August). *An analysis of relapse determinants for treated smokers.* Paper presented at the 89th Annual Meeting of the American Psychological Association, Los Angeles, CA.

Condiotte, M. M., & Lichtenstein, E. (1981). Self-efficacy and relapse in smoking cessation programs. *Journal of Consulting and Clinical Psychology, 49,* 648–658.

Conger, J. C., & Keane, S. P. (1981). Social skills intervention in the treatment of isolated or withdrawn children. *Psychological Bulletin, 90,* 478–495.

Darley, J., & Fazio, R. (1980). Expectancy confirmation processes arising in the social interaction sequence. *American Psychologist, 35,* 867–881.

Devins, G. M., Binik, Y. M., Gorman, P., Dattell, M., McClosky, B., Oscar, G., & Briggs, J. (1982). Perceived self-efficacy, outcome expectancies, and negative mood states in end-stage renal disease. *Journal of Abnormal Psychology, 91,* 241–244.

DiClemente, C. C. (1981). Self-efficacy and smoking cessation maintenance: A preliminary report. *Cognitive Therapy and Research, 5,* 175–187.

DiClemente, C. C. (1986). Self-efficacy and the addictive behaviors. *Journal of Social and Clinical Psychology, 4,* 302–315.

DiClemente, C. C., Gordon, J. R., & Gibertini, M. (1983, August). *Self-efficacy and determinants of relapse in alcoholism treatment*. Paper presented at the annual meeting of the American Psychological Association, Anaheim, CA.

Dolce, J. J. (1987). Self-efficacy and disability beliefs in behavioral treatment of pain. *Behaviour Research and Therapy, 25*, 289–299.

Dweck, C. S., & Liggett, E. L. (1988). A social-cognitive approach to motivation and personality. *Psychological Review, 95*, 256–273.

Emmons, R. A. (1992). Abstract versus concrete goals: Personal striving level, physical illness, and psychological well-being. *Journal of Personality and Social Psychology, 62*, 292–300.

Fiske, S.T., & Taylor, S. E. (1991). *Social cognition* (2nd ed.). New York: McGraw-Hill.

Forsterling, F. (1986). Attributional conceptions in clinical psychology. *American Psychologist, 41*, 275–285.

Frank, J. D., & Frank, J. B. (1991). *Persuasion and healing: A comparative study of psychotherapy* (3rd. ed.). Baltimore, MD: Johns Hopkins University Press.

Godding, P. R., & Glasgow, R. E. (1985). Self-efficacy and outcome expectancy as predictors of controlled smoking status. *Cognitive Therapy and Research, 9*, 583–590.

Goldfried, M. R., & Robins, C. (1982). On the facilitation of self-efficacy. *Cognitive Therapy and Research, 6*, 361–380.

Goozh, J. S., & Maddux, J. E. (1993). *Self-presentational concerns, social anxiety, and depression: The influence of self-efficacy, outcome expectancy, and outcome value*. Unpublished manuscript, George Mason University, Fairfax, VA.

Greenwald, A. G. (1980). The totalitarian ego: Fabrication and revision of personal history. *American Psychologist, 35*, 603–618.

Harvey, J. H., Weary, G., Maddux, J. E., Jordan, J., & Galvin, K. (1985). Attitude change theory, research, and clinical practice. In G. Stricker & R. Keisner (Eds.), *From research to clinical practice* (pp. 139–156). New York: Plenum Press.

Hollon, S. H., & Beck, A. T. (1986). Research on cognitive therapies. In S. L. Garfield & A. E. Bergin (Eds.), *Handbook of psychotherapy and behavior change* (pp. 443–482). New York: Wiley.

Ingram, R. E., Kendall, P. C., & Chen, A. H. (1991) Cognitive–behavioral interventions. In C. R. Snyder & D. R. Forsyth (Eds.), *Handbook of social and clinical psychology* (pp. 509–522). New York: Pergamon.

Jones, E. E. (1986, October 3). Interpreting interpersonal behavior: The effects of expectancies. *Science, 243*, 41–46.

Kanfer, F. H. (1984). Introduction. In R. P. McGlynn, J. E. Maddux, C. D. Stoltenberg, & J. H. Harvey (Eds.), *Social perception in clinical and counseling psychology* (pp. 1–6). Lubbock, TX: Texas Tech Press.

Kanfer, R., & Zeiss, A. M. (1983). Depression, interpersonal standard-setting, and judgements of self-efficacy. *Journal of Abnormal Psychology, 92*, 319–329.

Kazdin, A. E. (1979). Imagery elaboration and self-efficacy in the covert modeling treatment of unassertive behavior. *Journal of Consulting and Clinical Psychology, 47*, 725–733.

Kent, G., & Gibbons, R. (1987). Self-efficacy and the control of anxious cognitions. *Journal of Behavior Therapy and Experimental Psychiatry, 18*, 33–40.

Kirsch, I. (1985). Response expectancy as a determinant of experience and behavior. *American Psychologist, 40*, 1189–1202.

Kirsch, I. (1986). Early research on self-efficacy: What we already know without knowing we knew. *Journal of Social and Clinical Psychology, 4*, 339–358.

Kirsch, I. (1990). *Changing expectations: A key to successful psychotherapy*. Pacific Grove, CA: Brooks/Cole.

Kirsch, I., Mearns, J., & Catanzaro, S. (1990). Mood-regulation expectancies as determinants of dysphoria in college students. *Journal of Counseling Psychology, 3*, 306–312.

Kobasa, S. C. (1979). Stressful life events and health: An inquiry into hardiness. *Journal of Personality and Social Psychology, 37,* 1–11.

Korchin, S. J. (1976). *Modern clinical psychology: Principles of intervention in the clinic and community.* New York: Basic Books.

Leary, M. R. (1983). *Understanding social anxiety: Social, personality, and clinical perspectives.* Beverly Hills, CA: Sage.

Leary, M. R., & Atherton, S. C. (1986). Self-efficacy, social anxiety, and inhibition in social encounters. *Journal of Social and Clinical Psychology, 4,* 258–267.

Leary, M. R., & Maddux, J. E. (1987). Toward a viable interface between social and clinical/counseling psychology. *American Psychologist, 42,* 904–911.

Leary, M. R., Maddux, J. E., & Kowalski, R. N. (1987). *Goal-attainment expectancies, self-presentational outcomes, and social anxiety.* Unpublished manuscript, Wake Forest University, Winston-Salem, N.C.

Lewinsohn, P. M., Mischel, W., Chaplin, W., & Barton, R. (1980). Social competence and depression: The role of illusory self-perceptions. *Journal of Abnormal Psychology, 89,* 203–212.

Livesley, W. J., Jackson, D. N., & Schroeder, M. L. (1992). Factorial structure of traits delineating personality disorders in clinical and general populations samples. *Journal of Abnormal Psychology, 101,* 432–440.

Locke, E. A., & Latham, G. P. (1990). *A theory of goal-setting and task performance.* Englewood Cliffs, NJ: Prentice-Hall.

Maddux, J. E. (1993). The mythology of psychopathology: A social cognitive view of deviance, difference, and disorder. *The General Psychologist, 29,* 34–45.

Maddux, J. E., Norton, L. W., & Leary, M. R. (1988). Cognitive components of social anxiety: An investigation of the integration of self-presentation theory and self-efficacy theory. *Journal of Social and Clinical Psychology, 6,* 180–190.

Mahoney, M. J. (1991). *Human change processes.* New York: Basic Books.

Markus, H., & Nurius, P. (1986). Possible selves. *American Psychologist, 41,* 954–969.

Marlatt G. A., & Gordon, J. R. (Eds.). (1985). *Relapse prevention.* New York: Guilford.

Mearns, J. (1991). Coping with a breakup: Negative mood regulation expectancies and depression following the end of a romantic relationship. *Journal of Personality and Social Psychology, 60,* 327–334.

Myerson, W. A., Foreyt, J. P., Hammond, G. S., & DiClemente, C. C. (1980, November). *Self-efficacy: The development of a brief scale for prediction of success in a smoking cessation program.* Paper presented at the 14th Annual Convention of the Association for Advancement of Behavior Therapy, New York, NY.

Nikki, R. M., Remington, R. E., & MacDonald, G. A. (1984). Self-efficacy, nicotine fading/self-monitoring and cigarette smoking behaviour. *Behaviour Research and Therapy, 22,* 477–485.

O'Leary, A. (1985). Self-efficacy and health. *Behavior Therapy and Research, 23,* 437–452.

Ozer, E., & Bandura, A. (1990). Mechanisms governing empowerment effects: A self-efficacy analysis. *Journal of Personality and Social Psychology, 58,* 472–486.

Persons, J. B. (1986). The advantages of studying psychological phenomena rather than psychiatric diagnosis. *American Psychologist, 41,* 1252–1260.

Persons, J. B. (1989). *Cognitive therapy in practice: A case formulation approach.* New York: Norton.

Persons, J. B. (1991). Psychotherapy outcome studies do not accurately reflect current models of psychotherapy: A proposed remedy. *American Psychologist, 46,* 99–106.

Prochaska, J. O., DiClemente, C. C., & Norcross, J. C. (1992). In search of how people change: Applications to addictive behaviors. *American Psychologist, 47,* 1102–1114.

Reiss, S. (1991). Expectancy model of fear, anxiety, and panic. *Clinical Psychology Review, 11*, 141–153.

Riskind, J. R. (1982). The client's sense of personal mastery: Effects of time perspective and self-esteem. In I. L. Janis (Ed.), *Counseling on personal decisions* (pp. 247–262). New Haven: Yale University Press.

Rosenbaum, M., & Hadari, D. (1985). Personal efficacy, external locus of control, and perceived contingency of parental reinforcement among depressed, paranoid, and normal subjects. *Journal of Personality and Social Psychology, 49*, 539–547.

Rothbaum, F., Weisz, J. R., & Snyder, S. S. (1982). Changing the world and changing the self: A two-process model of perceived control. *Journal of Personality and Social Psychology, 42*, 5–37.

Saltzer, E. B. (1981). Cognitive moderators of the relationship between behavioral intentions and behaviors. *Journal of Personality and Social Psychology, 41*, 260–271.

Scheier, M. F., & Carver, C. S. (1988). A model of behavioral self-regulation: Translating intention into action. In L. Berkowitz (Ed.), *Advances in Experimental Social Psychology* (Vol. 21, pp. 322–343). San Diego, CA: Academic Press.

Schlenker, B. R., & Leary, M. R. (1982). Social anxiety and self-presentation: A conceptualization and model. *Psychological Bulletin, 92*, 641–669.

Schneider, J. A., O'Leary, A., & Bandura, A. (1985). *The development of a scale to assess self-efficacy in bulemics.* Unpublished manuscript, Stanford University, Stanford, CA.

Seligman, M. E. P. (1990). *Learned optimism.* New York: Knopf.

Shaywitz, S. E., Escobar, M. D., Shaywitz, B. A., Fletcher, J. M., & Makuck, R. (1992). Evidence that dyslexia may represent the lower tail of a normal distribution of reading ability. *New England Journal of Medicine, 326*, 145–150.

Smith, M. L., Glass, G. V., & Miller, T. I. (1980). *The benefits of psychotherapy.* Cambridge, MA: Harvard University Press.

Snyder, C. R., & Forsyth, D. R. (Eds.). (1991). *Handbook of social and clinical psychology.* New York: Pergamon.

Stamfl, T. G., & Levis, D. J. (1967). Essentials of implosive therapy. *Journal of Abnormal Psychology, 72*, 270–276.

Stanley, M. A., & Maddux, J. E. (1986a). Self-efficacy expectancy and depressed mood: An investigation of causal relationships. *Journal of Social Behavior and Personality, 4*, 575–586.

Stanley, M. A., & Maddux, J. E. (1986b). Self-efficacy theory: Potential contributions to understanding cognitions in depression. *Journal of Social and Clinical Psychology, 4*, 268–278.

Swann, W. B., Jr. (1983). Self-verification: Bringing social reality into harmony with the self. In J. Suls & A. G. Greenwald (Eds.), *Social psychology perspectives* (Vol. 2, pp. 33–66). Hillsdale, NJ: Erlbaum.

Swann, W. B., Jr. (1984). Quest for accuracy in person perception: A matter of pragmatics. *Psychological Review, 91*, 457–477.

Taylor, S. E. (1983). Adjustment to threatening events: A theory of cognitive adaptation. *American Psychologist, 38*, 1161–1173.

Taylor, S. E. (1989). *Positive illusions: Creative self-deception and the healthy mind.* New York: Basic Books.

Taylor, S. E., & Brown, J. D. (1988). Illusion and well-being: A social psychological perspective on mental health. *Psychological Bulletin, 2*, 193–210.

Tesser, A., & Paulhus, D. (1983). The definition of self: Private and public self-evaluation management strategies. *Journal of Personality and Social Psychology, 44*, 672–682.

Thompson, S. C. (1981). Will it hurt less if I can control it? A complex answer to a simple question. *Psychological Bulletin, 90*, 89–101.

Thompson, S. C. (1991). Intervening to enhance perceptions of control. In C. R. Snyder &

D. R. Forsyth (Eds.), *Handbook of social and clinical psychology* (pp. 607–623). New York: Pergamon.

Trull, T. (1992). DSM-III-R personality disorders and the five-factor model of personality: An empirical comparison. *Journal of Abnormal Psychology, 101,* 553–560.

Turk, D. C., & Salovey, P. (Eds.). (1988). *Reasoning, inference, and judgment in clinical psychology.* New York: Free Press.

Turner, S. M., McCann, B. S., Beidel, D. C., & Messick, J. E. (1986). DSM-III classification of the anxiety disorders. *Journal of Abnormal Psychology, 95,* 168–172.

Wakefield, J. C. (1992). The concept of mental disorder: On the boundary between biological facts and social values. *American Psychologist, 47,* 373–388.

Watson, P. J., Sawrie, S. M., & Biderman, M. D. (1991). Personal control, assumptive worlds, and narcissism. *Journal of Social Behavior and Personality, 6,* 929–941.

Wegner, D. M. (1989). *White bears and other unwanted thoughts: Suppression, obsession, and the psychology of mental control.* New York: Penguin Books.

Weinberg, R. S., & Agras, W. S. (1984). *The Weight Reduction Efficacy Questionnaire.* Unpublished manuscript, Stanford University, Stanford, CA.

Weinberg, R. S., Hughes, H. H., Critelli, J. W., England, R., & Jackson, A. (1984). Effects of preexisting and manipulated self-efficacy on weight loss in a self-control program. *Journal of Research in Personality, 18,* 352–358.

Williams, L. S. (1990). Guided mastery treatment of agoraphobia: Beyond stimulus exposure. *Progress in Behavior Modification, 26,* 89–121.

Williams, L. S., Dooseman, G., & Kleinfield, E. (1984). Comparative effectiveness of guided mastery and exposure treatments for intractable phobias. *Journal of Consulting and Clinical Psychology, 52,* 505–518.

Williams, L. S., & Watson, N. (1985). Perceived danger and perceived self-efficacy as cognitive determinants of acrophobic behaviors. *Behavior Therapy, 16,* 136–146.

Wolpe, J. (1958). *Psychotherapy by reciprocal inhibition.* Stanford, CA: Stanford University Press.

Wood, R. E., & Bandura, A. (1989). Impact of conceptions of ability on self-regulatory mechanisms and complex decision making. *Journal of Personality and Social Psychology, 56,* 407–415.

Wurtele, S. K. (1986). Self-efficacy and athletic performance: A review. *Journal of Social and Clinical Psychology, 4,* 290–301.

Yeates, K. O., Schultz, L. H., & Selman, R. L. (1990). Bridging the gap in child-clinical assessment: Toward the application of social-cognitive developmental theory. *Clinical Psychology Review, 10,* 567–588.

CHAPTER 3

SELF-EFFICACY, ANXIETY, AND PHOBIC DISORDERS

S. LLOYD WILLIAMS

Anxiety and phobic disorders are among the most prevalent, distressing, and disabling of psychosocial problems. They are problems that have long fascinated psychological theorists, and were the first phenomena to which self-efficacy theory was applied (Bandura, 1977; Bandura & Adams, 1977; Bandura, Adams, & Beyer, 1977). Since that initial work, considerable additional research has addressed how people's views of their own coping abilities bear on diverse adjustment problems (Maddux, 1991). This chapter reviews the status of self-efficacy perceptions as causes of anxiety and phobia, and whether self-efficacy theory is heuristic in developing improved treatments. The focus is on current causation rather than historical etiology. The aim is not to systematically address every constellation of responses that might be labeled an anxiety disorder*, but to examine the

---

*The term *anxiety disorders* is used in an informal and nonmedical sense. Social cognitive theory does not consider psychological problems as "mental illnesses," since that would be a pointless and misleading medicalization of human experience (Bandura, 1969, 1978a). Nor does social cognitive theory accept that human problems can be neatly arrayed in a catalog that dictates how they shall be characterized for all occasions and circumstances. Human problems can and must be viewed in different ways for different purposes. Enshrining a few arbitrary combinations of problematic phenomena as fixed "mental disorders" in diagnostic

---

S. LLOYD WILLIAMS • Department of Psychology, Lehigh University, Bethlehem, Pennsylvania 18105.

Self-Efficacy, Adaptation, and Adjustment: Theory, Research, and Application, edited by James E. Maddux. Plenum Press, New York, 1995.

influence of self-efficacy perceptions on the functional impairment, scary thoughts and feelings, and physiological arousal that characterize anxiety-related problems.

THE MEANING OF ANXIETY

Anxiety, an aversive experience of distress, is a major psychological problem not only in so-called anxiety disorders, but in life generally. What exactly is anxiety? The term has come to denote a diverse array of emotional, attitudinal, cognitive, perceptual, physiological, and behavioral responses. This expansive scope has been sustained partly because it could not be shown that any particular index of anxiety strongly predicts problem behavior (Williams, 1987, 1988). The result has been a frequent confusion between anxiety *per se* and numerous other responses that are merely correlated with anxiety.

Being anxious means primarily feeling anxious. The essence and *sine qua non* of anxiety is the subjective feeling of fear* (Williams, 1987). Operationally, feeling anxious means a self-judgment of fear intensity, as on a rating scale from *Not Afraid* to *Extremely Afraid*. Some have argued that because subjective fear is not public, it cannot by itself be proper data for the scientific study of fear (Lang, 1978). But nature presents anxiety to people primarily as an aversive feeling, and that is a good way to study it. This feeling is not merely operant "verbal behavior" or "language responding," but a personal reality of indisputable importance in its own right.

Nor is fear largely physiological arousal, since such arousal does not much correlate with feeling afraid (Lang, 1978; Morrow & Labrum, 1978; Williams, 1987). If physiology enters into it, it is mainly as subjectively felt by the client, which tends to be only weakly related with actual physiological arousal (e.g., Ehlers & Breuer, 1992; Mandler, 1962; Whitehead, Drescher, Heiman, & Blackwell, 1977). Physiological arousal without fear is commonplace, as when people exercise, feel exhilaration, or eat spicy food. And fear without physiological arousal is also common; even people having panic attacks do not always show autonomic increases (Barlow & Craske, 1988; Lang, 1978; Margraf, Taylor, Ehlers, Roth, & Agras, 1987; Taylor et al., 1986). Across a broad range of emotions, peripheral physiol-

---

manuals hampers more than it helps our ability to understand and alleviate psychological suffering (cf. Detre, 1985; Persons, 1986; Williams, 1985).

*This paper considers the terms *anxiety* and *fear* synonymous.

ogy tends to be an unreliable indicator of particular subjective feeling states (Lacey, 1967; Zajonc & McIntosh, 1992). The fact that fearful and nonfearful groups of people sometimes differ, on the average, in visceral activation, does not show that bodily arousal defines fear, because fearful and nonfearful groups will tend to differ markedly in all kinds of ways, including mood, self-efficacy, thoughts of danger, and many other reactions (Williams, 1985). Sad mood, low self-efficacy, autonomic arousal, and myriad other factors may be related to anxiety, and may affect anxiety, but it makes little sense to declare that they *define* anxiety.

Finally, anxiety is not behavior. To define fear as overt behavior, or to posit that behavior is a "system" of anxiety, is to undermine analysis of the relationship between emotion and behavior. Such an approach reduces the anxiety theory of neurotic behavior to the meaningless proposition that anxiety causes anxiety. Rather than simply issue a proclamation that anxiety is the basis of neurotic behavior, one must ask: What is the *evidence* that fear motivates avoidance? The answer does not inspire confidence in anxiety theory.

THE FAILURE OF ANXIETY THEORY

Self-efficacy theory was proposed at a time when the traditional anxiety-based theory of neurotic behavior was increasingly being recognized as inadequate. The theory that anxiety determines irrational avoidant behavior, and that reducing anxiety is necessary and sufficient to reduce avoidance, proved quite difficult to validate (Williams, 1987, 1988). Anxiety theory in its various forms, including the recent view that panic anxiety drives agoraphobic behavior, encounters the serious problem of explaining the consistently weak relationship between anxiety/panic, on the one hand, and dysfunctional avoidance behavior on the other (Bandura, 1969, 1978b; Carr, 1979; Craske & Barlow, 1988; Lang, 1978; Mineka. 1979: Rachman, 1976; Schwartz, 1986; Seligman & Johnston, 1973; Williams, 1987, 1988).

Both subjective fear/panic and physiological arousal are only weakly related with behavior. Much phobic avoidance occurs without fear or panic, as in housebound agoraphobics who remain completely free of anxiety (Spitzer & Williams, 1985), or bridge phobics who calmly plan vacation routes to avoid intimidating spans. Fear without notable avoidance is also commonplace, as in people who are frequent but fearful flyers. Similarly, many people remain agoraphobic for extended periods without having panic attacks, and others are panicky but not agoraphobic. More-over, the amount people benefit from treatment correlates little with how anxious they become during treatment (Mathews, Gelder, & Johnston, 1981; Rachman & Hodgson, 1974). The poor correlations make clear that anxiety and panic are not the major proximal determinants of phobic behavior (Williams, 1985, 1987). Anxiety is a serious problem in its own right, but it does not explain phobic behavior. A promising alternative view is that cognitive processes determine both anxiety and behavior.

SELF-EFFICACY THEORY

Self-efficacy theory posits that psychological treatment procedures of diverse forms benefit people partly by raising and strengthening their perceptions of self-efficacy (Bandura, 1977). In this view, it is their belief that they cannot cope with potential threats that make people anxious, avoidant, and beset with disturbing thoughts (Bandura, 1986). Perceived threat is a function of the relationship between appraisals of possible danger and of one's capabilities to deal with it. If people believe they can prevent, control, or cope with a potential difficulty, they will not see it as highly threatening, and they will have little reason to fear and avoid it. But if they judge themselves as lacking cognitive and behavioral coping capa-bilities, they will dwell on their vulnerabilities, perceive the situation as fraught with danger, and scare and inhibit themselves. Self-efficacy beliefs include not only judgments about whether one is capable of mounting and sustaining effective overt coping behaviors, but also whether one can exercise cognitive control over scary trains of thought. In the self-efficacy view, thought control inefficacy especially exacerbates feelings of anxiety and panic (Bandura, 1988).

Self-efficacy theory embodies predictions regarding the influence of self-efficacy judgments on other psychological responses, predictions re-garding factors that influence self-efficacy judgments, and principles for developing treatments to increase people's functional capabilities and decrease their distress. These aspects of the theory are discussed in the remainder of this chapter.

EFFECTS OF SELF-EFFICACY JUDGMENTS

In social cognitive theory, self-efficacy judgments exist in reciprocal causal relationship with other cognitive and emotional factors, and with behavior and the environment (see Chap. 1, this volume). This section of the present chapter examines evidence regarding the ways in which self-efficacy influences phobic behavior, thoughts, feelings, and physiological arousal.

SELF-EFFICACY INFLUENCE ON BEHAVIOR

Behavior is the most important dimension of psychological functioning that theories and treatments must address, because behavioral limitations and disabilities cause many of the material and psychosocial hardships that people with anxiety-related problems endure. Phobic and compulsive behavior often cost people their livelihoods, their ability to engage in desired social and recreational activities, and their sense of well-being and self-esteem. Moreover, phobic and compulsive behavior is often refractory to current treatments (Barlow, 1988). One of the most fundamental predictions of self-efficacy theory is that self-efficacy judgments strongly bear on phobic behavior.

Correlation between Self-Efficacy and Behavior

Testing the causal status of cognitive mediators requires initially showing that the postulated cause, in this case self-efficacy, does indeed correlate strongly with the effect to be explained, phobic disability. This is by no means a trivial test, because the correlations between phobic disability and its various proposed causes have tended to be weak (Williams, 1987, 1988). Strong correspondence between a proposed mediator and behavior encourages further exploration of the possible underlying causal processes, whereas weak correspondence encourages a search elsewhere.

A basic methodology for examining a proposed internal mediator's effect on behavior is to alternately measure the mediator and coping behavior in a number of subjects before and after diverse treatments. In self-efficacy research, people rate their self-efficacy by indicating their confidence that they could perform a graded sequence of phobia-related tasks. Then they display their actual capability by attempting the tasks. They then rate their self-efficacy again. Next, they are given treatment. After treatment, the measures are repeated. The repeated measurement of self-efficacy allows disentangling the effects of treatment from the effects of behavioral testing. Behavioral approach tests such as those used in self-efficacy research are highly reliable, valid, and meaningful measures of phobic disability (Williams, 1985).

The results of diverse studies with diverse phobic conditions show that regardless of whether treatment is vicarious, imaginal, or performance-based, a close correspondence exists between the level of self-efficacy and the level of actual functional capability (Bandura & Adams, 1977; Bandura, Adams, & Beyer, 1977; Bandura, Adams, Hardy, & Howells, 1980; Bandura, Reese, & Adams, 1982; Biran & Wilson, 1981; Bourque & Ladouceur, 1980; Emmelkamp & Felten, 1985; Ladouceur, 1983; Southworth & Kirsch, 1988; Williams, Dooseman, & Kleifield, 1984; Williams, Kinney, & Falbo, 1989; Williams & Rappoport, 1983; Williams, Turner, & Peer, 1985; Williams & Watson, 1985). Following diverse treatments, the correlations between self-efficacy and subsequent coping behavior average about .80.

Efficacy–Behavior Correlation Is Not an Artifact

The link between self-efficacy and behavior is not a mere methodological artifact of subjects' feeling social pressure to match their performances to their efficacy ratings. The phobia research procedure minimizes social pressure. Subjects complete the self-efficacy scales in relative or complete privacy. The efficacy ratings are not especially salient anyway, because they are embedded among other rating forms. When efficacy measures are more intrusive, ratings are found to be *less* congruent with behavior because subjects conservatively underestimate what they can do (Telch, Bandura, Vinciguerra, Agras, & Stout, 1982).

The psychological context of behavioral tests with phobic subjects renders the efficacy-matching hypothesis implausible. People come for treatment of a serious personal problem. They are encouraged to do as much as they can, and they have a strong personal stake in doing so. Given that subjects are confronting highly distressing phobic threats during the test, and that their efficacy judgments might have been recorded hours or even days earlier, perceived social pressure to play efficacy-matching games is trivial.

That self-efficacy measures do not have reactive effects upon behavior is clearly demonstrated by the pattern of discrepancies between prior self-efficacy judgments and subsequent coping behavior. If people were motivated to match behavior to judgment, they would more often err by overestimating than underestimating what they could do, because once their performance reached the level they had rated, they would simply stop to produce an exact match. In fact, however, many hundreds of behavioral test results indicate that at an initial assessment phase, severe phobics more often slightly surpass than fall short of what they think they can do (Williams & Bauchiess, 1992), and they are pleased, not chagrined, about it. Clearly they are unconcerned about efficacy-behavior matching. Other studies further corroborate that the mere act of rating self-efficacy has no bearing on subsequent coping behavior (Bandura, 1982; Gauthier & Ladouceur, 1981).

Self-Efficacy Is Not Merely "Willingness"

It has been suggested that when subjects rate self-efficacy scales, they are indicating their willingness, not their perceived ability (Kirsch, 1982, 1990). This analysis states that people with neuroses, despite rating their self-efficacy as zero for some tasks, in reality *can* do anything they want; they lack not ability, but incentives and desire.

Characterizing people with serious behavioral restrictions as lacking will, or as simply not wanting to behave properly, just does not square with the facts. Phobia fascinates precisely because it exemplifies a "paralysis of the will" in which seemingly sensible people, who possess the requisite rudimentary cognitive and motoric skills, who are aware that their fears are senselessness, and who have and perceive every reason to function normally, nevertheless *cannot*. Kirsch's (1982) finding that mildly fearful undergraduates (whose phobic disability was never actually tested) express increased willingness to approach a snake when offered strong make-believe incentives, says little about genuine phobic behavior or self-efficacy* People with phobias and compulsions pay frightfully high costs for their disabilities, not only in major financial setbacks, but in lost social and recreational functioning, and in lowered self-esteem. People who have abandoned fulfilling and lucrative careers because of a phobia or compulsion are not simply lacking inducements to be normal. Anguished agoraphobics who cannot attend their childrens' weddings are not merely being willfully obstinate. Phobic disability is genuine disability.

Anxiety disorders involve not only disability, but also routine avoidance of activities people could do if they tried (Williams, 1985).† In self-efficacy theory, such avoidance behavior certainly can be influenced by perceived incentives; "willingness" and action come from the combination

---

*Unlike the Kirsch (1982) study, most research on self-efficacy and phobia has selected severely phobic people from the community at large, who display actual disability on objective behavioral approach tests (Bandura, 1978, 1988; Williams, 1992).

†It is useful to distinguish between phobic avoidance and phobic disability (Williams, 1985). Often, phobic people are capable of doing more than they choose to do, and they may routinely avoid some activities that they could do if they tried. Incentives might well influence people to try some avoided tasks. But excepting mild cases, phobic people will be unable to do some tasks even when they perceive strong incentives and have ready opportunities to try (Williams, 1985).

of positive efficacy judgments and positive outcome expectations. Kirsch's (1982) finding was that incentives altered undergraduates' self-efficacy judgments, which should be largely independent of incentives. Therefore, Kirsch reasoned, the subjects must be "invoking a linguistic habit" (p. 133) of confusing their confidence in what they can do for their willingness to do.* It is not clear how (or that) these linguistically normal English speakers developed such a dysfunctional habit of misunderstanding the commonplace distinction between "confidence I can do" and "my willingness to do." Perhaps these subjects were simply bored and therefore inattentive to the instructions. Whatever the explanation, truly phobic individuals' self-efficacy ratings are far less amenable to influence by proffered hypothetical (or actual) incentives.

Finally, Kirsch (1990) argued that what motivates phobia is anticipated anxiety, and that self-efficacy predicts behavior only because self-efficacy is correlated with anticipated anxiety. A sizable body of empirical evidence establishes the inferiority of anticipated anxiety to self-efficacy in predicting and explaining neurotic behavior; this evidence is reviewed in a subsequent section (*Self-Efficacy Is Not Reducible to Expected Outcomes*). Phobic disability cannot be redefined as unwillingness, and low self-efficacy cannot be redefined as anticipated distress.

Self-Efficacy Causes and Reflects Behavior

The context of the high correlations between self-efficacy and behavior establish a strong case that self-efficacy is more than just a reflection of previous behavior. Cognitive causation is suggested by the power of self-efficacy judgments to predict posttreatment behavior even after treatments that were vicarious or imaginal, and which therefore benefited subjects without giving them any opportunity to actually attempt scary tasks. Severely snake-phobic subjects who view a therapeutic film will tend to experience widely varying degrees of therapeutic benefit, ranging from almost none to virtual complete elimination of the phobia. Increases in their confidence that they can cope, based on symbolic (vicarious or imaginal) experiences alone, measured after the treatment but before a posttreatment behavioral test, correspond well with gains they display in overt coping behavior (Bandura & Adams, 1977; Bandura et al., 1977, 1980, 1982).

Cognitive causation is also suggested strongly by evidence that generalized behavioral changes resulting from treatment of distinct dissimilar

---

*"Confidence" is the literal label of the 0–100 self-efficacy scale that subjects use, with 0 labeled *Cannot Do* and 100 labeled *Certain*.

phobias are more accurately predicted by changes in self-efficacy than by indices of previous behavior (Williams et al., 1989; see *Self-Efficacy Mediates Generalization of Behavior Change*). Even when people directly perform the target phobia-related activities during treatment, the resulting behavioral changes often are more accurately predicted by the level of self-efficacy instated by treatment, than by the level of behavioral accomplishment achieved during treatment (Bandura et al., 1977, 1980; Williams et al., 1984, 1989).

The superiority of self-efficacy judgments over past indices of behavior in predicting future behavior shows that self-efficacy is not simply an inert reflection of past behavior. Perceptions of self-efficacy are undoubtedly influenced by past behavior (See *Sources of Self-Efficacy*), but they in turn actively influence future behavior.

Self-Efficacy Is Not Reducible to Expected Outcomes

Some have argued that the factor causing maladaptive behavior is actually another psychological process that is correlated with perceived self-efficacy. Of course, such an argument requires specifying the alternative cause, since it is always possible merely to speculate that something else *might* be going on. Some have proposed that a third variable, which produces both self-efficacy phobic behavior, is conditioned anxiety (Eysenck, 1978; Wolpe, 1978), but we have already seen that anxiety is not a viable explanation of phobic behavior.

A number of more cognitively oriented theories of learning and motivation emphasize anticipated outcomes of behavior, that is, the consequences the person expects would follow from a given course of action. The difference between outcome expectations and self-efficacy judgments is clear and straightforward. Self-efficacy theory concerns one's self-perceived ability to execute and sustain a given course of action, overt or mental, irrespective of what would result from that action. For example, my belief that I can walk three blocks down the street is a perception of self-efficacy; my belief that I would faint (or die, or experience panic) if I were to walk three blocks, is an anticipated outcome.

Some have proposed that perceptions of self-efficacy might reduce to or derive from anticipated outcomes, and that people's expectations of negative outcomes underlie their avoidant behavior. Social cognitive theory acknowledges that outcome expectations can affect behavior independently of self-efficacy perceptions (Bandura, 1986a). Obviously, when other factors are equal, people are more apt to do what they expect to be enjoyable and rewarding than what they expect to be aversive and harmful. But self-efficacy judgments are partly independent of anticipated outcomes and constitute a partly independent source of motivation. I can judge myself quite capable of doing something that I think would produce undesirable outcomes (e.g., park illegally in Manhattan); and I can judge myself quite *un*able to do something that I think would produce desirable outcomes (e.g., compose lovely music).

Although efficacy judgments and outcome expectations are conceptually distinct, empirically they are not entirely independent. This is because outcomes often depend on how well one executes antecedent actions. Poor acting produces caustic reviews and scornful audiences, whereas good acting produces favorable reviews and appreciative audiences. Similarly, inept social approach can result in rejection and embarrassment, whereas adept approach would result in welcoming acceptance. Self-efficacy is not the sole determinant of expected outcomes, in part because outcomes sometimes bear little relation to antecedent behavior. But under the many circumstances in which proficient actions produce desirable outcomes but inept actions produce undesirable outcomes, then the outcomes I expect logically must be influenced by how well I think I can perform (see also Chap. 1, this volume).

The relationship between anticipated outcomes, self-efficacy, and phobic behavior has been examined in a number of studies by my colleagues and myself. In particular, we have examined three kinds of anticipated outcomes: perceived danger, anticipated anxiety, and anticipated panic, which I will cover in turn. It is clear that phobic people display all these patterns of thought to some extent. On the average, they do overestimate danger, and they anticipate becoming fearful and panicky. So the issue is whether perceived self-efficacy or one of these kinds of outcome expectations is more central to phobic behavior.

Self-Efficacy Is Not Reducible to Perceived Danger. One kind of outcome expectation often held to underlie phobic avoidance and disability is the belief that phobia-related activities will produce physical or psychosocial harm, such as dying, going crazy, or humiliating oneself (Beck, 1976; Beck, Emery, & Greenberg, 1985). In Beck's (1976) analysis, phobia is always linked to a particular theme of perceived danger, for example, height phobics think they would fall; social phobics expect humiliation and rejection; and agoraphobics anticipate losing control and dying.

An obvious difficulty with the perceived danger mediator is that phobic people are, by definition, aware that their phobia is irrational and out of proportion to the objective danger. Beck (1976; Beck et al., 1985) argued that although people might realize their fears are irrational when they are remote from the feared activities, as they approach closer, they perceive a catastrophic event as more and more likely. By the time they are in the situation they are sure that disaster is imminent.

This analysis encounters the serious problem that phobic people often avoid when they are far away from the feared activity, as in the bridge-phobic woman mentioned earlier, who never encounters a terrifying span because she calmly plans bridge-free routes in advance. Similarly, social phobics decline invitations to parties from the security of their living rooms. Clearly, whatever is inspiring their avoidance cannot be a factor that comes into play only when the person is just beginning to cross a bridge or enter a party.

But an even greater problem with perceived danger theory is that thoughts of danger tend to be only weakly related with phobic disability. Perceived danger and self-efficacy were measured in two studies with acrophobics (Williams & Watson, 1985; Williams et al., 1985) and two studies with agoraphobics, one of which was the generalization study described earlier (Williams et al., 1989, also Williams, 1991). In the studies with height phobics, perceived danger was measured as the rated likelihood of falling if one were to look down from each level of a tall building. This follows Beck's (1976) suggestion that acrophobia is inspired by an increased perception of the likelihood of falling. In the studies with agoraphobics, various areas of disability were behaviorally measured (e.g., driving, walking on the street, crossing bridges, etc.). For each, subjects were first asked whether they thought any particular negative consequence might occur if they were to do the activity. If so, they rated the likelihood of it occurring for each task of the behavioral test hierarchy. They also made self-efficacy ratings, and these and the danger ratings were then correlated with approach during the behavioral test.

The correlations between perceived danger and behavior tended to be variable but overall were low, averaging about .30 at the various assessment phases of the studies. To see whether perceived danger contributes anything to the prediction of behavior, partial correlation analyses were performed between self-efficacy and behavior with perceived danger held constant, and between perceived danger and behavior with self-efficacy held constant, with the results shown in Table 1. It is clear that self-efficacy is doing all the work, since every correlation between self-efficacy and behavior is significant when perceived danger is held constant, but the correlations between perceived danger and behavior all drop to insignificance when self-efficacy is held constant. Thus, perceived danger independently contributes essentially nothing to the prediction of behavior.

These findings indicate not only the importance of self-efficacy perceptions, but also that phobics are aware of the irrationality of their pho-

TABLE 1. Partial Correlation Analyses Predicting Behavior
from Perceived Self-Efficacy Holding Perceived Danger Constant,
and Vice Versa, by Study and Assessment Phase

Study/ Test Phase (n)	Self-Efficacy Predict Behavior (Perceived Danger Held Constant)	Perceived Danger Predict Behavior (Self-Efficacy Held Constant)
Williams & Waltson, 1985		
Pretreatment (15)	.62**	.19
Posttreatment (15)	.75***	−.38
Williams et al., 1985		
Pretreatment (38)	.45**	−.05
Posttreatment (38)	.91***	+.34[a]
Follow-up (38)	.90***	−.10
Williams, 1991		
Pretreatment (37)	.35*	−.20
Posttreatment (37)	.82***	−.08
Follow-up (26)	.84***	−.02

$*p < .05.$ $**p < .01.$ $***p < .001.$
[a]Significant in the direction contrary to expectation.

bias. Although many of these subjects did express some belief in danger, some did not, and others would give a relatively low probability of harm across all the tasks of the test, even though they were quite disabled. Thus, these people often display clear awareness that the activity is not actually very dangerous. In one of the studies (Williams & Watson, 1985), subjects rated their perceptions of danger not only prior to the behavioral test, but also while they were performing the tasks of the test. Even when they were in the phobic situation and highly anxious at the limit of their capabilities, some subjects insisted that they did not entertain any belief that they would fall or in another harmful consequence. An additional study found that while self-efficacy perceptions correlated significantly with speech-anxious behavior, negative-outcome expectations did not (Davison, Haaga, Rosenbaum, Dolezal, & Weinstein, 1991). It appears that thoughts of danger, like feelings of anxiety, are only diffuse and variable accompaniments of phobia, with little direct bearing on phobic behavior.

Self-Efficacy Is Not Reducible to Anticipated Anxiety/Panic. Another theory that emphasizes outcome expectations is the "fear-of-fear" concept, which holds that avoidance behaviors result from the motivation to avoid anxiety/panic and the expectation that approach might provoke it (e.g., Craske, Rapee, & Barlow, 1988; Kirsch, 1990). In this view, the avoidance is of aversive feelings, not of harm *per se*. Of course, fear-of-fear can be combined with perceived danger in theorizing that people avoid anxiety-provoking activities because they think anxiety will trigger a catastrophe, such as death or insanity. However, perceived danger has not fared well empirically, and in any case, it is conceivable that avoidance is motivated simply by the belief that it will prevent fear. Anticipated anxiety is a cognitive theory rather than an emotional theory, because it emphasizes not anxiety *per se*, but cognitive appraisals of context-specific vulnerability to anxiety.

In self-efficacy theory, anticipated anxiety and phobic behavior are correlated coeffects of low self-efficacy for coping cognitively and behaviorally with potential threats. People's anticipated anxiety was compared to their self-efficacy in seven studies, five of which were conducted with agoraphobics (Telch, Agras, Taylor, Roth, & Gallen, 1985; Arnow, Taylor, Agras, & Telch, 1985; Williams, 1991; Williams et al., 1989; Williams & Rappoport, 1983), one with a mixed group of agoraphobics and height phobics (Williams et al., 1984), and one with severe height phobics (Williams et al., 1985). Subjects then rated their self-efficacy (as described earlier), then their anticipated anxiety on a 0–10 scale of how anxious they thought they would become if they were to do each task in the behavioral hierarchy. Subjects then tried to do as many of the tasks as they could. These measures were gathered before and after treatment.

The correlations between anticipated anxiety and level of coping behavior were quite high, averaging about .70 across the various data sets, but these were consistently somewhat lower than the correlations between self-efficacy and behavior, which averaged about .80. Partial correlation analyses, presented in Table 2, showed that self-efficacy is consistently an accurate predictor of behavior, both in specific phobics and in agoraphobics, when anticipated anxiety is held constant, whereas anticipated anxiety generally loses predictive accuracy when self-efficacy is held constant.

Anticipated panic theory is a variant of fear-of-fear theory, in which agoraphobic people's thoughts about the likelihood of panic drive their avoidance behavior. This widely accepted theory was compared with self-efficacy theory in two studies that measured both mediators (Williams, 1991; Williams et al., 1989). Note that whereas anticipated panic is rated on a *likelihood* scale (0%–100%), anticipated anxiety is rated on a scale of anxiety *intensity* (0–10).

Anticipated panic correlated highly with anticipated anxiety (about .85), and with behavior (about .70). The results of partial correlation analyses of self-efficacy and anticipated panic as predictors of behavior showed that, as with anticipated anxiety, self-efficacy emerges as the overriding predictor of avoidance behavior, with anticipated panic inde-

TABLE 2. Partial Correlation Analyses Predicting Behavior
from Perceived Self-Efficacy Holding Anticipated Anxiety Constant,
and Vice Versa, by Study and Assessment Phase

Study/ Test Phase (n)	Self-Efficacy Predict Behavior (Anticipated Anxiety Held Constant)	Anticipated Anxiety Predict Behavior (Self-Efficacy Held Constant)
Williams & Rappoport, 1983		
Pretreatment 1 (20)	.40*	−.12
Pretreatment 2 (20)	.59**	−.28
Posttreatment (20)	.45*	.13
Follow-up (18)	.45*	.06
Williams et al., 1984		
Pretreatment (32)	.22	−.36*
Posttreatment (32)	.59**	−.21
Williams et al., 1985		
Pretreatment (38)	.25	−.36*
Posttreatment (38)	.72***	.05
Follow-up (38)	.66***	−.12
Arnow et al., 1985		
Pretreatment (24)	.77***	.17
Posttreatment (24)	.43*	−.08
Follow-up (24)	.88***	−.06
Telch et al., 1985		
Pretreatment (29)	−.28	−.56***
Posttreatment (29)	.48**	.15
Follow-up (29)	.42*	−.05
Williams, 1991		
Pretreatment (37)	.35*	−.20
Posttreatment (37)	.82***	−.08
Follow-up (26)	.84***	−.02

*$p < .05$. **$p < .01$. ***$p < .001$.

pendently contributing no significant predictiveness when self-efficacy is held constant.

So these results make clear that self-efficacy cannot easily be dismissed as a mere inert by-product of anticipated fear.

Self-Efficacy Mediates Generalization of Behavioral Change

The causal status of self-efficacy judgments is shown clearly in a recent study on generalization of behavioral change (Williams et al., 1989). In people with multiple phobias, treatment given for one phobia (e.g., driving) sometimes appears to produce marked improvements in a quite different phobia (e.g., heights or eating in restaurants) that was entirely untreated. Such generalized therapeutic changes, if indeed they occur, constitute a phenomenon well-suited to studying cognitive causation, because they occur without the person having had any learning experiences directly pertinent to the transfer phobia (or, in stimulus terms, without any "exposure" to transfer phobia stimuli).

Subjects were agoraphobic people who feared activities such as shopping, driving, walking, riding elevators, crossing bridges, and so on. Each subject completed behavioral tests in several areas of phobic disability, received brief performance-based treatment for one or two of the phobias, then completed the behavioral tests again in a midtreatment assessment phase. Subjects who still had more than one disabling phobia completed a second treatment phase with some phobias left untreated. Then they completed the behavioral tests again at a posttreatment and follow-up assessment phase. Subjects were required not to attempt phobia-relevant activities on their own between the pretest and the posttest.

The results showed that, first, the benefits did indeed transfer from the treated to the untreated phobic areas. The transfer phobias improved about half as much as the treated phobias, whereas control phobias did not improve in subjects who received no treatment. The degree of generalized change was highly idiosyncratic and variable within and between subjects, and could not be predicted simply by stimulus features shared by treated and transfer activities.

Second, perceived self-efficacy was the overriding predictor of the generalized benefits. Partial correlation analyses, shown in Table 3, indicate that even when controlling for the influence of the most recent previous behavior, anticipated anxiety, anticipated panic, or perceived danger, self-efficacy perceptions tended to strongly predict behavioral functioning. In contrast, with self-efficacy held constant, the various mediators showed little or no capacity to predict behavior. Previous behavior did not predict subsequent behavior in the transfer phobias, and did so in the treated phobias only weakly (Williams et al., 1989).

The consistent finding that self-efficacy perceptions predict coping behavior more accurately than does past behavior, and other kinds of thought processes and emotional reactions, strongly supports the view that self-efficacy judgments are important contributing causes of neurotic behavior. Additional issues have been raised about self-efficacy theory in critiques by various authors (e.g., Rachman, 1978), and these have been addressed in corresponding comments by Bandura (1978b, 1982, 1984, 1986b, 1991). Given the evidence in support of self-efficacy judgments as causes of behavior, it is of interest to examine their effect on other kinds of psychological responses, which will be examined in the following sections.

TABLE 3. Partial Correlations between Self-Efficacy
and Behavior Holding Alternate Factors Constant,
and between Alternate Factors and Behavior Holding Self-Efficacy
Constant, by Phobia Treatment Status and Assessment Phase[a]

		Treated phobias		Transfer phobias		
Alternate Factor	Pre	Mid	Post	Mid	Post	Follow-up
Self-Efficacy Predict Behavior, Alternate Factor Held Constant						
Perc. danger	.71***	.79***	.56***	.75***	.75***	.87***
Ant. anxiety	.45***	.65***	.47**	.53***	.36	.71***
Ant. panic	.71***	.63***	.41*	.51***	.41*	.75***
Previous beh.	—	.67***	.40*	.59***	.58**	.74***
Alternate Factor Predict Behavior, Self-Efficacy Held Constant						
Perc. danger	.02	−.21	−.20	.09	.11	−.02
Ant. anxiety	−.13	−.15	.02	−.15	−.16	−.03
Ant. panic	−.10	−.17	−.04	−.20*	−.40*	.05
Previous beh.	—	.49***	.33*	.19	.39	.54***

$*p < .05.$ $**p < .01.$ $***p < .001.$
[a]Data from Williams, Kinney, & Falbo, 1989.

SELF-EFFICACY INFLUENCE ON NEGATIVE COGNITIONS

The findings in the preceding section show clearly that self-efficacy perceptions account for behavioral disability with little help from other patterns of phobic thinking. These analyses suggest further that negative-outcome expectations are not an independent cause of behavior, but are rather a dependent effect of low self-efficacy. In self-efficacy theory, negative expectations are derived in part from perceptions of inefficacy for cognitive or behavioral coping with threats.

High correlations are found between self-efficacy and the various outcome expectations reported in the previous section. Across various data sets from different studies and assessment phases in the author's research program, the average correlation of self-efficacy with anticipated anxiety is about −.85, with anticipated panic about −.80, and with perceived danger about −.35 (Williams, 1991; Williams & Rappoport, 1983; Williams & Watson, 1985; Williams et al., 1984, 1985, 1989).

Evidence of a causal relationship between self-efficacy and outcome expectations is provided by a study with socially anxious individuals (Maddux, Norton, & Leary, 1988). Multiple regression analysis revealed that self-efficacy for skilled social behavior emerged as the best predictor of anticipated social anxiety, and negative-outcome expectations did not account for any additional variance. In a study with panic-disordered individuals using a cross-lagged panel design, Borden, Clum, and Salmon

(1991) repeatedly measured catastrophic cognitions and self-efficacy for coping with panic, and found that self-efficacy at an initial time tended to predict catastrophic thoughts at a future time, even with catastrophic thoughts at the initial time held constant. However, catastrophic thoughts did not predict future self-efficacy with current self-efficacy held constant. Although this preliminary study with a small sample of subjects requires replication, it is generally consistent with theory and evidence that low perceptions of self-efficacy and control create vulnerability to negative thoughts.

SELF-EFFICACY INFLUENCE ON ANXIETY

In self-efficacy theory, anxiety derives from a sense of inability to cope behaviorally and cognitively with potential threats (Bandura, 1988). Perceived threat is largely a function of how well one thinks one can deal with circumstances. A view down a steep, snowy hill can be either terrifying or delightful, depending on one's self-perceived skiing capabilities. When people have a diminished belief that they can exercise effective coping responses, they tend to become preoccupied with their deficiencies, and to ruminate about possible dangers. Nearly every activity and environment contains many potential hazards, of which people are fully aware. But they do not live in continual distress, because they judge themselves able to manage the hazardous elements, and they believe they can probably deal effectively with unforseen exigencies that might arise. Believing oneself unable to exercise control over potentially aversive or harmful events gives rise to anxiety.

Perceived Control

A growing convergence of theory and evidence in recent years testifies to the influential role of perceived control in ameliorating defensiveness and stress reactions. Perceived control is intimately related to perceived self-efficacy, since having control means being able to effectively exercise it. Without the self-efficacy belief that one can enact a controlling response, perceived control does not exist (See also Chap. 1, this volume).

It has long been known that having some control over aversive stimulation reduces fear. The perceived ability to mitigate, prevent, or terminate aversive events has benefits beyond merely being able to predict the events (Miller, 1979). A person who can influence the rate, intensity, or pattern of noxious stimulation will be left psychologically less distressed and vulnerable to fear than another who cannot exercise any influence, even when the two people experience the identical actual aversive stimulation (Miller, 1979; Mowrer & Viek, 1948; Seligman, 1975). Moreover, the benefits of perceived control do not require that the person actually make any controlling responses; the mere belief that one can respond effectively shields people from distress (Miller, 1979; Mineka & Kelly, 1989; Sanderson, Rapee, & Barlow, 1989).

The value of perceived control in preventing panic is well illustrated by Sanderson et al. (1989). Panic-disordered subjects completed a 15-minute trial of inhaling air that had been enriched with carbon dioxide. Prior to the trial, all subjects were told that when a light was illuminated, they would be able to reduce the amount of carbon dioxide they received by adjusting a dial, although they were encouraged to resist doing so. For half of the subjects, the light-signalling controllability was never illuminated during the trial, whereas for the other half, it was illuminated for the full 15 minutes. In actuality, the dial had no effect on carbon dioxide, and in any case, subjects did not try to manipulate it. Nevertheless, the group with illusory control had significantly fewer panic attacks, panic sensations, catastrophic thoughts, and lower subjective anxiety than did the group without control. Indeed, 80% of the subjects without control had a panic attack, whereas only 20% of the subjects with control panicked.

Thought-Control Efficacy and Anxiety

Self-efficacy was defined and measured originally as "coping self-efficacy," or confidence in one's ability to perform coping tasks (Bandura et al., 1977). Over a large number of data sets in the author and colleagues' research with phobias (e.g., Arnow et al., 1985; Telch et al., 1985; Williams & Rappoport, 1983; Williams & Watson, 1985; Williams & Zane, 1989; Williams et al., 1984, 1985, 1989), this kind of coping self-efficacy predicts people's anxiety during the behavioral tests at the level of about $r = .50$. But anticipated anxiety and anticipated panic tend to be more accurate than coping self-efficacy in predicting performance-related anxiety (Williams, 1985, 1986). Indeed, anticipated anxiety and anticipated panic predict performance anxiety at the level of about $r = .75$. Anticipated anxiety/panic consistently predict anxiety when self-efficacy is held constant, but with equal consistency self-efficacy loses its capacity to predict anxiety when anticipated anxiety/panic is held constant (Williams, 1985, 1986).

Especially challenging for self-efficacy theory are the circumstances that give rise to these correlations. That is, people can rate their self-efficacy as maximal for a task, but at the same time expect to become highly anxious doing the task. When the people later actually attempt the task, they typically are able to do it all, but they are very frightened while doing it. So this suggests that subjective fear arousal must come partly from another source than low coping self-efficacy.

A possible explanation of this pattern of results is Bandura's (1988) recent proposed expansion of self-efficacy theory to include self-efficacy for controlling scary trains of thought. The concept is that people anticipate and experience fear partly because they lack a sense of thought-control efficacy that would enable them to turn off frightening cognitions. So, even though they might be sure they could execute a task, they still expect and experience fear.

It is not the mere occurrence of a thought of danger that produces fear arousal. Most drivers imagine from time to time that a collision could occur, and most airplane passengers realize that their plane could crash. What prevents them from being gripped by fear is that they can easily dismiss such thoughts, keep them in perspective, and not apprehensively ruminate to the point of untoward distress. Support for this interpretation comes from findings that it is not the sheer frequency of distressing thoughts, but the perceived ability to turn them off, that bears more directly on fear arousal (Kent, 1987; Kent & Gibbons, 1987; Salkovskis & Harrison, 1984).

Recent data gathered by Zane (1990) compared thought-control self-efficacy to anticipated anxiety and anticipated panic in predicting fear arousal in agoraphobic individuals before and after treatment. The measure of thought-control self-efficacy asked people to judge how confident they were that they could control scary thoughts. Thought-control self-efficacy was generally more accurate than standard coping self-efficacy in predicting performance anxiety. Nevertheless, with anticipated panic or anticipated anxiety held constant, thought-control self-efficacy was a relatively weak predictor of anxiety, whereas with thought-control self-efficacy held constant, anticipated anxiety and panic remained strong predictors of anxiety. It appears that anticipations of panic/anxiety are related to anxiety arousal independently of self-efficacy. Because it is not clear how the mere anticipation of anxiety or of panic could cause one to become anxious or panicky, it seems that the determining cause must be a factor which, along with self-efficacy, contributes to anticipated fear. Whether that factor is a perception of danger or some other factor is not clear.

SELF-EFFICACY INFLUENCE ON PHYSIOLOGICAL AROUSAL

Coping self-efficacy appears to bear directly on physiological stress reactions. When phobic subjects' autonomic reactions are measured in relation to tasks for which they have varying strengths of self-efficacy, the results reveal that autonomic arousal is little elevated when coping with tasks they feel confident they can manage, but on tasks at a moderate level of efficacy, heart rate accelerates and blood pressure rises when anticipating and performing the tasks (Bandura et al., 1982). Subjects promptly refused to attempt tasks for which they have very low self-efficacy as too far beyond their coping capabilities to even try, in which case their subjective fear and cardiac reactivity subsided, but their blood pressure remained elevated. After subjects' perceptions of coping efficacy were strengthened to maximal levels via a brief guided mastery treatment procedure, they performed all of the previously threatening tasks without autonomic arousal (Bandura et al., 1982).

Heart rate and blood pressure changes in response to contact with phobic stressors are probably mediated by plasma catecholamines, specifically, plasma epinephrine and norepinephrine. In a study to determine whether people's perceptions of coping efficacy are linked directly to catecholamine secretion, severely spider phobic individuals observed a model demonstrate strategies for coping with spiders until they developed strong self-efficacy for some spider-related tasks, moderate self-efficacy for other tasks, and retained weak coping self-efficacy for yet other tasks (Bandura, Taylor, Williams, Mefford, & Barchas, 1985). Levels of plasma epinephrine, norepinephrine, and dopac were then monitored continuously while subjects attempted tasks corresponding to their strong, medium, and weak strengths of perceived self-efficacy (in counterbalanced order).

Plasma levels of all three catecholamines were significantly elevated in response to tasks attempted at a moderate strength of self-efficacy, compared to tasks performed at a high strength of self-efficacy. As in the earlier experiment, subjects quickly rejected the performance tasks for which their self-efficacy was very weak, and so their plasma epinephrine and norepinephrine levels remained low. Dopac, however, became significantly elevated for the tasks for which subjects had weak self-efficacy, evidently being affected by the mere mention of tasks that subjects judged to exceed their coping capabilities.

Following this assessment procedure, all subjects received a brief guided mastery treatment, in which the therapist first demonstrated a variety of means of effectively controlling spiders, and then guided and assisted the subjects in directly performing the tasks. The brief treatment raised all subjects' perceptions of self-efficacy for the tasks to maximal levels, and then the plasma catecholamine levels were again tested in response to the same three tasks. Results showed that there were no significant elevations in the levels of any of the catecholamines in response to the previously intimidating tasks after self-efficacy was raised to maximal levels (Bandura et al., 1985).

The findings reviewed thus far lend support to the conclusion that people's perceptions of their coping capabilities influence several important aspects of functioning. Low self-efficacy appears to be a major cause of phobic disability. In addition, self-efficacy appears to affect thoughts of aversive or hazardous outcomes, subjective feelings of fear, autonomic arousal, and plasma catecholamine release (see also O'Leary, this volume). It is important to consider not only the *effects* of self-efficacy perceptions, but their causes as well. Consideration of the sources of self-efficacy information will be informative for understanding the implications of self-efficacy theory for the treatment of anxiety disorders.

SELF-EFFICACY AND TREATMENT OF ANXIETY DISORDERS

SOURCES OF SELF-EFFICACY

If self-efficacy theory is to be useful for developing better treatments, it must specify the causes of self-efficacy. Bandura (1986a) has suggested four principal sources of information affecting perceptions of self-efficacy: performance accomplishments, vicarious experiences, verbal persuasion, and physiological states. Two additional sources of efficacy information, imaginal experiences and emotional states, also are discussed.

Performance Accomplishments

Direct performance experiences potentially have the greatest impact on self-efficacy perceptions, because firsthand successes and failures convey highly vivid and self-relevant information about what one can do. Self-efficacy and behavior are reciprocally related. Successes tend to increase self-efficacy, which in turn promotes further success; failures tend to lower self-efficacy and thereby limit further success. Although people weigh performance accomplishments heavily in judging their self-efficacy, they also consult other sources of information. As a result, self-judged capabilities often differ from previous accomplishments. When such discrepancies occur, it is self-efficacy that tends to be the better predictor of subsequent performance (Bandura & Adams, 1977; Bandura et al., 1977, 1980; Williams et al., 1984, 1989).

Vicarious Experiences

People's self-efficacy can be influenced powerfully by observing others. In vicarious modeling therapy, phobic clients view others coping successfully with phobia-related activities. Considerable evidence indicates that modeling can produce marked beneficial effects on self-efficacy, fear, and phobic behavior (Bandura et al., 1977; Bandura & Adams, 1977;

Rosenthal & Bandura, 1978). The likelihood of benefit is increased when clients perceive the model as similar to themselves. Similar or not, people sometimes conclude that other people's coping successes are irrelevant to their own capabilities. Vicarious successes therefore tend to be less potent than firsthand performance successes in enhancing self-efficacy (Bandura, Blanchard, & Ritter, 1969; Bandura et al., 1977; Rosenthal & Bandura, 1978).

Imaginal Experiences

In imaginal learning, clients imagine themselves or others succeeding in adaptive coping actions. In systematic desensitization (Wolpe, 1958), anxious clients visualize themselves performing a graduated sequence of progressively more scary tasks while remaining relaxed and very calm. In *implosion* (Stamfl & Levis, 1967), clients imagine themselves rapidly confronting their worst fears without relaxing. In *covert modeling* (Kazdin, 1984), clients imagine someone else coping with the phobic stressor.

A vast body of research reveals that imagined success experiences clearly benefit many anxious individuals, both lowering their fear and increasing their ability to behaviorally cope with former threats (Bandura, 1969; Kazdin, 1984; Leitenberg, 1976). Nonetheless, imaginal treatments for phobia are substantially less effective than performance treatments, because imagining oneself doing something is just not as convincing as actually doing it (Bandura et al., 1969; Crowe, Marks, Agras, & Leitenberg, 1972; Emmelkamp & Wessels, 1975; Johnston et al., 1976; Stern & Marks, 1973; Sherman, 1972; Thase & Moss, 1976; Ultee, Griffioen, & Schellekens, 1982; Watson, Mullett, & Pillay, 1973). The behavioral effects of visualizing oneself succeed are well predicted by changes in self-efficacy (Bandura & Adams, 1977; Bandura et al., 1980).

Verbal Persuasion

People can sometimes be led to a stronger belief in their own capabilities by persuasory dialogue. Because talking about coping is an indirect experience, it should be less potent than direct coping successes in improving self-efficacy. Verbal-cognitive therapies have indeed been found relatively weak for phobia, whether given alone or in combination with performance-based treatments (Biran & Wilson, 1981; Emmelkamp, Brilman, Kuiper, & Mersch, 1986; Emmelkamp, Kuipers, & Eggeraat, 1978; Emmelkamp & Mersch, 1982; Ladouceur, 1983; Williams & Rappoport, 1983). The benefits of verbal-cognitive therapy for agoraphobia were minimal even when treatment produced the targeted cognitive changes (Williams & Rappoport, 1983). In one study, performance mastery alone produced significantly better results than did a treatment combining performance and verbal-cognitive therapy (Ladouceur, 1983). Such findings do not preclude developing more effective verbal-cognitive procedures, of course, but indicate that the value of verbal-cognitive techniques in treating phobia has yet to be clearly demonstrated.

Physiological States

Physiological responses provide another source of efficacy information. People can interpret perceived autonomic arousal as a sign of impending inability to cope, or lack of arousal as a sign that they can handle the situation. Autonomic reactions are generally a fairly weak source of efficacy information, because people know from long experience that their viscera tell them relatively little about what they can do. People are notoriously poor at estimating their autonomic arousal (e.g., Ehlers, 1989; Ehlers & Breuer, 1992; Mandler, 1962), making it a treacherous guide. Even if they could accurately perceive their viscera, they would be badly misled because of the empirically poor relationship between physiological arousal and coping capabilities (Bandura, 1978b; Lang, 1978; Williams, 1987). Much latitude exists in how people can interpret the meaning of perceived arousal; a pounding heart can mean "fired up" for one person, but "terrified" for another. It is the interpretation more than the arousal *per se* that will determine the effects on self-efficacy.

Emotional States

People partly judge their self-efficacy by their subjective states of feeling and mood, which are not simply a function of physiological arousal. Indeed, the correlation between autonomic arousal and subjective feelings of fear is often near zero (e.g., Morrow & Labrum, 1978), as mentioned earlier. The causal relationship between subjective emotion and self-efficacy is reciprocal but asymmetrical, with self-efficacy exercising greater influence on emotion than emotion on self-efficacy. This is because emotional states are unstable and unreliable guides to effective behavior. People know that they often can perform reasonably well despite feeling scared, and that they can perform rather poorly despite freedom from fear (Bandura, 1988; Williams, 1987). Anxiety probably has some inhibiting effects on self-efficacy and thereby on behavior, but this has not been specifically demonstrated. Research has demonstrated that depressed mood can dampen self-efficacy (Kavanagh, 1992; Kavanagh &

Bower, 1985), just as low self-efficacy can dampen mood (Stanley & Maddux, 1986). Further research on the influence of emotion on self-efficacy is needed.

TREATMENT OF PHOBIC DISABILITY AND DISTRESS

Theories of personality and psychopathology must be judged in part by their capacity to help people change. In self-efficacy theory, the psychological *mechanism* of therapeutic change is cognitive, but the most powerful psychological *procedure* for instating change is behavioral. This is because people's judgments of what they can do are affected more by firsthand mastery experiences than by verbal–cognitive dialogue (Willams & Rappoport, 1983). Self-efficacy theory generally prescribes performance-based mastery experiences as central in treatment, because such direct success is the single most potent source of information for building a strong belief that one can cope (Bandura, 1977).

Performance-based treatments are widely recognized as the most effective approach for phobias (Barlow, 1988). However, the theory and practice of performance therapies often heavily emphasize the noncognitive concept of "exposure" to phobic stimuli (Marks, 1978). This likens treatment to a classical extinction procedure, in which doing phobia-related activities works by placing clients near to scary stimuli, until fear and avoidance somehow extinguish themselves over time.

The exposure metaphor does not specify what operationally defines exposure, what psychopathological factor creates neurotic emotions or behaviors, or what are the psychological mechanisms of therapeutic change (Rosenthal & Bandura, 1978; Williams, 1987, 1988, 1990). On a practical level, the exposure concept gives therapists little guidance in the best way to guide therapeutic performance beyond the vague principle of somehow bringing clients into prolonged commerce with phobic stimuli. Of course, domain-relevant information is necessary for learning in any domain, whether it be to master a phobia or a language. But that very broad generalization reveals precious little of specific value about how to teach German or how to help a phobic client who is struggling with a high balcony or a busy freeway.

In most accounts, "*in vivo* exposure" treatment seems to mean simply urging clients to go out between therapy sessions and put themselves in scary situations (Williams, 1990). Although exposure therapies achieve beneficial results in many cases, as currently implemented, they fail to benefit some clients, especially those with the most generalized and incapacitating phobias, and many clients are left with at least some phobic problems after treatment (Barlow, 1988; Gelder, 1977). Urging people to do the most terrifying activities for prolonged periods is evidently a prescription more easily given than filled. The limitations of exposure therapies call for a more specific technology of performance-based treatment.

In treatment based on self-efficacy theory, or *guided mastery therapy* (Williams, 1990), the emphasis is not on mere stimulus exposure, but on the quality and amount of information people gain about their developing capabilities. People are not passively absorbing stimuli for prolonged durations, but actively, and if possible rapidly, mastering a challenge. Three general strategies are used in guided mastery therapy (Williams, 1990). First, the therapist draws from a large repertoire of techniques designed to boost self-efficacy and performance by helping clients to do activities that they otherwise would find too difficult. The therapist might, for example, ride with a freeway phobic person the first time he or she drives the freeway, then follow in another car increasingly farther behind, until the client can drive it alone. The various performance aids are designed to create an interim increase in self-efficacy, to enable the person to tackle yet more challenging tasks, further boosting self-efficacy, and continuing in an ascending spiral of therapeutic change. Second, the therapist helps people increase the quality and proficiency of their performance by guiding them to abandon ritualistic defensive maneuvers and vary their performance. For example, the therapist might encourage the client to hold the steering wheel in a normal fashion rather than with "white knuckles," to turn off the car radio, and to change lanes and pass slow cars. Otherwise, these kinds of defensive activities undermine self-efficacy by circumscribing the sense of success, by vividly reminding people of their incompetence, and by leading them to attribute successes to the defensive maneuvers rather than to their growing capabilities (Kinney, 1992; Williams, 1985, 1990). Third, the therapist guides the person to do the tasks with increasing independence, without the presence of the therapist or other "safe" persons. When people are progressing well, the therapist provisionally withdraws the assistance, and ultimately arranges for people to have varied independent success experiences, so that their self-efficacy will be unconditional.

An exacting test of guided mastery is to compare it to similar or longer durations of "pure" stimulus exposure for phobia. Four experiments by the author and colleagues evaluated this question. In the first (Williams et al., 1984), we randomly assigned 32 severe driving and height phobics (about half of whom were agoraphobic) to 3 hours of individual guided mastery treatment, 3 hours of individual exposure treatment, or no treatment. In exposure, the therapist accompanied subjects to the treatment setting and strongly urged them to quickly confront the therapeutic tasks, and to persist despite anxiety. In guided mastery treatment, the therapist also encouraged rapid performance, but in addition gave subjects efficacy-based assistance and guidance when they were having trouble progressing.

The therapeutic improvements in approach behavior and self-efficacy are shown in Figure 1. Guided mastery treatment (the solid lines) was significantly and substantially more effective than exposure (the dashed lines) in increasing behavioral capabilities and self-efficacy, as well as in decreasing fear arousal. In addition, guided mastery subjects experienced significantly lower levels of anticipated anxiety and performance-related anxiety than did exposure subjects. Both treatments were more effective than the control condition.

A second study (Williams et al., 1985) compared guided mastery treatment to performance desensitization treatment. *Performance desensitization* is a popular variant of exposure treatment in which the therapist encourages phobic clients to approach phobic situations in a gradual way, so as to keep their anxiety arousal at relatively low levels. Subjects were 38 severely incapacitated height phobics who were randomly assigned to one of the two treatments or to a no-treatment control condition. Subjects were given a maximum of 3 hours of treatment, or less if they completed all of the therapeutic height tasks before 3 hours had elapsed. The results were essentially the same as in the previous experiment. Figure 2 shows the mean level of self-efficacy and behavioral approach by subjects in the three conditions at pretest, posttest, and at a 1-month follow-up. Guided mastery subjects improved significantly more than desensitization subjects, and mastery subjects remained less phobic than desensitization subjects at follow-up.

The significant therapeutic superiority of guided mastery treatment was also evident in subjects' anticipated anxiety and in their perceptions of danger in relation to the height tasks. It is noteworthy that due to their more rapid progress in treatment, guided mastery subjects received a significantly shorter duration of treatment than did the desensitization subjects, that is, less time of exposure resulted in greater therapeutic benefit.

A third study (Williams & Zane, 1989) compared guided mastery and flooding exposure therapy for 26 agoraphobics who became highly anx-

---→

FIGURE 1. Mean percent of tasks performed and mean level of self-efficacy before and after treatment, by subjects in the guided mastery, stimulus exposure, and control conditions. Note that self-efficacy was measured both before and after the behavioral test at each assessment phase (from Williams, Dooseman, & Kleifield, 1984).

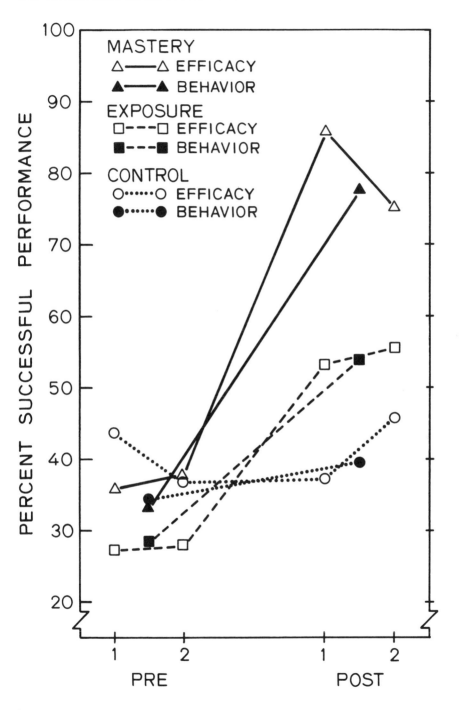

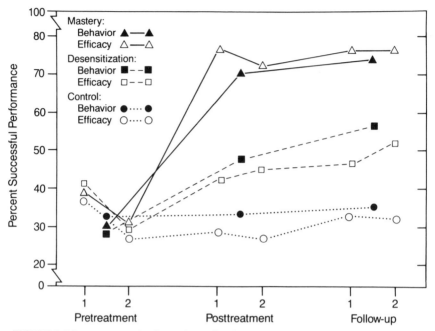

FIGURE 2. Mean percent of tasks performed and mean level of self-efficacy before and after treatment and at follow-up, by subjects in the guided mastery, performance desensitization, and control conditions. Note that self-efficacy was measured both before and after the behavioral test at each assessment phase (from Williams, Turner, & Peer, 1985).

ious during pretreatment behavioral tests, but were able to perform most or all tasks of the test. Subjects were randomly assigned to guided mastery, exposure, or no treatment. Both treatments embodied 1 hour of treatment per phobic area. Guided mastery treatment emphasized helping subjects perform tasks with fewer defensive maneuvers and in a varied proficient manner. Exposure treatment emphasized continuous full exposure to the scary stimuli. The results for the focal dependent variable, level of anxiety reached during the behavioral tests, are shown in Figure 3. Guided mastery treatment reduced anxiety significantly more than did exposure treatment, and the advantage of guided mastery over exposure significantly increased during the follow-up period. A similar fourth study (Zane & Williams, 1993), however, did not find an advantage for guided mastery over exposure.

In addition to the preceding findings, four studies similar in conception have been done by other investigators. The first (Bandura, Jeffrey, &

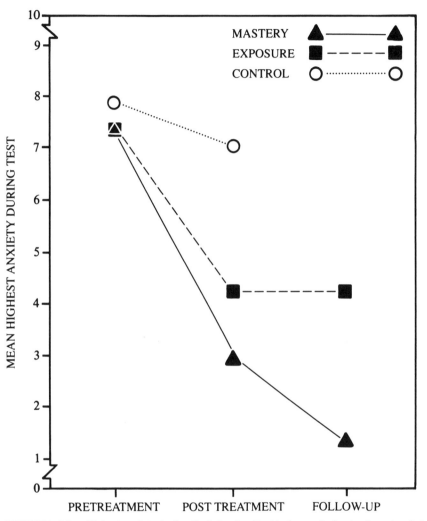

FIGURE 3. Mean highest anxiety during the behavioral test before and after treatment and at follow-up, by subjects in the guided mastery, stimulus exposure, and control conditions (from Williams & Zane, 1989).

Wright, 1974) compared guided mastery treatment given with a large or moderate number of therapist's aids, to a minimally aided exposure treatment for people with severe snake phobias. All three treatments were equated in exposure time and degree to which the therapist urged people to try to do the therapeutic tasks. The results showed that the treatments with guided mastery aids were significantly superior to the minimally aided exposure treatment.

In a similar study, O'Brien and Kelley (1980) varied the amount of active therapist-guided mastery assistance during performance treatment of snake fears, from none or little, to much or continuous therapist's assistance. The results showed that the groups with little or no aid benefited significantly less than did the more heavily aided groups.

It is worth noting that unlike most exposure therapists, who conduct treatment almost exclusively as "homework," the exposure therapists in the preceding studies were active, directly supervising participants' performance as they coped with real phobic threats. Nevertheless, their warm but firm encouragement to confront scary stimuli was significantly less effective than mastery-oriented technical guidance and assistance.

A recent study that compared homework exposure to guided mastery (Ost, Salkovskis, & Hellstrom, 1991) achieved results consistent with the earlier findings. Subjects received one of two treatments for their severe spider phobia. One treatment, which Ost et al. labeled "one-session treatment," was virtually identical with guided mastery or "participant modeling," as developed by Bandura et al. (1969, 1974, 1977, 1982, 1985) for snake and spider phobias. The other treatment was a homework-based exposure therapy conducted in a manner similar to the standard way in which agoraphobia therapies are carried out. The results showed that whereas the exposure homework program had very little beneficial effect, guided mastery resulted in near complete elimination of clients' phobias.

An additional published study did not find active-mastery-oriented therapist's assistance more beneficial than relatively or completely unaided performance therapy (Bourque & Ladouceur, 1980). The reasons for this negative finding are not clear, but in any case, the preponderance of the evidence, six of eight studies published to date, support the advantage of shifting the therapeutic emphasis from prolonged stimulus exposure and anxiety extinction to promoting rapid proficient performance accomplishments and a sense of mastery.

TREATMENT OF NONPHOBIC PROBLEMS

Self-efficacy-based therapy applied to phobias primarily targets overt performance, aiding and guiding it as a way of raising self-efficacy. Research reviewed in the previous section showed that this performance-based approach can improve upon mere exposure in increasing behavioral coping capabilities, reducing anxiety, and lowering negative thinking patterns. Since compulsions, like phobias, involve marked behavioral restrictions, guided mastery therapy for compulsions might employ therapeutic aids to help clients refrain from compulsive rituals after doing threatening tasks, using some of the techniques developed for phobias.

For treatment of problems that predominantly involve subjective states such as panic, obsessions, posttraumatic stress, or generalized anxiety, self-efficacy-based therapies have not been extensively developed. However, self-efficacy theory seems readily applicable to such states. Current theorizing in such problems as panic (Barlow, 1988) and posttraumatic stress (Foa, Zinbarg, & Rothbaum, 1992) emphasizes the importance of perceived control (see also Mineka & Kelly, 1989). The analyses and findings on perceived control are consistent with the self-efficacy view that treatments for panic, stress, and generalized anxiety, work in part by strengthening clients' beliefs that they have command of effective cognitive and behavioral coping responses.

Recent findings show that panic attacks can be rapidly, markedly, and enduringly reduced or eliminated by a variety of specific treatments, including applied relaxation therapy, cognitive therapy, respiratory control, and systematic panic induction, which are usually given in combination with encouragement to perform scary activities (Barlow, 1988; Rapee & Barlow, 1991). The success of these varied treatments suggests a common cognitive mechanism, with self-efficacy being a salient possibility (Borden, Clum, & Salmon, 1991).

In this view, panic and its negative sequelae result from a profound sense that one cannot control or manage scary thoughts and feelings. It is the sense of inability to prevent, control, or tolerate panic, and of inadequacy at controlling themselves during panic, that make people vulnerable to it (Bandura, 1988; Williams, 1990; Williams & Laberge, 1994). Support for this view comes from the finding presented earlier that when panic patients were given carbon dioxide inhalation with freedom to use an illusory means of control, only 20% panicked, but when they were given the same carbon dioxide inhalation without belief in control, 80% panicked (Sanderson et al., 1989).

Some components of a self-efficacy-based panic treatment have been suggested by Williams and Laberge (1994). In this approach, a variety of cognitive and behavioral exercises, as well as rational dialogue, are employed to convey a sense of efficacy. The treatment also involves helping people identify and eliminate subtle defensive maneuvers, which can undermine self-efficacy, and which are often practiced by people who display no gross disability or avoidance (Clark, 1989; Salkovskis, 1988; Williams, 1985). The usefulness of self-efficacy theory in helping people with generalized anxiety and post-traumatic stress remains to be explored.

FUTURE DIRECTIONS

Self-efficacy theory has demonstrated power to explain disparate phenomena involved in anxiety disorders, including aspects of neurotic behavior, cognition, physiology, and affect. It provides a cognitive mechanism that explains the beneficial effects of diverse treatments for neurotic problems. And it has been heuristic in fostering improvements in treatment techniques. Nonetheless, there are gaps in understanding, and a corresponding need for further investigation.

One issue concerns the relationship between self-efficacy and anxiety arousal. The findings presented earlier show that although self-efficacy for overt coping behavior is a very strong predictor of behavioral disability, it appears to be only a moderately strong predictor of subjective anxiety (Williams, 1986). Bandura (1988) has proposed that low self-efficacy for controlling scary thoughts is another efficacy-based source of anxiety. The concept of thought control self-efficacy broadens self-efficacy theory to include people's judgments that they can make subjective coping responses, and exercise cognitive control. This major extension of the theory appears to be a promising direction that might well increase its explanatory power. Nonetheless, preliminary evidence suggests that the predictive accuracy of anticipated anxiety remains, even when thought control self-efficacy is held constant. Whether this points to the operation of important psychological processes other than self-efficacy that give rise to anticipations of anxiety, remains to be determined, as does the issue of whether treatments need to be developed for altering these cognitive sources of anticipated anxiety.

Another issue that needs resolution is the role of danger perceptions in phobia. Perceived danger has been widely proposed as a central factor in neurotic problems (e.g., Beck et al., 1985; Clark, 1986), yet the evidence bearing on it as a causal process in anxiety disorders has been surprisingly sparse and indirect. It is not enough to show that anxiety-disordered people have elevated levels of danger ideation; rather, one must show that these ideas strongly predict and influence neurotic thought, feeling, and behavior. Relatively few studies have systematically gathered measures of expected danger in relation to anxiety-disordered behavior and feeling so as to put perceived danger theory to the test. The studies that have compared self-efficacy to perceived danger have found danger to be a highly variable and comparatively weak predictor of both neurotic behavior and neurotic anxiety (Williams & Watson, 1985; Williams et al., 1985, 1989). Yet, at the same time, fear without perceived danger seems powerfully counterintuitive and almost inconceivable. Indeed, in self-efficacy theory, danger perceptions are held to explain why low self-efficacy for some activities results in fear, but for most activities, low self-efficacy simply produces disinterest or other nonfearful response. It is important to further examine the role of danger ideation in anxiety disorders.

The majority of self-efficacy research to date has examined the effects of self-efficacy on other responses. It is vital also to understand the sources of self-efficacy, and how to influence these sources so as to most efficiently promote growth in self-efficacy. One important issue is the cognitive processing of efficacy-relevant information in anxiety disorders. A recent study considered whether attributional processes might influence the sense of self-efficacy that agoraphobic people derive from success experiences, and in particular whether attributions help explain why people differ in how much self-efficacy they gain from identical performance successes (Kinney, 1992). The findings showed a strong relationship between attributions and self-efficacy judgments in agoraphobic subjects. The more they attributed performance success to a therapist, the less their gains in self-efficacy and behavioral capabilities, an effect that held even when level of success was held constant. Understanding the factors that affect the formation of favorable and unfavorable attributions therefore would seem to have important implications for the design of treatments for anxiety and phobia.

An additional area requiring attention is the development of specific self-efficacy-based techniques for diverse anxiety-disordered conditions. Work has already been done for agoraphobia (Williams, 1990) and some specific phobias such as spiders (Bandura et al., 1985), snakes (e.g., Bandura et al., 1982), and heights (Williams et al., 1984, 1985). However, mastery-based procedures must be developed for such problems as social phobias and obsessive–compulsive problems, as well as the negative emotional and subjective states involved in panic attacks and obsessions.

In short, many significant challenges remain to our understanding the psychopathology and treatment of anxiety disorders. But the evidence reviewed here encourages optimism that self-efficacy theory can be of substantial help in meeting those challenges.

ACKNOWLEDGMENTS: This paper and much of the author's research reported in it were supported by United States Public Health Service grants R03-MH41595 and R29-MH43285.

REFERENCES

Arnow, B. A., Taylor, C. B., Agras, W. S., & Telch, M. J. (1985). Enhancing agoraphobia treatment outcome by changing couple communication patterns. *Behavior Therapy, 16*, 452–467.

Bandura, A. (1969). *Principles of behavior modification.* New York: Holt, Rinehart, & Winston.

Bandura, A. (1977). Self-efficacy: Toward a unifying theory of behavioral change. *Psychological Review, 84*, 191–215.

Bandura, A. (1978a). On paradigms and recycled ideologies. *Cognitive Therapy and Research, 2*, 79–103.

Bandura, A. (1979b). Reflections on self-efficacy. *Advances in Behaviour Research and Therapy, 1*, 237–269.

Bandura, A. (1982). The assessment and predictive generality of self-percepts of efficacy. *Journal of Behavior Therapy and Experimental Psychiatry, 13*, 195–199.

Bandura, A. (1984). Recycling misconceptions of perceived self-efficacy. *Cognitive Therapy and Research, 8*, 231–255.

Bandura, A. (1986a). *Social foundations of thought and action: A social cognitive theory.* Englewood Cliffs, NJ: Prentice-Hall.

Bandura, A. (1986b). The explanatory and predictive scope of self-efficacy theory. *Journal of Clinical and Social Psychology, 4*, 359–373.

Bandura, A. (1988). Self-efficacy conception of anxiety. *Anxiety Research, 1*, 77–98.

Bandura, A. (1991). Human agency: The rhetoric and the reality. *American Psychologist, 46*, 157–162.

Bandura, A., & Adams, N. E. (1977). Analysis of self-efficacy theory of behavioral change. *Cognitive Therapy and Research, 1*, 287–308.

Bandura, A., Adams, N. E., & Beyer, J. (1977). Cognitive processes mediating behavior change. *Journal of Personality and Social Psychology, 35*, 125–139.

Bandura, A., Adams, N. E., Hardy, A., & Howells, G. (1980). Tests of the generality of self-efficacy theory. *Cognitive Therapy and Research, 4*, 39–66.

Bandura, A., Blanchard, E. B., & Ritter, B. (1969). Relative efficacy of desensitization and modeling approaches for inducing behavioral, affective, and attitudinal changes. *Journal of Personality and Social Psychology, 13*, 173–199.

Bandura, A., Jeffrey, R. W., & Wright, C. L. (1974). Efficacy of participant modeling as a function of response induction aids. *Journal of Abnormal Psychology, 83*, 56–64.

Bandura, A., Reese, L., & Adams, N. E. (1982). Microanalysis of action and fear arousal as a function of differential levels of perceived self-efficacy. *Journal of Personality and Social Psychology, 43*, 5–21.

Bandura, A., Taylor, C. B., Williams, S. L., Mefford, I., & Barchas, J. (1985). Catecholamine secretion as a function of perceived coping self-efficacy. *Journal of Consulting and Clinical Psychology, 53*, 406–414.

Barlow D. H. (1988). *Anxiety and its disorders.* New York: Guilford.

Barlow, D. H., & Craske, M. G. (1988). The phenomenology of panic. In S. Rachman & J. D. Maser (Eds.), *Panic: Psychological perspectives* (pp. 11–35). Hillsdale, NJ: Erlbaum.

Beck, A. T. (1976). *Cognitive therapy and the emotional disorders.* New York: International Universities Press.

Beck, A. T., Emery, G., & Greenberg, R. L. (1985). *Anxiety disorders and phobias: A cognitive perspective.* New York: Basic Books.

Biran, M., & Wilson, G. T. (1981). Treatment of phobic disorders using cognitive and exposure methods: A self-efficacy analysis. *Journal of Consulting and Clinical Psychology, 49*, 886–899.

Borden, J. W., Clum, G. A., & Salmon, P. G. (1991). Mechanisms of change in the treatment of panic. *Cognitive Therapy and Research, 15,* 257–272.

Bourque P., & Ladouceur R. (1980). An investigation of various performance-based treatments with agoraphobics. *Behaviour Research and Therapy, 18,* 161–170.

Carr, A. T. (1979). The psychopathology of fear. In W. Slukin (Ed.), *Fear in animals and man* (pp. 199–235). New York: Van Nostrand Reinhold.

Clark, D. M. (1986). A cognitive approach to panic. *Behaviour Research and Therapy, 24,* 461–470.

Clark, D. M. (1989). Anxiety states: Panic and generalized anxiety. In K. Hawton, P. M. Salkovskis, J. Kirk, & D. M. Clark (Eds.), *Cognitive-behavioural treatment for psychiatric problems: A practical guide* (pp. 52–96). New York: Oxford.

Craske, M. G., & Barlow, D. H. (1988). A review of the relationship between panic and avoidance. *Clinical Psychology Review, 8,* 667–685.

Craske, M. G., Rapee, R. M., & Barlow, D. H. (1988). The significance of panic-expectancy for individual patterns of avoidance. *Behavior Therapy, 19,* 577–592.

Crowe, M., Marks, I., Agras, W., & Leitenberg, H. (1972). Time-limited desensitization, implosion, and shaping for phobic patients: A crossover study. *Behavior Research and Therapy, 12,* 319–328.

Davison, G. C., Haaga, D. A., Rosenbaum, J., Dolezal, S. L., & Weinstein, K. A. (1991). Assessment of self-efficacy in articulated thoughts: "States of mind" analysis and association with speech-anxious behavior. *Journal of Cognitive Psychotherapy, 5,* 83–92.

Detre, T. (1985). Is the grouping of anxiety disorders in DSM-III based on shared beliefs or data? In A. H. Tuma & J. D. Maser (Eds.), *Anxiety and the anxiety disorders* (pp. 783–786). Hillsdale, NJ: Erlbaum.

Ehlers, A. (1989). Interaction of psychological and physiological factors in panic disorder. In P. F. Lovibond & P. Wilson (Eds.), *Clinical and abnormal psychology* (pp. 1–13). Amsterdam: Elsevier.

Ehlers, A., & Breuer, P. (1992). Increased cardiac awareness in panic disorder. *Journal of Abnormal Psychology, 101,* 371–382.

Emmelkamp, P. M. G., Brilman, E., Kuiper, H., & Mersch, P. (1986). The treatment of agoraphobia: A comparison of self-instructional training, rational-emotive therapy, and exposure *in vivo. Behavior Modification, 10,* 37–53.

Emmelkamp, P. M. G., & Felten, M. (1985). The process of exposure *in vivo:* Cognitive and physiological changes during treatment of acrophobia. *Behaviour Research and Therapy, 23,* 219–223.

Emmelkamp P. M. G., Kuipers C. M., & Eggeraat, J. B. (1978). Cognitive modification versus prolonged exposure *in vivo:* A comparison with agoraphobics as subjects. *Behaviour Research and Therapy, 16,* 33–41.

Emmelkamp P. M. G., & Mersch P. P. (1982). Cognition and exposure *in vivo* in the treatment of agoraphobics: Short-term and delayed effects. *Cognitive Therapy and Research, 6,* 77–88.

Emmelkamp, P. M. G., & Wessels, H. (1975). Flooding in imagination vs. flooding *in vivo:* A comparison with agoraphobics. *Behaviour Research and Therapy, 13,* 7–16.

Eysenck, H. J. (1978). Expectations as causal elements in behavioural change. *Advances in Behaviour Research and Therapy, 1,* 171–175.

Foa, E. B., Zinbarg, R., & Rothbaum, B. O. (1992). Uncontrollability and unpredictability in post-traumatic stress disorder: An animal model. *Psychological Bulletin, 112,* 218–238.

Gauthier, J., & Ladouceur, R. (1981). The influence of self-efficacy reports on performance. *Behavior Therapy, 12,* 431–439.

Gelder, M. (1977). Behavioral treatment of agoraphobia. Some factors which restrict change after treatment. In J. C. Boulougouris & A. D. Rabavilas (Eds.), *The treatment of phobia and obsessive compulsive disorders* (pp. 7–12). New York: Pergamon.

Johnston, D. W., Lancashire, M., Mathews, A. M., Munby, M., Shaw, P. M., & Gelder, M. G. (1976). Imaginal flooding and exposure to real phobic situations: Changes during treatment. *British Journal of Psychiatry, 129,* 372–377.

Kavanagh, D. J. (1992). Self-efficacy and depression. In R. Schwarzer (Ed.), *Self-efficacy: Thought control of action* (pp. 177–193). Washington: Hemisphere.

Kavanagh, D. J., & Bower, G. H. (1985). Mood and self-efficacy: Impact of joy and sadness on perceived capabilities. *Cognitive Therapy and Research, 9,* 507–525.

Kazdin, A. E. (1984). Covert modeling. *Advances in Cognitive-Behavioral Research and Therapy, 3,* 103–129.

Kent, G. (1987). Self-efficacious control over reported physiological, cognitive and behavioural symptoms of dental anxiety. *Behaviour Research and Therapy, 25,* 341–347.

Kent, G. & Gibbons, R. (1987). Self-efficacy and the control of anxious cognitions. *Journal of Behavior Therapy and Experimental Psychiatry, 18,* 33–40.

Kinney, P. J. (1992). *The role of attributions in self-efficacy and behavioral changes following performance-based treatment of phobia.* Unpublished doctoral dissertation, Lehigh University, Bethlehem, PA.

Kirsch, I. (1982). Efficacy expectations or response predictions: The meaning of efficacy ratings as a function of task characteristics. *Journal of Personality and Social Psychology, 42,* 132–136.

Kirsch, I. (1990). *Changing expectations: A key to effective psychotherapy.* Pacific Grove, CA: Brooks-Cole.

Lacey, J. I. (1967). Somatic response patterning and stress: Some revisions of activation theory. In M. H. Appley & R. Trumbull (Eds.), *Psychological Stress: Issues in research* (pp. 14–42). New York: Appleton-Century-Crofts.

Ladouceur, R. (1983). Participant modeling with or without cognitive treatment of phobias. *Journal of Consulting and Clinical Psychology, 51,* 942–944.

Lang, P. J. (1978). Anxiety: Toward a psychophysiological definition. In H. S. Akiskal & W. L. Webb (Eds.), *Psychiatric diagnosis: Exploration of biological predictors* (pp. 365–389). New York: Spectrum.

Leitenberg, H. (1976). Behavioral approaches to treatment of neuroses. In H. Leitenberg (Ed.), *Handbook of behavior modification and behavior therapy* (pp. 124–167). Englewood Cliffs, NJ: Prentice-Hall.

Maddux, J. E. (1991). Self-efficacy. In C. R. Snyder and D. R. Forsyth (Eds.), *Handbook of social and clinical psychology* (pp. 57–78). New York: Pergamon.

Maddux, J. E., Norton, L. W., & Leary, M. R. (1988). Cognitive components of social anxiety: An investigation of the integration of self-presentation theory and self-efficacy theory. *Journal of Social and Clinical Psychology, 6,* 180–190.

Mandler, G. (1962). Emotion. In R. W. Brown, E. Galanter, E. Hess, & G. Mandler, *New Direction in Psychology I* (pp. 269–343). New York: Holt, Rinehart, & Winston.

Margraf, J., Taylor, C. B., Ehlers, A., Roth, W. T., & Agras, W. S., (1987). Panic attacks in the natural environment. *Journal of Nervous and Mental Disease, 175,* 558–565.

Marks, I. (1978). Behavioral psychotherapy of adult neurosis. In S. L. Garfield & A. E. Bergin (Eds.), *Handbook of psychotherapy and behavior change* (pp. 493–547). New York: Wiley.

Mathews, A. M., Gelder, M. G., & Johnston, D. W. (1981). *Agoraphobia: Nature and treatment.* New York: Guilford.

Miller, S. M. (1979). Controllability and human stress: Method, evidence and theory. *Behaviour Research and Therapy, 17,* 287–304.

Mineka, S. (1979). The role of fear in theories of avoidance learning, flooding, and extinction. *Psychological Bulletin, 86*, 985–1010.

Mineka, S., & Kelly, K. A. (1989). The relationship between anxiety, lack of control and loss of control. In A. Steptoe & A. Appels (Eds.), *Stress, personal control and health* (pp. 163–191). New York: Wiley.

Morrow, G. R., & Labrum, A. H. (1978). The relationship between psychological and physiological measures of anxiety. *Psychological Medicine, 8*, 95–101.

Mowrer, O. H., & Viek, P. (1948). An experimental analogue of fear from a sense of helplessness. *Journal of Abnormal and Social Psychology, 43*, 193–200.

O'Brien T., & Kelley, J. (1980). A comparison of self-directed and therapist-directed practice for fear reduction. *Behaviour Research and Therapy, 18*, 573–579.

Ost, L., Salkovskis, P. M., & Hellstrom, K. (1991). One-session therapist-directed exposure vs. self-exposure in the treatment of spider phobia. *Behavior Therapy, 22*, 407–422.

Persons, J. (1986). The advantages of studying psychological phenomena rather than psychiatric diagnoses. *American Psychologist, 11*, 1252–1260.

Rachman, S. (1976). The passing of the two-stage theory of fear and avoidance: Fresh possibilities. *Behaviour Research and Therapy, 14*, 125–131.

Rachman, S. (1978). Perceived self-efficacy: Analysis of Bandura's theory of behavioural change. *Advances in Behaviour Research and Therapy, 1*, [special issue edited by S. Rachman].

Rachman, S., & Hodgson, R. I. (1974). I. Synchrony and desynchrony in fear and avoidance. *Behaviour Research and Therapy, 12*, 311–318.

Rapee, R. M., & Barlow, D. H. (1991). The cognitive–behavioral treatment of panic attacks and agoraphobic avoidance. In J. R. Walker, G. R. Norton, & C. A. Ross (Eds.), *Panic disorder and agoraphobia: A comprehensive guide for the practitioner* (pp. 252–305). Pacific Grove, CA: Brooks/Cole.

Rosenthal, T. L., & Bandura, A. (1978). Psychological modeling: Theory and practice. In S. L. Garfield & A. E. Bergin (Eds.), *Handbook of psychotherapy and behavior change* (pp. 621–658). New York: Wiley.

Salkovskis, P. M. (1988). Phenomenology, assessment, and the cognitive model of panic. In S. Rachman & J. D. Maser (Eds.), *Panic: Psychological perspectives* (pp. 111–136). Hillsdale, NJ: Erlbaum.

Salkovskis, P. M., & Harrison, J. (1984). Abnormal and normal obsessions—A replication. *Behaviour Research and Therapy, 22*, 549–552.

Sanderson, W. C., Rapee, R. M., & Barlow, D. H. (1989). The influence of an illusion of control on panic attacks induced via inhalation of 5.5% carbon dioxide-enriched air. *Archives of General Psychiatry, 46*, 157–162.

Schwartz, B. (1986). *Psychology of learning and behavior*. New York: Norton.

Seligman, M. E. P. (1975). *Helplessness: On depression, development and death*. San Francisco: Freeman.

Seligman, M. E. P., & Johnston, J. C. (1973). A cognitive theory of avoidance learning. In F. J. McGuigan & D. B. Lumsden (Eds.), *Contemporary approaches to conditioning and learning* (pp. 69–110). Washington, DC: Winston.

Sherman, A. (1972). Real-life exposure as a primary therapeutic factor in desensitization treatment of fear. *Journal of Abnormal Psychology, 79*, 19–28.

Southworth, S., & Kirsch, I. (1988). The role of expectancy in exposure-generated fear reduction in agoraphobia. *Behaviour Research and Therapy, 26*, 113–120.

Spitzer, R. L., & Williams, J. B. W. (1985). Proposed revisions in the DSM-III classification of anxiety disorders based on research and clinical experience. In A. H. Tuma & J. D. Maser (Eds.), *Anxiety and the anxiety disorders* (pp. 759–773). Hillsdale, NJ: Erlbaum.

Stampfl, T. G., & Levis, D. J. (1967). Essentials of implosive therapy. *Journal of Abnormal Psychology, 72,* 496–503.

Stanley, M. A., & Maddux, J. E. (1986). Self-efficacy theory: Potential contributions to understanding cognitions in depression. *Journal of Social and Clinical Psychology, 4,* 268–278.

Stern, R. S., & Marks, I. M. (1973). A comparison of brief and prolonged flooding in agoraphobics. *Archives of General Psychiatry, 28,* 270–276.

Taylor, C. B., Sheikh, J., Agras, W. S., Toth, W. T., Margraf, J., Ehlers, A., Maddock, R. J., & Gossard, D. (1986). Ambulatory heart rate changes in patients with panic attacks. *American Journal of Psychiatry, 143,* 478–482.

Telch, M. J., Agras, W. S., Taylor, C. B., Roth, W. T., & Gallen, C. C. (1985). Combined pharmacological and behavioral treatment for agoraphobia. *Behaviour Research and Therapy, 23,* 325–335.

Telch, M. J., Bandura, A., Vinciguerra, P., Agras, A., & Stout, A. L. (1982). Social demand for consistency and congruence between self-efficacy and performance. *Behavior Therapy, 13,* 694–701.

Thase, M. E., & Moss, M. K. (1976). The relative efficacy of covert modeling procedures and guided participant modeling on the reduction of avoidance behavior. *Journal of Behavior Therapy and Experimental Psychiatry, 7,* 7–12.

Ultee, C. A., Griffioen, D., & Schellekens, J. (1982). The reduction of anxiety in children: A comparison of the effects of "systematic desensitization *in vitro*" and "systematic desensitization *in vivo*." *Behaviour Research and Therapy, 20,* 61–67.

Watson, J. P., Mullett, G. E., & Pillay, H. (1973). The effects of prolonged exposure to phobic situations upon agoraphobic patients treated in groups. *Behaviour Research and Therapy, 11,* 531–545.

Whitehead, W. E., Drescher, V. M., Heiman, P., & Blackwell, B. (1977). Relation of heart rate control to heartbeat perception. *Biofeedback and Self-Regulation, 2,* 371–392.

Williams, S. L. (1985). On the nature and measurement of agoraphobia. *Progress in Behavior Modification, 19,* 109–144.

Williams, S. L. (1986, August). Self-appraisal determinants of defensive behavior and emotional arousal. In R. Ganellen (Chair), *Agoraphobia: Cognitive contributions.* Symposium conducted at the meeting of the American Psychological Association, Washington, DC.

Williams, S. L. (1987). On anxiety and phobia. *Journal of Anxiety Disorders, 1,* 161–180.

Williams, S. L. (1988). Addressing misconceptions about phobia, anxiety, and self-efficacy: A reply to Marks. *Journal of Anxiety Disorders, 2,* 277–289.

Williams, S. L. (1990). Guided mastery treatment of agoraphobia: Beyond stimulus exposure. *Progress in Behavior Modification, 26,* 89–121.

Williams, S. L. (1991). Unpublished data.

Williams, S. L. (1992). Perceived self-efficacy and phobic disability. In R. Schwarzer (Ed.), *Self-efficacy: Thought control of action* (pp. 149–176). New York: Hemisphere.

Williams, S. L., & Bauchiess, R. (1992). *Cognitive factors influencing the persistence of agoraphobic avoidance and the rapidity of therapeutic change.* Unpublished manuscript, Lehigh University, Bethlehem, PA.

Williams, S. L., Dooseman, G., & Kleifield, E. (1984). Comparative effectiveness of guided mastery and exposure treatments for intractable phobias. *Journal of Consulting and Clinical Psychology, 52,* 505–518.

Williams, S. L., Kinney, P. J., & Falbo, J. (1989). Generalization of therapeutic changes in agoraphobia: The role of perceived self-efficacy. *Journal of Consulting and Clinical Psychology, 57,* 436–442.

Williams, S. L., & Laberge, B. (1994). Panic disorder with agoraphobia. In C. Last and M. Hersen (Eds.), *Adult behavior therapy casebook* (pp. 107–123). New York: Plenum.

Williams, S. L., & Rappoport, A. (1983). Cognitive treatment in the natural environment for agoraphobics. *Behavior Therapy, 14,* 299–313.

Williams, S. L., Turner, S. M., & Peer, D. F. (1985). Guided mastery and performance desensitization treatments for severe acrophobia. *Journal of Consulting and Clinical Psychology, 53,* 237–247.

Williams, S. L., & Watson, N. (1985). Perceived danger and perceived self-efficacy as cognitive determinants of acrophobic behavior. *Behavior Therapy, 16,* 237–247.

Williams, S. L., & Zane, G. (1989). Guided mastery and stimulus exposure treatments for severe performance anxiety in agoraphobics. *Behaviour Research and Therapy, 27,* 237–245.

Wolpe, J. (1958). *Psychotherapy by reciprocal inhibition.* Stanford, CA: Stanford University Press.

Wolpe, J. (1978). Self-efficacy theory and psychotherapeutic change: A square peg for a round hole. *Advances in Behaviour Research and Therapy, 1,* 231–236.

Zajonc, R. B., & McIntosh, D. N. (1992). Emotions research: Some promising questions and some questionable promises. *Psychological Science, 3,* 70–74.

Zane, G., & Williams, S. L. (1993). Performance-related anxiety in agoraphobia: Treatment procedures and cognitive mechanism of change. *Behavior Therapy, 24,* 625–643.

CHAPTER 4

SELF-EFFICACY AND ADDICTIVE BEHAVIORS

CARLO C. DiCLEMENTE, SCOTT K. FAIRHURST, and NANCY A. PIOTROWSKI

It was not long after Bandura introduced the construct of self-efficacy in 1977 that scientists and practitioners in the addictive behaviors began to use the construct in their theorizing and research. Marlatt and Gordon (1979) found a key role for self-efficacy in their model of relapse. Condiotte and Lichtenstein (1981), DiClemente (1981), and Shiffman (1982) began using self-efficacy to understand the process of smoking cessation. Heather, Rollnick and Winton (1982) and Litman and colleagues (1979) began discussing how efficacy could be used as a predictor of relapse in alcohol-dependence treatment. Self-efficacy demonstrated both conceptual and practical utility, as well as heuristic value, in these initial studies. Since 1977, many studies have used the construct with smoking, alcohol problems, drug abuse, and eating disorders. Measures of self-efficacy continue to prove valuable in the assessment and treatment of these addictive behaviors, particularly in the area of maintenance or relapse (DiClemente, 1986). However, questions and controversies surround the use and usefulness of self-efficacy with addictive behaviors. This chapter summarizes the issues that arise when applying self-efficacy to the addictive

CARLO C. DiCLEMENTE, SCOTT K. FAIRHURST, and NANCY A. PIOTROWSKI • Department of Psychology, University of Houston, Houston, Texas 77204.

Self-Efficacy, Adaptation, and Adjustment: Theory, Research, and Application, edited by James E. Maddux. Plenum Press, New York, 1995.

behaviors, as well as review studies that have used the construct with smoking, alcohol, drug abuse, and eating disorders.

APPLYING SELF-EFFICACY TO ADDICTION: FITS AND MISFITS

Self-efficacy theory proposes that efficacy evaluations will modulate effort expenditure as well as coping behaviors. These evaluations are understood to be behavior specific and related to past performance, verbal persuasion, vicarious experience, and emotional arousal. These particular aspects of self-efficacy theory make its application to the addictive behaviors quite intriguing for scientists and practitioners who view addictive behaviors from a biopsychosocial perspective (Donovan & Marlatt, 1988). By definition, *addictive behaviors* are those behaviors that are experienced by the individual and viewed by the society as being difficult or problematic to keep under personal control. For those who see addictions as completely beyond the control of the individual, the notion that one can feel efficacious about modification, control, or abstinence of these behaviors may seem a contradiction. However, many researchers and clinicians believe that the self-efficacy construct provides an avenue to explore self-evaluations of specific behaviors related to the execution or control of addictive behaviors.

Relapse and Efficacy

The most obvious area of application for self-efficacy was the problem of relapse. In trying to modify addictive behaviors, individuals often were not successful even after undergoing extensive and expensive treatment programs. Smokers, alcoholics, drug abusers, and individuals with eating disorders all experienced the same phenomenon (Carmody, 1990). In fact, the similar shape of the relapse curves for these different behaviors supported combining these behaviors together under the rubric of addictive behaviors (Hunt, Barnett, & Branch, 1971). In addition, similar situations or cues seemed to precipitate relapse across addictive behaviors (Marlatt & Gordon, 1979). These risky situations that cued the addictive behavior and precipitated relapse were the logical place to find a role for efficacy evaluations. Marlatt and J. R. Gordon (1979) Marlatt & J. R. Gordon (1985) developed a relapse model that included such self-efficacy evaluations (see Fig. 1). In their model, self-efficacy is an element of a complex process that includes outcome expectations, attributions, and the expected physiological effects of the substance or behavior. Self-efficacy acts as a moderator variable in the process of relapse. When faced with high-risk situations like

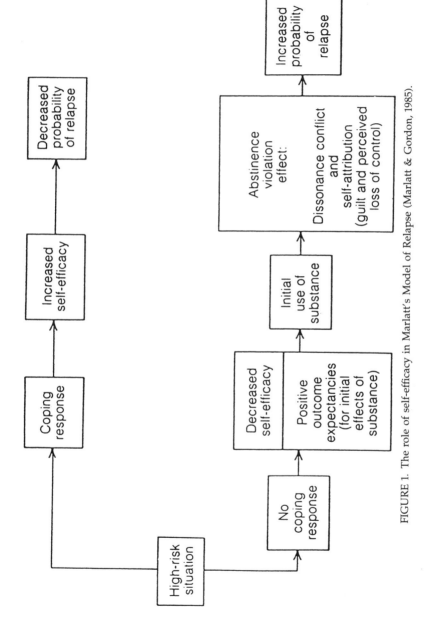

FIGURE 1. The role of self-efficacy in Marlatt's Model of Relapse (Marlatt & Gordon, 1985).

anger, anxiety, or social pressure to drink or use drugs, individuals can successfully perform adaptive coping behaviors or fail to cope. Self-efficacy for coping with each particular situation increases with success and decreases with failure. Decreased efficacy to cope with these situations, then, contributes to the probability of relapse. Marlatt and Gordon identified a coping self-efficacy that is related to the successful or unsuccessful modification of addictive behaviors.

INITIATION OF ADDICTIVE BEHAVIORS AND COPING EFFICACY

Another perspective that focuses on coping behavior and its relation to addictive behaviors is that proposed by Shiffman and Wills (1985). In this model, addictive behaviors are thought to begin as a coping response that is successful in the short term, but ultimately maladaptive. Thus, an adaptive coping repertoire would be needed to avoid short-term behavioral solutions that could develop into an addictive behavior. Once addicted, adaptive coping would need to be developed in order to modify those behaviors. Self-efficacy evaluations with respect to these adaptive coping behaviors play a key role in assessing vulnerability to initiation, as well as predicting the ability to modify or abstain from the addictive behavior.

INTERVENTION-RELATED EFFICACY

An intervention-focused application of self-efficacy concentrates on the role of efficacy evaluations in the control, modification, or cessation of a particular addictive behavior. Examples include individuals' self-evaluations of their abilities to abstain from smoking (DiClemente, 1981; DiClemente, Prochaska & Gibertini, 1985) or resist the urge to smoke (Condiotte & Lichtenstein, 1981), to avoid heavy drinking (Annis, 1982), to resist the urge to overeat (Glynn & Ruderman, 1986), to resist the use of cocaine, marijuana or speed (Hays & Ellickson, 1990), to avoid bulimic or anorexic behavior and control eating or maintain desired weight (Phelan, 1987), or to engage in a specific treatment regimen (Sallis et al., 1988). These efficacy evaluations are more directly related to the modification process for specific addictive behaviors and are differentiated by the behavior change goal of the addicted individual or the focus of the researcher.

ASSESSMENT AND APPLICATION OF SELF-EFFICACY ACROSS ADDICTIVE BEHAVIORS

The role that self-efficacy can play in the addictive behaviors is multi-faceted. Initiation, intervention, and relapse perspectives focus on different types of efficacy evaluations. The first challenge is to define the target behavior for which self-efficacy is to be assessed. As discussed previously,

1. *Coping* self-efficacy focuses on successful coping with specific situations, such as being assertive with friends or talking with someone when emotionally distressed instead of using the addictive behavior.
2. *Treatment behavior* self-efficacy involves the client's ability to perform treatment-relevant behaviors, such as self-monitoring or stimulus control (Overholser & Beck, 1985).
3. *Recovery* self-efficacy concentrates on a subject's ability to recover from a slip or temporary return to the addictive behavior (Cooney, Kopel, & McKeon, 1982; O'Leary, 1985).
4. *Control* self-efficacy focuses on the individual's confidence in the ability to control the behavior in a variety of provocative situations, for example, the ability to resist the urge to overeat or to not drink heavily (Annis, 1982; Glynn & Ruderman, 1986).
5. *Abstinence* self-efficacy involves the client's confidence in his or her ability to abstain from engaging in the addictive behavior in the various situations that are cues or triggers to perform that behavior (DiClemente, 1981; DiClemente, Prochaska & Gibertini, 1985).

For every application, it is important to specify the type of self-efficacy being evaluated. Although every application cannot be easily categorized, this review attempts to identify the types of self-efficacy evaluated in each study. The following sections discuss the application of self-efficacy to smoking, alcohol problems, drug abuse, and eating disorders, examining both the assessment and predictive ability of the specific self-efficacy assessed.

EFFICACY VS. OUTCOME EXPECTATIONS

Before exploring how self-efficacy evaluations for addictive behaviors can interact with treatment or change, it is important, at the outset, to review the distinction between efficacy expectations and outcome expectations. With respect to changing addictive behaviors, outcome expectations relate to the end state of sobriety, a drug-free life, or being thin, and what positive and negative experiences these states will bring with them. Expectations of what alcohol or drugs will do for or to an individual (e.g., decrease anxiety, increase sex drive) represent another type of outcome expectancy that has been related to the initiation and cessation of addictive behaviors (Brown, Goldman, Inn, & Anderson, 1980; Rohsenow, 1983; Southwick, Steele, Marlatt, & Lindell, 1981). Finally, expectations or estimations about the probability of some future event (e.g., "How confident are you that you will be abstinent from smoking or drinking in 1 month, or that you will be successful in stopping drinking 6 months from now?") seem best classified as combining both outcome success and efficacy expectations. Such estimations require individuals to evaluate both their confidence or efficacy to abstain across situations and time in order to assess the probability of future success. To respond to these types of inquiries, individuals would probably base future estimates on current performance and efficacy. However, predicting future outcomes seems more related to Bandura's definition of outcome expectations. The future orientation of these self-predictions involves an outcome estimate.

Outcome expectancies are hypothesized to be associated with, but independent of, efficacy evaluations. In the review of the articles for each addictive behavior this distinction is highlighted (see Chap. 1 for a detailed discussion of outcome expectancies).

EFFICACY EVALUATIONS AND THE PROCESS OF CHANGE

Efficacy evaluations represent an individual's confidence or belief in the ability to perform the particular target behavior. From an addictive behavior-change perspective, the target behavior is either control of or abstinence from the particular substance, be it alcohol, cocaine, cigarettes, or food. In either case, these efficacy evaluations should be relevant for assessing both entry into and active participation in treatment. However, if not understood in the context of the stages of behavior change, the direction of these relationships can sometimes be counterintuitive (see Fig. 2).

The process of modifying an addictive behavior follows a sequence of stages (Prochaska & DiClemente, 1992) from Precontemplation in which the individual is not seriously considering change, to a Contemplation stage that involves an evaluation of pros and cons of the behavior, as well as addressing the ambivalence about change. Outcome expectancies would be expected to be more salient as predictors in these early stages. As individuals move into the Preparation stage, they assess their resources and make a plan of action. In the Action stage, the plan for change is implemented and revised to meet new challenges. Changing addictive behaviors takes time and energy. The action phase can last for 3 to 6 months before the individual enters the Maintenance phase of change, where the challenge is sustaining long-term behavior change. Clearly, efficacy expectations related to behavior change would be most relevant in the Preparation and Action stages and would be expected to plateau in the Maintenance stage (DiClemente, 1986; DiClemente, Prochaska, & Gibertini, 1985).

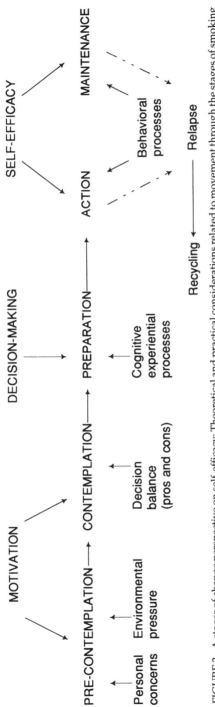

FIGURE 2. A stages of change perspective on self-efficacy: Theoretical and practical considerations related to movement through the stages of smoking cessation.

This relationship between self-efficacy and the stages of behavior change can help make sense of some confusing interactions between efficacy and treatment participation. Individuals with very high self-efficacy for avoiding overeating or abstaining from smoking would be unlikely to enter treatment, because they could achieve change with minimal assistance. Moderate to low levels of efficacy at pretreatment would seem preferable, because these individuals would need the persuasion, modeling, and other experiences provided by treatment. The level of efficacy upon entry, however, could impact attendance or drop out and affect the course of treatment. A quick rise in efficacy could indicate appropriate or inappropriate confidence in the ability to conquer the addiction, which could lead to early termination. Very low self-efficacy that continues during treatment could trigger discouragement and poor adherence to or drop out from treatment (DiClemente, 1991). In addition, efficacy evaluations should mediate treatment gains and the successful modification of the addictive behavior. Thus, maintenance and relapse are behavioral outcomes of treatment and change that should be predicted by efficacy evaluations. Finally, treatment and change, in turn, should influence an individual's efficacy evaluations according to the reciprocal determinism principle of social cognitive theory and the suggestion that enactment experiences are the most powerful source of self-efficacy (Bandura, 1986). Efficacy evaluations are moving targets that should anticipate and mirror actual changes in the addictive behavior and be influenced by these changes.

SELF-EFFICACY AND SMOKING BEHAVIOR

Abstinence self-efficacy for cigarette smoking has probably been the most studied of the addictive behavior efficacy evaluations. Several reasons account for this widespread application. First, smokers are less defensive than alcohol or drug dependent individuals in answering questions about their habit and can be recruited in large numbers. Moreover, taxonomies were developed for relevant situations considered to be relapse precipitants (Marlatt & Gordon, 1979) or prime smoking situations (Best & Hakstian, 1978). Typically, efficacy was assessed by giving a version of this list of situations or cues to individuals who were then asked to rate their confidence that they could resist the urge, abstain or refrain from smoking in each situation (see Table 1). Ratings were made on a Likert scale ranging either from 0 to 100 or from 1 to 5 or 10. Item scores were summed by situation subcategory or overall total to arrive at the individual's abstinence, control, or resistance self-efficacy. Types of situations identified in

TABLE 1. Sample Stems and Items
for Self-Efficacy Measures

Smoking
Confidence to Abstain from Smoking (1—*Not at All* to 5—*Extremely*)
1. When I am very anxious and stressed
2. With my spouse or close friend who is smoking
3. When I need a lift
Probability to be able to resist the urge to smoke (0–100)
1. When you feel frustrated
2. When you want something in your mouth
3. When you feel embarrassed
Eating/Diet
Probability of being able to resist the urge to overeat (0–100)
1. When tense
2. After an argument
3. When preparing food
Alcohol
I would be able to resist the urge to drink heavily (0–100)
1. If I felt I had let myself down
2. If I had trouble sleeping
3. If I passed by a liquor store
How confident that you would not drink (1–5)
1. When I am feeling angry inside
2. When I see others drinking at a bar or party
3. When I am physically tired

these scales were negative emotions, social pressure and influence; positive affect; social image; dieting or weight gain; craving or physiological cues; and testing willpower. Although these situations varied greatly, initial research indicated that a powerful first component or factor accounted for most of the variance (Baer & Lichtenstein, 1988; DiClemente et al., 1985). Investigators concluded that there appears to be one general efficacy for nonsmoking, rather that many separate, situation-specific efficacies. More recent analyses using confirmatory and causal modeling procedures, however, have demonstrated that situation specificity is an important first-order effect and that overall self-efficacy is an equally important second-order effect. (Velicer, DiClemente, Prochaska & Rossi, 1990). Thus, depending on the need and purpose in a particular setting, either specific subscales (e.g., relapse prevention training) or more global (e.g., comprehensive predictor variable) efficacy scores could be analyzed.

Efficacy evaluations in smoking have become routine in large-scale studies. However, efficacy is often evaluated with a single item representing an assessment of the subject's confidence to quit or be abstinent immediately posttreatment or 3 to 6 months later (Mothersill, McDowell, & Rosser, 1988; Norcross, Ratzin, & Payne, 1989; Wilson, Wallston, & King, 1990). As previously discussed, these items require both a current efficacy evaluation and a prediction of future behavioral outcomes. The majority of studies in the smoking literature, however, have used a current evaluation of abstinence or resistance self efficacy across multiple situations as the basic measure (Baer & Lichtenstein, 1988; Colletti, Supnick, & Payne, 1985; Condiotte & Lichtenstein, 1981; DiClemente et al., 1985; Kirscht et al., 1987, 1991; Owen, Ewins, & Lee, 1989; Strecher et al., 1985).

The extensive research on self-efficacy in smoking has enabled researchers to examine closely both the theoretical construct of self-efficacy and the construct's utility for addictive behaviors. The most relevant theoretical issues addressed in these studies focus on efficacy as a mediator of behavior change, the primacy of efficacy over simply measures of prior behavior, the proposed predictors of self-efficacy, and the relationship of self-efficacy to outcome expectancies and other important change constructs.

Initial studies of smoking abstinence self-efficacy supported the theoretical assumption that self-efficacy assessments were better predictors of successful cessation than past smoking behavior (Colletti et al., 1985; DiClemente, 1981); These findings also supported the theoretical assumption that efficacy evaluations were mediators of behavior change related to, but independent of, past behavior. Baer, Holt and Lichtenstein (1986) challenged this notion. Examining a series of partial correlations, they found support for efficacy as a unique predictor of success, but not for its role as a mediator. However, this finding needs confirmation from future research.

How efficacy evaluations develop and erode continues to be largely unknown and has not been systematically explored (DiClemente, 1986). Reported correlations in the literature give some glimpses into the process. Self-efficacy drops after a relapse crisis, whether that crisis was successfully met or not (Shiffman, 1984). Thus, confidence is shaken by serious temptations, cravings, or crises. Treatment and involvement in the process of changing addictive behaviors clearly affect self-efficacy by increasing the strength of these evaluations (Coehlo, 1984; Prochaska, Velicer, DiClemente, Guadagnoli, & Rossi, 1991). However, individuals who have made more attempts at quitting or are more experienced quitters do not necessarily have greater self-efficacy to avoid smoking (Haaga, 1989). Self-efficacy evaluations also were not found to be related to engaging in specific coping behavior in crisis situations (Shiffman, 1982, 1984).

It is clear from these studies that not all change activity is positively related to self-efficacy. In fact, some experiences of relapse and failure can erode an individual's confidence. In a large, longitudinal study that extensively analyzed smoking cessation coping activities, efficacy was found to be significantly but differentially related to the behavioral change process activity of self-changers (DiClemente et al., 1985; DiClemente & Prochaska, 1985). For smokers in the Action or Maintenance stage of quitting, higher efficacy was related to less process activities. The opposite was true for individuals in earlier stages of change, with greater efficacy significantly correlated with increased experiential and behavioral change process activity (DiClemente, 1986; DiClemente et al., 1985).

Different types of efficacy evaluations are related, but still appear to be independent. Brod & Hall (1984) found that a more generic self-efficacy was related to both a quality possession scale, consisting of self-reported personally efficacious qualities, and an abstinence self-efficacy evaluation at pretreatment. Each of these assessments seemed to tap different aspects or types of self-efficacy. Several studies have shown that outcome expectations and efficacy expectations for smoking cessation are correlated but not identical (Kirscht et al., 1987; Wilson et al., 1990). Different types of questions about an individual's efficacy will tap a different set of self-evaluations.

Recently researchers have been exploring the predictors of smoking abstinence self-efficacy by operationalizing the theoretical predictors of performance accomplishments, vicarious experience, verbal persuasion, and emotional arousal elaborated by Bandura (Fairhurst, 1990). Performance accomplishments, as measured by previous attempts to quit emerged as the strongest overall predictor. Most interesting was the finding that, like other practically and theoretically important constructs, predictors of efficacy varied according to subject's stage of change, supporting the argument for a stage-based understanding and evaluation of self-efficacy (DiClemente, et al., 1991).

Efficacy evaluations have proved to be powerful predictors in the smoking cessation literature. Treatment behavior efficacy and a generic cessation self-efficacy predicted joining or attending worksite and other treatment programs (Brod & Hall, 1984; Sussman et al., 1989). Though pretreatment abstinence efficacy has not always predicted posttreatment outcome (Garcia, Schmitz, & Doerfler, 1990; Owen et al., 1989); posttreatment abstinence efficacy has been quite predictive of outcomes that include relapse, time to relapse, abstinence, and maintenance. (Baer et al., 1986; Barrios & Niehaus, 1985; Coehlo, 1984; Condiotte & Lichtenstein, 1981; DiClemente, 1981; Prochaska, DiClemente, Velicer, Ginpil, & Norcross, 1985; Wojick, 1988; Yates & Thain, 1985).

In summary, the predictive ability and consistency of self-efficacy evaluations for smoking behavior have been impressive. Few constructs in the social sciences can boast such a record. In almost every case, efficacy evaluations, particularly abstinence efficacy evaluations, have been the most significant, or among the only significant, predictors of smoking cessation treatment outcome that emerged from studies that included a wide range of other predictors (DiClemente, 1986).

SELF-EFFICACY AND ALCOHOLISM TREATMENT

The application of self-efficacy in the area of alcohol problems has lagged behind the work in smoking cessation, even though the same relapse model and similar issues of motivation and change are relevant. Rollnick and Heather (1982) discussed both positive and negative self-efficacy as important constructs in alcoholism treatment. Positive efficacy related to mastery over abstinence; negative, to perceived weakness for alcohol. Using the same relapse categories Marlatt and Gordon (1979), several investigators have developed efficacy scales for alcoholism treatment. Annis developed and examined an instrument entitled the Situational Confidence Questionnaire (SCQ) (Annis & Graham, 1988) and a companion questionnaire called the Inventory of Drinking Situations (IDS) (Annis, Davis, Graham, & Levinson, 1987). Typically, subjects rate first how frequently they experience the urge to drink heavily in a variety of situations and settings (IDS), then rate their ability to resist the urge to drink heavily in these same situations (SCQ). A number of subscales are reported that clearly represent the Marlatt relapse categories. This questionnaire appears to have solid psychometric properties and would be quite relevant and useful for treatment assessments.

The Annis scales target drinking heavily and the ability to control heavy drinking as the focus for efficacy evaluations. A similar scale developed by DiClemente and colleagues (1983) assessed subjects' confidence to abstain from drinking in a range of situations similar to the Marlatt relapse categories. The Alcohol Abstinence Self-Efficacy Scale (AASE) assesses both temptation to drink and confidence to abstain from drinking in the same set of situations. The AASE is similar to a smoking abstinence self-efficacy scale developed by the same author (DiClemente, Carbonari, Montgomery & Hughes, 1994). Four subscales of the AASE have been identified: negative affect, social pressure, physical and other concerns, and resisting urges (DiClemente et al., 1994). Correlation of AASE subscales with Alcohol Use Inventory scales and stage-of-change measures supported the independence of the self-efficacy scales, as well as their differential relationships with drinking patterns and motivation. Additionally, there were no significant male versus female differences found on the AASE measure, indicating that it can be used with both genders. These two scales (SCQ and AASE), with their emphases on control or abstinence, have been used by most investigators to examine efficacy related to alcohol problems.

Several studies have explored alcohol control self-efficacy, that is, confidence to refrain from drinking heavily. Fromme, Kivlahan and Marlatt (1986) assessed alcohol control efficacy expectations by adapting the DiClemente and colleagues (1983) abstinence measure for use with individuals in a secondary prevention program. Self-efficacy scores for these problem drinkers were not correlated with amount of alcohol consumption as self-monitored by subjects. However, efficacy increased from pretreatment to 4-month follow-up. Annis and Davis (1988) also examined control efficacy using the SCQ with a small group of problem drinkers presenting for treatment. Self-efficacy to resist the urge to drink heavily was reported to be related to the specific posttreatment relapse situations, particularly for individuals who engaged in heavy drinking episodes. Similar to the previous study, efficacy expectations increased significantly from intake to 6-month follow-up.

Several studies examined control self-efficacy with inpatient samples of subjects. These studies found that efficacy to resist the urge to drink heavily increased during treatment and that efficacy at intake was strongly associated with average daily drinking at 3 months following treatment (Solomon & Annis, 1990). Burling, Reilly, Moltzen, & Ziff (1989) found that individuals with lower self-efficacy levels at intake received longer hospital stays and greater benefit at discharge. Abstainers at follow-up experienced an increase in efficacy during treatment that doubled that of subjects who relapsed. Annis, Davis, Graham, and Levinson (1987) examined control self-efficacy after inpatient treatment prior to aftercare. They found that subjects who had "differentiated" alcohol control efficacy expectations, that is, more variability in ratings of risk situations, benefitted most from a relapse prevention program when compared with traditional aftercare. There were no differences found for subjects who reported more "generalized" evaluations (equal risk across most situations) of self-efficacy.

Abstinence self-efficacy was examined by Miller, Ross, Emmerson, and Todt (1989). They modified the SCQ to focus on *abstinence* (avoid drinking altogether) rather than *control* (avoid drinking heavily), and used it to compare groups of Veterans Administration medical center patients. One group was abstinent a minimum of 12 months at testing (long-term sober, $n = 25$), and another group of patients was entering inpatient alcohol treatment (short-term sober, $n = 46$). These investigators found significant differences in abstinence self-efficacy between these two groups overall and in 7 of 8 SCQ subscales. A stepwise discriminant function using all 8 subscales correctly classified 92% of the long-term sober and 65% of the short-term sober patients. Performance accomplishments (length of abstinence) clearly affected self-efficacy evaluations in this study, providing support for the construct validity of the efficacy measure and some support for the theoretical assumptions of the construct as well.

DiClemente and Hughes (1990) assessed abstinence self-efficacy expectations in the context of the stages of change with individuals ($n = 224$) who came for an outpatient alcoholism treatment program. Subjects were classified as precontemplators, ambivalent, participation/prepared, uninvolved/discouraged, or contemplators, based on their profiles on a Stages of Change scale, called the University of Rhode Island Change Assessment (URICA). Both temptations to drink and abstinence self-efficacy were related to subjects' stage of change regarding their alcohol problem. Subjects classified as uninvolved or discouraged with respect to change demonstrated the highest levels of temptation and the lowest levels of self-efficacy. Precontemplators, who are resisting change or unconvinced of a problem, reported the lowest levels of temptation and were the only group to have efficacy levels greater than temptation levels. Thus, these individuals saw themselves as either having fewer problems with temptation to drink, or being so confident that they could abstain that they need not change. This study also reported on the difference between temptation and confidence scores for subjects in different stages, as well as the correlation between temptation and confidence scores. There were significant differences among groups on these derived scores with contemplation and preparation subjects demonstrating the most consistent relationship between temptation and efficacy ratings. The authors contended that using these alternative ways to assess self-efficacy evaluations, instead of simply reporting means and standard deviations, can increase the understanding of efficacy evaluations and improve the precision of predictions.

In terms of prediction, few studies have clearly tested the relationship between efficacy evaluations and outcomes. It is clear that efficacy evaluations increase during the course of treatment and at followup (Annis & Davis, 1988; Burling et al., 1989; Solomon & Annis, 1990). Posttreatment control self-efficacy has been related to relapse events (Annis & Davis, 1988), average daily drinking levels (Solomon & Annis, 1990), and posttreatment abstinence (Burling et al., 1989). However, control self-efficacy has not always been a successful predictor of abstinence at follow-up, even when assessed at the end of treatment (Burling et al., 1989). Long-term sobriety, on the other hand, has been related to abstinence self-efficacy (Miller et al., 1989). In addition, certain treatments have been found to affect self-efficacy differentially, with specific skills training superior to more generic interventions (Burling et al., 1989; Donovan & Ito, 1988).

Self-efficacy evaluations related to alcohol consumption can be differentiated into subgroups of related situations that reflect, more or less, Marlatt's relapse categories. However, the subcategories can vary from 8 (Annis, & Graham, 1988) to 4 (DiClemente et al., 1983). In addition, different factors have been found when Annis's SCQ has been refactored (Sandahl, Lindberg, & Ronnberg, 1990). Thus, the number and stability of the factors may vary by population and differ, depending on whether investigators are assessing abstinence or control self-efficacy. It must be noted that the populations used in the described studies ranged from college students in a secondary prevention program (Fromme et al., 1986), to inpatient alcoholics (Solomon & Annis, 1990), to individuals with one or more years of sobriety (Miller et al., 1989). Some investigators have applied self-efficacy in the context of primary prevention (Gottlieb, Mullen, & McAllister, 1987; Meier & Sampson, 1989). In fact, there is a growing literature on *resistance self-efficacy*, the perceived ability to resist pressure to drink or use drugs among adolescents (Hays & Ellickson, 1990; Rohrbach et al., 1987). However, these studies are beyond the scope of the current review.

Although implications of this diverse research for self-efficacy theory are not yet clear, several findings are notable. Fromme and colleagues (1986) did not find clear correspondence between actual level of drinking and alcohol control self-efficacy. This lack of correspondence presents a challenge to the theory, but could be explained by a population bias, an overconfidence bias, or the brief span of time between assessments, as the authors point out. Cooney, Gillespie, Baker, & Kaplan (1987) did find that nonalcoholics compared to a group of alcoholics experienced decreased self-efficacy to cope with future temptation after exposure to alcohol cues. Relationships found between smoking abstinence self-efficacy and the stages of change are beginning to be replicated to some extent with alcohol abstinence self-efficacy (DiClemente & Hughes, 1990). Efficacy evaluations appear interrelated with subjects' current stage status for drinkers entering outpatient treatment.

Self-efficacy assessments with alcohol-related problems pose unique challenges for theoretical and practical reasons. Type of efficacy assessed, the amount of pressure to report overly positive or, in some cases, overly negative self-evaluations, and the possible differential goals of treatment (abstinence vs. control) make the assessment and evaluation of efficacy difficult. On the positive side, there is much room for additional research to address practical and theoretical issues with important consequences for efficacy application and theorizing.

SELF-EFFICACY AND DRUG ABUSE

The issues and difficulties described above in regard to applying self-efficacy theory to alcohol problems are compounded when applied to drug abuse and dependence. There is little research and focus on self-efficacy in the area of substance abuse when alcohol and smoking are separated out. In a recent comprehensive review of assessment of addictive behaviors (Donovan & Marlatt, 1988), the chapters on cocaine, cannabis, and heroin had little or no reference to the assessment of self-efficacy. Recently, Annis (1990) discussed the application of self-efficacy in substance abuse. However, empirical evidence in substances other than alcohol and nicotine were notably absent.

The dearth of efficacy measures and research in the area of drug abuse treatment is most probably related to the skepticism about self-report among drug abusers, particularly when the drugs of abuse are illegal. Another contributing factor to suspect self-report is the rather high levels of sociopathy in the drug-abusing population, which might skew the reports to what the investigator wanted to hear rather than providing a more objective self-assessment. Although self-deception, social desirability, and deceit are significant barriers to accurate evaluation of self-efficacy to abstain from or to control use of substances, these barriers are not insurmountable and are also present to a lesser extent with alcohol and smoking, where efficacy has been used successfully. Self-reports of drug abusers can be reliable and accurate, however, the reliability evaluations of self-reports are marked by wide variations among studies reporting findings of accuracy of self-report based on samples and procedures used to obtain the self-reports (Maisto et al., 1990).

In an early study that examined self-efficacy with heroin users, Crowder (1982) predicted that relapsers would have diminished self-efficacy. However, he measured efficacy postrelapse using an attributional questionnaire and equated self-efficacy to the subject's attribution of failure to low ability. Although he stated that he did not find support for this component of the Marlatt model of relapse, his measure of efficacy is indirect at best and *post hoc*. The study seems to confound efficacy and outcome expectancies, as we have seen with other studies of addictive behaviors, and includes an attribution of failure component.

As reported in the alcohol section, some researchers have discussed a resistance self-efficacy with regard to alcohol and drugs. These studies focus on adolescents' efficacy to resist pressure to use (Hays & Ellickson, 1990) or efficacy to refuse drugs (Rohrbach et al., 1987). Hays and Ellickson found that, although self-efficacy and perceived pressure to use drugs were generalizable across substances, subjects distinguished between their capacity to resist across substances. Rorhbach and colleagues (1987) found that refusal self-efficacy increased with training and was related to prevention program outcomes and decreased use of drugs.

Researchers should apply caution, but not total skepticism when attempting to assess efficacy in the area of illegal substance abuse. There is clearly room for more studies focused on abstinence or coping self-efficacy with drug abusers and refusal self-efficacy with potential users.

SELF-EFFICACY AND EATING DISORDERS

Eating disorders such as obesity and problems of weight control, as well as problematic eating such as bulimia and anorexia, have often been included in the category of addictive behaviors because of their appetitive nature, very high relapse rates, and the experience of loss of control. Weight control self-efficacy to perform behaviors that lead to *weight loss* has been examined in a number of ways. In fact, the assessment of self-efficacy varies greatly from study to study and is more diverse than in smoking or alcohol efficacy research. Efficacy evaluations have included confidence to resist the urge to eat (Glynn & Ruderman, 1986), confidence to perform all of the different behaviors involved in weight loss (Sallis et al., 1988), and confidence to perform the tasks taught in a weight control program (Overholser & Beck, 1985). Other researchers have examined what appear to be better classified as outcome expectancies or combinations of outcome and efficacy expectancies (see Chap. 1). For example, Mitchell and Stuart (1984) examined subjects' confidence to reach the goal weight. Weinberger et al. (1984) studied individuals' certainty that they could lose a certain amount of weight. Rodin, Elias, Silberstein, & Wagner (1988) explored the subject's ability to lose weight and maintain weight loss, as did Blair, Lewis, & Booth (1989). Others have assessed subjects' confidence to motivate themselves to perform the tasks involved in weight loss for at least 6 months (Sallis et al., 1988). Finally, Patsis and Hart (1991) evaluated the individual's difficulty in controlling eating. With such variety in the assessment of the construct, it is difficult to summarize the findings and make generalizable conclusions. Let the reader beware.

Glynn and Ruderman's (1986) Eating Self-Efficacy Scale (ESES) is becoming a standard measure in the field. They modeled their scale after a smoking abstinence scale developed by Condiotte and Lichtenstein (1981) and used many of the situations from that instrument, while adding items specific to eating behavior. The scale was developed with nonclinical samples, using an assessment of the difficulty controlling overeating as the general question for each situation. When they applied the scale to a clinical sample of individuals attempting to lose weight, they changed the questionnaire stem to assess the individual's ability to resist the urge to eat in each situation. In using the questionnaire, some researchers have employed the original controlling overeating stem (Patsis & Hart, 1991), and others have used the prompt of resisting the urge to overeat or refraining from overeating (Forster & Jeffrey, 1986).

Glynn and Ruderman and other investigators have found two basic subcomponents in their efficacy scales that were similar to those found in the smoking scales (DiClemente, 1986). "Negative Affect Situations" provided the first and strongest component and included items such as overeating when depressed and overeating after an argument. The second component was labeled "Socially Acceptable Situations" and included overeating when tempting food is in front of you and overeating with family members. The authors provide substantial convergent validity data for the ESES subscales. Scores on these scales were significantly related to percentage overweight (males $r = .30$; females $r = .28$) and to a dieting restraint scale (males $r = .40$; females $r = .52$). Since these correlations are positive, they relate to the efficacy measured as "Difficulty Controlling Overeating" rather than "Ability to Resist the Urge to Eat."

On the theoretical side, there have been some very interesting findings with regard to the efficacy construct and how it works in weight control. Chambliss and Murray (1979) found that a self-efficacy enhancing treatment group had greater weight loss than a comparison group. However, this effect appeared to work for subjects with an internal rather than external locus of control. Male and female differences have been found in the responsiveness of efficacy evaluations to treatment, with females showing greater changes in self-efficacy in response to treatment (Forster & Jeffrey, 1986). However, in another study, posttreatment self-efficacy predicted greater weight loss for men, but not for women (Patsis & Hart, 1991). Efficacy evaluations are not completely contingent on the amount of weight loss during treatment (Bernier & Avard, 1986). Outcome and efficacy expectations are related but, as in the smoking cessation literature, they appear to be quite separate and unique evaluations (Edell et al., 1987).

Efficacy evaluations with weight control have also demonstrated predictive power. Efficacy to resist the urge to overeat increases during the course of treatment (Glynn & Ruderman, 1986; Forster & Jeffrey, 1986). Expectations that seem more like outcome expectancies than efficacy expectancies (i.e., subjects' confidence in reaching their goal weight, confidence in losing a certain amount of weight, or confidence in their ability to lose weight and maintain that loss) have been able to predict dropout from a weight control program (Mitchell & Stuart, 1984), as well as weight loss (Weinberger et al., 1984), and the maintenance of that weight loss (Blair, Booth, Lewis, & Wainright, 1989). Although one early study found that efficacy to perform treatment behaviors did not predict posttreatment eating styles (Overholser & Beck, 1985), most studies that use efficacy to resist the urge to eat or refrain from overeating have found these efficacy evaluations to be predictive of weight loss during the active phase of treatment (Glynn & Ruderman, 1986; Forster & Jeffrey, 1986). In addition, posttreatment efficacy evaluations have been related positively to maintenance (Patsis & Hart, 1991; Rodin et al., 1988).

Despite all the difficulties and differences in the assessment of self-efficacy related to eating behavior in weight control, the role that efficacy appears to play is quite similar to that in smoking cessation, where the assessments have been a bit more uniform. Efficacy evaluations appear to be useful and unique predictors of weight loss. Few constructs predict weight loss and maintenance of that loss in as consistent a fashion as self-efficacy focused on overeating behaviors.

Self-efficacy has also been applied to eating disorders other than obesity. Several authors have examined efficacy related to binge eating (Gormally, Black, Daston, & Rardin, 1982; Mizes, 1988) and bulimia (Etringer, Altmaier, & Bowers, 1989; Lehman & Rodin, 1989; Phelan, 1987). These studies usually focused on a coping self-efficacy (the ability to nurture oneself in ways other than eating), or more specific efficacy evaluations concerning either controlling eating or maintaining desirable weight (Phelan, 1987). In every case, women who engaged in bulimic behavior had lower self-efficacy than either normals or women with weight problems. Additionally, Phelan noted that this lowered efficacy appears to increase as a result of treatment. Although closely related to bulimia and the types of efficacy assessed in this area, self-efficacy with anorexia has not received a significant amount of research attention.

THE FUTURE OF SELF-EFFICACY
IN THE ADDICTIVE BEHAVIORS

The preceding review of self-efficacy theory as applied to the addictive behaviors offers not only a perspective on what has been done, but also a vision of what needs to be done in this area. The important areas for continued and future development seem to be assessment, treatment utility, and research. Issues in each of these areas are outlined and discussed in the following sections of the chapter.

Issues of Assessment

When it comes to assessing self-efficacy in addictive behaviors, the key question is always "Efficacy to perform what specific behavior?" The review clearly demonstrates the wide variation in types of efficacy assessed by researchers and clinicians within and across specific addictive behaviors. Future applications need to pay particular attention to the specific addictive behavior targeted. Smoking, heroin use, and bulimia are very different behaviors in topography, social acceptance, and personal meaning. Treatment and change of these different behaviors have some unique characteristics. Evaluating efficacy with these behaviors requires knowledge of these differences and creative specific application in order to provide valuable and relevant efficacy assessments. This is not a plea for a proliferation of new measures. In the areas where self-efficacy has been applied most extensively (smoking, eating, and alcohol), researchers and clinicians should use or adapt existing measures, so that results can be compared and some sense of norms for particular populations can be developed.

Assessment of self-efficacy is only as accurate as the question asked by the interviewer or researcher. Since the target behavior can include controlled use, resisting urges, using alternative coping skills, practicing program techniques, and abstinence, special attention must be given to the setting and the type of population involved when designing questions to assess efficacy. While piloting these questionnaires, researchers should debrief subjects to evaluate what the individual understands the questions to mean and how he or she arrived at the response. In this way we can begin to tease out efficacy from outcome expectations in our assessment. Questions that are complex and involve different types of expectations have problems with reliability and predictive utility. Questions that are too global have problems with specificity and sensitivity. Questions and settings that have excessive social desirability or pressure clearly compromise accurate self-evaluation.

The challenge in future assessments of self-efficacy in addictive behaviors appears to be in assessing enough of the domains that are relevant to accomplish a complete efficacy evaluation. Both outcome and efficacy expectations appear to relate to certain specific types of behavioral outcomes. Assessing both would insure the ability to examine the relationship of these expectancies on current and future behaviors. The type of efficacy evaluated is closely related to the goals of the individual, as well as the objectives of the programs or treatments being used to change both efficacy and behavior. An individual with a goal of moderation of drinking in an abstinence-oriented alcoholism treatment program would probably respond differently to an abstinence or control self-efficacy questionnaire by virtue of the two different objectives, and the mismatch between personal and program goals. Researchers may be better off assessing both types of efficacy evaluations and empirically examining the discrepancies.

The situations or cues used in the efficacy assessment also need to be relevant and comprehensive in order to insure good efficacy assessments. There seem to be identifiable subcomponents in efficacy evaluations when the focus is on cues to drink, smoke, or overeat. Relapse precipitants identified by Marlatt and Gordon are clearly relevant cues for most addictive behaviors, with social pressure and negative emotions as two common key dimensions. These have been most useful in abstinence or control self-efficacy. However, even with other types of self-efficacy evaluations (e.g., treatment or dieting efficacy), scales should include specific tasks that vary in difficulty, performed under a variety of circumstances. This would insure that the efficacy assessed met the criteria for the construct as originally outlined by Bandura.

One final note about single-item assessments of self-efficacy. There is some evidence that correlations between the single-item score and a longer, more in-depth assessment of efficacy can be quite high depending on the similarity of the items. However, most often, single-item efficacy assessments involve complex questions and attempt to capture expectancies about present and future behavior. These often involve assessments of both efficacy and outcome expectancies for the subjects. If one-item assessments must be used, multiple simple and clear questions would make results more interpretable.

TREATMENT UTILITY

The application of self-efficacy to the treatment of addictive behaviors has proven valuable for both research and clinical practice. Expectancies related to treatment behaviors or likelihood of success have predicted participation in treatment or drop out. End of treatment efficacy has been associated with maintenance or relapse and with posttreatment level of use for alcohol control self-efficacy. Not all studies, however, replicate these findings. The diversity of scales purporting to assess the same or similar self-efficacy construct make comparisons quite difficult. In addition, the use of subject samples from heterogeneous populations, ranging from nonclinical to outpatient and inpatient treatment seekers, to self-changers, increases the variability and clouds comparisons among studies. Researchers and clinicians alike should take the following preliminary steps before entering the area and applying self-efficacy to their favorite addictive behavior:

1. Identify the type of self-efficacy most appropriate for the question, problem, and population of interest. Is the interest in abstinence self-efficacy in a dependent heroin user on an inpatient unit, or in control self-efficacy with problem drinkers?
2. Examine the literature to see if other researchers have assessed a similar question, problem, and population. If not, are there any similarities in previous studies? Look across addictive behaviors for similarities. For example, a number of studies of smoking cessation and self-efficacy could provide good background information for assessing cocaine abstinence self-efficacy.
3. Try to use or adapt a previously developed scale if it has demonstrated good psychometric properties.
4. Make sure that the question you ask is the one you mean to ask. Be clear about the content and structure of the questions that you use to assess self-efficacy. Efficacy in one's ability to overcome a lapse is different from the ability to avoid a lapse. Seeing a bar, being at a bar, and being offered a drink at a bar are three different cues. With these few preliminary steps, the application of self-efficacy to addictive behaviors will be more appropriate and useful.

FLUIDITY OF SELF-EFFICACY EVALUATIONS

Efficacy evaluations are quite fluid and theoretically should shift as behaviors change. In many studies, efficacy has been found to shift during treatment and during the posttreatment period. *When* and *how often* to assess efficacy expectations become quite important questions, particularly for addictive behaviors. Exposure to cues and relapse crises affects efficacy evaluations. A sophisticated application of efficacy would entail a repeated assessment over the course of an active treatment or change phase and a realistic appraisal of how efficacy measured at one point in time should predict behavior at a second point in time. Researchers who assess pretreatment efficacy and expect it to predict behavior at a 12-month follow-up seem to be naive in light of the fluidity of efficacy assessments and the multiple paths that the course of change can take posttreatment, as demonstrated by Mermelstein, Gruder, Karnity, Reichman, & Flay (1991).

ACCURACY OF SELF-EFFICACY EVALUATIONS

Accuracy of self-assessment and self-report is an issue, particularly with addictive behaviors. At times, efficacy evaluations appear stronger or weaker than current behavior warrants. There is an assumption, particularly when it comes to addictive behaviors, that subjects deny the problem and fail to tell the truth. However, as Miller and Rollnick (1991) pointed out, denial is often the result of the communication patterns between a confrontive interviewer and client and not a characteristic of the addicted individual. Exaggeration, overestimation, pessimism, and underestimation are possible with every kind of efficacy evaluation (Bandura, 1986). Self-regulation requires accurate and appropriate self-assessments, even though these assessments may appear illogical to an external observer. However, it must be noted that efficacy differences have consistently been found among individuals at different points in the cycle of change. Although there may be inaccuracies in some subjects' self-assessments, large groups of subjects representing different stages show consistent patterns that would be inconsistent with wholesale and indiscriminate falsification of self-efficacy evaluations (DiClemente & Prochaska, 1985; DiClemente et al., 1991).

RESEARCH ISSUES

In addition to the above considerations, several important issues arise for researchers. In developing studies and communicating results, uniform and clear definitions of self-efficacy are necessary. Vague references to self-efficacy, indirect assessments, or the use of related constructs tied loosely to self-efficacy add confusion, not clarity, to an already complex area of study.

Although replication of a previous study is not very exciting or creative, replicability is the life blood of science. Many researchers attempt to change the question, population, and assessment instruments when designing a new study. This leap to what, at best, could be called generalizability misses the essential need for replication prior to generalization. With every addictive behavior, findings about the role of self-efficacy need to be replicated with large samples of similar subjects. Researchers conducting large-scale studies or evaluations of addictive behavior treatments have a wonderful opportunity to add efficacy evaluations so that major findings can be replicated.

Needless to say, the assessment instruments should be standardized and have demonstrated solid reliability and validity. Many investigators have paid close attention to the construction and evaluation of their self-efficacy instruments (Annis & Graham, 1988; Colletti et al., 1985; Condiotte & Lichtenstein, 1981; DiClemente et al., 1983, 1985, 1994; Glynn & Ruderman, 1986). Other investigators who wish to develop efficacy assessments for addictive behaviors should follow their lead. Continued and new evaluations of the psychometric properties of the assessments, rather than the development of new instruments, needs to be a high priority.

Research on self-efficacy is at different stages of development with each specific addictive behavior. Critical studies are needed in smoking, eating disorders, alcohol consumption, and drug abuse. The following is an outline of the major areas to be addressed.

Smoking. For smoking cessation there is a substantial body of research on the measurement of self-efficacy and its relationship to outcomes of interest. However, additional research is needed to examine shifts in efficacy during treatment and maintenance and the relationship of these shifts to abstinence outcomes. Erosion of efficacy prior to a slip or relapse, as well as the recovery or decline of efficacy after a slip or relapse, needs to be examined (Shiffman, 1984). Since there are well-defined instruments in this area, smoking abstinence self-efficacy represents a perfect place to do research into the efficacy construct itself with more microanalytic studies. Exploration of the predictors of self-efficacy, accuracy of self-assessment, and relationships between assessments of cue strength (temptations to smoke), and efficacy to abstain are important questions that provide rich opportunities for research.

Alcohol problems. Compared to smoking cessation, efficacy with alcohol problems is not as well developed an area of research. Replication of initial findings with alcohol control self-efficacy is needed. The relationship between abstinence self-efficacy and abstinence or relapse still needs to be established and replicated. The relationship between control and abstinence self-efficacy could be profitably pursued. The effects of pressure to enter treatment on efficacy evaluations and the impact of overconfidence or discouragement bias on self-efficacy are important areas to examine. The effect of lapses and relapses on efficacy evaluations is another area where important findings have yet to be discovered. Finally, the influence of self-help programs and particularly Alcoholics Anonymous on efficacy evaluations presents a fascinating challenge to investigators (DiClemente, 1993).

Eating Disorders. In the area of eating disorders, researchers need to focus on particular target behaviors, such as overeating or dieting. Refinement of scales and replication of early findings are top research priorities in this area. The relationship between efficacy and outcome expectancies could be easily examined in the area of weight control, where weight loss goals and consequences are clear and measurable. Multiple types of efficacy evaluations (control of weight, ability to self-nurture without food, resisting the urge to binge or purge) are most relevant for bulimic and anorexic behaviors and provide interesting opportunities for research.

Drug Abuse. In the area of illegal substance abuse, the field of research is wide open. Initial studies are needed to assess the ability of subjects to report usable evaluations of self-efficacy. The question of whether to assess each substance separately or to develop a more general efficacy evaluation for abstinence or use of multiple illegal substances is also important. Control versus abstinence self-efficacy is another important but not particularly popular area of needed research. Proponents of zero tolerance for drug use view any type of controlled use as problematic. However, goals other than abstinence are needed at times and are particularly appropriate for methadone maintenance programs.

THE CONTRIBUTION AND PROMISE OF SELF-EFFICACY WITH THE ADDICTIVE BEHAVIORS

Using self-efficacy theory in the study of addictive behaviors has proved to be a rewarding endeavor both for those interested in self-efficacy theory and those interested in specific addictive behaviors. The studies reviewed in this chapter support both the relevance and value of the self-efficacy construct for examining addictive behaviors. The clear contribution of self-efficacy evaluation for understanding modification of addictive behaviors is evident from the extensive review of the literature presented here. Treatment, relapse prevention, and self-change have all been shown to modify efficacy evaluations. Efficacy evaluations increase as individuals change the addictive behavior and maintain that change over time. Efficacy evaluations are related in a predictable manner to the stages of change and have a significant relationship with the processes of change or coping activities employed by individuals at different stages of change. Using efficacy in the context of the stages of change of the transtheoretical model seems particularly fruitful (Prochaska & DiClemente, 1992).

In fact, self-efficacy theory has already enlivened discussions of addiction etiology and treatment. Self-regulation is a controversial issue in addictive behaviors, where loss of control is a defining feature. Efficacy to resist, abstain, or control addictive behaviors can inform as well as enliven debate on these issues. Among intriguing questions that can be posed and answered by using self-efficacy with addictive behaviors are the following: Should efficacy evaluations be a secondary outcome measure to evaluate program effectiveness, or should they actually be primary outcome variables if the individual never succeeds in modifying significantly the addictive behavior during treatment? Does efficacy change at the threat of relapse, even if there is a successful resolution of the relapse crisis, as Shiffman has found? How do support and support groups affect efficacy evaluations? What are the negative predictors or factors that undermine or erode efficacy during and after treatment?

As with any useful construct, the potentials for use and misuse are significant. Rushing to use self-efficacy evaluations to guide treatment without attention to measurement and without adequate evaluation seems a bit premature. Efficacy assessments appear most useful in relapse prevention programs. The proliferation of studies using the term *self-efficacy* without adequate definition and proper distinctions is an undesirable result of the popularity enjoyed by self-efficacy theory. The potential in this area, on the other hand, is enormous. We have only just begun to understand and appreciate the role self-efficacy theory plays and can play in addictive behavior research and treatment. The richness and flexibility of application across behaviors allows programs and studies to assess different efficacies and evaluate a wide range of behaviors and expectancies about those behaviors.

REFERENCES

Annis, H. M. (1982). *Inventory of drinking situations.* Ontario, Canada: Addiction Research Foundation.

Annis, H. M. (1986). A relapse prevention model for treatment of alcoholics. In W. R. Miller & N. Heather (Eds.), *Treating addictive behaviors: Processes of change* (pp. 407–421). New York, NY: Plenum Press.

Annis, H. M. (1990). Relapse to substance abuse: Empirical findings within a cognitive-social learning approach. *Journal of Psychoactive Drugs, 22*(2), 117–124.

Annis, H. M., & Davis, C. S. (1988). Assessment of expectancies. In D. M. Donovan & G. A. Marlatt (Eds.), *Assessment of Addictive Behaviors* (pp. 84–111). New York: Guilford.

Annis, H. M., & Davis, C. S. (1989). Relapse prevention training: A cognitive–behavioral approach based on self-efficacy theory. [Special Issue, Relapse: Conceptual research and clinical perspectives.] *Journal of Chemical Dependency Treatment, 2*(2), 81–103.

Annis, H. M., Davis, C. S., Graham, M., & Levinson, T. (1987). A controlled trial of relapse prevention procedures based on self-efficacy theory. Unpublished manuscript cited in Annis, H. M., & Davis, C. S. (1989) Relapse Prevention.

Annis, H. M., & Graham, J. M. (1988). *Situational Confidence Questionnaire (SCQ) user's guide.* Toronto: Addiction Research Foundation.

Baer, J. S., Holt, C. S., & Lichtenstein, E. (1986). Self-efficacy and smoking reexamined: Construct validity and clinical utility. *Journal of Consulting and Clinical Psychology, 54*(6), 846–852.

Baer, J. S., & Lichtenstein, E. (1988). Classification and prediction of smoking relapse episodes: An exploration of individual differences. *Journal of Consulting and Clinical Psychology, 56*(1), 104–110.

Bandura, A. (1977). Self-efficacy: Toward a unifying theory of behavior change. *Psychological Review, 84*, 191–215.

Bandura, A. (1986). *Social foundations of thought and action: A social cognitive theory.* Englewood Cliffs, NJ: Prentice-Hall.

Barrios, F. X., & Niehaus, J. C. (1985). The influence of smoker status, smoking history, sex, and situational variables on smokers' self-efficacy. *Addictive Behaviors, 10*(4), 425–429.

Becona, E., & Frojan, M. J. (1988). Comparison between two self-efficacy scales in maintenance of smoking cessation. *Psychological Reports, 61*(2), 359–362.

Bernier, M., & Avard, J. (1986). Self-efficacy, outcome, and attrition in a weight reduction program. *Cognitive Therapy and Research, 10*(3), 319–338.

Best, J. A., & Haskstian, A. R. (1978). A situation-specific model for smoking behavior. *Addictive Behaviors, 3*(2), 79–92.

Blair, A. J., Booth, D. A., Lewis, V. J., & Wainwright, C. J. (1989). The relative success of official and informal weight reduction techniques: Retrospective correlational evidence. *Psychology and Health, 3*(3), 195–206.

Blair, A. J., Lewis, V. J., & Booth, D. A. (1989). Behavior therapy for obesity: The role of clinicians in the reduction of overweight. [Special Issue: Health psychology: Perspectives on theory, research and practice.] *Counseling Psychology Quarterly, 2*(3), 289–301.

Breteler, M. H., Mertens, E. H., & Rombouts, R. (1988). De motivatie tot verandering van rookgedrag: Modeltoetsing bij patienten met harten longklachten. [The motivation for change of smoking behavior: Developing a model for patients with cardiovascular and pulmonary complaints]. *Tijdschrift voor Alcohol, Drugs en Andere Psychotrope Stoffen, 14*(1), 22.

Brod, M. I., & Hall, S. M. (1984). Joiners and nonjoiners in smoking treatment: A comparison of psychosocial variables. *Addictive Behaviors, 9*(2), 217–221.

Brown, S. A., Goldman, M. S., Inn, A., & Anderson, L. R. (1980). Expectations of reinforcement from alcohol: Their domain and relation to drinking patterns. *Journal of Consulting and Clinical Psychology, 48*, 419–426.

Brownell, K. D., Marlatt, G. A., Lichtenstein, E., & Wilson, G. T. (1986, July). Understanding and preventing relapse. *American Psychologist, 41*(7), 765–782.

Burling, T. A., Reilly, P. M., Moltzen, J. O., & Ziff, D. C. (1989). Self-efficacy and relapse among inpatient drug and alcohol abusers: A predictor of outcome. *Journal of Studies on Alcohol, 50*(4), 354–360.

Carey, M. P., Snel, D. L., Carey, K. B., & Richards, C. S. (1989). Self-initiated smoking cessation: A review of the empirical literature from a stress and coping perspective. *Cognitive Therapy and Research, 13*(4), 323–341.

Carmody, T. P. (1990). Preventing relapse in the treatment of nicotine addiction: Current issues and future directions. *Journal of Psychoactive Drugs, 22*(2), 211–238.

Chambliss, C. A., & Murray, E. J. (1979). Efficacy attribution, locus of control of weight loss. *Cognitive Therapy and Research, 3*, 349–353.

Coelho, R. J. (1984). Self-efficacy and cessation of smoking. *Psychological Reports, 54*(1), 309–310.

Colletti, G., Supnick, J. A., & Payne, T. J. (1985). The Smoking Self-Efficacy Questionnaire (SSEQ): Preliminary scale development and validation. *Behavioral Assessment, 7*(3), 249–260.

Condiotte, M. M., & Lichtenstein, E. (1981). Self-efficacy and relapse in smoking cessation programs. *Journal of Consulting and Clinical Psychology, 49*, 648–658.

Cooney, N. L., Gillespie, R. A., Baker, L. H., & Kaplan, R. F. (1987). Cognitive changes after alcohol cue exposure. *Journal of Consulting and Clinical Psychology, 55*(2), 150–155.

Cooney, N. L., Kopel, S. A., & McKeon, P. (1982). *Controlled relapse training and self-efficacy in ex-smokers.* Paper presented at the annual meeting of the American Psychological Association, Washington, D.C.

Corcoran, K. J., & Rutledge, M. W. (1989). Efficacy expectation changes as a function of hypothetical incentives in smokers. *Psychology of Addictive Behaviors, 3*(1), 22–28.

Corty, E. (1983). The test-retest reliability of measures used in cigarette smoking research. *Addictive Behaviors, 8*(3), 315–317.

Crowder, R. L. (1982). Methadone-maintained males' reactions to success and failure: Causal attributions, self-efficacy, and attitudes toward heroin. *Drug and Alcohol Dependence, 10*, 367–381.

Devins, G. M., & Edwards, P. J. (1988). Self-efficacy and smoking reduction in chronic obstructive pulmonary disease. *Behaviour Research and Therapy, 16*(2), 127–135.

DeVries, H., Dijkstra, M., & Kuhlman, P. (1988). Self-efficacy: The third factor besides attitude and subjective norm as a predictor of behavioral intentions. *Health Education Research, 3*(3), 273–282.

DiClemente, C. C. (1981). Self-efficacy and smoking cessation maintenance: A preliminary report. *Cognitive Therapy and Research, 5*(2), 175–187.

DiClemente, C. C. (1986). Self-efficacy and the addictive behaviors. [Special Issue: Self-efficacy theory in contemporary psychology]. *Journal of Social and Clinical Psychology, 4*(3), 302–315.

DiClemente, C. C. (1991). Motivational interviewing and the stages of change. In W. R. Miller & S. Rollnick (Eds.), *Motivational interviewing: Preparing people to change addictive behavior* (pp. 191–202). New York: Guilford.

DiClemente, C. C. (1993). A.A. and the structure of change. In B. S. McCrady, & W. R. Miller (Eds.), *Research on Alcoholics Anonymous: Opportunities and alternatives* (pp. 79–97). New Brunswick: Rutgers University Press.

DiClemente, C. C., Carbonari, J. P., Montgomery, R. P. G., & Hughes, S. O. (1994). An alcohol abstinence self-efficacy scale. *Journal of Studies on Alcohol, 55*, 141–148.

DiClemente, C. C., & Gordon, J. R. (1982). Developing a self-efficacy scale for alcoholism treatment: An abstract. *Alcoholism: Clinical and Experimental Research, 6*, 1983.

DiClemente, C. C., Gordon, J. R., & Gibertini, M. (1983). *Self-efficacy and determinants of relapse in alcoholism treatment.* Paper presented at the annual meeting of the American Psychological Association, Anaheim, CA.

DiClemente, C. C., & Hughes, S. O. (1990). Stages of change profiles in alcoholism treatment. *Journal of Substance Abuse, 2*, 217–235.

DiClemente, C. C., & Prochaska, J. O. (1982). Self-change and therapy change of smoking behavior: A comparison of processes of change in cessation and maintenance. *Addictive Behaviors, 7*, 133–142.

DiClemente, C. C., & Prochaska, J. O. (1985). Processes and stages of change: Coping and competence in smoking behavior change. In S. Shiffman & T. A. Wills (Eds.), *Coping and Substance Abuse* (pp. 319–343). New York: Academic Press.

DiClemente, C. C., Prochaska, J. O., Fairhurst, S. K., Velicer, W. F., Velasquez, M. M., & Rossi, J. S. (1991). The process of smoking cessation: An analysis of precontemplation, contemplation and preparation stages of change. *Journal of Consulting and Clinical Psychology, 59*(2), 295–304.

DiClemente, C. C., Prochaska, J. O., & Gibertini, M. (1985). Self-efficacy and the stages of self-change of smoking. *Cognitive Therapy and Research, 9*(2), 181–200.

Dobbelaere, L. (1985). Assessment of therapiegerichte diagnostiek toegepast op alcoholmisbruik: Een exploratief onderzoek. [Assessment of directed therapeutic diagnosis applied to the misuse of alcohol: An explorative research]. *Gedragstherapie, 18*(1), 53–62.

Donovan, D. M., & Ito, J. R. (1988). Cognitive–behavioral relapse prevention strategies and aftercare in alcoholism rehabilitation. [Special Issue: Nontraditional approaches to treating alcohol-dependent veterans]. *Psychology of Addictive Behaviors, 2*(2), 74–81.

Donovan, D. M., & Marlatt, A. (1988). *Assessment of addictive behaviors.* New York: Guilford.

Dowd, E. T., Lawson, G. W., & Petosa, R. (1986). Attributional styles of alcoholics. *International Journal of the Addictions, 21*(4–5), 589–593.

Edell, B. H., Edington, S., Herd, B., O'Brien, R. M., & Witkin, G. (1987). Self-efficacy and self-motivation as predictors of weight loss. *Addictive Behaviors, 12*(1), 63–66.

Etringer, B. D., Altmaier, E. M., & Bowers, W. (1989). An investigation into the cognitive functioning of bulimic women. *Journal of Counseling and Development, 68*(2), 216–219.

Fairhurst, S. K. (1990). *Predictors of smoking abstinence self-efficacy.* Unpublished masters thesis, University of Houston, Houston, TX.

Forster, J. L., & Jeffery, R. W. (1986). Gender differences related to weight history, eating patterns, efficacy expectations, self-esteem, and weight loss among participants in a weight reduction program. *Addictive Behaviors, 11*(2), 141–147.

Fromme, K., Kivlahan, D. R., & Marlatt, G. A. (1986). Alcohol expectancies, risk identification, and secondary prevention with problem drinkers. *Advances in Behaviour Research and Therapy, 8*(4), 237–251.

Garcia, M. E., Schmitz, J. M., & Doerfler, L. A. (1990). A fine-grained analysis of the role of self-efficacy in self-initiated attempts to quit smoking. *Journal of Consulting and Clinical Psychology, 58*(3), 317–322.

Gilbert, D. G., & Spielberger, C. D. (1987). Effects of smoking on heart rate, anxiety, and feelings of success during social interaction. *Journal of Behavioral Medicine, 10*(6), 629–638.

Glynn, S. M., & Ruderman, A. J. (1986). The development and validation of an eating self-efficacy scale. *Cognitive Therapy and Research, 10*(4), 403–420.

Godding, P. R., & Glasgow, R. E. (1985). Self-efficacy and outcome expectations as predictors of controlled smoking status. *Cognitive Therapy and Research, 9*(5), 583–590.

Godin, G., & Lepage, L. (1988). Understanding the intentions of pregnant nullipara to not smoke cigarettes after childbirth. *Journal of Drug Education, 18*(2), 115–124.

Gormally, J., Black, S., Daston, S., & Rardin, D. (1982). The assessment of binge eating severity among obese persons. *Addictive Behaviors, 7*, 47–55.

Gottlieb, N. H., Mullen, P. D., & McAlister, A. L. (1987). Patients' substance abuse and the primary care physician: Patterns of practice. *Addictive Behaviors, 12*(1), 23–32.

Haaga, D. A. (1989). Articulated thoughts and endorsement procedures for cognitive assessment in the prediction of smoking relapse. *Psychological Assessment, 1*(2), 112–117.

Hays, R. D., & Ellickson, P. L. (1990). How generalizable are adolescents' beliefs about pro-drug pressures and resistance self-efficacy? *Journal of Applied Social Psychology, 20*(4), 321–340.

Heather, N., Rollnick, S., & Winton, M. (1982). A comparison of objective and subjective measures of alcohol dependence as predictors of relapse following treatment. *British Journal of Clinical Psychology, 22*, 11–17.

Hunt, W. A., Barnett, L. W., & Branch, L. G. (1971). Relapse rates in addiction programs. *Journal of Clinical Psychology, 27*, 455–456.

Johnson, C. A., & Solis, J. (1983). Comprehensive community programs for drug abuse prevention: Implications of the community heart disease prevention programs for future research. *National Institute on Drug Abuse Research Monograph Series, 47*, 76–114.

Jones, W., & Clifford, P. (1990). The privatization of treatment services for alcohol abusers: Effect on the Black community. *Journal of the National Medical Association, 82*(5), 337–342.

Kirmil, G. K., Eagleston, J. R., Thoresen, C. E., & Zarcone, V. P. (1985). Brief consultation and stress management treatments for drug-dependent insomnia: Effects on sleep quality, self-efficacy, and daytime stress. *Journal of Behavioral Medicine, 8*(1), 79–99.

Kirsch, I. (1986). Early research on self-efficacy: What we already know without knowing we knew. [Special Issue: Self-efficacy theory in contemporary psychology]. *Journal of Social and Clinical Psychology, 4*(3), 339–358.

Kirscht, J. P., Janz, N. K., Becker, M. H., Eraker, S. A., Billi, J. E., & Woolliscroft, J. O. (1987). Beliefs about control of smoking and smoking behavior: A comparison of different measures in different groups. *Addictive Behaviors, 12*(2), 205–208.

Lawrance, L. (1989). Validation of a self-efficacy scale to predict adolescent smoking. *Health Education Research, 4*(3), 351–360.

Lawrance, L., & Rubinson, L. (1986). Self-efficacy as a predictor of smoking behavior in young adolescents. *Addictive Behaviors, 11*(4), 367–382.

Lehman, A. K., & Rodin, J. (1989). Styles of self-nurturance and disordered eating. *Journal of Consulting and Clinical Psychology, 57*(1), 117–122.

Litman, G. K., Eiser, J. R., Ranson, N. S. B., & Oppenheim, A. N. (1984). Differences in relapse precipitants and coping behavior between alcohol relapsers and survivors. *Behavior Therapy, 17,* 89–94.

Litman, G. K., Stapleton, J., Oppenheim, A. N., Peleg, M., & Jackson, P. (1984). The relationship between coping behaviors, their effectiveness, and alcoholism relapse and survival. *British Journal of Addiction, 79,* 283–291.

Love, S. Q., Ollendick, T. H., Johnson, C., & Schlesinger, S. E. (1985). A preliminary report of the prediction of bulimic behaviors: A social learning analysis. *Bulletin of the Society of Psychologist in Addictive Behaviors, 4*(2), 93–101.

Maddux, J. E., & Rogers, R. W. (1983). Protection motivation and self-efficacy: A reviewed theory of fear appeals and attitude change. *Journal of Experimental Social Psychology, 19*(5), 469–479.

Maisto, S. A., McKay, J. R., & Connors, G. J. (1990). Self-report issues in substance abuse: state of the are future directions. *Behavioral Assessment, 12*(1), 117–134.

Marlatt, G. A., Curry, S., & Gordon, J. R. (1986). *A comparison of treatment approaches in smoking cessation.* Unpublished manuscript, University of Washington, Seattle, WA.

Marlatt, G. A., & Gordon, J. R. (1979). Determinants of relapse: Implications for the maintenance of behavior change. In P. Davidson (Ed.), *Behavioral medicine: Changing health lifestyles* (pp. 410–452). New York: Brunner/Mazel.

Marlatt, G. A., & Gordon, J. R. (Eds.). (1985). *Relapse prevention: Maintenance strategies in the treatment of addictive behaviors.* New York: Guilford.

McColl, M. A., Friedland, J., & Kerr, A. (1986). When doing is not enough: The relationship between activity and effectiveness in anorexia nervosa. [Special Issue: The evaluation and treatment of eating disorders]. *Occupational Therapy in Mental Health, 6*(1), 137–150.

McIntyre, K. O., Lichtenstein, E., & Mermelstein, R. J. (1983). Self-efficacy and relapse in smoking cessation: A replication and extension. *Journal of Consulting and Clinical Psychology, 51*(4), 732–633.

Meier, S. T., & Sampson, J. P. (1989). Use of computer-assisted instruction in the prevention of alcohol abuse. *Journal of Drug Education, 19*(3), 245–256.

Mermelstein, R., Gruder, C. L., Karnity, T., Reichman, S., & Flay, B. (1991). *Assessment of change following a cessation attempt: Description of new smoking outcome categories.* Poster presented at the 12th Annual Meeting of the Society of Behavioral Medicine, Washington, DC.

Miller, P. J., Ross, S. M., Emmerson, R. Y., & Todt, E. H. (1989). Self-efficacy in alcoholics: Clinical validation of the Situational Confidence Questionnaire. *Addictive Behaviors, 14*(2), 217–224.

Miller, W .R., & Rollnick, S. (1991). *Motivational interviewing: Preparing people to change addictive behavior.* New York: Guilford.

Mitchell, C., & Stuart, R. B. (1984). Effect of self-efficacy on dropout from obesity treatment. *Journal of Consulting and Clinical Psychology, 52,* 1100–1101.

Mizes, J. S. (1988). Personality characteristics of bulimic and noneating disordered female controls: A cognitive–behavioral perspective. *International Journal of Eating Disorders,* 7(4), 541–550.

Mothersill, K. J., McDowell, I., & Rosser, W. (1988). Subject characteristics and long-term postprogram smoking cessation. *Addictive Behaviors, 13*(1), 29–36.

Nicki, R. M., Remington, R. E., & MacDonald, G. A. (1984). Self-efficacy, nicotine-fading/self-monitoring and cigarette-smoking behaviour. *Behaviour Research and Therapy, 22*(5), 477–485.

Norcross, J. C., Ratzin, A. C., & Payne, D. (1989). The ringing in the New Year: The change processes and reported outcomes of resolutions. *Addictive Behaviors, 14*(2), 205–212.

O'Leary, A. (1985). Self-efficacy and health. *Behaviour Research and Therapy, 23*(4), 437–451.

Overholser, J., & Beck, S. (1985). Assessing generalization of treatment effects and self-efficacy in the modification of eating styles in obese children. *Addictive Behaviors, 10*(2), 145–152.

Owen, N., Ewins, A. L., & Lee, C. (1989). Smoking cessation by mail: A comparison of standard and personalized correspondence course formats. *Addictive Behaviors, 14*(4), 355–363.

Patsis, P., & Hart, K. E. (1991). *Coping and self-efficacy in weight-loss maintenance.* Paper presented at the convention of the Society of Behavioral Medicine, Washington, DC.

Phelan, P. W. (1987). Cognitive correlates of bulimia: The Bulimic Thoughts Questionnaire. *International Journal of Eating Disorders, 6*(5), 593–607.

Prochaska, J. O., Crimi, P., Lapsanksi, D., Martel, L., & Reid, P. (1982). Self-change processes, self-efficacy and self-concept in relapse and maintenance of cessation of smoking. *Psychological Reports, 51,* 983–990.

Prochaska, J. O., & DiClemente, C. C. (1992). Stages of change in the modification of problem behaviors. In M. Hersen, R. M. Eisler, & P. M. Miller (Eds.), *Progress in Behavior Modification* (Vol. 28, pp. 184–214). Sycamore, IL: Sycamore.

Prochaska, J. O., DiClemente, C. C., & Norcross, J. C. (1992). In search of how people change: Applications to addictive behaviors. *American Psychologist, 47*(9), 1102–1114.

Prochaska, J. O., DiClemente, C. C., Velicer, W. F., Ginpil, S. E., & Norcross, J. C. (1985). Predicting change in smoking status for self-changers. *Addictive Behaviors, 10*(4), 395–406.

Prochaska, J. O., Velicer, W. F., DiClemente, C. C., Guadagnoli, E., & Rossi, J. (1991). Patterns of change: Dynamic typology applied to smoking cessation. *Multivariate Behavioral Research, 26*(1) 83–107.

Reynolds, R. (1985). Tailoring smoking cessation: Can we do more with what we know? *Behavior Therapist, 8*(7), 125–151.

Reynolds, R. V., Tobin, D. L., Creer, T. L., Wigal, J. K., & Wagner, M. D. (1987). A method of studying controlled substance use: A preliminary investigation. *Addictive Behaviors, 12*(1), 53–62.

Rodin, J., Elias, M., Silberstein, L. R., & Wagner, A. (1988). Combined behavioral and pharmacologic treatment for obesity: Predictors of successful weight maintenance. *Journal of Consulting and Clinical Psychology, 56*(3), 399–404.

Rohrbach, L. A., Graham, J. W., Hansen, W. B., & Flay, B. R. (1987). Evaluation of resistance skills training using multitrait–multimethod role play skill assessments. [Special Issue: Drugs]. *Health Education Research, 2*(4), 401–407.

Rohsenow, D. J. (1983). Drinking habits and expectancies about alcohol's effects for self versus others. *Journal of Consulting and Clinical Psychology, 51,* 752–756.

Rollnick, S., & Heather, N. (1982). The application of Bandura's self-efficacy theory to abstinence-oriented alcoholism treatment. *Addictive Behaviors, 7*(3), 243–250.

Sabogal, F., Otero-Sabogal, R., Perez-Stable, E. J., Marin, B. V., & Marin, G. (1989). Perceived self-efficacy to avoid cigarette smoking and addiction: Differences between Hispanics and non-Hispanic Whites. *Hispanic Journal of Behavioral Sciences, 11*(2), 136–147.

Sallis, J. F., Pinski, R. B., Grossman, R. M., Patterson, T. L., & Nader, P. R. (1988). The development of self-efficacy scales for health-related diet and exercise behaviors. *Health Education Research, 3,* 283–292.

Sandahl, C., Lindberg, S., & Ronnberg, S. (1990). Efficacy expectations among alcohol-dependent patients: A Swedish version of the Situational Confidence Questionnaire. *Alcohol and Alcoholism, 25*(1), 67–73.

Schneider, J. A., O'Leary, A., & Agras, W. S. (1987). The role of perceived self-efficacy in recovery from bulimia: A preliminary examination. *Behaviour Research and Therapy, 25*(5), 429–432

Schoeneman, T. J., Stevens, V. J., Hollis, J. F., & Cheek, P. R. (1988). Attribution, affect, and expectancy following smoking cessation treatment. *Basic and Applied Social Psychology, 9*(3), 173–184.

Shiffman, S. (1982). Relapse following smoking cessation: A situational analysis. *Journal of Consulting and Clinical Psychology,* (50), 71–86.

Shiffman, S. (1984). Cognitive antecedents and sequelae of smoking relapse crises. *Journal of Applied Social Psychology, 14*(3), 296–309.

Shiffman, S., & Wills, T. A. (1985). *Coping and Substance Abuse.* New York: Academic Press.

Solomon, K. E., & Annis, H. M. (1990). Outcome and efficacy expectancy in the prediction of posttreatment drinking behaviour. *British Journal of Addiction, 85*(5), 659–665.

Southwick, L., Steele, C., Marlatt, A., & Lindell, M. (1981). Alcohol-related expectancies: Defined by phase of intoxication and drinking experience. *Journal of Consulting and Clinical Psychology, 5,* 713–721.

Stall, R., Coates, T. J., & Hoff, C. (1988). Behavioral risk reduction for HIV infection among gay and bisexual men: A review of results from the United States. [Special Issue: Psychology and AIDS]. *American Psychologist, 43*(11), 878–885.

Strecher, V. J., Becker, M. H., Kirscht, J. P., Eraker, S. A., & Graham-Thomas, R. P. (1985). Psychosocial aspects of change in cigarette-smoking behavior. *Patient Education and Counseling, 7*(3), 249–262.

Strecher, V. J., DeVellis, B. M., Becker, M. H., & Rosenstock, I. M. (1986). The role of self-efficacy in achieving health behavior change. *Health Education Quarterly, 13*(1), 73–92.

Strober, M., & Humphrey, L. L. (1987). Familial contributions to the etiology and course of anorexia nervosa and bulimia. [Special Issue: Eating disorders]. *Journal of Consulting and Clinical Psychology, 55*(5), 654–659.

Sussman, S., Whitney-Saltiel, D. A., Budd, R. J., Spiegel, D., Brannon, B. R., Hansen, W. B., Johnson, C. A., & Flay, B. R. (1989). Joiners and nonjoiners in worksite smoking treatment: Pretreatment smoking, smoking by significant others, and expectation to quit as predictors. *Addictive Behaviors, 14*(2), 113–119.

Teichman, M. (1986). A relapse inoculation training for recovering alcoholics. *Alcoholism Treatment Quarterly, 3*(4), 133–139.

Tipton, R. M., & Worthington, E. L. (1984). The measurement of generalized self-efficacy: A study of construct validity. *Journal of Personality Assessment, 48*(5), 545–548.

Tunstall, C. D., Ginsberg, D., & Hall, S. M. (1985). Quitting smoking. *International Journal of the Addictions, 20*(6–7), 1089–1112.

Velicer, W. F., DiClemente, C. C., Rossi, J. S., & Prochaska, J. O. (1990). Relapse situations and self-efficacy: An integrative model. *Addictive Behaviors, 15*(3), 271–283.

Wagner, S., Halmi, K. A., & Maguire, T. V. (1987). The sense of personal ineffectiveness in patients with eating disorders: One construct or several? *International Journal of Eating Disorders, 6*(4), 495–505.

Walker, W. B., & Franzini, L. R. (1985). Low-risk aversive group treatments, physiological feedback, and booster sessions for smoking cessation. *Behavior Therapy, 16*(3), 263–274.

Weinberg, R. S., Hughes, H. H., Critelli, J. W., England, R., & Jackson, A. (1984). Effects of preexisting and manipulated self-efficacy on weight loss in a self-control program. *Journal of Research in Personality, 18*, 352–358.

Wilson, D. K., Wallston, K. A., & King, J. E. (1990). Effects of contract framing, motivation to quit, and self-efficacy on smoking reduction. *Journal of Applied Social Psychology, 20*(7), 531–547.

Wilson, G. T., Rossiter, E., Kleifield, E. I., & Lindholm, L. (1986). Cognitive–behavioral treatment of bulimia nervosa: A controlled evaluation. *Behaviour Research and Therapy, 24*(3), 277–288.

Wojcik, J. V. (1988). Social learning predictors of the avoidance of smoking relapse. *Addictive Behaviors, 13*(2), 177–180.

Yates, A. J., & Thain, J. (1985). Self-efficacy as a predictor of relapse following voluntary cessation of smoking. *Addictive Behaviors, 10*(3), 291–298.

CHAPTER 5

SELF-EFFICACY AND DEPRESSION

James E. Maddux and Lisa J. Meier

Problems of adaptation and adjustment manifest themselves in both affective and behavioral difficulties. When people decide, however, to seek professional assistance for their problems in adjustment, they usually do so not because they view their behavior as dysfunctional, but because they are in emotional distress. Among the painful emotional states, depression is the most common problem leading to referral to medical or psychological professionals (Goodwin & Guze, 1984). Although depression has been investigated from a variety of theoretical perspectives (e.g., psychoanalytic, existential, behavioral), in recent years social cognitive approaches have predominated. Those that have received the most attention are the helplessness/hopelessness model (Abramson, Seligman, & Teasdale, 1978; Alloy, Kelly, Mineka, & Clements, 1990) and Beck's cognitive model (Beck, 1976). The application of self-efficacy theory to depression has received less attention than these other two models, but holds promise for contributing to our understanding of depression. This chapter presents a self-efficacy theory of depression, reviews empirical studies of the application of self-efficacy theory to understanding depression, and discusses the relationship between self-efficacy theory and helplessness/hopelessness theory and cognitive theory. A basic premise of this chapter

JAMES E. MADDUX and LISA J. MEIER • Department of Psychology, George Mason University, Fairfax, Virginia 22030.

Self-Efficacy, Adaptation, and Adjustment: Theory, Research, and Application, edited by James E. Maddux. Plenum Press, New York, 1995.

is that self-efficacy theory is not an alternative or competing approach to understanding depression, but it is compatible with other theories. Depression can be viewed as a *mood* that is experienced in varying degrees by most people at one time or another, or as a *mood disorder* or clinical syndrome that is experienced in full by a much smaller number of people. In the social cognitive view, normal experiences of distressing mood and maladaptive behavior and so-called mood and behavioral disorders differ in degree rather than kind (Maddux & Lewis, this volume). Thus, the distinction between sadness or depressed mood and a depressive disorder is not important for understanding the role of self-efficacy in depression. Therefore, studies on normal sad or depressed mood, including experimentally induced transient moods, are important in their own right and may add to our understanding of the mood disturbances that lead people to seek professional assistance.

SELF-EFFICACY THEORY OF DEPRESSION

Self-efficacy theory is concerned with the relationship between cognitions of self-devaluation and coping inability and the initiation and persistence of coping behaviors in the face of obstacles—concerns that are highly relevant to understanding depression. At least three types of self-efficacy beliefs influence depression (Bandura, 1992). First, people may feel unable to attain standards of achievement or performance that would bring personal satisfaction (e.g., Kanfer & Zeiss, 1983). Second, people may believe that they are incapable of developing satisfying and supportive relationships with others (e.g. Anderson & Arnoult, 1985; Yusaf & Kavanagh, 1990). Third, they may believe they are unable to control disturbing depressive ruminations (e.g., Kavanagh & Wilson, 1989). In addition, research suggests that depression is associated with two types of outcome expectancies: expectancies concerning the occurrence of positive and negative life events, and expectancies for the effectiveness of mood regulation strategies (Alloy, Albright, & Clements, 1987; Franko, Powers, Zuroff, & Moskowitz, 1985; Kirsch, Mearns, & Cantanzaro, 1990; Mearns, 1991). Each of these relationships will be discussed in greater detail. The social cognitive model of psychological adaptation and adjustment assumes that cognition, affect, and behavior are related reciprocally. Each factor influences the others, and a change in one leads inevitably to a change in the others (Maddux & Lewis, this volume). This same principle of reciprocal causality applies to the relationships among self-efficacy, depressed mood, and performance attainments (e.g., Kavanagh, 1992). According to this principle, self-efficacy beliefs influence mood and performance. In addition, emotional states and performance attainments are important sources of self-efficacy information (See Maddux, Chap. 2, this volume). Mood may influence self-efficacy directly or indirectly by hindering cognitive and behavioral effectiveness and goal attainment. Finally, emotional states influence performance and vice versa (Kavanagh, 1992).

The original formulation of self-efficacy theory (Bandura, 1977a) suggested that either low self-efficacy expectancies or low outcome expectancies can lead to apathy and low rates of initiation of behaviors, lack of interest and persistence in a task, and feelings of worthlessness and inadequacy. A revision of self-efficacy theory (Bandura, 1982, 1986) provided more detailed predictions about the relationships among self-efficacy expectancy, outcome expectancy, outcome value, and depression. According to this reformulation, when an outcome is highly valued, depression is likely when outcome expectancy is high and self-efficacy expectancy is low (Bandura, 1982, 1986). When people believe that highly desired outcomes (high outcome value) are obtainable through the performance of certain behaviors (high outcome expectancy), and believe that they are incapable (relative to capable others) of performing the requisite behaviors (low self-efficacy expectancy), they display low rates of behavioral initiative and persistence, self-devaluation, and depressed affect.

This self-denigrating, despondent response differs from the response people exhibit when they perceive low self-efficacy along with *low* outcome expectancy (Bandura, 1982, 1986). Under this condition, people perceive that the environment is unresponsive not only to their own efforts, but also to the efforts of others. Because people who believe the environment is generally unresponsive believe that they are unlikely to achieve their desired goals, they experience apathy and resignation; however, because they do not view themselves as deficient or defective relative to other people, they do not experience the important depressive features of self-devaluation and despondency.

These different predictions concerning self-efficacy expectancy, outcome expectancy, and depression have not been systematically and thoroughly investigated. Research supports both predictions to some degree. Some studies suggest that depression occurs only when outcome expectancy is high and self-efficacy is low (e.g., Olioff, Bryson, & Wadden, 1989). Other studies, however, have shown that depression occurs when either self-efficacy or outcome expectancy is low (e.g., Goozh & Maddux, 1992; Jacobs, Prentice-Dunn, & Rogers, 1984). Related research on personal goals has shown that positive mood is associated with the perceived attainability of highly valued personal goals, but this research has not distinguished between self-efficacy and outcome expectancies (e.g., Brunstein, 1993).

The nature of the outcome over which personal control is desired may differentiate affective and behavioral responses to perceived inefficacy (Bandura, 1982). Low self-efficacy for gaining highly valued or rewarding outcomes is likely to lead to despondency and, in extreme cases, depression; low self-efficacy for avoiding aversive outcomes may lead to anxiety. Also, in some situations, perceived inefficacy leads to both anxiety and depression. The distinction between types of life events and their relationship with depression and anxiety has not been investigated thoroughly. Low self-efficacy for preventing generic negative life events appears to be associated with both depression and anxiety, and the differentiating conditions, such as types of negative life events, are not yet clear (e.g., Goozh & Maddux, 1993; Tilley & Maddux, 1992). (A thorough discussion of the differentiation of depression from anxiety and their comorbidity is beyond the scope of the chapter. Interested readers should consult Alloy et al., 1990.)

SELF-EFFICACY AND MOOD: COVARIATION AND CAUSE

The relationship between cognition and emotion in general, and cognition and depression in particular, has long been a topic of research, and the question of whether cognitions are a correlate of depression, a cause of depression, or both, remains a source of controversy (e.g., Coyne & Gotlib, 1983; Lewinsohn, 1974; Schreiber, 1978; Shaw & Dobson, 1981). The research on the relationship between self-efficacy and depression does not settle the cognition–emotion controversy, but it does provide strong evidence that self-efficacy beliefs influence mood. Studies of self-efficacy and depression have examined the covariation of self-efficacy beliefs and mood, the influence of self-efficacy on mood, and the influence of mood on self-efficacy.

Covariation of Self-Efficacy and Depression

A number of studies have demonstrated that depressed mood and symptoms of depressive disorders are associated with self-efficacy expectancies. For example, Devins et al. (1982) found that self-efficacy expectancy and outcome expectancy independently predicted depression and self-esteem in patients with end-stage renal disease. These findings seem to support Bandura's (1977a) earlier hypotheses that depression will occur when either self-efficacy or outcome expectancy is low. Devins et al. (1982), however, used global rather than behavior-specific measures of self-efficacy and outcome expectancy. Self-efficacy theory emphasizes the use of measures specific to the behavior or behavioral domain under consideration. Kanfer and Zeiss (1983) examined the relationship between performance standards and self-efficacy for interpersonal functioning among depressed and nondepressed college students. Although ratings of minimally acceptable performance standards in the two groups did not differ, depressed college students had significantly lower self-efficacy expectancies than did nondepressed college students for various interpersonal behaviors at home, work, school, and in social settings. Thus, the significant discrepancy between standards and self-efficacy in the depressed group occurred because self-efficacy was low, not because standards were exceptionally high. The results suggest that, contrary to some cognitive theories (e.g., Beck, 1976), absolute performance standards for interpersonal effectiveness may not be as important in eliciting depression as the perceived discrepancy between standards and belief in ability to achieve them. This finding was given additional support by Ahrens, Zeiss, and Kanfer (1988), who found that depressed subjects set lower interpersonal goals than nondepressed subjects, and that depressed subjects failed to exhibit the self-enhancing evaluation of their interpersonal competence that was characteristic of nondepressed persons.

The work of Anderson and colleagues suggests that perceived uncontrollability of outcomes is the heart of the cognitive problem in depression and low self-efficacy expectancy (particularly for interpersonal behaviors) resulting from internal attributions about incompetence is the factor most responsible for the perception of the uncontrollability of outcomes (Anderson & Arnoult, 1985; Anderson, Horowitz, & French, 1983). These findings are consistent with those of Kanfer and Zeiss (1983) in supporting the primacy of low self-efficacy expectancies in depressive cognition.

Rosenbaum and Hadari (1985) examined self-efficacy expectancies and outcome expectancies in groups of normal subjects, depressed psychiatric patients, and paranoid psychiatric patients. Both paranoid and depressed patients reported lower self-efficacy expectancies than nonpatients. Also, the three groups differed in outcome expectancies. Paranoid persons perceived outcomes to be under the control of powerful others, and depressed persons perceived outcomes to be controlled by chance. The authors suggested that low self-efficacy may be a nonspecific factor in psychological dysfunction and that differences in outcome expectancies may determine the specific nature of the dysfunction. The notion that low self-efficacy is a characteristic of generic psychological dysfunction is given some support by studies suggesting that low self-efficacy is an important feature of both anxiety and depression (Goozh & Maddux,

1992; Maddux, Norton, & Leary, 1988; Riskind & Maddux, 1993; Tilley & Maddux, 1992; see also Williams, this volume). Olioff et al. (1989) examined the relative contributions of negative automatic thoughts (via the Automatic Thoughts Questionnaire; Hollon & Kendall, 1980) and self-efficacy for academic success to subsequent depression in a sample of undergraduate students. Self-efficacy was measured by having each student list 10 activities they perceived to produce undergraduate academic success (an outcome expectancy rating), check each activity they believed they would be able to carry out well during that school term, and rate their confidence about each judgment on a scale of 0 to 100. Two self-efficacy measures were computed, a total self-efficacy score and a specific self-efficacy score for the activity rated as most important to academic success—the activity with the highest outcome expectancy.

When initial level of depression, stressful life events, social supports, and their interaction were statistically controlled, automatic thoughts and *specific* self-efficacy both predicted the development of mild depressive features 4 weeks later. The total self-efficacy score was not a significant predictor of depressive features. Because the specific self-efficacy rating involved the activity with the highest outcome expectancy, the findings provide some support for the hypothesis that depression is most likely to occur when people believe that effective means exist for achieving what they want (high outcome expectancy) but believe that they are personally incapable of implementing these means (low self-efficacy).

Three related studies (Cozzarelli, 1993; Major, Cozzarelli, Cooper, Testa, & Mueller, 1990; Mueller & Major, 1989) examined the relationship between individual differences in self-efficacy for coping with abortion and postabortion adjustment. In a study by Mueller and Major (1989), perceived coping self-efficacy was measured by asking women about to have an abortion to indicate the extent to which they believed they could implement each of ten postabortion behaviors that facilitate good adjustment (e.g., ability to carry on with normal daily activities, ability to think about babies without distress). Adjustment to abortion—defined as the women's physical complaints, mood, anticipation of future negative consequences, and depression—was measured 30-minutes and 3-weeks postabortion. Women with high coping self-efficacy prior to the abortion experienced better moods, and anticipated fewer negative consequences immediately postabortion than women with low self-efficacy. These differences persisted to the 3-week follow-up. The findings on the relationship between self-efficacy and depression were essentially replicated by Major et al. (1990) and Cozzarelli (1993).

Fretz, Kluge, Ossana, Jones, and Merikangas (1989) examined self-efficacy, attitudes toward retirement, knowledge about aging and retirement, planfulness for retirement, job commitment, and social support as predictors of anxiety and depression about retirement. Level of self-efficacy was measured by asking subjects to respond "yes" or "no" to whether they thought they had the ability to adjust to retirement; strength of self-efficacy was assessed by having subjects indicate the probability (the chance out of 100) that they would be able to adjust to retirement. Both level of self-efficacy and strength of self-efficacy were significant predictors of depression beyond what could be predicted by demographic variables, income, and health. Planfulness was also a significant predictor of depression. This self-efficacy measure, however, seems more a measure of general control beliefs than of self-efficacy specifically, because the subjects were asked about their ability to achieve a certain goal (adjustment) rather than their ability to engage in behaviors that might lead to that goal (see Maddux, this volume; Kirsch, this volume).

Davis-Berman (1990) examined the influence of physical self-efficacy (Physical Self-Efficacy Inventory; Ryckman, Robbins, Thornton, & Cantrell, 1982) in the emotional adjustment of older adults (mean age of 81.1 years). Physical self-efficacy was a better predictor of depression than either general self-efficacy (General Self-Efficacy Inventory; Sherer et al., 1982) or objective measures of physical status. However, the degree to which the Physical Self-Efficacy Scale measures self-efficacy is questionable. For example, items from the scale include: "I have excellent reflexes"; "I have poor muscle tone"; "I take pride in my ability in sports." These items seem to measure physical health self-concept and self-esteem, not self-efficacy for physical activities.

Olioff and Aboud (1991) examined the relationship between parenting self-efficacy and postpartum depression among a group of 40 primiparous women. Self-efficacy for parenting was assessed by asking women to indicate their degree of confidence in their ability to implement 10 self-generated "good mothering" behaviors. Self-efficacy and self-esteem were assessed during the ninth month of pregnancy. Parenting self-efficacy significantly predicted postpartum depressed mood beyond what was predicted by self-esteem and prepartum mood. Self-esteem also added significantly to the prediction of postpartum mood. In addition, parenting self-efficacy was not associated with mood until 6 weeks after the women gave birth—not during the ninth month of pregnancy. Cutrona and Troutman (1986) provided additional support for the link between parenting self-efficacy and postpartum depression.

Goozh and Maddux (1993) examined the role of self-presentational concerns, self-efficacy, outcome expectancy, and outcome value in social anxiety and depressed mood. Results generally supported the utility of distinguishing among presentational self-efficacy, presentational outcome expectancy, and presentational outcome value. Presentational self-efficacy was the best predictor of situational depressed mood; presentational outcome expectancy and outcome value were significant predictors of depressed mood, but were significantly weaker predictors than self-efficacy.

Self-Efficacy and Treatment of Depression

The preceding studies examined the relationship between self-efficacy and common experiences of depressed mood or sadness. Although social cognitive theory assumes a continuity between normal affect and affective experiences that lead people to seek professional help, demonstration that self-efficacy is associated with depressive "disorders" lends additional credibility to the construct. Several treatment outcome studies have provided evidence for a strong association between self-efficacy and depression. Kavanagh and Wilson (1989) tested the contribution of self-efficacy expectancies to response to cognitive treatment of depression. They gave clinically depressed volunteers self-efficacy questionnaires and other measures before and after they were treated with 9 weeks of group cognitive therapy for depression. Depression was measured immediately before treatment, during treatment, immediately after the 9 weeks of treatment, and during a 12-month follow-up period. They found that improvements in depression during treatment were significantly correlated with self-efficacy regarding control of mood. Self-efficacy regarding control of negative cognitions identified subjects who relapsed over the next 12 months.

Yusaf and Kavanagh (1990) explored the relationship among self-efficacy, mood, and performance within the context of a treatment study. One self-efficacy measure corresponded to components of the treatment program and treatment goals (i.e., control of tension, control of enjoyability, control of negative thoughts, social competence, and control of mood). The second self-efficacy measure focused on self-efficacy for assertion and athletic activities, which were not specific treatment goals. The treatment group was provided 10 sessions of treatment that included relaxation training, increasing pleasant activities, controlling negative thoughts, and increasing assertion and positive social interactions. A wait-list control group received treatment after the completion of the study. Measures of self-efficacy, automatic thoughts, and depression were taken before treatment, at the end of treatment, and 12 weeks following treatment.

The treatment and control groups showed an equally significant decrease in depression. Changes in 10 of the 13 target measures were associ-

ated with improvements in depression for subjects who received treatment, whereas little relationship existed between depression and the specific target variables in the control group. (See also Teasdale, 1985; Zeiss,
Lewinsohn, & Munoz, 1979). Self-efficacy for athletics and assertiveness
(Scale 2) also contributed significantly to the variance between groups.
Treatment subjects gained more confidence about controlling mood, but
according to depression scores, were not better able to do this than the
control group. Subjects who were more depressed and had the least self-
efficacy for controlling mood at pretest were more depressed at posttest,
whether or not they received treatment.

EFFECTS OF INDUCED SELF-EFFICACY ON MOOD

The studies described in the previous section provide strong evidence
for a significant covariation between self-efficacy and depressed mood but
cannot be used as evidence that low self-efficacy causes depressed mood.
Causal relationships between self-efficacy and mood are best explored by
experiments that manipulate one variable and then assess the impact of
these induced changes on another variable (e.g., Kavanagh, 1992). Several
experimental studies have investigated the causal relationship between
self-efficacy expectancy and depression by manipulating self-efficacy and
assessing changes in mood, performance on various tasks or activities, or
self-esteem. Some of these studies also have attempted to manipulate
outcome expectancies and assess their impact on mood.

Davis and Yates (1982) attempted to induce self-efficacy expectancies
and outcome expectancies for an anagram task and examined their effects
on performance and depressed affect. As predicted by Bandura's revised
model of self-efficacy and depression, performance deficits on the anagram tasks and depressed affect occurred only when outcome expectancy
was high and self-efficacy expectancy was low, although only for male
subjects. This study, however, contains two major problems. First, outcome
expectancy was manipulated by presenting to subjects information indicating that either most students or few students solved the anagrams to be
presented. This procedure, however, because it addressed subjects' beliefs
about their own abilities (via comparison to others) to solve the anagrams
rather than their beliefs about the possible results (e.g., reward, praise) of
solving the anagrams, seems more a manipulation of self-efficacy expectancy than outcome expectancy. Second, the manipulation of self-efficacy
expectancy was partially ineffective for female subjects. In at least one
condition (low self-efficacy expectancy/high outcome expectancy), female
subjects failed to change their ratings of self-efficacy expectancy following
the manipulation.

In a follow-up to Davis and Yates (1982), Bloom, Yates, and Brosvic (1983) examined the finding that females were less susceptible than males to the depressive effects of manipulations of self-efficacy expectancy and outcome expectancy. The self-efficacy manipulation in Bloom et al. (1983), unlike the manipulation in Davis and Yates (1982), was effective for both male and female subjects. Bloom et al. (1983) also replicated the gender effect found in Davis and Yates (1982); males exhibited greater performance deficits on anagram tasks and greater depressed affect than females when self-efficacy expectancy was low and outcome expectancy was high. However, because the manipulation of outcome expectancy in Bloom et al. (1983) was the same as in Davis and Yates (1982), these results are also questionable. Furthermore, because all subjects received only manipulations for low self-efficacy and high outcome expectancy, the study did not provide comparisons of the effect of different conditions of self-efficacy and outcome expectancy on depression.

Jacobs, Prentice-Dunn, and Rogers (1984) found independent effects for self-efficacy expectancy and outcome expectancy on degree of persistence at an unsolvable design problem; high levels of each created greater persistence. These results appear to support Bandura's (1977a) earlier predictions, rather than the more recent interactive predictions (Bandura, 1982), although their relevance to depression is questionable because Jacobs et al. (1984) did not assess affect or self-esteem.

Schwartz and Fish (1989) examined the effect of induced self-efficacy on mood and performance on an anagram task. They randomly assigned depressed and nondepressed subjects to anagram-training groups. Half the subjects were told that their anagram-solving skills were better than most other students—a high self-efficacy induction. The other half were told that their anagram-solving skills were about the same as other students—a low (or lower) self-efficacy induction. Before and after the self-efficacy inductions, subjects completed depression and self-efficacy measures. After the self-efficacy inductions, subjects completed a more difficult anagram-solving task, and depression was again assessed.

Although the self-efficacy manipulation was not successful in producing group differences in self-efficacy for solving anagrams, greater success in training led to increases in self-efficacy, regardless of group assignment. Higher posttraining self-efficacy was associated with significant decreases in depressive affect for depressed subjects but not nondepressed subjects (probably because their low depression scores left little room for change). Depressed subjects showed an increase in depression when confronted with a difficult task, regardless of degree of success on the final task. The investigators suggested that the increase in self-efficacy among the depressed subjects was transient and that they quickly became demoralized and more depressed when confronted with a more difficult task, which may have prompted a reappraisal of self-efficacy (as suggested by Bandura, 1982).

Mueller and Major (1989), described in part earlier, also examined the effect of interventions designed to alter causal attributions and self-efficacy for coping with abortion on postabortion adjustment and coping. They randomly assigned women waiting to have an abortion to one of three experimental groups. The first group received a 7-minute pre-abortion intervention aimed at altering attributions for an unwanted pregnancy by minimizing self-character blame, the extent to which women attributed the pregnancy and abortion to internal, stable, and global aspects of the self. The second group received a 7-minute preabortion verbal persuasion intervention designed to raise perceived self-efficacy for coping with the abortion. A control group received standard information about abortion and clinic services. Perceived coping self-efficacy, character self-blame, and adjustment to abortion were measured as noted previously. Adjustment to abortion was measured 30-minutes and 3-weeks postabortion. The self-efficacy intervention provided a more powerful immediate intervention for postabortion depression than did the attributional intervention, although no effects of the interventions were observed on adjustment 3-weeks postabortion. The investigators suggested that this may indicate that the 7-minute "intervention" was not sufficiently strong to affect long-term adjustment.

Tilley and Maddux (1992) tested the hypothesis that depression and anxiety are both caused by low self-efficacy for control over negative life events, but are differentiated by the type of negative life event—that depression is associated with expectations of the nonoccurrence or loss of valued outcomes and that anxiety is associated with the occurrence of aversive or harmful outcomes. Vignettes describing important life events were used to manipulate self-efficacy expectancy for preventing negative life events and the type of event (preventing an aversive outcome vs. preventing the loss of a valued outcome). Each vignette was followed by items designed to assess self-efficacy expectancy, outcome value, and depressed or anxious mood. The results indicated that subjects in the low self-efficacy condition indicated greater anxious mood and greater depressed mood than subjects in the high self-efficacy condition, but type of negative life event did not discriminate anxious from depressed mood.

Goozh (1992) manipulated self-efficacy expectancy, outcome expectancy, and outcome value for self-presentational concern and examined the effects of these induced beliefs on mood. As predicted, low self-efficacy for successful execution of self-presentational skills in a variety of interpersonal situations produced greater depressed mood than high self-efficacy.

Low outcome expectancy for self-presentational skills also produced greater depressed mood than high outcome expectancy. The interaction between self-efficacy and outcome expectancy on mood was also significant, such that the greatest depressed mood was produced under low self-efficacy and low outcome expectancy. Contrary to predictions from self-efficacy theory, low outcome value also produced greater depressed mood; subjects who were induced to believe that self-presentational success was relatively unimportant displayed greater depressed mood than those who placed greater importance on self-presentational success.

EFFECTS OF INDUCED MOOD ON SELF-EFFICACY

Relatively few studies have attempted to determine to what degree mood determines self-efficacy. In perhaps the first such study, Kavanagh and Bower (1985) examined the effect of induced mood on self-efficacy for a variety of behavioral domains (e.g., romantic activities, social skills, assertion skills, athletic ability). Happy, sad, and neutral moods were induced via recall under hypnosis of highly emotional successful or failed romantic experiences or an emotionally neutral event. Inducing a happy mood increased self-efficacy for a range of interpersonal and athletic behaviors. These findings were supported by Kavanagh and Hausfield (1986), who found that induced happy moods resulted in increased self-efficacy for muscle strength activities, and by Wright and Mischel (1982), who found that induced happiness and sadness led to self-efficacy differences on a perceptual task. Kavanagh and Bower (1985) suggested that the efficacy changes under different mood conditions were the result of an association between negative mood and mood congruent cognitions—that high self-efficacy expectancies are associated with and triggered by a happy mood, and low self-efficacy expectancies are linked to and made more salient by a sad mood (i.e., network theory; Bower, 1981).

A later study by Bower (1987) suggested that the influence of induced mood on self-efficacy may be mediated by changes in performance attainments. Induced happy and sad moods (induced by music and recall of romantic experiences) produced expected differences in persistence on an anagram task but did not produce differences in self-efficacy measured before the task. After the task, however, happy subjects had higher self-efficacy than sad subjects. Thus, induced mood produced differences in performance, which then were associated with differences in self-efficacy.

Stanley and Maddux (1986b) examined the effects of induced self-efficacy on mood and induced mood on self-efficacy. The first of two experiments demonstrated that induced self-efficacy expectancies for an anticipated social interaction significantly influenced mood; low self-efficacy expectancies created greater depressed mood than high self-efficacy expectancies. In the second experiment, however, neither depressed nor elated mood had an effect on self-efficacy expectancies for the anticipated interaction. Although these results suggest that the causal relationship between self-efficacy expectancies and depressed mood occurs in only one direction, a more powerful mood induction (such as that used in Kavanagh & Bower, 1985) probably would be necessary to influence self-efficacy expectancies for an anticipated social interaction.

The most compelling evidence for the influence of mood on self-efficacy is presented by Salovey and Birnbaum (1989) in three experiments on the effect of induced sad, happy, and neutral moods on the health beliefs of healthy and sick people. Subjects induced to feel sad reported lower self-efficacy for health-promoting and illness-alleviating behaviors than happy or neutral subjects. In addition, among healthy subjects, sad subjects provided more pessimistic probability estimates of future negative health-relevant events than happy subjects. Effects of mood on outcome expectancies were marginal but in the same direction as the effects on self-efficacy. Finally, Salovey and Rosenhan (1989) found that induced mood also influences self-efficacy for interpersonal helping behavior.

OUTCOME EXPECTANCIES AND DEPRESSION

The distinction between self-efficacy expectancies and outcome expectancies is important is self-efficacy theory, although their relationship and their independent and interactive effects on mood and behavior remain a source of controversy (see Chap. 1, this volume). As noted in the previous section, however, few studies of depression have clearly differentiated self-efficacy from outcome expectancies and examined their relationship to depression. Therefore, comparing the strength of the association between self-efficacy and depression with that of outcome expectancy and depression is difficult. The few relevant studies reviewed previously, however, suggest that low outcome expectancies for positive events and high outcome expectancies for negative events are associated with depressed mood.

Several studies not discussed in previous sections have examined the relationship between outcome expectancies and depression (although without also examining self-efficacy) and also have found that outcome expectancies are strongly associated with depression. These studies have examined two types of outcomes expectancies, life-event expectancies and mood regulation expectancies.

OUTCOME EXPECTANCIES FOR LIFE EVENTS

A number of studies have shown that depressed people either have a pessimistic outcome expectancy bias or lack the optimistic outcome expectancy bias that seems characteristic of nondepressed people (e.g., Alloy, Albright, & Clements, 1987). For example, depressed people believe that positive events are less likely to occur to themselves than to other people, that negative events are more likely to occur to themselves and others than are positive events, and that negative events are more likely to occur to themselves than to others (e.g., Pietromonaco & Markus, 1985; Pyszcynski, Holt, & Greenberg, 1987; Salovey & Birnbaum, 1989). In addition, non-depressed people are more likely to view positive events as more probable than negative events, a bias not shared by depressed people (Pyszczynski et al., 1987), and overestimate the covariance between their own behavior and positive outcomes (Kayne & Alloy, 1988). Self-focus seems to enhance the pessimism of depressed people (Pyszczynski et al., 1987). Evidence that these negative outcome expectancies are characteristic of depression is also provided by research on the helpless/hopelessness models of depression (e.g., Alloy et al., 1987; Alloy et al., 1990).

Left unresolved by these studies, however, is the question of the degree to which outcome expectancies for negative life events influence depression independent of self-efficacy for coping with these events, and the degree to which these negative outcome expectancies are caused by low self-efficacy. Part of the problem, once again, lies in the difficulty researchers have had in differentiating self-efficacy from outcome expectancies. For example, one recent study (Weiss, Sweeney, Proffitt, & Carr, 1993) seemed to find that outcome expectancies contributed to the prediction of depressed mood in children, independent of self-efficacy beliefs. However, the measures in this study do not provide a clean separation of self-efficacy and outcome expectancy.

OUTCOME EXPECTANCIES FOR MOOD REGULATION

When people feel bad, they often have difficulty imagining feeling good (e.g., Carson & Adams, 1980). People who lack strategies for managing or regulating negative affect, or who have low expectancies for success in regulating negative affect, may be more vulnerable to prolonged negative mood states than individuals who are able to employ such strategies and who believe in their effectiveness (Kirsch, 1990). In addition, a common mechanism in all effective treatments of depression may be the inducement of a strong belief that the depression can be alleviated and that the depressed behavior can influence mood (Kirsch, 1990; Teasdale, 1985).

Such expectancies for the occurrence of nonvolitional affective states have been referred to as *response expectancies* (Kirsch, 1985, 1990). Several studies have examined the relationship between expectancies for regulating negative mood state and depression.

Kirsch et al. (1990) found that expectancy for negative mood regulation among college students accounted for variance on measures of coping and depressed mood beyond the variance accounted for by stressful life events, family support, and personality variables. The more the subjects believed in the effectiveness of the mood regulation strategies, the less depressed they were, independent of the *use* of the coping behavior on which the expectancy was generated. Kirsch et al. suggested that mood enhancement is produced *not* by more persistent use of coping strategies, but by belief in the effectiveness of those strategies—by strong outcome expectancies. Once the negative mood state is alleviated, people no longer persist in their coping efforts. In contrast, those who attempt coping efforts with little confidence in their effectiveness remain dysphoric and persist in their coping efforts. This last speculation seems somewhat inconsistent with self-efficacy theory, which states that people are more likely to initiate and maintain behaviors when they believe they will be successful. However, at least two explanations for this apparent discrepancy can be offered. First, coping persistence can refer to at least two different coping styles, either persisting with one or two coping strategies until success is attained, or a more unsystematic style that consists of attempting to implement a large number of strategies in a helter-skelter fashion, but without persisting with any specific strategy. The style of persistence assessed in Kirsch et al. (1990) is not clear. In addition, Kirsch et al. did not measure self-efficacy for executing the mood regulation strategies. People with high self-efficacy for the mood regulation strategies are likely to persist with coping behaviors, even if they hold relatively weak beliefs in the effectiveness of the strategies, whereas those with both low efficacy expectancies and low outcome expectancies are unlikely to initiate or persist in coping efforts.

Mearns (1991) examined the relationship between mood regulation outcome expectancies and the severity of depression and use of coping strategies for individuals following the end of a romantic relationship. Mood regulation outcome expectancies were measured by the Negative Mood Regulation Scale (NMR; Catanzaro & Mearns, 1990), a 30-item self-report measure that asks respondents to rate the extent to which they think each of a variety of behavioral and cognitive strategies will work for them to alleviate a negative mood. Undergraduates completed the NMR, a depression inventory, and a relationship survey that assessed several aspects of relationships that had been identified as important predictors of postrelationship depression (e.g., intensity of the subject's love for the partner, duration of the relationship). Subjects also rated the frequency with which they had employed each of 41 coping behaviors since the end of the relationship. As predicted, mood regulation expectancies were negatively correlated with depression in the first week following the breakup. Mood regulation expectancies also were positively related to active coping attempts following the end of that relationship.

Doerfler and Richards (1981) explored differences between people who successfully coped with depression on their own and those who had not. They interviewed 13 depressed women who had attempted to cope with their depression on their own for at least 2 weeks. In an interview, subjects described their depression self-control strategies. Analysis of the interview data suggested that successful subjects initiated more social changes than unsuccessful subjects and believed more strongly in the effectiveness of their own positive coping statements.

THEORETICAL ISSUES

The major social cognitive theories of depression are concerned primarily with perceptions of personal control over positive and negative events. Each contends that, when depressed, people believe they have little control over the good and bad things that happen to them and that such beliefs can cause depressed affect. Beliefs about personal control are the heart of self-efficacy theory; thus integration of self-efficacy theory with the other major models may facilitate the development of a single comprehensive social cognitive theory of depression.

SELF-EFFICACY THEORY AND BECK'S COGNITIVE THEORY

According to Beck's cognitive model of depression (Beck, 1967, 1976; Beck, Rush, Shaw, & Emery, 1979), depressed persons hold negative views of themselves, their world, and their future. They see themselves as defective, inadequate, deprived, and incapable of achieving the success and happiness that others seem capable of achieving; they see their world as too demanding, uncaring, and fraught with obstacles and problems; and they view their condition as hopeless and anticipate that life will continue to be full of hardship, pain, frustration, and deprivation (Beck et al., 1979). This cognitive schema (or negative cognitive triad) is activated by circumstances similar to those responsible for creating the negative concepts in the first place and is the proximal cause of depression.

The negative view of self can be seen as a generalized low self-efficacy expectancy that is the product of, and is manifested in, numerous situation-specific and behavior-specific low self-efficacy expectancies (Stanley & Maddux, 1986a; Kanfer & Zeiss, 1983). Depressed persons view themselves as generally incompetent and incapable, perhaps particularly incapable of performing those behaviors that others seem able to perform to achieve highly desired goals (high outcome expectancy and high outcome value with low self-efficacy expectancy).

The negative view of the world can be viewed as a set of low outcome expectancies, a set of perceptions of response–outcome noncontingency. Depressed persons see their world as filled with frustrations and obstacles to be overcome. They believe environmental events are uncontrollable, because nothing works to change certain undesirable situations or to obtain personal attributes, relationships, or goals considered important to happiness and self-worth.

The depressed person's negative view of the future can be expressed as a set of expectations that the world will continue to be as it is (low outcome expectancies) and that they will continue to be incapable and incompetent (low self-efficacy expectancies) in obtaining those things considered to be important to happiness and self-worth (high outcome value).

SELF-EFFICACY THEORY AND HELPLESSNESS/HOPELESSNESS THEORY

The relationship between "learned helplessness" and human depression has been subject of study for over two decades. During that time, the helplessness model of depression has been revised several times. The most recent version is *hopelessness theory* (Alloy et al., 1990). The helplessness and hopelessness models are concerned primarily with perceptions of the controllability of important outcomes, which is also the major focus of self-efficacy theory. Although self-efficacy is concerned primarily with expectancies about future negative life events, the helplessness/hopelessness model is concerned primarily with causal attributions or explanations for negative events that have already occurred. The central prediction of the helplessness/hopelessness theories is that individuals who habitually explain negative life events as caused by internal, stable, and global factors (e.g., general incompetence) are likely to become depressed when such events occur (Peterson & Seligman, 1984). This depressive explanatory style influences the types of attributions made for specific negative life events and expectations about the controllability of future aversive outcomes. Explanatory style is a risk factor or distal cause of depression, and expectations are the proximal and sufficient cause (Peterson & Seligman, 1984).

The more recent hopelessness theory proposes that a proximal and sufficient cause of depression is the expectation that a highly desired outcome is unlikely to occur, or that a highly aversive outcome is likely to occur—a *negative outcome expectancy*—and the expectation that no response at one's disposal will change the likelihood of the occurrence of these outcomes—a *helplessness expectancy* (Alloy et al., 1990). Thus, hopelessness consists of the combination of negative outcome expectancy and helplessness expectancy.

Expectancies are accorded more attention in the recent hopelessness model than in previous versions, but are not described with the same degree of precision and clarity as in self-efficacy theory. The distinction between self-efficacy expectancy and outcome expectancy may add clarity and precision to the concept of helplessness expectancy. People may feel helplessness for one or both of two reasons; they may believe that no response exists that might influence an aversive outcome, or they may believe that some responses might influence these outcomes, but they are personally and uniquely incapable of executing these responses. The former belief is an outcome expectancy; the latter is a self-efficacy expectancy. Thus, a helplessness expectancy can consist of low outcome expectancies, low self-efficacy expectancies, or both. Research strongly supports making the general distinction between self-efficacy expectancy and outcome expectancy (e.g., Maddux, Norton, & Stoltenberg, 1986; Maddux, this volume) and suggests that the distinction is useful in understanding anxious and depressed mood (e.g., Goozh & Maddux, 1993; Maddux et al., 1988; Tilley & Maddux, 1992). In addition, according to self-efficacy theory, depression will occur only when the individual believes that some responses might prevent the negative event but that he/she is unable to execute the responses (Bandura, 1982). Thus, this hypothesis suggests that a helplessness expectancy consists of high outcome expectancy and low self-efficacy expectancy. The relationship between a helplessness expectancy and both self-efficacy expectancy and outcome expectancy has not been explored empirically, although several studies (to be described) have examined the role that self-efficacy and outcome expectancy jointly play in depressed mood.

The distinction between "personal helplessness" and "universal helplessness," proposed in an earlier version of learned helplessness theory (Abramson, Seligman, & Teasdale, 1978), also has parallels in self-efficacy theory. Personal helplessness is the perception that one is uniquely deficient in the ability to control specific outcomes; universal helplessness is the belief that no one is able to control the outcome in question (Abramson et al., 1978). Universal helplessness can consist of a universal low outcome expectancy (no response can control a particular outcome) or a universal low self-efficacy expectancy (no one is capable of performing the behavior that might produce the outcome). Personal helplessness, however, is a combination of high outcome expectancy and low self-efficacy expectancy. Personally helpless individuals believe that certain behaviors are likely to lead to desired outcomes, that other people are capable of performing these behaviors, but that they themselves are not (Stanley & Maddux, 1986a).

SELF-EFFICACY AND CAUSAL ATTRIBUTIONS

Attributional theories share with self-efficacy theory a concern for understanding beliefs about personal control and the effects of such beliefs on emotions and actions. Although many studies have addressed the relationship between attributions and depression (see Brewin, 1985; Robins, 1988; Sweeney, Anderson, & Bailey, 1986 for reviews), few studies have examined the relationship between causal attributions and self-efficacy and their combined influence on mood (see also Maddux, Chap. 1, this volume). The helplessness/hopelessness model of depression proposes that self-efficacy beliefs are an outgrowth of attributional/explanatory style (Peterson & Stunkard, 1992). Scheier and Carver's (1988) model of behavioral self-regulation also proposes that attributions influence behavior via expectancies. Bandura (1992), however, has argued that self-efficacy beliefs influence causal attributions (e.g., Alden, 1986; McAuley, Duncan, & Elroy, 1989). The few studies of depression that have examined both attributions and expectancies have not produced conclusive findings concerning the relationships among attributions, expectancies, and depression. For example, Riskind, Rholes, Brannon, and Burdick's (1987) "confluence hypothesis" proposes that expectancies mediate causal attributions for negative life events and depressive symptoms and that the relationship between attributional style and depression depends upon the relationship between attributions and expectancies. In an examination of this hypothesis, undergraduate students completed measures of attributional style, depression, and positive and negative expectations about the future (e.g., "I will be able to make friends with people I really like."). Six weeks later, depression was again assessed. Although initial depression was the most important predictor of later depression, attributional style predicted a significant additional portion of the variance in later depression. The expectancy measure alone was not a significant predictor of later depression, but the expectancy–attribution interaction was. The results suggest that causal attributions and expectancies work together to produce depression, but do not suggest that attributions cause expectancies or vice versa. In addition, Riskind et al. (1987) did not distinguish between self-efficacy and outcome expectancy; their expectancy measure seems to include both constructs.

Mueller and Major (1989) examined the interaction between character self-blame (internal and stable attribution) and self-efficacy for specific coping behaviors on postabortion adjustment of women who were about to have abortions. Both attributional style and self-efficacy independently predicted immediate postabortion adjustment. Contrary to the results of Riskind et al. (1987), the interaction between attributions and self-efficacy did not predict postabortion adjustment.

Two studies by Hull and Mendolia (1991) indicated that the relationships among attributions, expectancies, and mood are somewhat complex, as might be expected. Using structural modeling techniques, Hull and Mendolia (1991) provided strong evidence of a direct relationship between expectancies and depression, a direct relationship between attributional style for *negative events* and depression, and indirect relationships between attributional style for *positive and negative events* and depression mediated by expectancies.

Schiaffino and Revenson (1992) have provided the most complete analysis of the relationships among attributions, self-efficacy, and outcome expectancy, although the complexity of their findings raises as many questions as they answer. In a study of coping with a chronic illness, rheumatoid arthritis (RA), Schiaffino and Revenson (1992) provided evidence that causal attributions and self-efficacy interact in influencing depression and physical disability. Self-efficacy was negatively related to depression for subjects who made internal, stable, global attributions for RA flare-ups; however, self-efficacy had little relationship to depression for subjects who made external, unstable, specific attributions for flare-ups. The pattern of relationships was different for physical disability. For subjects who made internal, stable, global attributions, self-efficacy was (surprisingly) positively related to disability; but for subjects who made external, unstable, specific attributions, self-efficacy and disability were negatively related.

Additional clarification of the relationship between causal attributions and self-efficacy and the manner in which attributions and self-efficacy interact to influence mood awaits future research. The relationship is likely to be bidirectional. Explanations of past and recent events no doubt influence perceptions of personal competence and efficacy, and perceptions of efficacy probably influence interpretations and explanations of events. For example, people who feel strongly confident in their abilities in a specific domain are more likely to attribute temporary failure in this domain to lack of effort rather than to lack of ability.

SUMMARY AND FUTURE DIRECTIONS

Despite a few measurement problems and some inconsistent findings, research generally indicates that self-efficacy beliefs are strongly associated with depressed mood. Low self-efficacy for achieving personal standards, interpersonal success and satisfaction, and controlling cognitions are each predictive of depressed mood. Thus, strong evidence exists for self-efficacy/mood covariation. In addition, in some studies, experimentally induced low self-efficacy beliefs produced a stronger depressed mood than induced high self-efficacy beliefs, providing evidence that low self-efficacy causes depressed mood. Finally, some studies indicate that inducing a depressed mood can produce low self-efficacy, although the evidence for this causal direction is not as strong as is evidence for the other direction.

Two types of outcome expectancy also seem associated with depression: expectancies for negative and positive life events, and expectancies for mood regulation. Depressed people hold pessimistic beliefs concerning the likelihood of negative and positive life events. In addition, expectations that specific strategies will prove effective in alleviating depressed mood predict lower depressed mood following negative life events. So far, however, studies of mood regulation expectancies have examined outcome expectancies but not self-efficacy expectancies for specific mood control strategies.

A comparison with two other major social cognitive theories of depression indicates that self-efficacy theory offers an analysis of depression that is compatible with these theories, yet provides a conceptualization and assessment of expectancies for personal control that allows self-efficacy theory to be integrated with these other models and provide them with greater clarity and precision. Research supports the utility of the distinction between self-efficacy expectancy and outcome expectancy and suggests that both may contribute to depressed mood. The concept of a helplessness expectancy from the recent hopelessness theory and the earlier distinction between universal helplessness and personal helplessness may benefit from a reconceptualization based on the distinction between self-efficacy and outcome expectancy. The depressive cognitive schema in Beck's cognitive theory also consists largely of attitudes and beliefs that closely resemble self-efficacy, outcome expectancy, and outcome value. The relationship between causal attributions and self-efficacy and their interactive impact on mood is in need of further theoretical and empirical exploration.

Because the role of self-efficacy in depression has received relatively little attention from researchers, a number of questions and issues are in need of empirical investigation.

1. *The relationship between self-efficacy and outcome expectancy and their independent and interactive influence on mood.* Both self-efficacy and outcome

expectancy appear to be associated with mood, but how they are related to each other and how they influence mood interactively remains unclear.

2. *The relationship between helplessness/hopelessness theory and self- efficacy theory.* The concepts of hopelessness and helplessness are capable of definition as interactions of self-efficacy expectancy and outcome expectancy. The relationship between measures of helplessness and hopelessness and measures of self-efficacy and outcome expectancy requires exploration.

3. *The causal relationship between self-efficacy and mood.* Studies clearly demonstrate that self-efficacy and mood covary, and experimental studies that have induced self-efficacy or mood and examined the effect of one on the other suggest that the causal relationship is reciprocal. Additional controlled experimental studies are necessary to clarify this relationship.

4. *Mood regulation expectancies.* A few studies have demonstrated that expectations for success in regulating negative affect predict negative affect and coping. These studies, however, have assessed mood regulation outcome expectancies rather than self-efficacy expectancies. The predictive utility of mood regulation expectancy measures will probably be enhanced by inclusion of the measurement of self-efficacy for specific mood regulation strategies.

5. *Anxiety and depression covariation.* Studies have shown not only that anxiety is a common feature of depression, but also that depression is frequently found with anxiety states (e.g., Dobson, 1985; Watson & Clark, 1984). Understanding the relationship between depression and anxiety may be enhanced by understanding similarities and differences in associated cognitions. Self-efficacy appears to be associated with both depressed mood and anxiety; however, research needs to address the conditions under which low self-efficacy will lead to depression, anxiety, or both.

6. *Clearer definition and measurement of self-efficacy and outcome expectancy.* The large variation in definition and measurement of self-efficacy across studies has made comparison of findings among studies difficult, not only in studies of self-efficacy and depression, but also in other studies (Maddux, Chap. 1, this volume). These measurement problems have also led to difficulty in clarifying the relationship between self-efficacy expectancy and outcome expectancy. Greater clarity and consistency in the measurement of self-efficacy and outcome expectancy is essential to understanding the relationship between these cognitions and mood.

7. *Employment of measures of self-efficacy (and outcome expectancy) in evaluations of clinical interventions.* The few intervention studies that have employed self-efficacy measures suggest that they predict intervention success. In addition, direct facilitation of self-efficacy holds promise as an intervention target. Evaluations of the success of interventions for depres-

sion might benefit by measures of self-efficacy and outcome expectancy for specific intervention components and techniques (e.g., assertiveness training, mood regulation techniques).

REFERENCES

Abramson, L. Y., Seligman, M. E. P., & Teasdale, J. D. (1978). Learned helplessness in humans: Critique and reformulation. *Journal of Abnormal Psychology, 87,* 49–74.

Ahrens, A. H., Zeiss, A. M., & Kanfer, R. (1988). Dysphoric deficits in interpersonal standards, self-efficacy, and social comparison. *Cognitive Therapy and Research, 12*(1), 53–67.

Alden, L. E. (1986). Self-efficacy and causal attributions for social feedback. *Journal of Research in Personality, 20,* 460–473.

Alloy, L. B., Albright, J. S., & Clements, C. M. (1987). Depression, nondepression, and social comparison biases. In J. E. Maddux, C. D. Stoltenberg, & R. Rosenwein (Eds.), *Social processes in clinical and counseling psychology* (pp. 94–112). New York: Springer-Verlag.

Alloy, L. B., Kelly, K. A., Mineka, S., & Clements, C. M. (1990). Comorbidity in anxiety and depressive disorders: A helplessness/hopelessness perspective. In J. D. Maser & C. R. Cloniger (Eds.), *Comorbidity in anxiety and mood disorders* (pp. 499–553). Washington, DC: American Psychiatric Press.

Anderson, C. A., & Arnoult, L. H. (1985). Attributional style and everyday problems in living: Depression, loneliness, and shyness. *Social Cognition, 3,* 16–35.

Anderson, C. A., Horowitz, L. M., & French, R. (1983). Attributional style of lonely and depressed people. *Journal of Personality and Social Psychology, 45,* 127–136.

Bandura, A. (1977a). Self-efficacy theory: Toward a unifying theory of behavioral change. *Psychological Review, 84,* 191–215.

Bandura, A. (1977b). *Social learning theory.* Englewood Cliffs, NJ: Prentice-Hall.

Bandura, A. (1982). Self-efficacy mechanisms in human agency. *American Psychologist, 37,* 122–147.

Bandura, A. (1986). *Social foundations of thought and action: A social cognitive theory.* Englewood Cliffs, NJ: Prentice-Hall.

Bandura, A. (1989). Human agency in social cognitive theory. *American Psychologist, 44,* 1175–1184.

Bandura, A. (1992). Exercise of personal agency through the self-efficacy mechanism. In R. Schwarzer (Ed.), *Self-efficacy: Thought control of action* (pp. 3–38). Washington, DC: Hemisphere.

Beck, A. T. (1967). *Depression: Clinical, experimental, and theoretical aspects.* New York: Harper & Row.

Beck, A. T. (1976). *Cognitive therapy and the emotional disorders.* New York: International University Press.

Beck, A. T. (1978). *Beck Depression Inventory.* Philadelphia, PA: Center for Cognitive Therapy.

Beck, A. T., & Emery, G. (1985). *Anxiety disorders and phobias: A cognitive perspective.* New York: Basic Books

Beck, A. T., Rush, J. A., Shaw, B., & Emery, G. (1979). *Cognitive therapy of depression.* New York: Guilford.

Bloom, C. P., Yates, B. T., & Brosvic, C. M. (1983, August). *Self-efficacy reporting, sex-role stereotype, and sex differences in susceptibility to depression.* Paper presented at the annual meeting of the American Psychological Association, Anaheim, CA.

Bower, G. H. (1981). Mood and memory. *American Psychologist, 36,* 129–148.

Bower, G. H. (1987). Commentary on mood and memory. *Behaviour Research and Therapy, 25,* 443–455.

Brewin, C. R. (1985). Depression and causal attribution: What is their relation? *Psychological Bulletin, 98,* 297–309.

Brunstein, J. C. (1993). Personal goals and subjective well-being: A longitudinal study. *Journal of Personality and Social Psychology, 65,* 1061–1070.

Burns, D. D., Shaw, B. F., & Croker, W. (1987). Thinking styles and coping strategies of depressed women: An empirical investigation. *Behaviour Research and Therapy, 25,* 223–225.

Carson, T. P., & Adams, H. E. (1980). Activity valence as a function of mood change. *Journal of Abnormal Psychology, 89,* 368–377.

Catanzaro, S. J., & Mearns, J. (1990). Measuring generalized expectancies for negative mood regulation: Initial scale development and implications. *Journal of Personality Assessment, 54,* 546–563.

Coyne, J. C., & Gotlib, I. H. (1983). The role of cognition in depression: A critical approach. *Psychological Bulletin, 94,* 472–505.

Cozzarelli, C. (1993). Personality and self-efficacy as predictors coping with abortion. *Journal of Personality and Social Psychology, 65,* 1224–1236.

Crocker, J., Alloy, L. B., & Kayne, N. T. (1988). Attributional style, depression, and perceptions of consensus for events. *Journal of Personality and Social Psychology, 54,* 840–846.

Cutrona, C. E., & Troutman, B. R. (1986). Social support, infant temperament, and parenting self-efficacy: A mediational model of postpartum depression. *Child Development, 57,* 1507–1518.

Davis-Berman, J. (1988). Self-efficacy and depressive symptomatology in older adults: An exploratory study. *International Journal of Aging and Human Development, 27,* 35–43.

Davis-Berman, J. (1990). Physical self-efficacy, perceived physical status, and depressive symptomatology in older adults. *The Journal of Psychology, 124,* 207–215.

Davis, F. W., & Yates, D. T. (1982). Self-efficacy expectancies versus outcome expectancies as determinants of performance deficits and depressive affect. *Cognitive Therapy and Research, 6,* 23–35.

Devins, G. M., Binik, Y. M., Gorman, P., Dattell, M., McClosky, B., Oscar, G., & Briggs, J. (1982). Perceived self-efficacy, outcome expectancies, and negative mood states in end stage renal disease. *Journal of Abnormal Psychology, 91,* 241–244.

Dobson, K. (1985). The relationship between anxiety and depression. *Clinical Psychology Review, 5,* 307–324.

Doerfler, L. A., & Richards, C. S. (1981). Self-initiated attempts to cope with depression. *Cognitive Therapy and Research, 5,* 367–371.

Ellis, A. (1984). Rational-emotive therapy. In R. J. Corsini (Ed.), *Current Psychotherapies* (3rd ed., pp. 196–238). Itasca, IL: Peacock.

Franko, D. L., Powers, T. A., Zuroff, D. C., & Moskowitz, D. S. (1985). Children and affect: Strategies for self-regulation and sex differences in sadness. *American Journal of Orthopsychiatry, 55,* 210–219.

Fretz, B. R., Kluge, N. A., Ossana, S. M., Jones, S. M., & Merikangas, M. W. (1989). Intervention targets for reducing preretirement anxiety and depression. *Journal of Counseling Psychology, 36,* 301–307.

Goodwin, D. W., & Guze, S. B. (1984). *Psychiatric diagnosis* (3rd ed.). New York: Oxford University Press.

Goozh, J. S. (1992). *Understanding social anxiety via self-presentational theory.* Unpublished doctoral dissertation. George Mason University, Fairfax, VA.

Goozh, J. S., & Maddux, J. E. (1993). Self-presentational concerns, social anxiety, and depression: The influence of self-efficacy, outcome expectancy, and outcome value. Unpublished manuscript. George Mason University, Fairfax, VA.

Hollon, S. D., & Garber, J. (1980). A cognitive–expectancy theory of therapy for helplessness and depression. In J. Garber, & M. E. P. Seligman (Eds.), *Human helplessness: Theory and applications* (pp. 173–195). New York: Academic Press.

Hollon, S. D., & Kendall, P. C. (1980). Cognitive self-statements in depression: Development of an Automatic Thoughts Questionnaire. *Cognitive Therapy and Research, 4*, 383–395.

Hull, J. G., & Mendolia, M. (1991). Modeling the relations of attributional style, expectancies, and depression. *Journal of Personality and Social Psychology, 61*, 85–97.

Jacobs, B., Prentice-Dunn, S., & Rogers, R. W. (1984). Understanding persistence: An interface of control theory and self-efficacy theory. *Basic and Applied Social Psychology, 5*, 333–347.

Kaghe, N. T., & Alloy, L. B. (1988). Clinician and patient as aberrant actuaries: Expectation-based distortions in assessment of covariation. In L. Y. Abramson (Ed.), *Social cognition and clinical psychology: A synthesis*. New York: Guilford.

Kanfer, F. H., & Hagerman, S. (1980). The role of self-regulation. In L. P. Rehm (Ed.), *Behavior therapy and depression: Present status and future directions* (pp. 143–179). New York: Academic Press.

Kanfer, R., & Zeiss, A. M. (1983). Depression, interpersonal standard settings, and judgments of self-efficacy. *Journal of Abnormal Psychology, 92*, 319–329.

Kavanagh, D. J. (1992). Self-efficacy and depression. In R. Schwarzer (Ed.), *Self-efficacy: Thought control of action* (pp. 177–194). Washington, DC: Hemisphere.

Kavanagh, D. J., & Bower, G. H. (1985). Mood and self-efficacy: Impact of joy and sadness on perceived capabilities. *Cognitive Therapy and Research, 9*, 507–525.

Kavanagh, D. J., & Hausfeld, S. (1986). Physical performance and self-efficacy under happy and sad moods. *Journal of Sports Psychology, 8*, 112–123.

Kavanagh, D. J., & Wilson, P. H. (1989). Prediction of outcome with group cognitive therapy for depression. *Behavior Research and Therapy, 27*, 333–343.

Kirsch, I. (1985). Response expectancy as a determinant of experience and behavior. *American Psychologist, 40*, 1189–1202.

Kirsch, I. (1990). *Changing expectations: A key to successful psychotherapy*. Pacific Grove, CA: Brooks/Cole.

Kirsch, I., Mearns, J., & Catanzaro, S. J. (1990). Mood-regulation expectancies as determinants of dysphoria in college students. *Journal of Counseling Psychology, 37*, 306–312.

Lewinsohn, P. M. A. (1974). A behavioral approach to depression. In R. J. Friedman & M. M. Katz (Eds.), *The psychology of depression: Contemporary theory and research*. Washington, DC: Winston.

Lubin, B. (1965). Adjective Checklist for measurement of depression. *Archives of General Psychiatry, 12*, 57–62.

Lubin, B. (1967). *Depression adjective checklists*. San Diego, CA: Educational and Industrial Testing Service.

Maddux, J. E., Norton, L. W., & Leary, M. R. (1988). Cognitive components of social anxiety: An investigation of the integration of self-presentation theory and self-efficacy theory. *Journal of Social and Clinical Psychology, 6*, 180–190.

Maddux, J. E., Norton, L. W., & Stoltenberg, C. D. (1986). Self-efficacy expectancy, outcome expectancy, and outcome value: Relative effects on behavioral intentions. *Journal of Personality and Social Psychology, 51*, 783–789.

Maddux, J. E., & Stanley, M. A. (1986). Self-efficacy theory in contemporary psychology: An overview. *Journal of Social and Clinical Psychology, 4*, 249–255.

Maddux, J. E., Stanley, M. A., & Manning, M. M. (1987). Self-efficacy theory and research:

Applications in clinical and counseling psychology. In J. E. Maddux, C. D. Stoltenberg, & R. Rosenwein (Eds.), *Social processes in clinical and counseling psychology* (pp. 39–55). New York: Springer-Verlag.

Major, B., Cozzarelli, C., Schiacchtiano, A. M., Cooper, M. L., Testa, M., & Mueller, P. M. (1990). Perceived social support, self-efficacy, and adjustment to abortion. *Journal of Personality and Social Psychology, 59,* 452–463.

Manning, M. M., & Wright, T. L. (1983). Self-efficacy expectancies, outcome expectancies, and the persistence of pain control in childbirth. *Journal of Personality and Social Psychology, 45,* 421–431.

McAuley, E., Duncan, T. E., & McElroy, M. (1989). Self-efficacy cognitions and causal attributions for children's motor performance: An explanatory investigation. *Journal of Genetic Psychology, 150,* 65–73.

Mearns, J. (1991). Coping with a breakup: Negative mood regulation expectancies and depression following the end of a romantic relationship. *Journal of Personality and Social Psychology, 60,* 327–334.

Moos, R. H., Cronkite, R. C., Billings, A. G., & Finney, J. W. (1983). Health and Daily Living Form Manual. Stanford, CA: Stanford University School of Medicine.

Moos, R. H., & Moos, B. S. (1986). *Family environment scale manual* (2nd ed.). Palo Alto, CA: Consulting Psychologists Press.

Mueller, P., & Major, B. (1989). Self-blame, self-efficacy, and adjustment to abortion. *Journal of Personality and Social Psychology, 57,* 1059–1068.

Olioff, M., & Aboud, F. E. (1991). Predicting postpartum dysphoria in primiparous mothers: Roles of perceived parenting self-efficacy and self-esteem. *Journal of Cognitive Psychotherapy, 5,* 3–14.

Olioff, M., Bryson, S. E., & Wadden, N. P. (1989). Predictive relation of automatic thoughts and student efficacy to depressive symptoms in undergraduates. *Canadian Journal of Behavioral Science, 21,* 353–363.

Perry, M. A., & Furukawa, M. J. (1986). Modeling Methods. In F. H. Kanfer & A. P. Goldstein (Eds.), *Helping people change: A textbook of methods* (3rd ed., pp. 66–110). New York: Pergamon.

Peterson, C., & Seligman, M. E. P. (1984). Causal explanations as a risk factor for depression: Theory and evidence. *Psychological Review, 91,* 347–374.

Peterson, C., & Stunkard, A. J. (1992). Cognates of personal control: Locus of control, self-efficacy, and explanatory style. *Applied and Preventive Psychology, 1,* 111–117.

Pietromonaco, P. R., & Markus, H. (1985). The nature of negative thoughts in depression. *Journal of Personality and Social Psychology, 48,* 799–807.

Pyszczynski, T., Holt, K., & Greenberg, J. (1987). Depression, self-focused attention, and expectancies for positive and negative future life events for self and others. *Journal of Personality and Social Psychology, 52,* 994–1001.

Radloff, L. S. (1977). The CES-D Scale: A new self-report depression scale for research in the general population. *Applied Psychological Measurement, 3,* 385–401.

Rehm, L. P. (1977). A self-control model of depression. *Behavior Therapy, 8,* 787–804.

Riskind, J. H., & Maddux, J. E. (1993). Loomingness, helplessness, and fearfulness: An integration of harm-looming and self-efficacy models of fear. *Journal of Social and Clinical Psychology, 12,* 73–89.

Riskind, J. H., Rholes, W. S., Brannon, A. M., & Burdick, C. A. (1987). Attributions and expectations: A confluence of vulnerabilities in mild depression in a college student population. *Journal of Personality and Social Psychology, 53,* 349–354.

Robins, C. J. (1988). Attributions and depression: Why is the literature so inconsistent? *Journal of Personality and Social Psychology, 54,* 880–889.

Rosenbaum, M., & Hadari, D. (1985). Personal efficacy, external locus of control, and perceived contingency of parental reinforcement among depressed, paranoid, and normal subjects. *Journal of Personality and Social Psychology, 49,* 539–547.

Ryckman, R., Robbins, M., Thornton, B., & Cantrell, P. (1982). Development and validation of a physical self-efficacy scale. *Journal of Personality and Social Psychology, 42,* 891–900.

Salovey, P., & Birnbaum, D. (1989). Influence of mood on health-relevant cognitions. *Journal of Personality and Social Psychology, 57,* 539–551.

Salovey, P., & Rosenhan, D. L. (1989). Mood and prosocial behavior. In H. L. Wagner & A. S. R. Manstead (Eds.), *Handbook of social psychophysiology* (pp. 371–391). Chichester, UK: Wiley.

Scheier, M. F., & Carver, C. S. (1988). A model of behavioral self-regulation: Translating intention into action. *Advances in Experimental Social Psychology, 21,* 303–346.

Schiaffino, K. M., & Revenson, T. A. (1992). The role of perceived self-efficacy, perceived control, and causal attributions in adaptation to rheumatoid arthritis: Distinguishing mediator from moderator effects. *Personality and Social Psychology Bulletin, 18,* 709–718.

Schreiber, M. J. (1978). Depressive cognitions [letter to the editor]. *American Journal of Psychiatry, 135,* 1570.

Schwartz, J., & Fish, J. M. (1989). Self-efficacy and depressive affect in college students. *Journal of Rational-Emotive and Cognitive-Behavior Therapy, 7,* 219–236.

Shaw, B. F., & Dobson, K. S. (1981). Cognitive assessment of depression. In T. V. Merluzzi, C. R. Glass, & M. Genest (Eds.), *Cognitive assessment* (pp. 361–387). New York: Guilford.

Sherer, M., Maddux, J. E., Mercadante, B., Prentice-Dunn, S., Jacobs, B., & Rogers, R. W. (1982). The self-efficacy scale: Construction and validation. *Psychological Reports, 51,* 663–571.

Stanley, M. A., & Maddux, J. E. (1986a). Self-efficacy expectancy and depressed mood: An investigation of causal relationships. *Journal of Social Behavior and Personality, 1,* 575–586.

Stanley, M. A., & Maddux, J. E. (1986b). Self-efficacy theory: Potential contributions to understanding cognitions in depression. *Journal of Social and Clinical Psychology, 4,* 268–278.

Sweeney, P. D., Anderson, K., & Bailey, S. (1986). Attributional style in depression: A meta-analytic review. *Journal of Personality and Social Psychology, 50,* 974–991.

Teasdale, J. D. (1985). Psychological treatments for depression: How do they work? *Behaviour Research and Therapy, 23,* 157–165.

Tilley, C. L. (1989). *Discriminating anticipated depressed and anxious moods: An evaluation of the specificity of negative expectancies for controlling different negative life events.* Unpublished doctoral dissertation, George Mason University, Fairfax, VA.

Tilley, C. L., & Maddux, J. E. (1992). *Anxiety, depression, and self-efficacy for preventing negative life events: An experimental investigation.* Unpublished manuscript, George Mason University, Fairfax, VA.

Watson, D., & Clark, L. A. (1984). Negative affectivity: The disposition to experience aversive emotional states. *Psychological Bulletin, 96,* 465–490.

Weiner, B., & Litman-Adizez, T. (1980). An attributional approach to learned helplessness and depression. In J. Garber & M. E. P. Seligman (Eds.), *Human helplessness: Theory and applications* (pp. 50–57). New York: Academic Press.

Weiss, J. R., Sweeney, L., Profitt, V., & Carr, T. (1993). Control-related beliefs and self-reported depressive symptoms in late childhood. *Journal of Abnormal Psychology, 102,* 411–418.

Wetzel, J. W. (1984). *Clinical handbook of depression.* New York: Gardner Press.

Wright, J., & Mischel, W. (1982). Influence of affect on cognitive social learning person variables. *Journal of Personality and Social Psychology, 43,* 901–914.

Yusaf, S. O., & Kavanagh, D. J. (1990). Mechanisms of improvement in treatment for depression: Test of a self-efficacy and performance model. *Journal of Cognitive Psychotherapy: An International Quarterly, 4,* 51–70.

Zeiss, A. M., Lewinsohn, P. M., & Munoz, R. F. (1979). Nonspecific improvement effects in depression using interpersonal skills training, pleasant activity schedules, or cognitive training. *Journal of Consulting and Clinical Psychology, 47,* 427–439.

Part III

APPLICATIONS IN HEALTH PSYCHOLOGY

CHAPTER 6

SELF-EFFICACY AND HEALTHY BEHAVIOR
PREVENTION, PROMOTION, AND DETECTION

JAMES E. MADDUX, LAWRENCE BRAWLEY, and ANGELA BOYKIN

People do not always act in their own best interest. Too many of us smoke too much, drink too much, eat too much, drive too fast, get too much sun, engage in high-risk sexual activities, fail to wear seat belts—the list goes on. Psychologists have devoted much effort to understanding why people engage in behavior that seems self-destructive, and why they fail to do what they surely know is good for them, or at least will be in the long run (e.g., Baumeister & Scher, 1988). Health psychologists have been among the most active in the search for an understanding of why people engage in unsafe and unhealthy behaviors and why they have such great difficulty altering unhealthy behavior patterns and adapting healthier ones. Beliefs about personal control or efficacy are featured prominently in each of the

JAMES E. MADDUX and ANGELA BOYKIN • Department of Psychology, George Mason University, Fairfax, Virginia 22030.   LAWRENCE BRAWLEY • Department of Kinesiology, University of Waterloo, Waterloo, Ontario, Canada N2L 3G1.

Self-Efficacy, Adaptation, and Adjustment: Theory, Research, and Application, edited by James E. Maddux. Plenum Press, New York, 1995.

major models or theories of health-related behavior change. This chapter is concerned with the role of perceived personal control in people's decisions about behaviors that affect their physical health, with a major focus on self-efficacy theory and research.

Beliefs about self-efficacy influence health in two ways. First, self-efficacy influences the adoption of healthy behaviors, the cessation of unhealthy behaviors, and the maintenance of these behavioral changes in the face of challenge and difficulty. Second, self-efficacy affects the body's physiological responses to stress, including the immune system. This chapter is concerned with the first route of influence. Chapter 8 by O'Leary and Brown, in this volume, is concerned with the second.

TYPES OF HEALTH BEHAVIOR: PREVENTION, PROMOTION, AND DETECTION

A discussion of the role of self-efficacy and other social cognitive factors in health behavior is aided by an understanding of the basic types of health behavior that have been the target of research. Because social cognitive theories are concerned with the role of expected and desired consequences, a classification of health behavior should emphasize the *goals* people are trying to attain when they engage in behaviors that affect their health. The three major types of health behaviors that have been examined in research are *prevention*, *promotion*, and *detection* behaviors. This typology is based on the expected consequences of the behavior rather than on the topography of the behavior. Research has shown that self-efficacy is important in each of these types of health behaviors, as the examples provided below briefly demonstrate.

An awareness of the different goals to which people aspire when engaging in health behavior is crucial to predicting and changing behavior for at least two reasons. First, people differ in the goals to which they aspire when initiating health behaviors. For example, some people may be more interested in promotion goals than prevention goals when beginning an aerobics class. Second, the reasons people attempt to maintain health behaviors over time may differ from those reasons that led to the initiation of the behavior (e.g., H. Leventhal, Diefenbach, & E. A. Leventhal, 1992). For example, a person's goals for continuing to attend aerobics classes may change over time from prevention goals to promotion goals. Understanding the different goals to which people aspire and the individual differences in goals and changes in goals enhances our understanding of the initiation and maintenance of health behavior.

PREVENTION

Prevention behaviors are behaviors that people engage in or cease engaging in because they believe these behaviors or their cessation will prevent or reduce their risk for future health problems. Prevention behaviors are sometimes referred to as *protection* behaviors (e.g., protection motivation theory, Maddux & Rogers, 1983; Rogers, 1975). Common prevention behaviors include changes in diet and exercise that reduce risk for cardiovascular disease (Ewart, Chap. 7, this volume), abstinence from smoking (DiClemente, Fairhurst, & Piotrowski, Chap. 4, this volume), wearing a seatbelt, using sunscreens, and practicing safe sexual behaviors, such as using a condom. Some prevention behaviors, such as fastening a seatbelt or wearing a condom, are single acts that are relatively simple to perform. Prevention regimens or routines, however, involve multiple acts that often must be performed on a daily basis, such as the self-care regimen of the person with diabetes mellitus.

Diabetic Regimen Compliance

The self-care regimen for diabetes mellitus provides a useful context in which to examine the role of self-efficacy beliefs in adherence to prevention behaviors. Diabetes mellitus, a chronic condition characterized by insufficient glucose production and metabolism, affects approximately 7% of the population (Glatthaar, Welborn, Stenhouse, & Garcia-Webb, 1985). Because diabetes is rarely managed successfully with medication alone, its management usually requires major changes in behavior, and includes following a strict program of diet, exercise, medication, and blood glucose self-monitoring. This regimen must be followed on a daily basis for life (Cox & Gonder-Frederick, 1992). The multifaceted nature of this treatment contributes to the problem of noncompliance (e.g., Goodall & Halford, 1991). Compliance with one aspect of the regimen does not guarantee compliance with the other aspects (Glasgow, McCaul, & Schafer, 1987; Orme & Binik, 1989).

Numerous studies have found positive relationships between self-efficacy or outcome expectancy and compliance with one or more aspects of the diabetic control regimen. Many of these studies, however, have methodological problems. For example, some diabetes-regimen self-efficacy scales contain items that assess outcome expectancy rather than self-efficacy (Crabtree, 1986; Grossman, Brink, & Hauser, 1987; Padgett, 1991). In some studies, compliance has been assessed by metabolic rather than behavioral measures (e.g., Glasgow et al., 1989; Grossman et al., 1987;

Padgett, 1991). Although metabolic control is the goal of compliance, the relationship between compliance behaviors and metabolic measures is less than perfect; thus, metabolic measures should not be used as measures of compliance in place of behavioral measures.

The most methodologically sound studies have found that self-efficacy is a good predictor of compliance with various aspects of the regimen (e.g., Glasgow et al., 1989; Kingery & Glasgow, 1989; McCaul, Glasgow, & Schafer, 1987). Outcome expectancies also have been found to predict compliance, but not as well as self-efficacy (e.g., McCaul et al., 1987). Outcome value (e.g., the importance of metabolic control) has been neglected in the study of diabetic-regimen compliance and deserves attention. Typically, these studies have examined one or more aspects of the regimen but, to date, no comprehensive studies have examined self-efficacy, outcome expectancy, and outcome value for all the major aspects of the diabetic regimen. Such studies are needed in light of the fact that self-efficacy for one skill does not guarantee self-efficacy for another, and compliance with one aspect of the regimen does not guarantee compliance with other aspects.

PROMOTION

Promotion behaviors are those behaviors that people engage in not because they are interested primarily in preventing ill health, but because they want to maintain or improve their current state of good health (Matarazzo, Weiss, Herd, Miller, & Weiss, 1984; Stanley & Maddux, 1986; Stokols, 1992). Promotion behaviors are sometimes referred to as *health enhancement* behaviors (e.g., Matarazzo et al., 1984). Common promotion behaviors include regular exercise, diet modification, and stress management among people who are currently healthy and are striving to improve their health rather than merely prevent health problems.

Because the distinction between prevention and promotion depends not on the nature of the behavior but on the goals to which the person aspires, the distinction is sometimes subtle. What begins as a prevention behavior may evolve into a promotion behavior as the individual's goals shift from simply preventing illness to attaining an exceptional level of health. For example, middle-aged executives who have had a mild heart attack may begin an exercise regimen primarily to prevent another heart attack, but they may maintain their regimen over the long run or even increase the rigor of their regimen beyond what is required for risk reduction because they develop a desire for better-than-average health and fitness.

Some prevention behaviors are promotion behaviors, and vice versa. However, some prevention behaviors do not directly promote or enhance health. For example, wearing a seatbelt while riding in a moving automobile reduces the risk of being seriously injured in an accident, but does not make one healthier. Likewise, wearing a condom during sex reduces the risk of disease, but does not otherwise enhance health.

Self-Efficacy and Exercise

Health-promotion regimens often include exercise because of its impact on physical health (Dishman & Sallis, 1994; Dubbert, 1992) and psychological well-being (Casperson, Powell, & Merritt, 1994; McAuley, 1994). Such benefits, however, often take many months to accrue (Dishman, 1988; Dubbert, 1992; Haskell, 1994; Rejeski, 1994). Relatively few people (perhaps one in five) engage in regular exercise for a period of time sufficient to secure these benefits (Dubbert, 1992). The attrition rate for both clinical and community-based exercise programs can be as high as 50% within the first 3 to 6 months of participation (Brawley & Rodgers, 1993; Dishman, 1988). Social cognitive variables, including self-efficacy, seem to play a major role in this attrition.

Among those who initiate exercise programs, those who develop strong beliefs of self-efficacy based on early success are more likely to persist than those who experience initial failure and the resulting feelings of low self-efficacy. Self-efficacy theory also predicts that persistence with an exercise program is influenced by beliefs about the ability to make regular exercise a part of daily living. Research suggests that self-efficacy expectancy, outcome expectancy, and outcome value are important in the initiation and maintenance of a variety of exercise programs, including weight training and aerobics (e.g., Brawley & Rodgers, 1993; Brawley & Horne, 1988; Desharnais, Bouillon, & Godin, 1986; Dzewaltowski, Noble, & Shaw, 1990; Garcia & King, 1991; McAuley, 1991, 1994; McAuley & Courneya, 1993; McAuley & Jacobson, 1991; Poag-Ducharme & Brawley, 1991a, 1991b; Rodgers & Brawley, 1991a, 1991b). This research, conducted in a variety of settings (e.g., universities, work sites), has examined both structured (programmed and supervised) and unstructured (self-regulated) exercise programs, and has employed a variety of people (college-age to elderly, blue-collar and white-collar workers, men and women). Most of these studies have focused on prediction of exercise at one point in time, but others have examined exercise intensity and duration.

Because exercise and most other promotion behaviors must be performed consistently over time to be beneficial, the influence of various social cognitive factors beyond the initiation and the early period of performance is important. For example, a beginning exerciser may successfully maintain an exercise program for several weeks, but then return to a sedentary pattern for a period before resuming a pattern of consistent performance. Several studies have examined changes in the relationship between self-efficacy and exercise as the individual attempts to establish a consistent pattern of exercise behavior. These studies have found that self-efficacy predicts exercise behavior at different stages of exercise experience and that the relative influence of self-efficacy and outcome expectancy may change with experience (e.g., Marcus, Selby, Niaura, & Rossi, 1992; McAuley, 1991; McAuley & Jacobson, 1991; McAuley & Rowney, 1990; Poag-DuCharme & Brawley, 1993).

For example, Rodgers and Brawley (1993) assessed self-efficacy and outcome expectancy/value (the product of outcome expectancy and outcome value) in the study of a university sample of beginning weight trainers. An initial 2-day "How to Weight Train" workshop increased weight-training self-efficacy and outcome expectancy/value (i.e., the belief that weight training will increase strength and the value of this result). Preclinic outcome expectancy/value was a better predictor of initial weight-training intentions than was self-efficacy. However, self-efficacy was a better predictor than outcome expectancy/value of participants' intentions to continue weight training on their own beyond the workshop. In contrast to this study of beginning exercisers, Desharnais et al. (1986) found that, among experienced exercisers, both self-efficacy and outcome expectancy/value predicted intentions to exercise.

The findings of these two studies suggest that people who have little or no prior experience with a specific exercise behavior may base their decision to try it largely on their beliefs about the probability and value of possible benefits. However, because initial experience with exercise strongly influences self-efficacy (e.g., Ewart, Taylor, Reese, & Debusk, 1983), they quickly develop beliefs about self-efficacy that become the primary determinant of persistence. The difference in the influence of self-efficacy and outcome expectancy/value at different degrees of experience may be due to the difference in the power of proximal and distal consequences. The benefits of an exercise program (or other promotion behavior) may take months or even years to accrue, but the difficulties and discomforts that may lead to lower self-efficacy and discouragement are immediate.

Poag-DuCharme and Brawley (1993) examined the attendance of adult females initiating unstructured, self-regulated patterns of exercise. They assessed self-efficacy, intentions, and attendance over a 16-week period. Two types of self-efficacy were assessed: self-efficacy for scheduling exercise, and self-efficacy for overcoming exercise barriers. Both self-efficacy measures predicted intentions to exercise at onset and mid-program (week 9); however, only self-efficacy for scheduling predicted attendance at the exercise site during weeks 9 through 16. Also, for those people who adhered to the program, scheduling self-efficacy accounted for variance beyond that accounted for by past behavior. McAuley (1993) reported similar findings.

Poag-DuCharme and Brawley (1993) examined 207 adults, who already were regular exercisers, over the course of a 12-week structured community-based program. Three types of self-efficacy were assessed: self-efficacy for the exercise components, self-efficacy for scheduling, and self-efficacy for overcoming barriers. The types of self-efficacy that predicted exercise intentions varied at different points in the program. Exercise-component self-efficacy predicted intentions early in the program; all three self-efficacy measures predicted intentions at midpoints, and both exercise-component and scheduling self-efficacy predicted intentions in the later weeks of the program. In addition, both scheduling self-efficacy and intentions independently contributed to the prediction of class attendance, more so in the later weeks (7–12) than the earlier part of the program. More recently, Poag-DuCharme (1993) demonstrated that self-efficacy mediated the perceived influence of exercisers' goals on attendance and intended exercise intensity at two different points in an exercise program. These studies and others (e.g., McAuley, 1992, 1993) suggest the need to study changes in the relationship between self-efficacy and exercise over time.

DETECTION

Detection behaviors provide information about the presence or absence of an unhealthy or potentially unhealthy condition. Unlike prevention and promotion behaviors, detection behaviors do not directly reduce one's risk of disease or enhance one's state of health. Breast self-examinations do not prevent breast tumors or affect their growth, and HIV-screening tests do not reduce the risk of HIV infection or enhance the immune system. Instead, the information provided by these detection behaviors and others influences health *only* if the individual uses the information to make decisions about prevention and promotion behaviors, such as seeking early treatment or changing personal habits to reduce the disease's progression. The link between detection information and behavior depends in part on the individual's interpretation of the information (e.g., certainty–uncertainty; see Cioffi, 1991, 1994). Thus, social cognitive theory and research on detection behavior must take into account the fact that *informa-*

tion is the most immediate consequence of performance. Detection behaviors may be performed by the individual (e.g., breast self-examinations, blood pressure self-monitoring) or by a health professional (e.g., mammogram, HIV-seropositivity testing, tuberculosis screening).

Some detection behaviors, such as going to a clinic for a mammogram, a tuberculosis screening, or an HIV-seropositivity test, require little skill on the part of the individual and are, therefore, unlikely to be significantly influenced by beliefs about self-efficacy for their performance. For example, a woman's self-efficacy for correctly performing a mammogram will have no impact on her decision to seek one, because only trained medical professionals perform mammograms. Her self-efficacy for getting herself to the clinic probably will be important, but getting oneself to a clinic is not a detection behavior. Decisions to seek detection behaviors performed by health professionals (e.g., HIV testing) are often very difficult and distressing, but these decisions are probably more influenced by fear and anticipated fear than by self-efficacy for any particular behavior (See Maddux, Chap. 1, this volume; Kirsch, Chap. 12, this volume). Some self-performed detection behaviors, such a breast self-examinations, require considerable skill in proper execution *and* regular performance, and are therefore more likely to be influenced by self-efficacy beliefs.

Self-Efficacy and Breast Self-Examinations

About 10% of American women eventually will develop breast cancer (American Cancer Society, 1988). Despite advances in medical technology, about 95% of breast cancers are discovered by women themselves (American Cancer Society, 1988), usually by accident, when the tumor is large enough to be easily detected (Foster et al., 1978; Ogawa, Tominaga, Yoshida, Kubo, & Takeuchi, 1987). Cancers detected at an earlier stage, however, mean a better prognosis for the patient (Miller, Chamberlain, & Tsechkovski, 1985; Seidman, Gelb, Silverberg, LaVerda, & Lubera, 1987). Breast self-examination (BSE) is an effective method of early detection of tumors (Cady, 1986). Although studies indicate the BSE is easily learned, only 14–40% of American women perform BSE regularly (Alagna & Reddy, 1984; Morra, 1985).

Several of the major variables employed in social cognitive models of health behavior have been shown to be associated with regular performance of BSE. Research on perceived vulnerability, usually referred to in the BSE literature as susceptibility to breast cancer, generally has found that women with higher rates of BSE practice perceive themselves as more susceptible to breast cancer than do women with lower rates of BSE practice (Cole & Gorman, 1984; Hisrchfield-Bartek, 1982; Kelly, 1979; Massey, 1986; Ronis & Harel, 1989), although exceptions do exist (Rutledge, 1987; Bennett, Lawrence, Fleischmann, Gifford, & Slack, 1983).

Response efficacy, which is an outcome expectancy, has been defined in the BSE research as the perceived benefits of early detection of breast cancer and has been found to be an important predictor of BSE (e.g., Ronis & Harel, 1989; Ronis & Kaiser, 1989). However, because BSE is a detection behavior, not a prevention behavior, measures of response efficacy should examine beliefs about the effectiveness of BSE in providing accurate information about the presence or absence of breast tumors. At least one study assessed response efficacy in this way and found that it was predictive of intentions to perform BSE (Rippetoe & Rogers, 1987).

At least two BSE studies have examined outcome value. Kelly (1979) found that women who practiced BSE also believed that early detection is important. Also, Ronis and Harel (1989) found that women perceive breast cancer as potentially more severe when treated late than when treated early, a finding that suggests that women value the detection information provided by BSE.

A number of studies have examined the importance of self-efficacy for correct BSE performance, although most of these studies have not employed the term self-efficacy. These studies have generally shown that the belief that one can perform BSE correctly is positively associated with its performance (e.g., Alagna, Morokoff, Bevett, & Reddy, 1987; Rippetoe & Rogers, 1987; Ronis & Kaiser, 1989). Because the effectiveness of BSE as a detection behavior depends not only on performing it correctly, but also on performing it regularly, assessing only self-efficacy for correct performance may not be sufficient for predicting regular performance. Self-efficacy theory stipulates that specificity of a self-efficacy measures and the target behavior is important in determining the predictive utility of the measure. This principle was supported by Buckner and Maddux (1994) who found that self-efficacy for remembering to perform BSE monthly was a strong independent predictor of self-reported monthly BSE. The distinction between self-efficacy for performing BSE and self-efficacy for remembering to perform BSE had not been previously demonstrated. These results suggest that measures of self-efficacy for BSE and other health behaviors (detection, prevention and promotion) should not be limited to assessing perception of competence with the behavior in question, but should include assessment of self-efficacy for performing the behavior daily, weekly, or monthly (depending on the recommendation) and integrating it into one's life. In fact, self-efficacy for remembering to perform a health behavior is likely to be much more important than self-efficacy for simply performing the behavior correctly, because so many health behaviors require the frequent or scheduled performance of a behavior that requires a low level of skill for correct performance (e.g., taking a pill, buckling a seatbelt, using a condom, brushing or flossing teeth).

SELF-EFFICACY IN MODELS OF HEALTH BEHAVIOR

Self-efficacy can be best understood and appreciated by understanding its role in a comprehensive model of health decisions and actions. The self-efficacy construct, in some form, plays an important role in the social cognitive models of health behavior that have received the most empirical investigation and support: the health belief model (Rosenstock, 1974), protection motivation theory (Maddux & Rogers, 1983; Rogers, 1975, 1983), and the theory of reasoned action/planned behavior (Ajzen & Madden, 1986; Fishbein & Ajzen, 1975).

HEALTH BELIEF MODEL

The health belief model (HBM) was developed by social psychologists in the 1950s to attempt to explain the public's poor compliance with public health programs, such as immunizations and tuberculosis screenings (Janz & Becker, 1984; Rosenstock, 1974). The HBM consists of the following four major cognitive components:

1. Perceived susceptibility—individuals' assessment of their risk for a particular health threat
2. Perceived severity of the health threat
3. Perceived benefits of the behavior recommended to reduce the threat
4. Perceived barriers to action—individuals' perception of the possible undesirable consequences that might result from performance of the recommended prevention behavior.

In addition, the likelihood of taking action is influenced by a *cue-to-action*—an external event (e.g., mass-media message) or internal event (e.g., symptom of possible illness) that prompts the individual to act on the aforementioned beliefs (Janz & Becker, 1984; Prentice-Dunn & Rogers, 1986; Rosenstock, 1974).

The HBM has received considerable support in numerous investigations of preventive health behaviors and compliance with medical regimens (Janz & Becker, 1984; Rosenstock, 1974), although applications to exercise have been scant. The strongest support has been found for the impact of perceived barriers, probably because of the relationship between perceived barriers and perceived self-efficacy, and the weakest for perceived severity (consistent with research using protection motivation theory). Recent research has shown that *social support* is important in addition to the original components (e.g., Kelly, Zyzanski, & Alemagno, 1991; Uzark, Becker, Dielman, & Rocchini, 1987; Zimmerman & Conner, 1989), consistent with research on self-efficacy and cardiovascular rehabilitation (Ewart, Chap. 7, this volume) and the role of perceived social norms in the theory of reasoned action/planned behavior. Also, HBM researchers have begun to incorporate a self-efficacy factor into the model (Rosenstock, Strecher, & Becker, 1988).

PROTECTION MOTIVATION THEORY

Protection motivation theory (PMT) was developed originally to explain inconsistencies in the research on fear appeals and attitude change (Rogers, 1975) but since that time has been employed primarily as a model for health decision making and action. PMT is concerned with decisions to protect oneself from harmful or stressful life events, although it can also be viewed as a theory of coping with such events (e.g., Rippetoe & Rogers, 1987). In PMT, decisions to engage (or not engage) in health-related behaviors are influenced by two primary cognitive processes: *threat appraisal*, an evaluation of the factors that influence the likelihood of engaging in a potentially unhealthy behavior (e.g., smoking, sex without a condom); and *coping appraisal*, an evaluation of the factors that influence the likelihood of engaging in a recommended preventive response (e.g., exercise, using a condom). The most common index of protection motivation is a measure of *intentions* to perform the recommended preventive behavior, as defined by the theory of reasoned action/planned behavior.

Threat appraisal is influenced primarily by *perceived vulnerability*, the person's estimation of the degree of risk for specific health hazard if current unhealthy behaviors are continued (e.g., risk for developing lung cancer if one continues smoking) and *perceived severity*, the person's evaluation of the degree of harm, discomfort, or damage that will result from the specified health hazard (e.g., the perceived severity of lung cancer). As perceived vulnerability and perceived severity increase, the probability of engaging in the unhealthy behavior decreases. However, the probability of performing the unhealthy behavior is *increased* by the perceived intrinsic rewards (e.g., pleasure) and extrinsic rewards (e.g., approval) that result from the behavior.

Coping appraisal is influenced primarily by *response efficacy*, the person's estimation of the likelihood of the effectiveness of a proposed coping strategy in preventing the specified health hazard (e.g., that quitting smoking will reduce one's risk for lung cancer) and *self-efficacy*, belief in the ability to implement the recommended coping behavior or strategy (e.g., the belief that one can quit smoking). As response efficacy and self-efficacy increase, so does the probability of engaging in the recommended preventive behavior. In addition, however, the probability of performing the preventive coping response is decreased by the perceived response costs (e.g., loss of pleasure, loss of social support).

Strong support has been found for the effect of perceptions of vulnerability, response efficacy, and self-efficacy on health-related intentions and behavior (e.g., Maddux & Rogers, 1983; Stanley & Maddux, 1986; Wurtele, 1986; Wurtele & Maddux, 1987). Perceived severity has not proven a robust variable (see previous section on the health belief model), possibly because of the lack of variability of peoples' perceptions of the severity of most of the health threats examined in PMT research (e.g., cancer, heart disease). Research has demonstrated that PMT is a useful model for understanding not only self-protective behavior, but also behavior that protects specific significant others (e.g., Campis, Prentice-Dunn, & Lyman, 1989), endangered animal species (e.g., donating money to an animal protection society; Shelton & Rogers, 1981), and society at large (e.g., engaging in nuclear war prevention activities; Axelrod & Newton, 1991).

THEORY OF REASONED ACTION AND PLANNED BEHAVIOR

The theory of reasoned action (Fishbein & Ajzen, 1975) and its recent extension, the theory of planned behavior (Ajzen, 1985, 1988), assume that people make rational decisions about their behavior based on information or beliefs about the behavior and its consequences—what consequences they expect and the importance of those consequences. Both theories propose that behavioral *intentions* are the most important determinants and predictors of behavior and that intentions are a function of *attitudes* toward the behavior and goal in question and the person's perceptions of *social norms* regarding the behavior.

The assessment of attitudes toward the behavior consists of assessments of beliefs about expected consequences and the evaluation or importance of those consequences. Social-norm measures assess a person's belief that specific important others believe that the person should or should not perform the behavior and the person's motivation to comply with these other people. Thus, perceptions of social norms influence intentions because of the person's expectations regarding the possible reactions of others and the importance or value of those reactions. For this reason, both the attitudes and social-norm components can be defined in terms of expected outcomes and the importance or value of those outcomes.

The theory of planned behavior (TPB) builds on the theory of reasoned action by proposing that for behaviors that are difficult to execute, prediction of intentions and behavior must include an assessment of the person's *control* over the execution of the behavior. However, in TPB, the assessment of *perceived behavioral control* is used as a proxy measure of actual control. Therefore, the control component of TPB is similar to a self-efficacy expectancy, in that it involves perceptions that one possesses both the resources and opportunities to execute the behavior or attain the goal (Ajzen, 1985). Perceived control is viewed as a direct determinant of behavior, as well as an indirect determinant of behavior via its effect on intentions.

Although the *definition* of perceived behavioral control is highly similar to self-efficacy expectancy, its *measurement* presents some ambiguities. Early studies assessed perceived control in terms of perceived barriers to performing the behavior (e.g., Ajzen & Madden, 1986). Such measurement makes perceived control more similar to the perceived barriers component of the health belief model than to self-efficacy expectancy. Also unclear is whether perceived control should be measured as control over the behavior, or control over goal attainment (e.g., Madden, Ellen, & Ajzen, 1992). The assessment of perceived control in some TPB studies is concerned with the expectation of attaining a specific goal, rather than performing specific behaviors or executing a specific plan of action that is expected to lead to the goal. For example, in Schifter and Ajzen's (1985) study of weight loss, perceived control was measured by items concerning "the likelihood that if you try you will manage to reduce weight over the next 6 weeks" and "your best estimate that an attempt on your part to reduce weight will be successful." These measures do not address the persons' beliefs about their ability to perform effectively a behavior or execute a plan of action that may lead to weight loss, such as "reducing your caloric intake by 25%" or "engaging in moderate exercise three times a week." Instead, these items entail a somewhat vague assessment of the effectiveness of "trying" and "attempting."

One of the major strengths of TRA/TPB is its emphasis on measures that are specific to the behavior, context, and goal in question. The theory recognizes, for example, that there are a wide variety of healthy behaviors, that these behaviors can be performed at various times and in various settings, and that people engage in healthy behaviors for a variety of goal-related reasons. An accurate TRA/TPB-based assessment and prediction of healthy behavior takes into account this complexity and specificity. Numerous studies have indicated that the TRA/TPB is a useful model for understanding and predicting healthy behavior (e.g., Brawley & Rodgers,

1992; Godin, 1993; Godin & Shephard, 1990; McAuley & Courneya, 1993; Rodgers & Brawley, 1993; Yordy & Lent, 1993).

COMMON THEORETICAL ELEMENTS

The preceding models share the assumption that human beings are goal-directed, self-regulating, and capable of forethought, planning, and fairly rational decision making. However, the similarities among these models goes beyond their general assumptions about human nature. They also share a number of specific components or ingredients that should compel researchers to view these models not as competitors to be pitted against one another, but rather as complementary and amenable to integration. Taken together, these models suggest that a small number of major factors influence health decisions and behaviors: (a) outcome expectancies (perceived vulnerability, response efficacy/expected benefits, and expected costs); (b) outcome value; (c) self-efficacy expectancy; and (d) intention.

OUTCOME EXPECTANCIES

An outcome expectancy concerns our belief that certain behaviors probably will or will not result in certain outcomes (or goals, if they are desired outcomes). In the prediction of health behavior, the following three kinds of outcome expectancies are important:

1. Perceived vulnerability or susceptibility to a health threat
2. The efficacy of the recommended health behavior in reducing the probability of the threat and other expected benefits
3. Expected costs.

Outcome expectancies also can be categorized into *stimulus expectancies*, beliefs about external events that might result from an action, and *response expectancies*, beliefs about nonvolitional responses, such as emotions or pain (Kirsch, 1985). Although both types of outcome expectancies are important, for many behaviors, response expectancies may be more important than stimulus expectancies. Most people wish to avoid injury and illness because they are uncomfortable and painful conditions, in addition to being inconvenient, impractical, and often expensive. The major desired and expected outcomes that lead people to engage in health promotion behaviors are feelings of physical and psychological well-being, not additional material goods or financial rewards. Even increased physical attractiveness is valued more for its desired emotional benefits than its material benefits. In addition, the major costs associated with most protection, promotion, and detection behaviors are stimulus expectancies (e.g., anxiety, pain, discomfort, inconvenience, loss of pleasure).

Because perceived vulnerability or susceptibility, as defined by the health belief model and protection motivation theory, concerns an expected event, it is an outcome expectancy. In studies of protection behavior, it is assumed that subjects are not engaging in the recommended protective behavior under investigation; thus, implicit in the assessment of perceived vulnerability in these studies is the assumption that persons are to estimate their vulnerability to a health threat should they *not* engage in a recommended behavior or should they continue engaging in their current pattern of behavior. Recent research has provided some evidence for the importance of making the conditional nature of vulnerability measures explicit (e.g., "If you do not quit smoking now, how likely are you to develop lung cancer?"; Ronis, 1992). Although detection behaviors do not directly reduce the risk of an unhealthy condition or directly improve health, conditional measures of perceived vulnerability in detection studies nonetheless may be useful (e.g., "If you do not begin performing breast self-examinations, how likely are you to die of breast cancer?") The notion of perceived vulnerability will be less important for people with health promotion goals because they are not motivated primarily by preventing negative health outcomes.

Of the theories described in this chapter, only the theory of reasoned action/planned behavior does not specify a perceived vulnerability component. Because TRA/TPB was not developed specifically for health behaviors, the omission of perceived vulnerability is understandable. In TRA/TPB, assessments of attitude toward the behavior, which deal with expected consequences and their importance, may presuppose that people engage in protection and detection behaviors because they perceive some personal vulnerability; however, direct assessment of perceived vulnerability may be important in TRA/TPB research involving health behavior.

Both the health belief model and protection motivation theory include outcome expectancy in their consideration of the expected benefits (desired outcomes) and costs (undesired outcomes) of the recommended health behavior. For most health protection and promotion behaviors, the expected desired outcomes (e.g., improved health) are distal, whereas the expected undesired outcomes (e.g., discomfort, inconvenience) are proximal. Some detection behaviors (e.g., breast self-examination) provide proximal benefits in the form of information, although the major benefits that result from accurate detection—morbidity reduction through early treatment—are distal. TRA/TPB includes outcome expectancy in the assessment of attitudes toward the behavior (i.e., expected outcomes) and social norms (i.e., probable reactions of other people). These attitudes and social norms are essentially types of expected benefits and costs.

OUTCOME VALUE

Outcome value, or goal value, is the value or importance attached to specific goals or outcomes in specific contexts or situations, sometimes referred to as *reinforcement value* (Rotter, 1954) or *incentive value* (McClelland, 1985). An outcome or goal can be important because we wish to attain it (money, better health) or because we wish to avoid it (e.g., cancer, obesity). In protection motivation theory and the health belief model, the perceived severity of the health-threat component is an outcome value. In the TRA/TPB, outcome value is evident in the assessment of attitudes toward the behavior (evaluation of expected outcomes) and social norms (importance placed on reactions of significant others).

SELF-EFFICACY EXPECTANCY

Self-efficacy has been incorporated into the health belief model, protection motivation theory, TRA/TPB. As noted previously, however, the lack of clarity in the definition and measurement of perceived behavior control in studies of TRA/TPB raises some questions about its similarity to self-efficacy. To be fair, however, self-efficacy also has been defined and measured differently across studies by different researchers. Thus, it is difficult to decide to which self-efficacy measure we should compare measures of perceived behavior control to determine their similarity.

INTENTION

An intention is what one says one plans to do. Research on the TRA has shown that intentions are good predictors of behavior. Research on the TPB has shown that behavior is directly influenced by both intentions and self-efficacy/perceived behavioral control. People seem capable of acting without making conscious decisions to act (i.e., without developing an intention or plan) based on their expectations for success.

Intention seems to be a simple notion, and its definition and measurement are rather straightforward under most conditions. However, in a number of common situations relevant to health and exercise behavior, the distinctions between intentions, self-efficacy expectancy, and outcome expectancy become fuzzy. Specifically, some researchers have raised questions about these distinctions in situations in which performing a behavior may lead to immediate, involuntary aversive reactions, such as fear, pain, or discomfort (see Maddux, Chap. 1, this volume; Kirsch, Chap. 12, this volume). Because expected pain and discomfort are common perceived barriers to exercise behavior, these questions should be of interest to health behavior theorists and researchers.

SELF-EFFICACY AND HABIT

A *habit* is a behavior that has been performed repeatedly and is now performed automatically, without benefit of a conscious decision that involves the consideration of at least one other alternative course of action (Ronis, Yates, & Kirscht, 1989). Many important health-related behaviors become habitual only with great difficulty, if at all, for example, exercise (Dishman, 1982; Belisle, Roskies, & Levesque, 1987) dental flossing (McCaul, Glasgow, & O'Neill, 1992), and using safety belts (Rudd & Geller, 1985). Because behaviors that are initiated are not always maintained, understanding how behaviors become habits is important for understanding the role of self-efficacy and other social cognitive factors in health behavior.

Habit theory (Ronis et al., 1989) is based on the distinction between *controlled cognitive processes*—those that are intentional and require conscious effort—and *automatic cognitive processes*—those that are so well learned through repetition that they do not require conscious effort, but are set in motion by situational cues (Schneider & Shiffrin, 1977). According to habit theory, a frequently repeated health behavior (e.g., toothbrushing, wearing seatbelts) may eventually come under the control of situational cues. Infrequently repeated behaviors (e.g., vaccinations, medical checkups, HIV testing) remain under the control of conscious cognitive processes and deliberate decisions.

Situational cues can be important in at least two ways—as *cues-to-decisions* and as *cues-to-action*. For frequently repeated behaviors that come under the control of situational cues, the situation contains cues-to-action. For health behaviors that never become habitual and that continue to be influenced primarily by controlled cognitive process decisions, situational cues will retain indirect influence over these behaviors, because the situation will contain cues-to-decision that elicit controlled cognitive processes and decision making. For example, clear weather or the sight of one's running shoes or bicycle may initiate a process of deciding whether or not to go for a run or a ride. Seeing a television commercial for athletic gear or a health club may be a cue for deciding whether to exercise. These cues to not elicit the behavior itself, but they do elicit the social cognitive factors involved in deciding and intending.

The distinction between cues-to-decision and cues-to-action suggests that social cognitive factors such as self-efficacy may be most influential at the initiation of health behavior and in the early stages of performance, but may become less important with repeated performance. For example, as behaviors become habitual, self-efficacy expectancies are likely to remain highly correlated with behavior, but are less likely to *influence* behavior, because habitual behaviors are automatic and not the result of decisions. Also, outcome expectancies and outcome value may lose their influence as behaviors becomes habitual, because the reasons for engaging in the behavior may move out of awareness.

HABITS AND STAGES OF CHANGE

Behavior change, including changes in healthy behavior, is best understood as occurring in stages or steps (e.g., Brawley & Rodgers, 1992; Prochaska, DiClemente, & Norcross, 1992; Schwarzwer, 1992; Weinstein & Sandman, 1992), and the factors that influence behavior may change from one stage to another. Therefore, we need dynamic (rather than static) models that acknowledge that different issues and perhaps different decision rules may be involved at different stages (e.g., initiation vs. maintenance; Weinstein, 1993; Weinstein & Sandman, 1992). Habit theory also deals with changes in the influence of the factors that determine behavior and therefore needs to be incorporated into these dynamic stage models of change.

The transtheoretical model (Prochaska et al., 1992) and the precaution-adoption-process model (Weinstein, 1988; Weinstein & Sandman, 1992) are the most well-developed stage models. Although the number and names of the stages differ among the models, the models agree on the importance of distinguishing between awareness of a health issue, engagement in or contemplation of the issue (e.g., thinking about the pros and cons of changing behavior), committing and planning to change behavior, actively changing behavior, and maintaining the behavior change. Implicit in each model is the assumption that behavior change begins largely under the control of deliberate cognitive processes (contemplation, decisions, intentions, plans), but gradually becomes controlled more by automatic cognitive processes. As the new behavior is repeated over time, situational cues-to-decision develop, eliciting the cognitive process that results in decisions and intentions. As these cues become more numerous and powerful, the person enters the maintenance stage in which situational cues easily elicit the decision-making process, but elicit few actual behaviors. Because the elicited cognitive process does not always result in an intention to engage in health-related behavior, the person may experience relapse. However, the person also relapses because few behaviors are automatically elicited by situational cues, which have not yet become cues-to-action. As more behaviors come under the control of automatic cognitive processes (e.g., turning left to go to the health club rather than right to go home, buckling a seatbelt), the person relapses less often.

As decisions and intentions lead to action, and as actions are maintained and repeated over time, actions may come to be performed automatically in response to situational cues such that they are no longer under volitional control. In some cases a *habit stage* may evolve in which behavior is primarily controlled by cues-to-action. For example, frequent repetition of buckling a seatbelt when getting in the driver's side of one's own car probably will lead to automatic performance of buckling under those specific conditions, although buckling the seatbelt when getting into the passenger side of someone else's car may still require engagement of controlled cognitive processes.

The key to bringing multiple-act health regimens under the control of automatic processes and making them habitual is in the consistent pairing of discrete preparatory behaviors with specific situational cues (e.g., running or walking at the scheduled time and from the same place everyday). As cues-to-decision become cues-to-action and the person moves through these stages of change, behavior comes increasingly under the control of automatic processes, and the cognitive variables emphasized in the models described here become increasingly less influential.

TOWARD AN INTEGRATED MODEL

Despite the scores of published studies on social cognitive models of healthy behavior, no consensus has yet been achieved concerning which model is the most useful. Empirical comparisons pitting one model against another have been few (only four such published studies between 1974 and 1991, according to Weinstein, 1993). More important, studies that place one model in competition against another are unlikely to be informative, given the strong similarities among the models. A better approach is to attempt to incorporate the major features of the relevant models into a single model and then attempt to determine the relative importance of the features of the new inclusive model.

Because it includes most of the major components of the other models, the theory of planned behavior provides a good vehicle for integration. The TPB offers the following advantages:

1. Perceived behavioral control includes (although it is not identical to) the notion of self-efficacy.

2. It includes a perceived social-norms component that is not featured prominently in the other models.
3. The definition and measurement of attitudes toward the behavior incorporates outcome expectancy and outcome value in its assessment of beliefs about expected consequences and the importance of those consequences.
4. The theory includes intention as a variable that links attitudes and beliefs to behavior.

Modifications of the theory of planned behavior drawn from the other models would include the following:

1. Perceived vulnerability or susceptibility (as found in the health belief model and protection motivation theory) may be incorporated into the attitude component as an outcome expectancy for the negative health consequences that might result from maintaining one's present health behavior (e.g., "If I continue my sedentary life style, I will increase my chances of developing heart disease.").
2. A perceived severity component (as found in the health belief model and protection motivation theory) may be incorporated into the attitude component in the form of the importance of the negative health consequences of maintaining one's current health behavior.
3. Incorporating the concept of situational cues and the distinction between cues-to-decision and cues-to-action may provide a foundation for expanding the theory of planned behavior into a stage or phase theory. This revision would include the concept of habit and would assume (as do other stage models) that people move in and out of stages or phases as they attempt to make difficult behavioral changes.

Figure 1 offers an integrated model based on the TPB that incorporates what research on the other models tells us about the important influences on health and exercise behavior. In this model, behavior is the result of three influences: intentions, self-efficacy for the new behavior, and cues-to-action. Intentions are the most immediate and powerful determinant of behavior. Self-efficacy influences behavior both directly and indirectly through its influence on intentions (i.e., intentions may mediate the influence of self-efficacy). Situational cues influence behavior directly when a behavior has been performed repeatedly in the presence of the same cues and is prompted automatically by these cues. When situational cues automatically prompt behavior, we refer to these cues as cues-to-action and to the behavior as a habit.

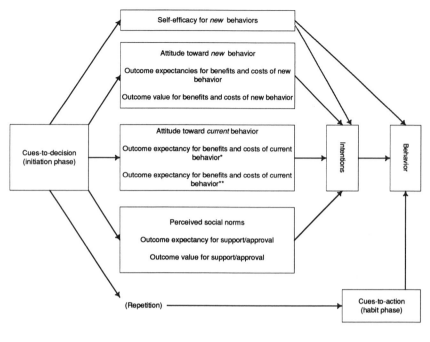

*Includes perceived vulnerability to negative health consequences.

**Includes perceived severity of negative health consequences.

FIGURE 1. A revised theory of planned behavior that incorporates situational cues and habits.

Intentions are determined by four factors: self-efficacy for the new behavior, attitude toward the new behavior, attitude toward the current behavior, and perceived social norms. Independent assessment of attitudes toward the current (unhealthy) and new (healthier) behavior is important, because people who consider changing their behavior will engage in a comparative analysis of the benefits and costs of the current and new behaviors. Attitude toward the current and new behaviors consists of outcomes expectancies (expected benefits and costs) and outcome value (importance of these benefits and costs). Assessment of attitude toward the new behavior must also include an assessment of perceived vulnerability to the relevant negative health outcomes and perceived severity of these expected negative health outcomes (as noted in protection motivation theory and the health belief model).

Self-efficacy expectancy for the new behavior replaces perceived behavioral control. Perceived behavioral control incorporates both self-efficacy expectancy and outcome expectancy, which theory and research suggest should be given separate consideration. Thus, perceived personal control should be defined and measured as a self-efficacy expectancy rather than a hybrid of self-efficacy expectancy and outcome expectancy. Another reason for limiting the definition and measurement of perceived control to self-efficacy is that outcome expectancies are already incorporated in the model in the assessment of attitudes toward the behavior (e.g., expected outcomes and their value or importance). Thus, including outcome expectancies in a measure of perceived control would be redundant. The extensive theory and research on the development of self-efficacy and its influence on behavior would then be directly applicable to this new definition of perceived behavioral control.

Attitudes toward the current and new behaviors are defined and measured as outcome expectancies and outcome values, as currently practiced in TPB research. Because perceived social norms also are concerned with expected consequences and the importance of these consequences (i.e., the expected reactions of others and the importance of those reactions), perceived social norms could be assessed by a combination of outcome expectancy measures (e.g., "If I attend my aerobics class, my spouse me will approve of/support me.") and outcome value measures (e.g., "The approval/support of my spouse is very important to me.") The research on TRA/TPB suggests that the strong influence of social norms warrants giving expected social outcomes consideration separate from other types of expected nonsocial outcomes.

These cognitive influences are triggered by situational cues that may be either external (e.g., a Nike commercial on television that triggers cognitions about the pros and cons of exercise) or internal (e.g., a cough that triggers cognitions about trying to quit smoking). When situational cues trigger the cognitive process that leads to behavioral intentions to behave but do not automatically prompt the behavior itself, we call them cues-to-decision. For complex sequences of behaviors that require some deliberation and planning for their execution, cues-to-decision will remain important over time. However, if the decision-making process and the behavior are repeated sufficiently over time in the presence of the same cues, these initial cues-to-decision may become cues-to-action, a process that may take considerable time for some behaviors. As cues-to-decision become cues-to-action and behavior becomes less deliberate and more automatic, the individual gradually moves into the habit phase, in which he acts without the social-cognitive information processing (i.e., considering beliefs, expectancies, and social norms) that may have influenced the initial intentions to act. Thus, the social cognitive factors important for the initiation of a behavior and the early period of maintenance may, for some behaviors, become less important over time.

SUMMARY

The models and theories that have guided the vast majority of the research on health behavior share a number of basic assumptions about the rational nature of humankind and the importance of beliefs, expectancies, and intentions in predicting and determining behavior (see also Weinstein, 1993). Because these models assume that expected consequences are powerful determinants of behavior, knowing people's reasons for doing what they do is essential when trying to predict what they will do, or when trying to get them to change what they do. Therefore, understanding theory and research on health behavior will be aided by understanding the different types of health-related goals to which people may aspire—protection, promotion, and detection goals.

These models also share a number of specific variables: outcome expectancy, outcome value, self-efficacy expectancy, and intention. The notion of habit development and the role of situational cues in habit development suggest that modification of these social cognitive models may be necessary. Specifically, the idea that over time, behaviors move from the influence of controlled cognitive processes to automatic (cue-based) cognitive processes suggests that the social cognitive factors that are crucial in the initial stages of the performance of health behavior may become less crucial as behavior is performed with sufficient frequency and consistency.

Because these models are more similar to than different from each other, research that pits one model against another in an attempt to support one and refute the other may not be the most productive use of researchers' efforts. Instead, theorists and researchers might better direct their energies toward integrating the major models into a single model and then conducting research that examines the relative importance of various social cognitive variables in the context of different health behaviors and situations. The goal of this kind of research would not be the determination of which model is better than the others, or even which variables are more important than others, but instead to determine the relative utility of variables and changes in relative utility with different behaviors and situations and over time. (See Weinstein, 1993, for details on research strategies.) Because of its inclusiveness, the theory of planned behavior, with some simple but essential modifications, may provide a good foundation on which to build an integrated model.

REFERENCES

Ajzen, I. (1985). From intentions to actions: A theory of planned behavior. In J. Kuhl & J. Beckman (Eds.), *Action control: From cognition to behavior* (pp. 11–39). Heidelberg: Springer.

Ajzen, I. (1988). *Attitudes, personality, and behavior.* Chicago: Dorsey Press.

Ajzen, I., & Madden, T. J. (1986). Prediction of goal-directed behavior: Attitudes, intentions, and perceived behavioral control. *Journal of Experimental Social Psychology, 22,* 453–474.

Alagna, S. W., Morokoff, P. J., Bevett, J. M., & Reddy, D. M. (1987). Performance of breast self-examination by women at high risk for breast cancer. *Women and Health, 12,* 29–47.

Alagna, S. W., & Reddy, D. (1984). Predictors of proficient technique and successful lesion detection in breast self-examination. *Health Psychology, 3,* 113–127.

American Cancer Society. (1988). *Cancer facts & figures—1988.* New York: Author.

Axelrod, L. J., & Newton, J. W. (1991). Preventing nuclear war: Beliefs and attitudes as predictors of disarmist and deterrentist behavior. *Journal of Applied Social Psychology, 21,* 29–40.

Bandura, A. (1977). Self-efficacy: Toward a unifying theory of behavioral change. *Psychological Review, 84,* 191–215.

Bandura, A. (1986). *Social foundations of thought and action.* New York: Prentice-Hall.

Bandura, A. (1989). Human agency in social cognitive theory. *American Psychologist, 44,* 1175–1184.

Baumeister, R. F., & Scher, S. J. (1988). Self-defeating behavior patterns among normal individuals: Review and analysis of common self-destructive tendencies. *Psychological Bulletin, 104,* 3–22.

Belisle, M., Roskies, E., & Levesque, J. M. (1987). Improving adherence to physical activity. *Health Psychology, 6,* 159–172.

Bennett, S. E., Lawrence, R. S., Fleischmann, K. H., Gifford, C. S., & Slack, W. V. (1983). Profile of women practicing breast self-examination. *Journal of the American Medical Association, 249,* 488–491.

Brawley, L. R., & Horne, T. E. (1987, August). *Predictors of fitness class adherence: The use of attitudinal models.* Report: Project No. 8606-4042-2042, Canadian Fitness and Lifestyle Research Institute, Ottawa.

Brawley, L. R., & Horne, T. E. (1988, December). *Refining attitude–behavior models to predict adherence in normal and socially supportive conditions: Part I & II.* Report: Project No. 8706-4042-2099, Canadian Fitness and Lifestyle Institute, Ottawa.

Brawley, L. R., & Rodgers, W. M. (1992). Social psychological aspects of fitness promotion. In P. Seraganian (Ed.), *Exercise psychology: The influence of physical exercise on psychological processes* (pp. 254–298). New York: Wiley.

Brawley, L. R., & Rodgers, W. M. (1993). Social psychological aspects of fitness promotion. In P. Seraganian (Ed.), *Exercise psychology: The influence of physical exercise on psychological processes* (pp. 254–298). New York: Wiley.

Brown, J. D. (1991). Staying fit and staying well: Physical fitness as a moderator of life stress. *Journal of Personality and Social Psychology, 60,* 555–561.

Buckner, E., & Maddux, J. E. (1994). *Self-efficacy and breast self-examination: Performing versus remembering.* Unpublished manuscript, George Mason University, Fairfax, VA.

Cady, B. (1986, April). Breast cancer screening and diagnosis in a primary care practice. *Primary Care and Cancer,* 28–38.

Campis, L. K., Prentice-Dunn, S., & Lyman, R. D. (1989). Coping appraisal and parents' intentions to inform their children about sexual abuse: A protection motivation theory analysis. *Journal of Social and Clinical Psychology, 8,* 304–316.

Carver, C. S., & Scheier, M. F. (1982). Control theory: A useful conceptual framework for personality, social, clinical, and health psychology. *Psychological Bulletin, 92*, 111–135.

Carver, C. S., & Scheier, M. F. (1990). Origins and functions of positive and negative affect: A control-process view. *Psychological Review, 97*, 19–35.

Casperson, C. J., Powell, K. E., & Merritt, R. K. (1994). Measurement of health status and well-being. In C. Bouchard, R. J. Shephard, & T. Stephens (Eds.), *Physical Activity, fitness, and health: International proceedings and consensus statement* (pp. 180–202). Champaign, IL: Human Kinetics.

Cioffi, D. (1991). Asymmetry of doubt in medical self-diagnosis: The ambiguity of "uncertain wellness." *Journal of Personality and Social Psychology, 61*, 969–980.

Cioffi, D. (1994). When good news is bad news: Medical wellness as a nonevent. *Health Psychology, 13*, 63–72.

Cole, C. F., & Gorman, L. M. (1984). Breast self-examination: practices and attitudes of registered nurses. *Oncology Nursing Forum, 11*, 37–41.

Corcoran, K. J. (1991). Efficacy, "skills," reinforcement, and choice behavior. *American Psychologist, 46*, 155–157.

Corcoran, K. J., & Rutledge, M. W. (1989). Efficacy expectation changes as a function of hypothetical incentive in smokers. *Psychology of Addictive Behaviors, 3*, 22–28.

Cox, D. J., & Gonder-Frederick, L. (1992). Major developments in behavioral diabetes research. *Journal of Consulting and Clinical Psychology, 55*, 139–144.

Crabtree, M. K. (1986). Self-efficacy and social support as predictors of diabetic self-care. *Dissertation Abstracts International, 47*, 2369–2620.

Desharnais, R., Bouillon, J., & Godin, G. (1986). Self-efficacy and outcome expectations as determinants of exercise adherence. *Psychological Reports, 59*, 1157–1159.

Dishman, R. K. (1982). Compliance/adherence in health-related exercise. *Health Psychology, 1*, 237–267.

Dishman, R. K. (1988). *Exercise adherence: Its impact on public health.* Champaign, IL: Human Kinetics.

Dishman, R. K. (1993). Exercise adherence. In R. N. Singer, M. Murphy, & L. K. Tennant (Eds.), *Handbook of research on sport psychology* (pp. 779–798). New York: Macmillan.

Dishman, R. K., & Sallis, J. F. (1994). Determinants and interventions for physical activity and exercise. In C. Bouchard, R. J. Shephard, & T. Stephens (Eds.), *Physical activity, fitness, and health: International proceedings and consensus statement* (pp. 214–238). Champaign, IL: Human Kinetics.

Dubbert, P. M. (1992). Exercise in behavioral medicine. *Journal of Consulting and Clinical Psychology, 60*, 613–618.

Dzewaltowski, D. A., Noble, J. M., & Shaw, J. M. (1990). Physical activity participation: Social cognitive theory versus the theories of reasoned action and planned behavior. *Journal of Sport and Exercise Psychology, 12*, 388–405.

Eagley, A. H., & Chaiken, S. (1993). *The psychology of attitudes.* Fort Worth: Harcourt Brace Jovanovich.

Ewart, C. K. (1991). Social action theory for a public health psychology. *American Psychologist, 46*, 931–946.

Ewart, C. K., Taylor, B., Reese, L. B., & DeBusk, R. F. (1983). Effects of early postmyocardial infarction exercise testing on self-preception and subsequent physical activity. *The American Journal of Cardiology, 51*, 1076–1080.

Fishbein, M., & Ajzen, I. (1975). *Belief, attitude, intention, and behavior: An introduction to theory and research.* Reading, MA: Addison-Wesley.

Foster, R. S., Lang, S. P., Costanza, M. C., Worden, J. K., Haines, C. R., & Yates, J. W. (1978).

Breast self-examination practices and breast-cancer stage. *The New England Journal of Medicine, 299,* 265–270.

Garcia, A. W., & King, A. C. (1991). Predicting long-term adherence to aerobic exercise: A comparison of two models. *Journal of Sport and Exercise Psychology, 13,* 394–410.

Glasgow, R. E., McKaul, K. D., Schafer, L. C. (1987). Self-care behaviors and glycemic control in Type I diabetes. *Journal of Chronic Disease, 5,* 399–412.

Glasgow, R. E., Toobert, D. J., Riddle, M., Donnelly, J., Mitchell, D. L., & Calder, D. (1989). Diabetes-specific social learning variables and self-care behaviors among persons with Type II diabetes. *Health Psychology, 8,* 285–303.

Glatthaar, C., Welborn, T. A., Stenhouse, N. S., & Gracia-Webb, P. (1985). Diabetes and impaired glucose tolerance: A prevalence estimate based on the Busselton 1981 survey. *Medical Journal of Australia, 143,* 436–440.

Godin, G. (1993). The theories of reasoned action and planned behavior: Overview of findings, emerging research problems, and usefulness for exercise promotion. *Journal of Applied Sport Psychology, 5,* 141–157.

Godin, G., & Shephard, R. J. (1990). Use of attitude–behavior models in exercise promotion. *Sports Medicine, 10,* 103–121.

Goodall, T. A., & Halford, W. K. (1991). Self-management of diabetes mellitus: A critical review. *Health Psychology, 10,* 1–8.

Grossman, H. Y., Brink, S., & Hauser, S. T. (1987). Self-efficacy in adolescent girls and boys with insulin-dependent diabetes mellitus. *Diabetes Care, 10,* 324–329.

Haskell, W. L. (1994). Dose-response issues from a biological perspective. In C. Bouchard, R. J. Shephard, & T. Stephens (Eds.), *Physical activity, fitness, and health: International proceedings and consensus statement* (pp. 1030–1039). Champaign, IL: Human Kinetics.

Hirshfield-Bartek, J. (1982). Health beliefs and their influence on breast self-examination practices in women with breast cancer. *Oncology Nursing Forum, 9,* 77–81.

Janz, N. K., & Becker, M. H. (1984). The Health Belief Model: A decade later. *Health Education Quarterly, 11,* 1–47.

Kelly, P. T. (1979). Breast self-examinations: Who does them and why? *Journal of Behavioral Medicine, 2,* 31–38.

Kelly, R. B., Zyzanski, S. J., & Alemagno, S. A. (1991). Prediction of motivation and behavior change following health promotion: Role of health beliefs, social support, and self-efficacy. *Social Science and Medicine, 32,* 311–320.

Kingery, P. M., & Glasgow, R.E. (1989). Self-efficacy and outcome expectancies in the self-regulation of non-insulin dependent diabetes mellitus. *Health Education, 20,* 13–19.

Kirsch, I. (1982). Efficacy expectations or response predictions: The meaning of efficacy ratings as a function of task characteristics. *Journal of Personality and Social Psychology, 42,* 132–136.

Kirsch, I. (1985). Self-efficacy and expectancy: Old wine with new labels. *Journal of Personality and Social Psychology, 49,* 824–830.

Kirsch, I. (1986). Early research on self-efficacy: What we already know without knowing we knew. *Journal of Social and Clinical Psychology, 4,* 339–358.

Lau, R. R., Hartman, K. A., & Ware, J. E. (1986). Health as a value: Methodological and theoretical considerations. *Health Psychology, 5,* 25–43.

Lazarus, R. S., & Folkman, S. (1984). *Stress, coping, and appraisal.* New York: Springer.

Leary, M. R., & Maddux, J. E. (1987). Toward a viable interface between social and clinical/counseling psychology. *American Psychologist, 42,* 904–911.

Leventhal, H., Diefenbach, M., & Leventhal, E. A. (1992). Illness cognition: Using common sense to understand treatment adherence and affect cognition interaction. *Cognitive Therapy and Research, 16,* 143–163.

Madden, T. J., Ellen, P. S., & Ajzen, I. (1992). A comparison of the theory of planned behavior and the theory of reasoned action. *Personality and Social Psychology Bulletin, 1*, 3–9.

Maddux, J. E. (1991). Self-efficacy. In C. R. Snyder & D. R. Forsyth (Eds.), *Handbook of social and clinical psychology* (pp. 57–78). New York: Pergamon.

Maddux, J. E., Norton, L. W., & Stoltenberg, C. D. (1986). Self-efficacy expectancy, outcome expectancy, and outcome value: Relative effects on behavioral intentions. *Journal of Personality and Social Psychology, 51*, 783–789.

Maddux, J. E., & Rogers, R. W. (1983). Protection motivation and self-efficacy: A revised theory of fear appeals and attitude change. *Journal of Experimental Social Psychology, 19*, 469–479.

Maddux, J. E., Sherer, M., & Rogers, R. W. (1982). Self-efficacy expectancy and outcome expectancy: Their relationships and their effects on behavioral intentions. *Cognitive Therapy and Research, 6*, 207–211.

Maddux, J. E., & Stanley, M. A. (1986). Self-efficacy theory in contemporary psychology: An overview. *Journal of Social and Clinical Psychology, 4*, 249–255.

Maddux, J. E., Stoltenberg, C. D., & Rosenwein, R. (Eds.). (1987). *Social processes in clinical and counseling psychology*. New York: Springer-Verlag.

Manning, M. M., & Wright, T. M. (1983). Self-efficacy expectancies, outcome expectancies, and the persistance of pain control in childbirth. *Journal of Personality and Social Psychology, 45*, 421–431.

Marcus, B. H., Selby, V. C., Niaura, R. S., & Rossi, J. S. (1992). Self-efficacy and the stages of exercise behavior change. *Research Quarterly for Exercise and Sport, 63*, 60–66.

Massey, V. (1986). Perceived susceptibility to breast cancer and the practice of breast self-examination. *Nursing Research, 35*, 183–185.

Matarazzo, J. D., Weiss, S. M., Herd, J. A., Miller, N. E., & Weiss, S. M. (1984). *Behavioral health: A handbook of health enhancement and disease prevention*. New York: Wiley.

McAuley, E. (1991). Efficacy, attributional, and affective responses to exercise participation. *Journal of Sport and Exercise Psychology, 13*, 382–393.

McAuley, E. (1992). The role of efficacy cognitions in the prediction of exercise behavior of middle-aged adults. *Journal of Behavioral Medicine, 15*, 65–88.

McAuley, E. (1993). Self-efficacy and the maintenance of exercise participation in older adults. *Journal of Behavioral Medicine, 16*, 103–113.

McAuley, E. (1994). Physical activity and psychosocial outcomes. In C. Bouchard, R. J. Shephard, & T. Stephens (Eds.), *Physical activity, fitness, and health: International proceedings and consensus statement* (pp. 551–568). Champaign, IL: Human Kinetics.

McAuley, E., & Courneya, K. S. (1993). Adherence to exercise and physical activity as health-promoting behaviors: Attitudinal and self-efficacy influences. *Applied and Preventative Psychology, 2*, 65–77.

McAuley, E., & Jacobson, L. (1991). Self-efficacy and exercise participation in sedentary adult females. *American Journal of Health Promotion, 5*, 185–191.

McAuley, E., & Rowney, T. (1990). Exercise behavior and intentions: The mediating role of self-efficacy cognitions. In L. VanderVelden & J. H. Humphrey (Eds.), *Psychology and sociology of sport* (Vol. 2, pp. 3–15). New York: AMS Press.

McClelland, D. C. (1985). How motives, skills, and values determine what people do. *American Psychologist, 40*, 812–825.

McCaul, K. D., Glasgow, R. E., & O'Neill, H. K. (1992). The problem of creating habits: Establishing health-protective dental behaviors. *Health Psychology, 11*, 101–110.

McCaul, K. D., Glasgow, R. E., & Schafer, L. C. (1987). Diabetes regimen behaviors. *Medical Care, 25*, 868–881.

Miller, A. B., Chamberlain, J., & Tsechkovski, M. (1985). Self-examination in the early detection of breast cancer. *Journal of Chronic Disease, 38*, 527–540.

Morra, M. (1985). Breast self-examination today: An overview of its use and its value. *Seminar in Oncology Nursing, 1*, 170–175.

Ogawa, H., Tominaga, S., Yoshida, F., Kubo, K., & Takeuchi, S. (1987). Breast self-examination practice and clinical stages of breast cancer. *Japanese Journal of Cancer Research, 78*, 447–452.

Orme, C. M., & Binik, Y. M. (1989). Consistency of adherence across regimen demands. *Health Psychology, 8*, 27–43.

Padgett, D. K. (1991). Correlates of self-efficacy beliefs among patients with non-insulin dependent diabetes mellitus in Zagreb, Yugoslavia. *Patient Education and Counseling, 18*, 139–147.

Poag-DuCharme, K. A. (1993). *Goal-related perceptions of social-cognitive predictors of exercise behavior.* Unpublished dissertation. University of Waterloo, Waterloo, Ontario.

Poag-DuCharme, K. A., & Brawley, L. R. (1991a, October). *The goal dynamics of fitness classes: A preliminary analysis.* Paper presented at the annual meeting of the Canadian Society for Psychomotor Learning and Sport Psychology, London, Ontario.

Poag-DuCharme, K. A., & Brawley, L. R. (1991b, October). *The relationship of self-efficacy and social support to exercise intentions in the aged.* Paper presented at the annual meeting of the Canadian Society for Psychomotor Learning and Sport Psychology, London, Ontario.

Poag-DuCharme, K. A., & Brawley, L. R. (1993). Self-efficacy theory: Use in the prediction of exercise behavior in the community setting. *Journal of Applied Sport Psychology, 5*, 178–194.

Prentice-Dunn, S., & Rogers, R. W. (1986). Protection motivation theory and preventive health: Beyond the health belief model. *Health Education Research: Theory and Practice, 1*, 153–161.

Prochaska, J. O., DiClemente, C. C., & Norcross, J. C. (1992). In search of how people change: Applications to addictive behaviors. *American Psychologist, 47*, 1102–1114.

Rejeski, W. J. (1994). Dose-response issues from a psychosocial perspective. In C. Bouchard, R. J. Shephard, & T. Stephens (Eds.), *Physical activity, fitness, and health: International proceedings and consensus statement* (pp.1040–1055). Champaign, IL: Human Kinetics.

Rejeski, W. J., & Brawley, L. R. (1988). Defining the boundaries of sport psychology. *The Sport Psychologist, 2*, 231–242.

Rippetoe, P. A., & Rogers, R. W. (1987). Effects of components of protection motivation theory on adaptive and maladaptive coping with a health threat. *Journal of Personality and Social Psychology, 52*, 596–604.

Rodgers, W. M., & Brawley, L. R. (1991a). The role of outcome expectancies in participation motivation. *Journal of Sport and Exercise Psychology, 13*, 411–427.

Rodgers, W. M., & Brawley, L. R. (1991b, June). *Evaluating fitness messages promoting involvement: Effects on attitudes and behavioural intentions.* Paper presented at the annual meeting of North American Society for the Psychology of Sport and Physical Activity, Kent, Ohio.

Rodgers, W. M., & Brawley, L. R. (1993). Using both self-efficacy theory and the theory of planned behavior to discriminate adherers and dropouts from structured programs. *Journal of Applied Sport Psychology, 5*, 195–206.

Rogers, R. W. (1975). A protection motivation theory of fear appeals and attitude change. *Journal of Psychology, 91*, 93–114.

Rogers, R. W. (1983). Cognitive and physiological processes in fear appeals and attitude change: A revised theory of protection motivation. In J. T. Cacioppo & R. E. Petty (Eds.), *Social psychophysiology: A sourcebook* (pp. 153–176). New York: Guilford.

Ronis, D. L. (1992). Conditional health threats: Health beliefs, decisions, and behaviors among adults. *Health Psychology*, 11, 127–134.

Ronis, D. L., & Harel, Y. (1989). Health beliefs and breast examination behaviors: Analyses of linear structural equations. *Psychology and Health*, 3, 259–285.

Ronis, D. L., & Kaiser, M. K. (1989). Correlates of breast self-examination in a sample of college women: Analyses of structural linear equations. *Journal of Applied Social Psychology*, 19, 1068–1084.

Ronis, D. L., Yates, J. F., & Kirscht, J. P. (1989). Attitudes, decisions, and habits as determinants of behavior. In A. R. Pratkanis, S. J. Breckler, & A. G. Greenwald (Eds.), *Attitude structure and function* (pp. 213–239). Hillsdale, NJ: Erlbaum.

Rosenstock, I. M. (1974). The health belief model and preventive health behavior. *Health Education Monographs*, 2, 354–386.

Rosenstock, I. M., Strecher, V. J., & Becker, M. H. (1988). Social learning theory and the health belief model. *Health Education Quarterly*, 15, 175–183.

Rotter, J. B. (1954). *Social learning and clinical psychology*. New York: Prentice-Hall.

Rudd, J. R., & Geller, E. S. (1985). A university-based incentive program to increase safety belt use: Toward cost-effective institutionalization. *Journal of Applied Behavior Analysis*, 18, 215–226.

Rutledge, D. N. (1987). Factors related to women's practice of breast self-examination. *Nursing Research*, 36, 117–121.

Schifter, D. B., & Ajzen, I. (1985). Intention, perceived control, and weight loss: An application of the theory of planned behavior. *Journal of Personality and Social Psychology*, 49, 843–851.

Schneider, W., & Shiffrin, R. M. (1977). Controlled and automatic human information processing: I. Detection search, and attention. *Psychological Review*, 84, 1–66.

Schwarzer, R. (1992). Self-efficacy in the adoption and maintenance of health behaviors: Theoretical approaches and a new model. In R. Schwarzer (Ed.), *Self-efficacy: Thought control of action* (pp. 217–244). Washington, DC: Hemisphere.

Seidman, H., Gelb, S. K., Silverberg, E., LaVerda, N., & Lubera, J. A. (1987). Survival experiences in the breast cancer detection demonstration project. *CA-A Cancer Journal for Clinicians*, 37, 258–290.

Shelton, M. L., & Rogers, R. W. (1981). Fear-arousing and empathy arousing appeals to help: The pathos of persuasion. *Journal of Applied Social Psychology*, 4, 366–378.

Snyder, C. R., & Forsyth, D. R. (Eds.). (1991). *Handbook of social and clinical psychology: The health perspective*. New York: Pergamon.

Stanley, M. A., & Maddux, J. E. (1986). Cognitive processes in health enhancement: Investigation of a combined protection motivation and self-efficacy model. *Basic and Applied Social Psychology*, 7, 101–113.

Stokols, D. (1992). Establishing and maintaining health environments: Toward a social ecology of health promotion. *American Psychologist*, 47, 6–22.

Strickland, B. R. (1989). Internal–external control expectancies: From contingency to creativity. *American Psychologist*, 44, 1–12.

Taylor, S. E. (1983). Adjustment to threatening events. *American Psychologist*, 38, 1161–1173.

Teasdale, J. D. (1978). Self-efficacy: Toward a unifying theory of behavioural change? In S. Rachman (Ed.), *Advances in behaviour research and therapy* (vol. 1, pp. 211–215). Oxford: Pergamon.

Uzark, K. C., Becker, M. H., Dielman, T. E., & Rocchini, A. P. (1987). Psychosocial predictors of compliance with a weight control intervention for obese children and adolescents. *Journal of Compliance in Health Care*, 2, 167–178.

Weinstein, N. D. (1988). The precaution adoption process. *Health Psychology*, 7, 355–386.

Weinstein, N. D. (1993). Testing four competing theories of health-protective behavior. *Health Psychology, 12*, 324–333.

Weinstein, N. D., & Sandman, P. M. (1992). A model of the precaution adoption process: Evidence from home radon testing. *Health Psychology, 11*, 170–180.

Wurtele, S. K. (1986). Self-efficacy and athletic performance: A review. *Journal of Social and Clinical Psychology, 4*, 290–301.

Wurtele, S. K., & Maddux, J. E. (1987). Relative contributions of protection motivation theory components in predicting exercise intentions and behavior. *Health Psychology, 6*, 453–466.

Yordy, G. A., & Lent, R. S. (1993). Predicting aerobic exercise participation: Social cognitive, reasoned action, and planned behavior models. *Journal of Sport and Exercise Psychology, 15*, 363–374.

Zimmerman, R. S., & Conner, C. (1989). Health promotion in context: The effects of significant others on health behavior change. *Health Education Quarterly, 16*, 57–75.

CHAPTER 7

SELF-EFFICACY AND RECOVERY FROM HEART ATTACK

IMPLICATIONS FOR A SOCIAL COGNITIVE ANALYSIS OF EXERCISE AND EMOTION

CRAIG K. EWART

Coronary heart disease continues to be the leading health threat to citizens of developed nations; in the United States alone, diseases of the heart and vasculature cause over a half-million premature deaths annually while contributing to nearly as many cases of preventable disability (Gunby, 1992). One's chances of surviving a heart attack (acute myocardial infarction, AMI) have increased in recent years due to important innovations in emergency and postcoronary care. Yet survivors still face disabling difficulties that most health care providers are ill-prepared to detect and poorly equipped to treat (Ben-Sira & Eliezer, 1990; Fontana, Kerns, Rosenberg, & Colonese, 1989).

Most of these problems, and the disabilities they cause, are attributable to psychological and behavioral difficulties rather than to biology. The unheralded onset of AMI, and its mortal danger, leaves patients feeling

CRAIG K. EWART • School of Public Health, Johns Hopkins University, Baltimore, Maryland 21205.

Self-Efficacy, Adaptation, and Adjustment: Theory, Research, and Application, edited by James E. Maddux. Plenum Press, New York, 1995.

helpless and afraid. Many become so frightened that they restrict their activities far more than is medically necessary, and thereby deprive themselves of rewards they formerly derived from work, family, friendships, and ordinary day-to-day pursuits. Patients' despair at their seeming helplessness may be deepened even further by family members' well-meaning efforts to discourage physical activity or to avoid discussing topics that might be upsetting. Unfortunately, such protectiveness tends to retard recovery by prolonging the patient's physical inactivity and social isolation, while straining relationships within the family (Coyne & Smith, 1991).

Self-efficacy theory provides a useful framework for explaining problematic emotional and behavioral responses to AMI, and generates practical methods for detecting and modifying psychological barriers to recovery. Viewed more broadly, studies of self-efficacy in coronary patients also may help us understand how, and under what conditions, physical exercise enhances emotional adjustment and psychological well-being in people who are healthy. Answers to this larger question must be found if exercise is to be used effectively as a preventive public health strategy aimed at reducing cardiovascular risk and improving quality of life. The first part of this chapter summarizes research suggesting how patients' self-efficacy appraisals influence their behavioral responses to AMI. In the remaining part of the chapter, these and other findings are used to create a model suggesting how physical exertion, self-efficacy, and emotion are causally related, and to suggest how exercise training might be used more effectively to promote psychological adjustment and enhance quality of life in people who have not developed coronary disease.

RECOVERY AFTER ACUTE MYOCARDIAL INFARCTION

Patients who have suffered AMI or undergone coronary artery bypass graft (CABG) are considered to be at low risk of recurrent AMI in the near future if they do not exhibit severe exercise-induced ischemia or severe left ventricular dysfunction; in the 33–50% of patients who fit the low-risk profile, annual mortality is less than 2% (DeBusk et al., 1986). Low-risk patients need less medical treatment than patients at higher risk, and if they become normally active (avoiding prolonged bed rest), they experience a rapid increase in functional capacity during the first 6 months after AMI, even without formal exercise training. This comparatively rapid recovery of physical capability allows low-risk patients to return to work much sooner than patients at higher risk. Indeed, after 3 to 6 months of recovery, low-risk patients have been found to exhibit a functional exercise capacity similar to that of healthy men in their 50s (DeBusk et al., 1986).

EXERCISE IN PHASE 1 REHABILITATION

Three weeks after AMI, low-risk patients are encouraged to begin exercising at gradually increasing frequencies, durations, and intensities by engaging in progressive walking, jogging, cycling, swimming, or similar activities. The goal is to exercise at intensities ranging from 70–85% of peak heart rate (measured during a symptom-limited exercise test) for 20–30 minutes per day, from 3 to 5 days per week. Patients may be encouraged to exercise at home, and are given a portable monitor to help them maintain their exercise heart rate within the recommended range (Miller, Haskell, Berra, & DeBusk, 1984). Patients who have undergone CABG can exercise safely and without discomfort after 3 to 4 weeks postsurgery. CABG patients are generally advised to engage in walking and stationary cycling rather than jogging, because the former activities are less likely to result in nonunion of the sternum. (The sternum is surgically cut apart during the bypass operation to permit access to the heart; the two parts are rejoined and must grow together again during recovery.) Getting involved in a regimen of progressive walking or stationary cycling is especially important for CABG patients, because they tend to experience physical deconditioning during the bed rest that follows surgery. This deconditioning causes fatigue, which patients misconstrue as a sign of cardiac illness, when it is, in fact, quite reversible with a program of moderate walking.

Return to Work

Resuming work is far less likely to cause medical problems than patients often believe. Only 5% of patients in the United States now engage in physically demanding occupational work, so very few are advised to seek less demanding job assignments. Moreover, despite the fact that blood pressure tends to be higher in the work environment than at home (Pickering, 1989), AMI occurs no more frequently in one setting than the other (DeBusk et al., 1986). By 3 months after AMI, low-risk patients are able to exercise safely at intensities that are far more demanding than those they experience on the job. After 3 months, low-risk patients usually are not advised to delay returning to work on medical grounds. Indeed, at this point in their recovery, many patients find the prospect of not working to be a source of significant hardship and stress.

EXERCISE IN PHASE 2 REHABILITATION

After the first 3 months post-AMI, participation in regular physical exercise continues to be beneficial. A program of regular exercise reduces fatigue, promotes a sense of vigor, and facilitates return to normal activities. The benefits of continuing participation in an exercise-rehabilitation program are indicated by a meta-analysis of 22 randomized trials of exercise rehabilitation: Participation in rehabilitative exercise was associated with a 20% reduction in mortality during the first 3 years after AMI (O'Connor et al., 1989). Although this reduction in mortality may also have been influenced by changes in diet, smoking, or stress frequently targeted by rehabilitation programs, the well-documented effects of exercise in improving cardiovascular function in healthy individuals supports the view that patients who avoid exercising after AMI may be at somewhat greater risk than those who exercise regularly.

SELF-EFFICACY AND RECOVERY

Self-efficacy theory has proven to be extremely useful in understanding, measuring, and modifying psychological reactions that contribute to unnecessary anxiety and functional disability after AMI or CABG. The theory suggests that fear and activity restriction may result from inaccurate self-appraisals of one's physical capabilities. Moreover, the theory proposes that the most effective way to reduce this disability is to alter dysfunctional self-appraisals by identifying feared activities and helping patients perform them in carefully graduated "doses," thus gradually building a sense of mastery. Self-efficacy enhancement may also be achieved vicariously by having patients observe others like themselves performing these activities, by teaching physicians and nurses to offer persuasive reassurance, and by providing appropriate interpretations of internal bodily sensations in order to keep patients from misconstruing and "pathologizing" their meaning. Much of this can be accomplished during routine care by appropriately trained personnel, and does in fact take place in well-designed cardiac rehabilitation programs.

The potential value of a self-efficacy approach to cardiac rehabilitation is suggested by research Ewart and colleagues have conducted over the past decade. This research began with an attempt to identify patients' significant fears and to develop valid self-efficacy measures for each area of concern. Scales were developed to measure self-appraised ability to walk and jog various distances, climb stairs, lift heavy objects, and engage in sexual activity; respondents were asked to report their confidence (on scales ranging from 0 = *Not at All Confident*, to 100 = *Completely Confident*) that they could perform successively more difficult levels of each activity.*

---

*Copies of self-efficacy scales used in the studies described in this chapter are available from the author.

In a preliminary validation study, patients who had recently suffered AMI completed these scales while waiting in the clinic lobby before taking their 3-week treadmill test, in the stress lab immediately after the test, and again in the lobby after the results of the test had been explained to them by a cardiologist and nurse.

As predicted, changes in self-efficacy scores following the test were compatible with the notion that patients' exercise experience, together with the cardiologist's comments during and after the evaluation, altered patients' perceptions of their physical capabilities: Self-efficacy increased in nearly all patients, with the exception of a small subgroup who experienced exercise-induced chest pain (angina) while walking on the treadmill (Ewart, Taylor, Reese, & DeBusk, 1983). As predicted by self-efficacy theory, self-efficacy gains were largest for activities that resembled the legwork performed on the treadmill (e.g., walking, jogging, stair climbing), and were smaller for less similar behaviors (e.g., lifting weights or engaging in sexual intercourse). Self-efficacy changes following the interpretive counseling by the cardiologist and the nurse indicated that advice from these providers helped patients generalize their exercise-test experience to lifting and sexual activity.

SELF-EFFICACY MEDIATES PHYSICAL ACTIVITY

The validation study suggested that self-efficacy scales measure patients' appraisals of their physical capabilities, but do these appraisals mediate involvement in physical exertion as the theory would assert? To evaluate this possibility, patients who participated in the validation study were equipped with a portable activity monitor and given activity diaries to complete daily for 1 week before taking the treadmill test, and again for 1 week after it. The activity data revealed that changes in jogging self-efficacy following the treadmill test predicted changes in daily-activity levels better than did the peak heart rate and maximal energy-expenditure levels observed during the test. The extent to which patients increased their physical activity levels the week after the test was more closely related to their self-appraised capabilities than to their actual biological condition.

Further evidence that self-efficacy mediates physical activity derives from a subsequent study of patients who participated regularly in a Phase 2 cardiac rehabilitation program. All had suffered AMI more than 6 months before the study began; they met three times each week for supervised group jogging sessions conducted at a community college. An important objective of Phase 2 rehabilitation is to ensure that patients continue to exercise regularly in bouts of sufficient duration and intensity to promote cardiovascular health without overexerting themselves and getting into trouble. One study goal was to determine if self-efficacy appraisals pre-dicted patient success in exercising within their prescribed "safe and effective" heart-rate range. Participants performed a maximal treadmill exercise test, completed the self-efficacy scales, and several weeks later, were individually monitored (via Holter recorder) as they engaged in one of their regular group-jogging sessions. The Holter data were examined later to determine if the number of minutes participants exercised within their prescribed heart-rate range were related to their jogging self-efficacy. Results disclosed that adherence to the prescribed range was predicted by self-appraised ability to jog, but not by the participant's actual perfor-mance during the maximal treadmill test. These findings strongly sup-ported the earlier discovery that self-efficacy appraisals are superior to functional exercise evaluation in predicting adherence to rehabilitative exercise regimens.

Specificity of Self-Efficacy

Bandura (1986) has emphasized repeatedly that self-efficacy percep-tions tend to be quite specific to behaviors and situations. Such specificity would have important implications for designing effective activity promo-tion programs in cardiac rehabilitation: The program's behavioral impact may be as much the function of the *variety* of exercises performed as of their exertional intensity and duration. Research with patients undergoing strength and endurance evaluation supports the specificity of physical self-efficacy appraisals. In the Phase 2 rehabilitation participants described earlier, self-perceived ability to lift various amounts of weight and do push-ups was correlated with subsequently measured arm strength, but was unrelated to aerobic power as measured by the maximal treadmill exercise test. Conversely, self-appraised ability to jog and climb stairs was correlated with aerobic power, but was unrelated to arm or leg strength. Participants were randomly divided into two groups that performed the arm and leg strength tests in counterbalanced order; results revealed that arm self-efficacy increased after arm-strength testing but not after the leg-strength tests. Assessment of leg strength had no effect on self-efficacy for the tasks requiring arm strength. These results support the view that exer-cise programs are more likely to succeed in promoting resumption of nor-mal activities if they include a variety of flexibility and strength-enhancing exercises in addition to conventional walking and jogging regimens.

Self-Efficacy Predicts Overexertion

Although excessive curtailment of physical exercise is a widespread problem after AMI, some patients appear overly confident and push themselves to achieve dangerous levels of physical exertion. Psychodynamic interpretations label this "denial," and ascribe it to unconscious fears (Hackett, Cassem, & Wishnie, 1968), yet it is also possible that these individuals have inappropriately high levels of confidence in their physical capabilities. Laboratory studies investigating the effects of self-efficacy on response to failure feedback support this possibility. In these studies, experimentally manipulated performance feedback is used to give subjects the impression that they exhibit high or low levels of ability in performing an unfamiliar task. After high- or low-self-efficacy for the task has been experimentally induced, subjects perform another task and afterward are told that they "failed." When asked to continue working on this task, subjects with low-induced self-efficacy become less involved in the task, whereas subjects with high levels of induced self-efficacy work harder than they did before (Bandura, 1986). If a high level of confidence in a given performance domain causes people to undertake more demanding performances and to persevere longer, it is conceivable that people with high levels of physical self-efficacy might be more prone to overexert themselves when exercising after AMI.

We investigated this possibility by examining the relationship between self-efficacy and overexertion during supervised group exercise in patients who participated in the Phase 2 rehabilitation study. *Overexertion* was defined as the number of minutes a participant's heart rate exceeded their recommended upper limit during a 20-minute group-jogging session (Ewart et al., 1986). Findings were consistent with results of the laboratory studies: Patients who had high levels of confidence in their ability to jog, as indicated by a self-efficacy score in the top one-third of the jogging self-efficacy distribution, greatly exceeded their prescribed upper heart-rate limit, whereas those in the lower two-thirds of the distribution did not. Over half (57%) of the patients with high jogging self-efficacy placed themselves in significant medical danger by exercising above their prescribed maximum heart rate for more than half of the exercise session. Patients whose self-efficacy scores were in the lower two-thirds of the distribution had an 81% chance of not overexerting themselves in this manner. These data suggest the importance of identifying patients who may feel overly self-efficacious after AMI and of providing counseling to help them avoid dangerous levels of physical activity. It may be that those at highest risk will prove to be people who led physically vigorous lives prior to AMI, and hence have a robust sense of confidence in their exertional capabilities.

INTERPERSONAL INFLUENCES ON SELF-EFFICACY

Patients' internal psychological processes are not the only barriers that prevent their becoming more active. As noted earlier, family members play an important role in determining how active the patient will become in the early weeks after AMI (Coyne & Smith, 1991). Typical is the wife of a patient in one of our early self-efficacy studies, who claimed she had hidden the keys to the family car to prevent her husband from driving two blocks to buy a magazine at a local convenience store. Spouses are frightened by their partners' heart attacks and they too feel helpless; their attempts to limit their partners' activity are understandable responses to being inadequately informed and all too frequently ignored.

If a cardiac patient engages in vigorous exercise during the early weeks after AMI, the exercise typically takes place in a medical setting, when the patient's spouse is not present. Spouses have little or no opportunity to observe their partners exercising strenuously yet safely. Self-efficacy theory suggests that the most convincing way to alter a spouse's appraisals of partner efficacy would be to arrange for the spouse to experience the same level of exertion the patient could safely tolerate. A study was conducted to test this hypothesis. Men participating in research on prognosis in early heart disease were randomly assigned to perform a 3-week maximal exercise test with: (a) wife absent; (b) wife present as observer; or (c) wife present to observe her husband on the treadmill, then *perform the test herself* (Taylor, Bandura, Ewart, Miller, & DeBusk, 1985). Patients and their wives completed the self-efficacy scales before the treadmill test, immediately after completing the test, and again after being informed of the test results. Wives rated their levels of confidence in their *husband's*—not their own—physical capabilities. The results revealed that only the wives who actually walked on the treadmill themselves subsequently increased their ratings to levels matching their husband's self-efficacy. Waiting in the lobby while her husband took the test, or merely watching him perform, had no appreciable effect on a wife's appraisals of her husband's capabilities. The findings suggest a simple and potentially effective method for creating a more supportive social environment for early exercise after AMI.

SELF-EFFICACY AND PSYCHOLOGICAL RESPONSES TO EXERCISE IN HEALTHY ADULTS

Findings summarized thus far support the hypothesis that inaccurate self-efficacy appraisals cause cardiac patients to inhibit their activities, prolong their disability, and elevate cardiovascular risk. The data are also compatible with the view that interventions to modify appraisals of physical self-efficacy may help patients become more active, shorten the length of their disability, and reduce their long-term risk. Yet exercise is widely recommended for health promotion and *primary*-risk reduction in people who have not developed symptoms of cardiovascular illness, and who are not inhibited by the anxieties patients experience after AMI. Not only are these healthier populations unburdened by excessive fear of exertion, they tend to view exercise as a way to reduce the normal stresses of daily living, to feel happier, and to improve the quality of their lives. Indeed, regular physical exercise has been recommended for amelioration of depression and enhancement of psychological adjustment (Folkins & Sime, 1981; Morgan, 1985).

Yet the question of using exercise to promote emotional adjustment poses new challenges to self-efficacy theory, and to social cognitive theory generally. Emotional responses are more difficult to define and measure than are physical exercise activities; to explain their relationship to self-efficacy and exercise, it is necessary first to analyze the event sequences or processes through which moods and emotions originate, to determine how affective responses and self-efficacy differ, and to specify the pathways by which physical exertion, affect, and self-appraisal might be causally related.

The remaining sections of this chapter consider these problems and develop a working social cognitive model to guide future investigation. First, alternative current approaches to the study of emotions are described, and an approach is proposed that is both compatible with available data and also capable of being incorporated within a social cognitive theoretical framework. Next, a model is outlined specifying the role of self-efficacy appraisals in the sequence of events leading from physical exertion to emotional experience. Data from recent self-efficacy research using pharmacologic treatments to manipulate physiological feedback are used to indicate the possible role of self-appraisal in determining the emotional benefits of exercise training.

APPROACHES TO EMOTION

Emotions have been studied in two fundamentally different ways. Investigators favoring a *categorical* approach have tried to identify basic emotions and to create models of each. Included in these models are the conditions known to evoke a particular category of emotion, and the cognitive, behavioral, and physiological responses that usually accompany it. "Fear" may be distinguished from "sadness," for example, by the fact that fear is triggered by the perception of threat or danger, and is accompanied by elevated heart rate and avoidance behavior, whereas sadness is a pattern of responses elicited by a perceived loss and characterized by hopelessness and passivity. The categorical tradition in emotion research is exemplified in the "motivational–relational" theory of Lazarus (1991a; 1991b), which classifies emotions on the basis of goal-appraisal processes. Events that appear to threaten, delay, or thwart a valued goal give rise to "negative" emotions, whereas "positive" emotions are elicited by events that are appraised to be goal-congruent. The family of negative emotions includes anger, fright–anxiety, guilt–shame, sadness, envy–jealousy, and disgust; the positive emotion family comprises happiness/ joy, pride, love/affection, and relief.

Each emotion subtype has its own core "relational theme": In *anger*, the relational theme is the perception of a "demeaning offense against me and mine"; the core theme of *happiness* is the appraisal that one "is making reasonable progress toward a goal" (Lazarus, 1991b, p. 122). Activation of a given relational theme sets in motion a distinctive sequence of cognitive, biological, and behavioral events that can vary in intensity and are specific to a particular emotion (e.g., trembling and indecision with fear, smiling and optimism with happiness). Motivational–appraisal models have proven useful in research on emotional factors in cardiovascular and immune diseases, in which experimental investigation suggests that different patterns of social behavior and physiological responding (blood pressure elevations, immune response suppression) are associated with the activation of different core relational themes (Ewart, 1993, 1991; Kiecolt-Glaser et al., 1993).

The other major approach to understanding emotion can be characterized as *dimensional*. Investigators pursuing this line of inquiry assume that the varied and seemingly endless number of emotion words used in everyday speech refer, in fact, to but a few underlying dimensions of affective experience. They try to uncover these dimensions by applying factor-analytic and clustering methods to people's ratings of emotion words in order to see which emotion descriptors tend to covary across individuals. One prominent dimensional model reduces human emotions to two independent factors reflecting *positive* and *negative* affective experiences (Watson, Clark, & Tellegen, 1988; Watson & Pennebaker, 1989). "Positive affect" describes the extent to which emotional experiences are characterized by feelings of energy, mental concentration, and pleasurable engagement; a person with a high score on the positive affect dimension feels enthusiastic, energetic, and alert, whereas a person with a low score feels sad and lethargic. "Negative affect," on the other hand, describes the degree to which emotions are characterized by feelings of anger, nervousness, fear, and disgust; a person with a high negative affect score feels frightened or furious, whereas an individual with a low score feels calm, serene, and free of annoyance or worry. Research within this two-factor paradigm has suggested that day-to-day fluctuations in negative affect are related to variations in "daily hassles," illness symptoms, and perceived stress, whereas fluctuations in positive affect are associated with variations in social interaction and physical activity (Watson & Pennebaker, 1989). Which of the two approaches to emotion is more likely to advance our understanding of exercise and affect? This depends, of course, on what one wants to know. To the investigator who wonders if specific physiological changes give rise to the pleasant emotions many people associate with exercising, a dimensional scheme such as the two-factor model is appealing. The Positive Affect And Negative Affect Scales (PANAS) developed by Watson et al. (1988) provide brief (10-item), psychometrically sound measures of each construct; the PANAS can be administered repeatedly over the course of an exercise bout to determine if levels of positive or negative affect vary with changes in perceived exertion, heart rate, endorphins, monoamines, body temperature, or other suspected physiological mediators of mood variation (Tuson & Sinyor, 1993). Moreover, the two-dimensional model's assumption that positive affect and negative affect fluctuate independently promotes a more differentiated view of exercise and affect than is attainable when investigators use instruments that were designed to facilitate psychiatric evaluation (e.g., the profile of Mood States (POMS; McNair, Lorr, & Droppleman, 1981). With the PANAS, for example, it is possible to determine if exercise of a given type, intensity, or duration reduces negative affect, increases positive affect, or accomplishes both goals (Ewart, 1992; 1989).

Yet the dimensional model's virtues of brevity and simplicity are seriously offset by an insensitivity to important differences between emotion types. Imagine, for example, we are trying to evaluate an exercise training program designed to help patients return to normal activities after acute myocardial infarction. Would it matter if the program succeeded in reducing patients' fears about becoming active, yet left many patients feeling frustrated or even angry at the manner in which the program was conducted? Or assume that Training Method A tended to "interest" program participants more than did Training Method B, but that Training Method B induced a stronger sense of "pride." Would we want to know this? If one adheres strongly to a *dimensional* view of emotion, the answer should be "No." From the perspective of the two-factor model, for example, when participants say they feel "afraid" or "angry" they simply are saying they feel *bad*, or are expressing negative affect; when they report feeling "interested" or "proud," they merely are claiming to feel *good*, or are expressing positive affect. Differences between feeling afraid as opposed to angry, interested as opposed to proud, are relatively unimportant if these words are only surface indicators of underlying negative or positive affectivity; what really matters if the *number* of positive or negative affect words endorsed—not their specific content. This view contrasts sharply, however, with the perspectives and concerns of those who provide health care: Whether a patient is afraid or angry, interested or satisfied, can have important implications for diagnosis, prognosis, and overall quality of life.

Many would argue, moreover, that emotions such as anger, shame, or pride differ substantially from affective states such as discomfort, pleasure, curiosity, or alertness, in that the former entail more extensive cognitive processing (e.g., appraisal). Some forms of exercise may serve to relieve discomfort, reduce fatigue, or increase alertness, whereas other training methods may be needed to foster cognitions that give rise to feelings of relief, happiness, or pride (Ewart, 1992,1989). When exercise is used to encourage a particular kind of emotional or psychological change, simple dimensional models and scales may prove to be inadequate.

Dimensional measures of positive and negative affect may tell us if exercises of a particular type, duration, or intensity make people feel "better" or "worse" in a general sense, and may suffice when one seeks to determine if affective responses to exertion are mediated by changes in endorphins, body temperature, or similar physiological processes. The dimensional approach would seem especially compatible with a general arousal theory of emotion (Schachter, 1966), the view that all emotion words describe one common, orchestrated pattern of physiological change. Yet the notion of general arousal is increasingly challenged by evidence of autonomic specificity for emotions such as anger, sadness, fear, and disgust, as well as for positive emotions (Davidson, Ekman, Saron, Senulis, & Friesen, 1990; Ekman, Levenson & Friesen, 1983; Levenson, 1988). Physiological specificity appears more consistent with categorical than with dimensional views of emotion.

Although it is less parsimonious than the dimensional approach, the categorical paradigm has the advantage of requiring investigators and program planners to formulate precise conceptual models to guide physical training interventions. Instead of assuming that physical exertion will alter broadly defined positive or negative affectivity, program designers must first identify the specific psychological goals that intervention should achieve. Should training attempt to alleviate affective states such as discomfort or fatigue? Should it increase participants' sense of vigor and alertness? Or should there be an attempt to stimulate cognitively based affective responses by fostering emotions such as pride, relief, and happiness, while reducing sadness and anxiety? When affective goals have been defined, categorical models of basic emotions can suggest specific steps to take in order to elicit desired affective responses. These models call attention to environmental and social–contextual aspects of exercise training as distinct from the exertional components. For example, a motivational–relational model implies that in addition to exercise type, duration, or intensity, the role of performance goals, feedback, social interaction, attentional focus, and similar factors affecting cognitive appraisal processes can be critical.

A Social Cognitive Model

A theory-based approach is needed if significant advances in our understanding of exercise and emotion are to be achieved. Although exercise is widely touted for its psychological benefits, much of the research on this question has been limited conceptually and findings are equivocal (Salazar, Petruzzello, Landers, Etnier, & Kubitz, 1993). Most investigators have focused on exercise *type* and *intensity*, paying little or no attention to social–contextual or other aspects of the training experience. Anxiety reduction is the one emotional outcome to be demonstrated with reasonable consistency across a number of studies; positive changes in emotions such as anger or sadness, or affective states such as vigor of fatigue, have been documented less consistently (Tuson & Sinyor, 1993). Because the majority of studies evaluate the short-term effects of exercising, we do not know if the psychological benefits that *have* been demonstrated tend to persist over time. It appears that intense exertion may help reduce states of fatigue or tension, yet it is unclear if these changes lead to longer term alterations of prevailing mood or emotion.

A further barrier to progress has been the influential assumption that psychological responses to exercise must be mediated by exertion-induced changes in physiological processes. Yet many studies that report beneficial psychological outcomes fail to find that they are correlated with measured physiological responses to training (Tuson & Sinyor, 1993). The lack of relationship between emotional outcomes and changes in physiological parameters such as heart rate, maximal oxygen uptake, or muscle strength, militates against the widely held notion—encouraged by the general arousal model—that exercise reduces autonomic arousal and thereby dampens the physiological underpinnings of negative emotions. Few researchers have pursued the possibility that affective responses to exercise are influenced by social-appraisal processes, and only indirectly by physiology.

How might exercising evoke emotion? The answer requires a model of the processes by which moods and emotions originate. A model of emotion processes in postcoronary exercise is outlined in Figure 1, which summarizes three essential elements of emotional experience that have figured prominently in analyses by social cognitive theorists. The type of

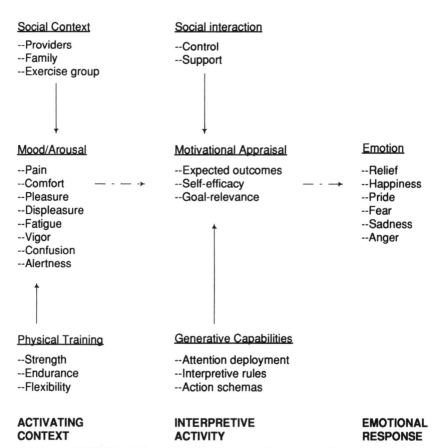

FIGURE 1. Model of Emotion Process in Postcoronary Exercise.

emotion experienced depends upon the activating context, which may include internal sensations of pain, comfort, fatigue, or energy, as well as external social cues, such as displays of threat or reassurance. These internal and external events may have little emotional impact if attention is directed elsewhere; if noticed but not carefully scrutinized, they may elicit diffuse states of pleasure or displeasure, vigor or lassitude. Affective states only evoke emotion when they have been appraised in light of one's predominant strivings or concerns. Eliciting events that appear to facilitate valued strivings leads to positive emotions, whereas events that appear to threaten such strivings lead to negative emotions. The specific type of positive or negative emotional experience (e.g., happiness or pride, fear of sadness) is determined by the nature of the appraisal. The specific emotional reaction, in turn, influences subsequent behavior.

For example, when first moving about after coronary artery bypass surgery, many patients experience sternal "clicking" sensations at the site where their surgically separated sternum was rejoined. Patients who appraise these clicks as signifying that the wound is breaking open are frightened and may become physically inactive. On the other hand, those who have been informed that clicking sensations are expected early concomitants of recovery-promoting physical activity may feel little or no fear; some even manage to take pride in the fact that they are being appropriately active. Figure 1 demonstrates that the patient's emotional reaction is determined by "outcome" appraisals (e.g., sternal clicking signals danger versus recovery), "self-efficacy" appraisals (e.g., sternal clicking is or is not a sign of disability), and "goal-relevance" appraisals (e.g., clicking does or does not threaten the attainment of a valued striving or goal). Moreover, it is suggested that these appraisals are heavily influenced by the individual's store of acquired knowledge and action schemas ("generative capabilities"), as well as the availability of supportive social relationships with family members, healthcare providers, and important others ("social interaction processes"). Patients who have learned that certain unfamiliar physical sensations are signs that they are making progress in recovery, and who receive encouragement from those they trust, are likely to form outcome, self-efficacy, and goal-relevance appraisals that foster feelings of happiness and pride, and that strengthen commitment to appropriate physical activity. Those who lack this information, or who are actively discouraged by persons they trust, are likely to form appraisals that lead to worry, sadness, and inactivity.

The important point here is that physical sensations, such as pain, muscle tension, or fatigue, influence but do not in themselves define emotional reactions to physical exercise. Emotional responses are as much the products of social contexts and interpretive activities as of the physiological changes induced by exertion. Emotional affects of exercising thus should vary, depending upon whether the exerciser attends to internal sensations as opposed to external environmental cues, and also on the ways in which somatic information is interpreted. Nor do outcome appraisals, self-efficacy judgments, or perceptions of goal relevance constitute emotions. Instead, they are appropriately construed as cognitive activities that help create emotions by transforming "simple" affective reactions, such as bodily pain or pleasure, into the more complicated experiences we call "fear," "sadness," "happiness," or "relief." Note, too, that via appraisal, even physically painful sensations may be transformed into positive emotions. For example, sensations of fatigue or muscle soreness may be viewed with pride if taken to signify success in pushing oneself beyond previous limits in the service of attaining a valued performance standard. Pride is the likely response if the exerciser judges the fatigue or soreness to be only temporary (outcome appraisal), views the performance that caused these sensations as signifying improved physical capability (self-efficacy appraisal), and sees this gain as helping to fulfill a valued striving (goal-relevance appraisal).

Mood Influences Self-Efficacy

Support for this sequence is found in research showing that affective states can influence self-efficacy appraisal processes (Maddux & Meier, Chap. 5, this volume). College students who rated their self-efficacy for athletic performances when in a pleasant mood (induced by recalling a pleasant romantic episode under hypnosis) reported higher levels of self-efficacy for athletic performances than they did when in an unpleasant mood (induced by recalling a romantic failure; Kavanagh & Bower, 1985). The finding that athletic self-efficacy increased or diminished following the recall of nonathletic experiences suggests that *mood,* and not the specific memory, altered self-efficacy. Bower's well-known studies of affect and memory suggest that memory is mood-dependent: People are more likely to recall experiences that match their current mood than to recall experiences that evoked feelings that are "incongruent" with current affect. For example,when sad, one is more likely to remember unhappy events than to recall moments of joy; when happy, it is easier to recall pleasant, as opposed to distressing, occurrences. In other words, when one is upset, memories of disappointing experiences become more accessible in short-term memory and thereby undermine self-efficacy. Cardiac patients who feel dejected are prone to gauge their capabilities in light of their physically weaker moments, whereas when they feel happy, their appraisals are guided by memories of their better performances.

To the extent that unpleasant moods undermine self-efficacy by biasing recall, providing prompt, specific, and credible performance feedback during and after exercise should help curtail this debilitating effect. Credible feedback reduces the likelihood that people will rely mainly on memories of past performances (possibly biased by mood-congruence effects) when estimating their current capabilities. Conversely, inducing pleasant moods by creating an enjoyable exercise environment may make it easier for participants to recall times when they felt better about themselves, and thereby increase their self-efficacy. There are limits to such self-efficacy enhancement, however. Because mood enhances appraisal by influencing the accessibility of past performances, the ability of pleasant moods to favorably bias self-appraisal is limited by the actual level or quality of past accomplishments.

Self-Efficacy Shapes Emotion

Figure 1 implies that self-efficacy appraisals shape emotional experiences. This influence is supported by experiments that manipulate failure feedback to subjects who report low or high levels of self-efficacy for a laboratory task. Subjects are randomly assigned to receive failure or success feedback on the task, regardless of how well they actually perform. Subjects with low levels of self-efficacy for the experimental task become sad and discouraged after being given feedback that they did not perform well, whereas subjects with high levels of self-efficacy for the task do not (Bandura, 1986). Presumably, individuals with low self-efficacy interpret the feedback as confirming their lack of ability, or helplessness, an interpretation conducive to the emotion of sadness (Lazarus, 1991b), whereas individuals with higher levels of self-efficacy do not succumb to negative self-evaluation, and hence do not become despondent. Despondence seems especially likely in persons who believe their failure to be prognostic of their success in other performance domains (outcome appraisals), and believe it threatens their ability to realize valued ambitions (goal appraisals).

Self-Efficacy Mechanisms of Emotional Change

The above analysis suggests that self-efficacy judgments belong to a class of appraisal processes that are distinct from moods and emotions, and play a pivotal role in transforming the former into the latter. Social cognitive theory suggests several important mechanisms through which this transformation may occur. First, people judge their capabilities by comparing their performances against their past attainments, and against performances by others whom they judge to be like themselves (Bandura, 1986). Seeing oneself exercise at intensities that compare favorably to exercises performed prior to one's illness, or are similar to activities of recovered patients, may alleviate anxiety, encourage optimism, and promote a sense of relief. Because even small performance changes can be reassuring, positive emotional responses may occur long before physiologically important gains in muscle strength or aerobic power can be demonstrated. Second, exertion may alter self-efficacy via internal feedback, as when a perceived lessening of exercise-induced discomfort, pain, or fatigue gives rise to favorable self-appraisal; the perception that a task is becoming less difficult to perform may strengthen self-efficacy, even in

the absence of more explicit performance feedback. Third, even unpleasant physical sensations, such as pain or fatigue, may increase self-efficacy
if construed as but the temporary consequence of performing at a more
demanding level. Finally, exercising in a pleasant environment with an
attentive staff and convivial social atmosphere may improve a patient's
mood, render favorable memories of past attainments more accessible to
short-term memory, enhance self-efficacy, and thereby promote feelings of
happiness and pride.

These mechanisms help explain why many of the studies that demonstrate psychological benefits of exercise fail to find a link between emotional gains and measured physiological changes. Positive emotions may
arise from self-efficacy enhancement due to performance gains, physiological sensations, and social influences that are not reflected in the measures of strength or aerobic power frequently used in gauging the physical
benefits of training. Conversely, physical performance gains may not increase self-efficacy if they go unnoticed by the exerciser, or if their implications are misinterpreted. Social cognitive analysis suggests, moreover, that
attempts to explain emotional reactions to exercise by measuring changes
in a single physiological index (e.g., endorphins, temperature, oxygen
uptake, heart rate) are not likely to prove very informative. Self-efficacy
appraisals are influenced by inputs from a variety of external and internal
sources; they are not simple transductions of physical capabilities or biological events.

DO HEART RATE AND PERFORMANCE CHANGES MEDIATE
EMOTIONAL RESPONSES TO AEROBIC EXERCISE?

Support for this view is provided by two recently published studies.
In one study (Desharnais, Jobin, Cote, Levesque, & Godin, 1993), enrollees
in a aerobic exercise program were randomly assigned to one of two
conditions: one group was told that exercise would improve their psychological well-being, whereas the other was not told this. During training,
the "psychological expectancy" group was repeatedly encouraged to "selectively attend to signs of psychological and biological improvement,"
whereas in the control group "emphasis was put only on the biological
aspect of the program (p. 151)." Although fitness increased to a similar
degree in both conditions, self-esteem improved only in the group that
received the psychological intervention. Although the authors of this
study attribute the increased self-esteem to "a strong placebo effect," their
procedure involved experimental manipulation of subjects' attentional
and appraisal processes, and hence constituted an active cognitive treat-

ment. Their results suggest that altered appraisal, rather than aerobic conditioning, led to improvements in self-esteem.

Further support for a social cognitive as opposed to physiological theory of affective response to exercise is found in a recent study that evaluated the combined effects of exercise training and sympatholytic drug intervention on self-efficacy, emotion, and physical performance in men with mild hypertension (Stewart, Kelemen, & Ewart, 1993). Fifty-two previously sedentary men (mean age = 45 years) participated in 10 weeks of circuit weight training after being randomized either to propanolol (a beta blocker), diltiazem (a calcium channel blocker), or placebo. Beta blockers lower blood pressure by reducing sympathetic drive to the heart, thereby limiting the heart-rate level attainable during a bout of exercise. Consequently, patients on beta blockers fail to achieve the full cardiovascular benefits of aerobic exercise training. Calcium channel blockers (e.g., diltiazem) lower blood pressure without affecting heart-rate response to exertion or limiting aerobic conditioning. Placebo, of course, affects neither the blood pressure nor the heart rate response to exercise. This design makes it possible to assess the degree to which heart rate feedback and treadmill performance gains contribute to the changes in self-efficacy and emotion that are believed to result from aerobic training.

If aerobic training enhances self-efficacy and improves emotional adjustment largely by increasing aerobic power (as indicated by exercise heart rate, maximal oxygen uptake, and treadmill exercise time), men receiving either diltiazem or placebo should exhibit greater improvements in self-efficacy and emotion following training than the men who receive propanolol. Unlike participants who received diltiazem or placebo, men taking propanolol would not find themselves sustaining increasingly higher heart rates during their exercise bouts, nor would they observe notable changes in their treadmill endurance times after training; they therefore would receive fewer internal or external cues that exercising had altered their physical condition. Moreover, the aerobic power hypothesis implies that in the diltiazem and placebo groups, changes in self-efficacy and affect should correlate with exercise-induced gains in aerobic capabilities. Conversely, if other elements of exercise training are responsible for improving self-efficacy and emotion, men in all three experimental conditions should report similar increments in self-efficacy and improved affect following training. In either event, however, the model outlined in Figure 1 predicts that changes in self-efficacy and affect will be correlated.

Before and after the 10-week training program, maximal oxygen uptake (VO_2 max) was measured during symptom-limited standard Bruce treadmill testing by expired gas analysis, and maximal arm and leg strength were tested using variable resistance weight machines. Self-efficacy scales (Ewart, 1990) were administered at these times to assess participants' self-appraised ability to engage in activities requiring arm strength (lifting, push-ups) and leg strength (walking, jogging, climbing stairs). Emotions (anxiety, dejection, anger) and mood/arousal states (vigor, fatigue, confusion) were also assessed using the Profile of Mood States (POMS). The exercise training program consisted of three group sessions per week for 10 weeks; sessions consisted of warm-up calisthenics, circuit weight training (30 min), and aerobics (20 min), which consisted of walking, jogging, and stationary cycling. As study drugs affected heart rate, participants were not taught to monitor their heart rate, nor was attention drawn to this variable.

The study yielded the following major findings:

1. As expected, propanolol limited the full conditioning benefits of exercise training: Aerobic power (VO_2 max) increased in men receiving diltiazem or placebo, but did not change significantly in men receiving propanolol.
2. Also as expected, arm and leg strength increased significantly and to a similar degree in all three groups.
3. Self-efficacy increased significantly in all groups, yet self-efficacy changes were uncorrelated with gains in aerobic power or arm/leg strength, suggesting that self-efficacy gains were not mediated by changes in aerobic power or muscle strength.
4. POMS Anxiety/Tension scores decreased and POMS Vigor scores increased to equivalent degrees in all groups.
5. Increases in self-efficacy were correlated with decreases in POMS Anxiety and Depression.

Thus, although self-efficacy appraisals were correlated with *baseline* arm and leg strength, exercise appeared to enhance self-efficacy by mechanisms that did not involve changes in muscle strength or maximal oxygen uptake. Men receiving propanolol experienced improvements in self-efficacy, despite their not having experienced the higher exercise heart rates or aerobic performance levels attained by men in the diltiazam and placebo groups. Although the propanolol group did achieve significant grains in arm and leg strength, these could not explain the self-efficacy changes, because gains in muscle strength were unrelated to gains in self-efficacy. The lack of a nonintervention control group leaves open the possibility that simply being in the study caused participants to rate their self-efficacy and emotional status more favorably at posttest ("Hawthorne effect"). Yet this interpretation of the results is weakened by the finding that participants failed to alter their ratings of POMS Fatigue or POMS Confusion, as well as by the fact that changes in self-efficacy, POMS

Anxiety, and POMS Depression did not correlate with the observed increments in POMS Vigor. Instead, the pattern of correlations seems to reflect several different underlying processes, some of which involved the reduction of negative emotions, possibly mediated by self-efficacy, whereas others involved increased activation and arousal.

In brief, exercise training appeared to improve participants' appraisals of their physical capabilities, and changes in self-appraisal were associated with reductions in negative emotions, such as anxiety and depression. Exercise training also appeared to increase Vigor, as reflected in higher scores on items describing levels of activation such as "Lively," "Vigorous," "Energetic," and "Full of pep," yet these changes in arousal were unrelated to changes in self-appraisal or emotion; self-efficacy changes were associated with emotional changes rather than with altered arousal. This is consistent with the notion (Fig. 1) that emotional responses are constituted through processes of self-appraisal, whereas simpler states of arousal, fatigue, pleasure, or displeasure, are not.

CONCLUSION

Studies of self-efficacy in patients recovering from AMI support the view that much of the disability patients experience after their infarct is attributable to inaccurate self-appraisals of their physical capabilities. Theory-based interventions that have proven to be effective in modifying these inhibiting self-appraisals can be implemented in the course of routine postcoronary care, and should be directed at family members as well as at the patient.

Research in cardiac patients has broader implications for understanding how regular physical exercise might enhance emotional adjustment and improve quality of life in healthy people who are without symptoms of cardiovascular disease. A social cognitive analysis of causal relationships between physical exertion, self-appraisal, and emotion suggests that perceptions of self-efficacy play a key mediating role in transforming internal exertion-induced sensations (e.g., reduced discomfort, increased vigor), performance feedback (e.g., improved running time), and social-contextual stimuli (e.g., convivial exchanges with fellow exercisers) into emotional responses such as relief, happiness, or pride. Research using pharmacological interventions to manipulate heart-rate feedback and performance gains during aerobic training suggests that self-efficacy appraisals are not mere transductions of physiological processes or performance gains, and suggests new directions for study of the mechanisms by which physical exercise may enhance emotional adjustment.

ACKNOWLEDGMENTS: Preparation of this chapter was supported in part by Grant No. R01-HL36298 from the National Heart, Lung, and Blood Institute of the National Institute of Health, Bethesda, Maryland.

REFERENCES

Bandura, A. (1986). *Social foundations of thought and action.* Englewood Cliffs, NJ: Prentice-Hall.

Bandura, A. (1990). Perceived self-efficacy in the exercise of personal agency. *Applied Sports Psychology, 2*, 128–163.

Bandura, A., & Cervone, D. (1983). Self-evaluative and self-efficacy mechanisms governing the motivational effects of goal systems. *Journal of Personality and Social Psychology, 45*, 1017–1028.

Ben-Sira, Z., & Eliezer, R. (1990). The structure of readjustment after heart attack. *Social Science and Medicine, 30*, 523–536.

Bersheid, E. (1983). Emotion. In H. Kelley, E. Bersheid, A. Christensen, J. H. Harvey, T. L. Huston, G. Levinger, E. McClintock, L. A. Peplau, & D. R. Peterson (Eds.), *Close relationships* (pp. 110–168). New York: Freeman.

Boutcher, S. H., & Landers, D. M. (1988). The effects of vigorous exercise on anxiety, heart rate, and alpha activity of runners and nonrunners. *Psychophysiology, 25*, 696–702.

Bower, G. H. (1981). Mood and memory. *American Psychologist, 36*, 129–148.

Brown, J. D. (1991). Staying fit and staying well: Physical fitness as a moderator of life stress. *Journal of Personality and Social Psychology, 60*, 555–561.

Cioffi, D. (1991). Beyond attentional strategies: A cognitive–perceptual model of somatic interpretation. *Psychological Bulletin, 109*, 25–41.

Coyne, J. C., & Smith, D. A. F. (1991). Couples coping with a myocardial infarction: A contextual perspective on wives' distress. *Journal of Personality and Social Psychology, 61*, 404–412.

Davidson, R. J., Ekman, P., Saron, C. D., Senulis, J. A., & Friesen, W. V. (1990). Approach–withdrawal and cerebral asymmetry: Emotional expression and brain physiology I. *Journal of Personality and Social Psychology, 58*, 330–341.

DeBusk, R. F., Blomqvist, C. G., Kouchoukos, N. T., Luepker, R. V., Miller, H. S., Moss, A. J., Pollock, M. L., Reeves, T. J., Selvester, R. H., Stason, W. B., Wagner, G. S., & Willman, V. L. (1986). Identification and treatment of low-risk patients after acute myocardial infarction and coronary-artery bypass graft surgery. *New England Journal of Medicine, 314*, 161–166.

Desharnais, R., Jobin, J., Cote, C., Levesque, L., & Godin, G. (1993). Aerobic exercise and the placebo effect: A controlled study. *Psychosomatic Medicine, 55*, 149–154.

Ekman, P., Levenson, R. W., & Friesen, W. V. (1983). Autonomic nervous system activity distinguishes among emotions. *Science, 221*, 1208–1210.

Emmons, R. A. (1986). Personal strivings: An approach to personality and subjective well-being. *Journal of Personality and Social Psychology, 51*, 1058–1068.

Ewart, C. K. (1989). Psychological effects of resistive weight training: Implications for cardiac patients. *Medicine and Science in Sports and Exercise, 21*, 683–688.

Ewart, C. K. (1990). A social problem-solving approach to behavior change in coronary heart disease. In S. Schumaker, E. Schron, & J. Ockene (Eds.), *Handbook of health behavior change* (pp. 153–190). New York: Springer.

Ewart, C. K. (1991). Social action theory for a public health psychology. *American Psychologist, 46*, 931–946.

Ewart, C. K. (1992). Self-efficacy and recovery from acute myocardial infarction. In R. Schwarzer (Ed.), *Self-efficacy: Thought control of action* (pp. 287–304). New York: Springer.

Ewart, C. K. (1993). Editorial: Marital interaction—The context for psychosomatic research. *Psychosomatic Medicine, 55,* 410–412.

Ewart, C. K., Stewart, K. J., Gillilan, R. E., & Kelemen, M. H. (1986). Self-efficacy mediates strength gains during circuit weight training in men with coronary artery disease. *Medicine and Science in Sports and Exercise, 18,* 531–540.

Ewart, C. K., Stewart, K. J., Gillilan, R. E., Kelemen, M. H., Valenti, S. A., Manley, J. D., & Kelemen, M. D. (1986). Usefulness of self-efficacy in predicting overexertion during programmed exercise in coronary artery disease. *American Journal of Cardiology, 57,* 557–561.

Ewart, C. K., & Taylor, C. B. (1985). The effects of early postmyocardial infarction exercise testing on subsequent quality of life. *Quality of Life and Cardiovascular Care, 1,* 162–175.

Ewart, C. K., Taylor, C. B., Reese, L. B., & DeBusk, R. F. (1983). Effects of early postmyocardial infarction exercise testing on self-perception and subsequent physical activity. *American Journal of Cardiology, 51,* 1076–1080.

Folkins, C. H., & Sime, W. E. (1981). Physical fitness training and mental health. *American Psychologist, 36,* 373–389.

Fontana, A. F., Kerns, R. D., Rosenberg, R. L., & Colonese, K. L. (1989). Support, stress, and recovery from coronary heart disease: A longitudinal causal model. *Health Psychology, 8,* 175–193.

Frijda, N. H., Kuipers, P., & Ter Schure, E. (1989). Relations among emotion, appraisal, and emotional action readiness. *Journal of Personality and Social Psychology, 57,* 212–228.

Gunby, P. (1992). Cardiovascular diseases remain nation's leading cause of death. *Journal of the American Medical Association, 267,* 335–336.

Hackett, T. P., Cassem, N. H., & Wishnie, H. A. (1968). The coronary care unit: An appraisal of its psychologic hazards. *New England Journal of Medicine, 279,* 1365–1370.

Kavanagh, D. J., & Bower, G. H. (1985). Mood and self-efficacy: Impact of joy and sadness on perceived capabilities. *Cognitive Therapy and Research, 9,* 507–525.

Kiecolt-Glaser, J. K., Malarkey, W. B., Chee, M. A., Newton, T., Cacioppo, J. T., Mao, J. Y., & Glaser, R. (1993). Negative behavior during marital conflict is associated with immuno-logical down-regulation. *Psychosomatic Medicine, 55,* 395–409.

Lazarus, R. S. (1991a). Progress on a cognitive–motivational–relational theory of emotion. *American Psychologist, 46,* 819–834.

Lazarus, R. S. (1991b). *Emotion and adaptation.* New York: Oxford University Press.

Levenson, R. W. (1988). Emotion and the autonomic nervous system: A prospectus for research on autonomic specificity. In H. Wagner (Ed.), *Social psychophysiology and emotion: Theory and clinical applications* (pp. 17–42). London: Wiley.

Martin, J. E., Dubbert, P. M., Katell, A. D., Thompson, J. K., Raczynski, J. R., Lake, M., Smith, P. O., Webster, J. S., Sikora, T., & Cohen, R. E. (1984). Behavioral control of exercise in sedentary adults: Studies 1 through 6. *Journal of Consulting and Clinical Psychology, 52,* 795–811.

McNair, D. M., Lorr, M., & Droppleman, L. F. (1981). *Manual for the Profile of Mood States.* San Diego, CA: Educational & Industrial Testing Service.

Miller, N. H., Haskell, W. L., Berra, K., & DeBusk, R. F. (1984). Home versus group exercise training for increasing functional capacity after myocardial infarction. *Circulation, 70,* 645–649.

Morgan, W. P. (1985). Affective beneficence of vigorous physical activity. *Medicine and Science in Sports and Exercise, 6,* 422–425.

O'Connor, G. T., Buring, J. E., Yusuf, S., Goldhaber, S. Z., Olmstead, E. M., Paffenbarger, R. S.,

& Hennekens, C. H. (1989). An overview of randomized trials of rehabilitation with exercise after myocardial infarction. *Circulation, 80*, 234–244.

Pennebaker, J. W. (1982). *The psychology of physical symptoms*. New York: Springer-Verlag.

Pickering, T. G. (1989). Ambulatory monitoring: Applications and limitations. In N. Schneiderman, S. Weiss, & P. Kaufman (Eds.), *Handbook of research methods in cardiovascular behavioral medicine* (pp. 261–272), New York: Plenum Press.

Ross, C. E., & Hayes, D. (1988). Exercise and psychologic well-being in the community. *American Journal of Epidemiology, 127*, 762–761.

Salazar, W., Petruzzello, S. J., Landers, D. M., Etnier, J. L., & Kubitz, K. A. (1993). Meta-analytic techniques in exercise psychology. In P. Seraganian (Ed.), *Exercise psychology: The influence of physical exercise on psychological processes* (pp. 122–145). New York: Wiley.

Schachter, S. (1966). The interaction of cognitive and physiological determinants of emotional state. In C. D. Spielberger (Ed.), *Anxiety and behavior* (pp. 193–224). New York: Academic Press.

Steptoe, A., & Cox, S. (1988). Acute effects of aerobic exercise on mood. *Health Psychology, 7*, 329–340.

Stewart, K. J., Kelemen, M. H., & Ewart, C. K. (1993). Relationships between self-efficacy and mood before and after exercise training. *Journal of Cardiopulmonary Rehabilitation, 14*, 35–42.

Taylor, C. B., Bandura, A., Ewart, C. K., Miller, N. H., & DeBusk, R. F. (1985). Exercise testing to enhance wives' confidence in their husband's capability soon after clinically uncomplicated myocardial infarction. *American Journal of Cardiology, 55*, 636–628.

Taylor, C. B., Sallis, J. F., & Needle, R. (1985). The relation of physical activity and exercise to mental health. *Public Health Reports, 100*, 195–202.

Tellegen, A. (1985). Structures of mood and personality and their relevance to assessing anxiety, with an emphasis on self-report. In A. H. Tuma & J. D. Maser (Eds.), *Anxiety and the anxiety disorders* (pp. 681–706). Hillsdale, NJ: Erlbaum.

Tuson, K. M., & Sinyor, D. (1993). On the affective benefits of acute aerobic exercise: Taking stock after twenty years of research. In P. Seraganian (Ed.), *Exercise psychology: The influence of physical exercise on psychological processes* (pp. 80–121). New York: Wiley.

Watson, D. W., Clark, L. A., & Tellegen, A. (1988). Development and validation of brief measures of positive and negative affect: The PANAS scales. *Journal of Personality and Social Psychology, 54*, 1063–1070.

Watson, D. W., & Pennebaker, J. W. (1989). Health complaints, stress, and distress: Exploring the central role of negative affectivity. *Psychological Review, 96*, 234–254.

CHAPTER 8

SELF-EFFICACY AND THE PHYSIOLOGICAL STRESS RESPONSE

Ann O'Leary and Shirley Brown

INTRODUCTION

In recent years there has been a dramatic increase in attention to the construct of *stress*. Whereas a few decades ago the term was hardly used, in the modern age most of us probably hear the term daily (Lazarus & Folkman, 1984). One reason for this increased attention has been our growing understanding of the effects of stress and other emotional processes on important health outcomes, such as cardiovascular disease and infectious illness (Contrada, Leventhal, & O'Leary, 1990). Stress can influence health through two pathways. The first involves its effects on the adoption of health-impairing behaviors, such as the use of tobacco, alcohol, or other recreational drugs—or avoiding medical care or treatment—whereas the second concerns its direct effects on tissues and organs. This second pathway is mediated by activity in the major stress-responsive body systems, whose neuroendocrine products (to be reviewed) mediate the process.

Psychologists have applied a variety of theoretical constructs to the area of stress psychobiology (reviewed in Miller & O'Leary, 1993). One

Ann O'Leary and Shirley Brown • Department of Psychology, Rutgers University, New Brunswick, New Jersey 08903.

Self-Efficacy, Adaptation, and Adjustment: Theory, Research, and Application, edited by James E. Maddux. Plenum Press, New York, 1995.

227

such approach is social cognitive theory (SCT), which features individuals' beliefs about their own competencies, or self-efficacy beliefs. A wide variety of studies conducted within the framework of SCT support the notion that individuals' beliefs about their abilities to achieve their goals and manage specific situations strongly influence motivational, behavioral, and emotional processes. This chapter explores the role of coping self-efficacy in modifying physiological stress responses. Self-efficacy beliefs have been shown to moderate several components of the physiological stress response, including activity of the sympathetic nervous system, the hypothalamic–pituitary–adrenal cortical system, the endogenous opioid system, and the immune system. Studies to be reviewed include both field and laboratory research.

A noted advantage of self-efficacy theory relative to other cognitive approaches to health is its specification of methods for positively modifying the suggested process. Graded mastery experience—for example, through goal-setting and practice in following the modeling of successful behavior by similar others—has been shown to readily enhance self-efficacy judgements and behavior (Bandura, Adams, Hardy, & Howells, 1980; Bandura, Jeffrey, & Wright, 1974). All of the studies described in this chapter involve experimental manipulation of self-efficacy as a method for establishing its causal role in psychobiological functioning.

OVERVIEW OF PHYSIOLOGICAL MECHANISMS

When organisms are confronted with situations that they appraise as potentially harmful or threatening to their comfort, they usually experience strong physiological reactions. Of the myriad physical responses that occur in response to stress (Asterita, 1985), several neuroendocrine pathways are held to be the most functionally related—and therefore the most responsive—to emotion and distress. These include the sympathetic adrenomedullary (SAM), the hypothalamic adrenocortical (HPAC), and the endogenous opioid systems. Although these systems are highly interrelated, it is nevertheless heuristic and feasible to distinguish among the broad psychological correlates of activity in each. At the end of this section we also present a very brief overview of the immune system.

THE SYMPATHETIC NERVOUS SYSTEM

The sympathetic nervous system (SNS), also called the autonomic nervous system, consists of two arms, the sympathetic and parasympathetic subsystems. Each of these comprises nerves that end in certain target organs, including the heart, lungs, digestive system, and kidneys. The SAM system is activated in situations that engender acute emotions, such as fear and anger, and serves to prepare the organism for "fight or flight." The effects of the sympathetic arm serve to ready the organism for rapid, acute energy expenditure, while the parasympathetic arm produces opposite effects and serves to modulate the sympathetic response. Another end organ, the adrenal gland, is innervated by sympathetic nerves, and when this system is activated, the medulla (inner core) of the adrenal gland secretes catecholamines, such as epinephrine and norepinephrine, into the blood stream, where they have the capacity to reach most other parts of the body. The sympathetic nervous system also innervates lymphoid organs, which contain many of the white blood cells that comprise the immune system.

The Hypothalamic–Pituitary–Adrenal Cortical System

In contrast, the activity of the HPAC system is associated with overwhelming threat, loss, and depression, and induces the organism to retreat and conserve energies. This system is part of the endocrine (hormonal) system, whose effects are generally slower than those of the nervous system. HPAC activation produces enhanced secretion of corticosteroid hormones, such as cortisol from the cortex (outer layer) of the adrenal glands.

It is important to be aware of the differences in the psychological underpinnings of these two systems, the SAM and the HPAC,while recognizing that many stressful situations will elicit activity in both systems. Both originate with central nervous system (CNS) activity, actually with cognitive appraisal processes in the cerebral cortex, and both involve activity in the brain's limbic system. However, their peripheral effects are quite different, and the types of appraisals that generate them differ, as described. These two systems have been respectively designated the *fight–flight* and *conservation–withdrawal* systems (Henry & Stephens, 1977), or the "effort" and "distress" systems (Frankenhuaser, 1983), based upon their differential functions.

The Endogenous Opioid System

The endogenous opioid system is complex, having both CNS and peripheral effects. Opioid peptides, which are molecularly similar to exogenous opiates (e.g., morphine and heroin) produce similar effects, such as analgesia, and also affect some homeostatic processes, such as the regulation of food intake and thermal regulation. They further serve to calm organisms that are under extremely stressful conditions (see Cohen, Pickar, & Dubois, 1983; G. A. Olson, R. D. Olson, & Kastin, 1992 for reviews). Activation of the stress-related component of this system takes place in association with helplessness—for example, after repeated electric shock when the organism has no means for terminating the stimulation—and during severe physical pain (Bolles & Fanselow, 1984; Shavit & Martin, 1987). Opioid activity can be blocked by administering naloxone or naltrexone, which occupy opiate receptors and thus prevent their effects. In general, it has been established that phenomena hypothesized to be mediated by opioids indeed are by demonstrating that they are reversed by the administration of such opioid antagonists. Furthermore, decrements in pain tolerance resulting from opioid antagonist administration imply ongoing activity of the opioid system, because analgesia is an established effect of opioid activity.

THE IMMUNE SYSTEM

The immune system is the body's means of maintaining its integrity against nonself material, such as infectious pathogens (e.g., bacteria, viruses, fungi, and parasites), and is also thought to play a role in cancer surveillance (for a more comprehensive overview of the immune system, see O'Leary, 1990). The leukocytes (i.e., the white blood cells) that comprise the immune system develop in the bone marrow and thymus and are stored in these and other lymphoid organs. There are numerous types of lymphocytes that can be distinguished on the basis of receptors on their surfaces. One major distinction exists between B-lymphocytes and T-lymphocytes. B-lymphocytes secrete molecules called antibodies, whereas some T-cells have cytotoxic capabilities and others communicate with other immune-system cells to enhance ("helper" T-cells) or to dampen ("suppressor" T-cells) immune responses. Natural killer (NK) cells destroy virally infected and dysplastic cells.

The effectiveness of the immune system can be measured in two ways. *Enumerative* assessment involves counting the cells of different types that are found in the blood. *Functional* measures evaluate how well the cells perform their functions. A common functional measure is the proliferative (replication) response of lymphocytes to stimulation by *mitogens*, foreign materials that are recognized as antigen by the cells, causing them to multiply.

HEALTH CONSEQUENCS OF STRESS SYSTEM ACTIVATION

There is documented evidence of many important health effects of prolonged or extreme activation of these systems. Excessive and frequent SNS activity appears to impact on the major cardiovascular diseases, especially coronary heart disease (CHD; reviewed in Haynes & Matthews, 1988). Adrenocortical activation has been found to be immunosuppressive in a variety of ways, and may thereby contribute to an increased incidence of infectious and autoimmune diseases, and even cancer (see Contrada et al., 1990; O'Leary, 1990). Asthma, diabetes, certain gastrointestinal disorders, headaches, hypertension, and stroke are among the other known stress-related disorders.

Given these relationships, the studies reviewed here are potentially relevant to the development of long-term health consequences, such as heart disease or cancer. However, because such diseases may take many years to develop, only those psychobiological processes that occur frequently are likely to influence such outcomes. The notion that efficacy beliefs are specific to particular domains is a central and distinguishing feature of self-efficacy theory. Although there may be some generalization of efficacy beliefs across domains that are perceived to require similar skills, such beliefs are held to be essentially unrelated in different domains. According to the theory, then, a person may expect to be successful at giving sales presentations and experience minimal stress when doing so, but become extremely distressed when required to socialize at a cocktail party. The frequency with which this individual encounters the latter situation will then have an impact on long-term stress-related health outcomes.

THEORETICAL BACKGROUND

Stress researcher Richard Lazarus and colleagues have observed that stress reactions occur following a *primary appraisal* of impending threat or harm (Lazarus, 1991; Lazarus & Folkman, 1984). Primary appraisal concerns what is at stake, what the organism has to lose. Another important link in the pathway from stressor to physical reaction is *secondary appraisal*, an assessment of the personal resources available for managing the potential stressor. Perceptions of self-efficacy to cope with existing stressors are a type of secondary appraisal. Coping can consist of behavioral or cognitive efforts to manage the stressor itself (so-called "problem-focused coping" in Lazarus's nomenclature) or to control one's emotional response to it ("emotion-focused coping"). Since individuals who judge themselves capable of managing or controlling a given stressor should be less anxious and less physiologically aroused, self-efficacy to cope with stress has been investigated as a factor that may buffer or dampen the physiological stress response.

Effects of behavioral and cognitive control over noxious conditions on the resulting stress reactions have been demonstrated for some time, and across a variety of potentially aversive, stressful, and painful events (reviewed in Bandura, 1986; Lazarus & Folkman, 1984). For example, aversive stimuli are perceived as less noxious when people believe that they have the option of terminating the stimulation, even if they never use that option (Glass, Reim, & Singer, 1971; Glass, Singer, Leonard, Krantz, & Cummings, 1973; Miller, 1980). Perceiving oneself as capable of coping with a stressor is equivalent to having control over the effects of that stressor. Thus, in recent years, self-efficacy beliefs have been assessed in several stress studies as potential buffers against physiological stress effects.

EVIDENCE FOR SELF-EFFICACY EFFECTS
ON STRESS PHYSIOLOGY

A number of studies have productively employed a phobic fear model for investigating the influence of self-efficacy on stress reactions. In these studies, individuals with severe phobias (usually of snakes or spiders) are treated by an SCT-generated approach in which therapeutic confrontation with the feared object gradually promotes mastery over the debilitating fear. Self-efficacy and physiological parameters are typically assessed before, during, and after the course of the therapy.

Phobic fear is an emotional state that is likely to engender SAM system activity. Indeed, in a study using the phobia paradigm, efficacy to handle a snake was manipulated to varying degrees of efficacy for task performance during phobia therapy, with some subjects receiving minimal therapy and therefore gaining small increases in efficacy, and others receiving moderate and large amounts of efficacy enhancement, respectively. Peripheral indices of sympathetic arousal—heart rate and blood pressure—were measured during anticipation and performance of tasks for which these differential levels of efficacy had been instated. Level of arousal varied as a function of perceived efficacy, as did subjective fear and actual enactive attainments (Bandura, Reese, & Adams, 1982). Whereas heart rate rose to its highest level during anticipation of tasks for which efficacy was moderate, it declined during anticipation of tasks for which efficacy was low, presumably because subjects did not plan to attempt these tasks. However, blood pressure remained high during anticipation of these tasks. During anticipation and performance of tasks for which efficacy was high, increases in heart rate and blood pressure were small. After successful treatment for the phobia was completed, the same tasks provoked only minimal sympathetic response. In a subsequent study of spider phobics (Bandura, Taylor, Williams, Mefford, & Barchas, 1985), assessment of blood levels of the catecholamines, epinephrine, norepinephrine, and dopac, provided a more direct measure of SAM activity. Based on the results of the Bandura et al. (1982) study, the investigators hypothesized that catecholamines would rise sharply during tasks for which subjects felt moderately efficacious, and also during those for which subjects felt inefficacious, unless they declined to attempt the task. As indicated by Figure 1, the predicted relationships were generally well supported: Catecholamine release was low during tasks for which subjects felt highly efficacious, higher for those associated with moderate levels of self-efficacy, and low for tasks associated with such weak self-efficacy that subjects had no intention of attempting them. The catecholamine dopac, which is related to CNS dopamine degradation, rose during anticipation of even low efficacy tasks; that is, while subjects merely contemplated performing them. In another phase of the study, changes in catecholamine levels were assessed as subjects completed each phase of treatment. These results also reflected the efficacy–stress relationship. Early in treatment, subjects evidenced high sympathetic activity, which then diminished as treatment progressed, but then increased at the end, when subjects were asked to suspend control and simply let the spider crawl over them.

Perceived coping efficacy also appears to influence the endogenous opioid response to stress. In a study investigating the mechanisms of cognitive control techniques for pain management (Bandura, O'Leary, Taylor, Gauthier, & Gossard, 1987), subjects were randomized to one of three interventions after a cold pressor pain performance assessment: training in cognitive pain control, receiving placebo medication, or a non-intervention control. In the Cognitive Coping condition, subjects received 30-minute instruction in a variety of pain-management techniques, including attention diversion, pleasant imagery, mental dissociation of the arm from the rest of the body, cognitive relabeling of pain as other types of sensation, and self-encouragement of coping efforts. The placebo was administered by a physician who conveyed an expectation that it was a powerful analgesic. Subjects in the Control condition simply waited for 30 minutes. Treatment effects on efficacy and pain tolerance were then assessed. Following the assessment, half of the subjects in each group were further randomized to receive either naloxone, an opiate antagonist, or a saline control injection. The study design is summarized in Figure 2. Figure 3 depicts the result of the interventions on perceived efficacy to tolerate and to reduce pain, and on actual pain tolerance. The cognitive coping training produced significant increases in both types of self-efficacy, as well as in pain tolerance, whereas the placebo medication enhanced self-efficacy to endure, but not to reduce, pain. In turn, both types of self-efficacy predicted actual pain tolerance, with cognitive copers exhibiting the greatest tolerance increases.

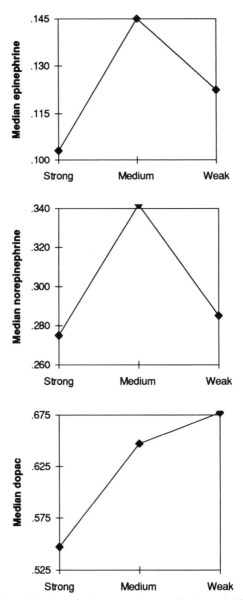

FIGURE 1. Median level of catecholamine secretion as a function of differential strength of perceived coping self-efficacy (Reprinted from Bandura, O'Leary, Taylor, Williams, Mefford, & Barchas, 1985).

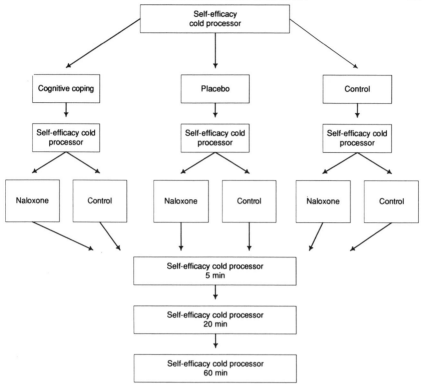

FIGURE 2. Design of study examining self-efficacy and cognitive control effects on endogenous opioid response (Adapted from Bandura, O'Leary, Taylor, Gauthier, & Gossard, 1987).

A central question of the study was whether, and to what extent, central opioid activity mediates the effectiveness of cognitive pain control techniques. It was reasoned that since naloxone blocks the effect of opioids, any mediating effect of opioids would be reversed by the large dose (10 mg) of naloxone administered. Subsequent to administration of the saline or the naloxone, the expected effect was detected: Endogenous opioid activity was implicated in the cognitive coping condition (see Fig. 4). However, pain tolerance was not completely *reversed* by the high dose of naloxone, as it would have been if the mechanism were fully mediated by opioids. Instead, subjects in the cognitive coping condition showed significantly less *increase* over time in their tolerance of the cold pressor pain. Furthermore, subjects with the largest increases in self-efficacy to reduce pain at the end of the training session were both more pain tolerant in subsequent trials and exhibited greater reactivity to naloxone.

These results were interpreted to reflect both opioid and nonopioid

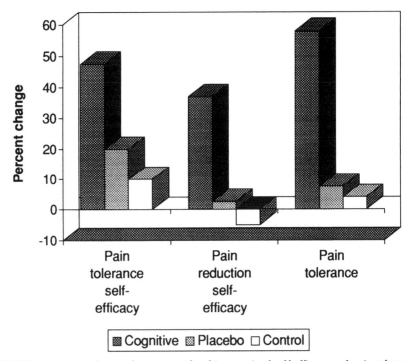

FIGURE 3. Percent changes from pretest level in perceived self-efficacy and pain tolerance achieved by people who were taught cognitive pain-control techniques, administered a placebo, or received no intervention (Reprinted from Bandura, O'Leary, Taylor, Gauthier, & Gossard, 1987).

mediation of pain tolerance in the cognitive copers. The pattern of results suggests that opioid mechanisms are activated in the latter phases of the tolerance test, when self-efficacy begins to break down and the tolerance limit is approached. Accordingly, subjects who perceived themselves as more efficacious were more likely to take on higher pain stimulation, and thus were more likely to exhibit opioid activity. This explanation is consonant with research indicating the role of opioids under conditions of stress and helplessness, and not under conditions of control.

Endogenous opioid mechanisms in reaction to purely *mental* stress have also been demonstrated in response to modification of self-efficacy (Bandura, Cioffi, Taylor, & Brouillard, 1988). To manipulate self-efficacy in this study, subjects were administered the stressor, a mental arithmetic task, under one of two conditions: either self-paced by the subject, or with pacing "yoked" to that of another randomly selected self-paced subject

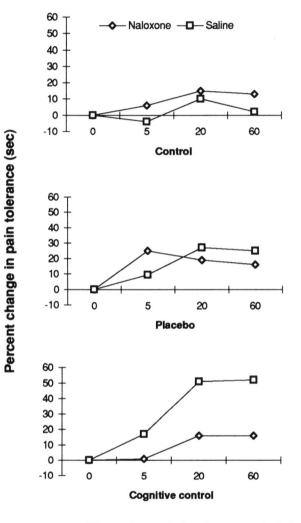

Time of post-injection tests (min)

FIGURE 4. Percent change in pain tolerance from the posttreatment level at each of three post injection periods as a function of whether people received saline or the opiate antagonist naloxone (Reprinted from Bandura, O'Leary, Taylor, Gauthier, & Gossard, 1987).

(and thus not under the target subject's control). This produced expected increases in self-efficacy for the self-paced group and decreases in the yoked group. Furthermore, the efficacy effects of the manipulation were corroborated by elevated measures of heart rate in low efficacy subjects but not in high efficacy ones.

Subsequent to this manipulation, subjects were randomly assigned to two further conditions, receiving either a naloxone or a saline injection, as in the cold pressor study previously described. A pain tolerance test was then administered to determine the effect of the injection. The rationale for this procedure was that if mental stress with low self-efficacy were accompanied by opioid activation, then naloxone should reduce performance on a pain tolerance test by blocking this activity. Indeed, subjects in the low-efficacy group who received naloxone were significantly less able to tolerate pain than low-efficacy subjects in the saline control condition. No differences were found between high-efficacy subjects who received naloxone versus saline, indicating that these subjects were not under stress and displayed no opioid activation. These results indicate that the self-efficacy manipulation activated opioid systems in the distressed subjects, and provide persuasive evidence that self-efficacy influences opioid reactions even to purely mental stressors.

Several studies have explored the impact of self-efficacy on the relationships between stress and immune function. One such investigation employed a naturalistic stressor—rheumatoid arthritis (RA)—to examine the impact of a self-efficacy enhancing stress-management intervention on measures of both local and systemic immunity (O'Leary, Shoor, Lorig, & Holman, 1988). It has been speculated that RA, a very painful and frequently debilitating joint condition, may have an autoimmune etiology in which the immune system treats parts of the joints as nonself. This could result from dysfunction of the suppressor T-cell system, whose immune-active cells are responsible for curtailing completed or improper immune reactions. Figure 5 depicts hypothesized interactions among immune-dysfunction and the common physical and psychological features of RA. In this model, immune-dysfunction and related autoimmune processes in the joints produce pain, which in turn leads to reduced activity and subsequent depression, as well as stress. Furthermore, psychological distress would seem likely to be associated with further immune impairment, given the growing literature on psychoneuroimmunology (see Herbert & Cohen, 1993; O'Leary, 1990 for reviews) and the literature relating stress to worse medical outcome in RA (Anderson, Bradley, Young, McDaniel, & Wise, 1985). Thus a vicious circle can be created for RA patients; however, it is one that might be expected to be broken by psychosocial intervention for

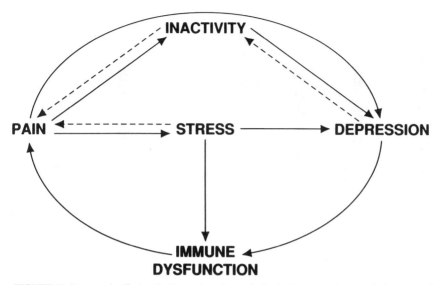

FIGURE 5. Proposed effects of physical and psychological comcomitants of rheumatoid arthritis on immune dysfunction (Adapted from O'Leary, Shoor, Lorig, & Holman, 1988).

the management of pain and stress (see McCracken, 1991, for a review of psychosocial interventions for arthritis).

In O'Leary et al. (1988) there were two conditions to which female subjects with RA were randomized. Half of the subjects received a 5-session cognitive–behavioral intervention that conferred techniques for pain and stress management and employed goal-setting for activity increase and the attainment of other life goals. The other treatment condition was a bibliotherapy control employing a popular "Helpbook" for arthritis management. The interventions were evaluated across a range of criteria. These included psychological measures—self-efficacy to manage pain specifically, and arthritis generally; coping; perceived stress and depression—and medical measures—self-monitored pain and ratings of joint impairment by rheumatologists blind to treatment condition. Finally, immune system measures—including the number of helper and suppressor T-cells and proliferative responses of lymphocytes to mitogen stimulation—were collected. All measures were obtained before and after the interventions to assess intervention effects.

As depicted in Figure 6, significant results differentiating the treatment and control groups were found for perceived self-efficacy, self-rated pain, and joint impairment. A marginally significant reduction in disability

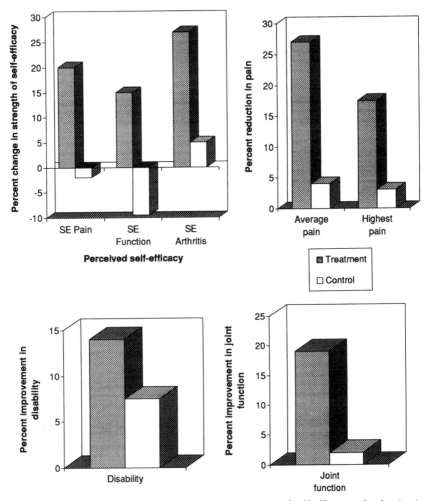

FIGURE 6. Changes exhibited by arthritis patients in perceived self-efficacy and reduction in pain and impairment of joints as a function training in self-regulatory techníques (Adapted from O'Leary, Shoor, Lorig, & Holman, 1988).

was also obtained. Those in the cognitive–behavioral intervention group also exhibited reductions in depression and stress, increased coping, and improved sleep quality. Furthermore, the extent of self-efficacy enhancement in these subjects was significantly correlated with treatment effectiveness. Whereas there were no significant effects of the intervention on systemic immune measures, subjects with higher ratings of efficacy and with more efficacy enhancement as a result of treatment exhibited greater numbers of suppressor T-cells and lower helper:suppressor T-cell ratios posttreatment (reflecting superior immune functioning in this disease model). Thus, efficacy was correlated with improved immune function, both cross-sectionally and longitudinally, although immunity did not change significantly among all subjects receiving the intervention. On the other hand, the significant reduction of joint inflammation, as rated by the rheumatologists, appears to reflect improved local immune and inflammatory processes (i.e., in the joints). The intervention therefore appeared to influence local, but not systémic, immune functioning.

Another recent study utilized the phobic-stress paradigm described earlier to study effects of self-efficacy on immunity (Wiedenfeld, O'Leary, Bandura, Brown, Levine, & Raska, 1990). The experimental stressor in this study was treatment for snake phobia, a guided mastery therapy that requires subjects to attempt increasingly difficult tasks as modeled by the therapist. The study followed a baseline-intervention-baseline (A-B-A) design, with assessments of psychological functioning, self-efficacy, immune function, and salivary cortisol in the first week repeated the second week, immediately following 4 hours of guided mastery therapy, and again 1 week later, after successfully completing a series of snake-handling tasks with full efficacy in the third week.

As illustrated in Figure 7, it was found that absolute numbers of several circulating lymphocyte types were significantly elevated during stress exposure in the second week. Intermediate values were obtained in the third week, reflecting either persistent enhancement following treatment or possibly in response to the excitement (also a SAM activator) of therapy "graduation" during the final week. This finding of apparent immune enhancement in connection with stress might be seen as contradicting other studies showing immune decrements in association with stress and depression. However, the finding does reproduce the demonstrated effects of epinephrine injection (Crary et al., 1983), and probably reflects movement of cells into the bloodstream from organs of storage (presumably following SAM innervation of lymphoid organs mentioned previously). The nature of this stressor, which is acute, short-lived, under the subject's control, and elicits a relatively "pure" emotional state of fear, makes it likely to be associated with a relatively pure SAM response and little HPAC activity. In fact, recall that catecholamine release was previously shown to be associated with phobic stress and coping, in the Bandura et al. (1992) study. Interestingly, a small subset of subjects, who instead exhibited *decrements* in immune measures during exposure to the stressor with recovery in the third week, also had substantially higher levels of salivary cortisol (reflecting HPAC activity) at the end of the

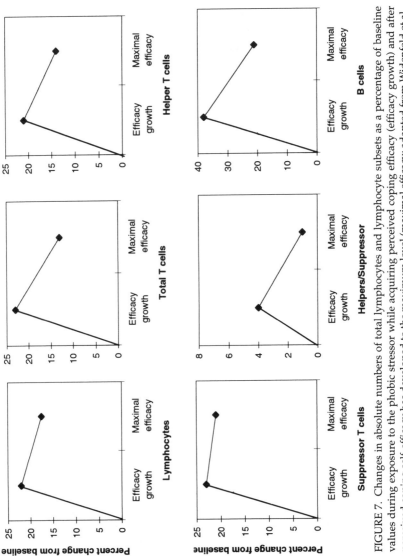

FIGURE 7. Changes in absolute numbers of total lymphocytes and lymphocyte subsets as a percentage of baseline values during exposure to the phobic stressor while acquiring perceived coping efficacy (efficacy growth) and after perceived coping self-efficacy has developed to the maximum level (maximal efficacy; adapted from Widenfeld et al., 1990).

therapy session, relative to those showing enhanced immunity. As for self-efficacy, the investigators found that its rate of growth related positively to amount of immune enhancement, and negatively to salivary cortisol concentration at the end of the stress-exposure session. On the basis of these results, the authors speculated that rapid increments in self-efficacy may be associated with SAM activity, or "effort" in Frankenhauser's nomenclature, whereas slower growth of efficacy may be associated with adrenocortical activity and "distress." The major finding of increases in numbers of lymphocytes circulating in the blood may also have an evolutionary basis, because organisms in "fight-or-flight" situations may have been likely to incur external wounds that might become infected were lymphocytes not rapidly deployed to the area.

DISCUSSION AND FUTURE DIRECTIONS

Social cognitive theory presents a comprehensive structure within which to examine the complexities of cognitive, affective, behavioral, and physiological phenomena of interest in health psychology. This chapter summarizes only one of the pathways—influences on stress physiology—by which self-efficacy can affect health. The fundamental nature of self-efficacy as it relates to stress is illustrated by efficacy contributions to a variety of physiological stress systems, including the sympathetic nervous system, the hypothalamic–pituitary–adrenal cortical system, the endogenous opioid system, and ultimately the immune system. Despite the fact that the cognitive appraisal underlying activity in these diverse systems may differ, the fundamental belief that "I can cope with this, I can manage the stressor using cognitive and/or behavioral means" underlies all of them. In some cases, efficacy beliefs are associated directly with a dampening of stress processes, in another case with an enhancement of them mediated by enhanced behavioral exposure to the stressor (as in the laboratory pain study by Bandura et al., 1987), and in still another case, faster growth of efficacy in a phobic stress situation was speculated to prevent HPAC activity while permitting SAM activity (the phobic stress immunology study by Wiedenfeld et al., 1990). The systematic delineation of these processes via microanalytic psychobiological procedures would constitute a significant research contribution in this area.

It must be emphasized that many of the physiological processes described are components of larger and far more complex systems. The immune system, for example, comprises intricate feedback mechanisms that in effect render terms such as "immune impairment" and "immune enhancement" overly simplistic. Within the neuroendocrine pathways, particularly the HPAC system, there are many additional hormones and hormonal interactions that are likely to have as yet poorly investigated influences on stress physiological relationships. Furthermore, the clinical relevance of some of these statistically significant findings, in most cases, remains to be supported by properly controlled studies. Nevertheless, knowledge of how self-efficacy affects these processes is a vital step toward a fuller understanding of the linkages among cognitive and affective factors, stress physiology, and disease processes. The increasing sophistication of multidisciplinary research is encouraging in this light.

It should also be emphasized that many health outcomes are potentially influenced by another pathway, that of health-impacting behaviors. For example, many behaviors that are damaging to health, such as increased use of nicotine, alcohol, and street drugs, are used to cope palliatively with stress, and may be further associated with reductions in sleep and poorer nutrition. Therefore it is incumbent upon investigators, particularly those conducting correlational field research, to design their methodologies so as to identify contributions from each health-related behavior, or at least to control statistically for the variables of less interest in a particular study.

There is a great need for the development of psychosocial interventions for stressful chronic illnesses. Self-efficacy theory, with its focus on effective intervention strategies such as guided mastery, is particularly suited to this endeavor. Chronic illness comprises a growing proportion of health difficulty as the population of the United States ages, and often stress accompanies the disease itself, its symptoms, or its treatment. In chronic cardiovascular disease (i.e., after a heart attack), it is possible to enhance self-efficacy for resuming activity using a treadmill procedure (Taylor, Bandura, Ewart, Miller, & DeBusk, 1985). Reducing stress in chronic-disease models could potentially have physiologically health-enhancing effects, as well as affective and behavioral ones. Some evidence for this has been obtained in rheumatoid arthritis studies as described previously, but developing self-efficacy-enhancing treatments for other illnesses, such as cancer, HIV illness, and diabetes, would be promising avenues to pursue.

REFERENCES

Anderson, K. O., Bradley, L. A., Young, L. D., McDaniel, L. K., & Wise, C. (1985). Rheumatoid arthritis: Review of psychological factors related to etiology, effects, and treatment. *Psychological Bulletin, 98*, 358–387.

Asterita, M. F. (1985). *The physiology of stress.* New York: Human Sciences Press.

Bandura, A. (1986). *Social foundations of thought and action: A social cognitive theory.* Englewood Cliffs, NJ: Prentice-Hall.

Bandura, A., Adams, N. E., Hardy, A. B., & Howells, G. N. (1980). Tests of the generality of self-efficacy theory. *Cognitive Therapy and Research, 4,* 39–66.

Bandura, A., Cioffi, D., Taylor, C. B., & Brouillard, M. E. (1988). Perceived self-efficacy in coping with cognitive stressors and opioid activation. *Journal of Personality and Social Psychology, 55,* 479–488.

Bandura, A., Jeffrey, R. W., & Wright, C. L. (1974). Efficacy of participant modeling as a function of response induction aids. *Journal of Abnormal Psychology, 83,* 56–64.

Bandura, A., O'Leary, A., Taylor, C. B., Gauthier, J., & Gossard, D. (1987). Perceived self-efficacy and pain control: Opioid and nonopioid mechanisms. *Journal of Personality and Social Psychology, 53,* 563–571.

Bandura, A., Reese, L., & Adams, N. E. (1982). Microanalysis of action and fear arousal as a function of differential levels of perceived self-efficacy. *Journal of Personality and Social Psychology, 43,* 5–21.

Bandura, A., Taylor, C. B., Williams, S. L., Mefford, I. N., & Barchas, J. D. (1985). Catecholamine secretion as a function of perceived coping self-efficacy. *Journal of Consulting and Clinical Psychology, 53,* 406–414.

Bolles, R. C., & Fanselow, M. S. (1984). Endorphins and behavior. *Annual Review of Psychology, 33,* 87–101.

Cohen, M. R., Pickar, D., & Dubois, M. (1983). The role of the endogenous opioid system in the human stress response. *Psychiatric Clinics of North America, 6,* 457–471.

Contrada, R. J., Leventhal, H., & O'Leary, A. (1990). Personality and health. In L. A. Pervin (Eds.), *Handbook of Personality: Theory and research* (pp. 638–669). New York: Guilford.

Crary, B., Hauser, S. L., Borysenko, M., Kutz, I., Hoban, C., Ault, K. A., Weiner, H. L., & Benson, H. (1983). Epinephrine-induced changes in the distribution of lymphocyte subsets in the peripheral blood of humans. *Journal of Immunology, 131,* 1178–1181.

Frankenhauser, M. (1983). The sympathetic–adrenal and pituitary–adrenal response to challenge: Comparison between the sexes. In T. M. Dembroski, T. H. Schmidt, & G. Blumchen (Eds.), *Biobehavioral bases of coronary heart disease* (pp. 91–105). New York: Karger.

Glass, D. C., Reim, B., & Singer, J. (1971). Behavioral consequences of adaptation to controllable and uncontrollable noise. *Journal of Experimental Social Psychology, 7,* 244–257.

Glass, D. C., Singer, J. E., Leonard, H. S., Krantz, D., & Cummings, H. (1973). Perceived control of aversive stimulation and the reduction of stress responses. *Journal of Personality, 41,* 577–595.

Haynes, S. G., & Matthews, K. A. (1988). Review and methodologic critique of recent studies on Type A behavior and cardiovascular disease. *Annals of Behavioral Medicine, 10,* 47–59.

Henry, J. P., & Stephens, P. M. (1977). *Stress, health, and the social environment.* New York: Springer.

Herbert, T. B., & Cohen, S. (1993). Stress and immunity in humans: A meta-analytic review. *Psychosomatic Medicine, 55,* 364–379.

Lazarus, R. (1991). *Emotion and adaptation.* New York: Oxford University Press.

Lazarus, R., & Folkman, S. (1984). *Stress, appraisal, and coping.* New York: Springer.

McCracken, L. M. (1991). Cognitive–behavioral treatment of rheumatoid arthritis: A preliminary review of efficacy and methodology. *Annals of Behavioral Medicine, 13,* 57–65.

Miller, S. M. (1980). Why having control reduces stress: If I can stop the roller coaster I don't want to get off. In J. Garber & M. E. P. Seligman (Eds.), *Human helplessness: Theory and research* (pp. 71–95). New York: Academic Press.

Miller, S. M., & O'Leary, A. (1993). Cognition, stress, and health. In K. Dodson & P. C. Kendall (Eds.), *Cognition and psychopathology* (pp. 159–189). New York: Academic Press.

O'Leary, A. (1990). Stress, emotion, and human immune function. *Psychological Bulletin, 108,* 363–382.

O'Leary, A., Shoor, S., Lorig, K., & Holman, H. R. (1988). A cognitive–behavioral treatment for rheumatoid arthritis. *Health Psychology, 7,* 527–544.

Olson, G. A., Olson, R. D., & Kastin, A. J. (1992). Endogenous opiates: 1991. *Peptides, 13,* 1247–1287.

Shavit, Y., & Martin, F. C. (1987). Opiates, stress, and immunity: Animal studies. *Annals of Behavioral Medicine, 9,* 11–20.

Taylor, C. B., Bandura, A., Ewart, C. K., Miller, N. H., & DeBusk, R. F. (1985). Raising spouse's and patient's perception of his cardiac capabilities after clinically uncomplicated myocardial infarction. *American Journal of Cardiology, 55,* 635–638.

Wiedenfeld, S. A., O'Leary, A., Bandura, A., Brown, S., Levine, S., & Raska, K. (1990). Impact of perceived coping efficacy on components of the immune system. *Journal of Personality and Social Psychology, 59,* 1082–1094.

PART IV

OTHER APPLICATIONS

CHAPTER 9

SELF-EFFICACY AND CAREER CHOICE AND DEVELOPMENT

GAIL HACKETT and NANCY E. BETZ

There are few other decisions that exert as profound an influence on people's lives as the choice of a field of work, or career. Not only do most people spend considerably more time on the job than in any other single activity (save, arguably, sleep), but also choice of occupation significantly affects lifestyle, and work adjustment is intimately associated with mental health and even physical well-being (Levi, 1990; Osipow, 1986). Despite the relative neglect of work/career issues in the field of psychology at large, researchers in the area of vocational psychology have been studying career choice and work adjustment for decades, and a number of theoretical models of career choice and development have been generated (Hackett & Lent, 1992).

Historically, trait and factor approaches (e.g., Dawis & Lofquist, 1984) have dominated the field. Trait and factor theories emphasize congruence (or matching) between job requirements and personal characteristics, such as interests, abilities, and personality, in the prediction of job choice and satisfaction (Hackett, Lent, & Greenhaus, 1991). In the past several decades, the original trait and factor perspectives have been updated to reflect a more complex person–environment interaction (e.g., Rounds & Tracey,

GAIL HACKETT • Division of Psychology in Education, Arizona State University, Tempe, Arizona 85287. NANCY E. BETZ • Department of Psychology, Ohio State University, Columbus, Ohio 43210.

Self-Efficacy, Adaptation, and Adjustment: Theory, Research, and Application, edited by James E. Maddux. Plenum Press, New York, 1995.

1990), but critics argue that even the updated trait and factor models remain limited in their ability to adequately capture the dynamic and complex processes involved in choosing a career (Hackett & Lent, 1992). Developmentally based career theories, that is, those theories that draw on developmental and self-concept psychology and focus on how interests, work values, and self-estimates of ability develop and interact with career exploration and choice behavior over the life span (e.g., Super, 1990), have also received a great deal of attention in the career literature.

Not until the mid-1970s was learning theory explicitly applied to the career decision-making process. Krumboltz, Mitchell, and Jones (1976) hypothesized the mechanisms whereby interests, work values, and career decision-making skills develop over time as a result of instrumental, associative, and vicarious learning experiences. The introduction of the idea that important aspects of the career development process might be learned and, therefore modifiable, was an important contribution to understanding career choice and development. As of the early 1980s, however, the *social learning* approach to career decision making had not yet incorporated some of the theoretical advances from current cognitive theories, especially Bandura's (1977) self-efficacy theory (Hackett & Lent, 1992).

Hackett and Betz (1981) recognized the importance of social cognitive perspectives in informing theory and research on career development, and proposed some of the ways in which self-efficacy theory could enrich career development theory. Specifically, they argued that self-perceptions of ability are more predictive of career choice behavior than commonly used objective ability measures. Hackett and Betz were particularly interested in explanations of women's career development. The problem of the underutilization of women's talents and abilities in career pursuits and the underrepresentation of women in higher status, higher paying male-dominated occupations has long been a concern of vocational theorists and researchers (Betz & Fitzgerald, 1987). Hackett and Betz (1981) hypothesized that traditionally feminine, sex-typed experiences in childhood often limit women's exposure to the sources of information necessary for the development of strong perceptions of efficacy in many occupational areas. Lowered perceived efficacy along important career-related dimensions could, in turn, unduly restrict the types of occupations considered (e.g., traditionally male- or female-dominated) and affect performance and persistence in the pursuit of a chosen occupation. Thus, Hackett and Betz argued that self-efficacy theory could partially explain the cognitive- and corollary-affective mediators of women's gender-role socialization experiences and the resulting gender differences in career-choice patterns observable in the workforce.

Research on career self-efficacy began with an emphasis on applications of self-efficacy theory to women's career development, but quickly moved to general applications for both men and women (Betz & Hackett, 1986; Lent & Hackett, 1987). The original statements and early research (Betz & Hackett, 1981; Hackett & Betz, 1981) focused on efficacy judgments concerning specific occupations, termed *occupational* or *career-related* self-efficacy. However, because the scope of the research has broadened considerably since the early 1980s, subsequent researchers often employ the term *career self-efficacy* to indicate self-efficacy in relation to the wide variety of career-related tasks, decisions, behaviors, and adjustment processes that are influential in determining career development (Betz & Hackett, 1986; Lent & Hackett, 1987). This chapter follows established practice in using *career self-efficacy* as an umbrella term and employs more specific terms (e.g., *occupational* or *career decision-making* self-efficacy) as they apply to topics under discussion.

Career development has been, historically, at the core of the field of counseling psychology (Hackett et al., 1991). However, interest in self-efficacy and vocational behavior extends beyond the issues of career choice and adolescent career development. Relevant studies on the self-efficacy of adult workers have appeared in the industrial/organizational literature. In addition, the educational process is intimately intertwined with preparation for work; studies on self-efficacy, education, and instruction are therefore also germane (see Schunk, Chap. 10, this volume). This chapter addresses research investigating the role of self-efficacy expectations in the consideration and choice of occupation. We also examine self-efficacy with regard to academic choices and persistence in academic programs, because these processes lead directly to occupational/career choices.

SELF-EFFICACY AND CHOICE BEHAVIOR

The career-choice literature has typically been divided into studies examining the *content* of career choices, that is, *what* the individual considers or chooses, and studies examining the *process* of choosing, or *how* the individual goes about making choices (Crites, 1981). Reflecting this distinction in the general literature, the sections that follow review research exploring both the content of career choice and the process of career decision making. Most of the extant research on career self-efficacy has addressed the content issue, but some investigations have explored process issues, such as the relations between self-efficacy and interests, academic achievement and persistence in academic programs, career decision making, and career indecision.

GENDER AND OCCUPATIONAL SELF-EFFICACY

In the first empirical test of the usefulness of self-efficacy theory in understanding career choices, Betz and Hackett (1981) examined gender differences in perceived efficacy and the relationships of occupational self-efficacy to vocational interests and the range of career options considered. This early attempt at operationalizing self-efficacy for occupations culminated in two measures. One measure requested that college students rate their confidence in their ability to successfully complete the educational requirements for 20 different occupations; the second measure asked for confidence estimates for performing the job duties of the same 20 occupations (10 *Nontraditional for Women* or male-dominated and 10 *Traditional for Women* or female-dominated, across six career fields).

The results of this initial investigation indicated no overall gender differences on either measure of occupational self-efficacy (Betz & Hackett, 1981). However, gender differences did emerge when the nontraditional and traditional occupations were examined separately. College men's occupational self-efficacy was equivalent across occupations, but women's occupational self-efficacy was significantly lower than men's for traditionally male-dominated occupations, and significantly *higher* for traditionally female-dominated occupations. In addition, occupational self-efficacy, in combination with gender and vocational interests, was significantly predictive of the range of occupations students had considered as viable options. Objective achievement measures (ACT test scores) were not predictive of the range of occupational alternatives considered.

Several subsequent studies replicated and extended the Betz and Hackett (1981) study, using modifications of their measure. Branch and Lichtenberg's (1987) findings were largely supportive, as were results reported by Layton (1984), who included measures of career salience and locus of control. As in the Betz and Hackett study, Layton found occupational self-efficacy to be predictive of the range of careers considered by college women. However, self-efficacy for occupations was not related to locus of control, nor was it predictive of career exploration behaviors (i.e., searching for career information). Furthermore, career salience was found to moderate the effects of occupational self-efficacy on career choices. That is, occupational self-efficacy was significantly predictive of consideration of career alternatives among women for whom a career was important, but was not as predictive for women who were less committed to having a career (Layton, 1984).

Results of studies investigating the career self-efficacy of minority high school equivalency students suggest gender differences in career self-efficacy that correspond to the percentages of males and females in varying occupations (Bores-Rangel, Church, Szendre, & Reeves, 1990; Church, Teresa, Rosebrook, & Szendre, 1992); these gender differences in occupational self-efficacy were significantly correlated with gender differences in occupational consideration. In the Church et al. (1992) study, the patterns of gender differences were found to exist whether the analysis was conducted at an aggregate level (across male- and female-dominated occupations) or at the level of specific occupations.

Post-Kammer and Smith (1985) found some gender differences in the occupational self-efficacy expectations of eighth and ninth graders. With these younger students, however, gender differences were not as pervasive as they were with college students, and vocational interests emerged as a stronger predictor of the occupations students had considered than did occupational self-efficacy. Post-Kammer and Smith (1986) modified Betz and Hackett's (1981) instrument to include a wider range of math/science-related occupations. With a sample of disadvantaged precollege students, gender differences in occupational self-efficacy emerged for math/science careers, but not for nonmath careers. Both self-efficacy and vocational interests predicted the range of occupations considered. The relative strength of the two predictors differed, however, by prediction equation. Self-efficacy contributed more to the prediction of math/science occupations than to non-math/science occupations. The strength of the predictors also varied as a function of gender. Occupational self-efficacy was the strongest predictor of occupational consideration for the women in the sample, whereas interests were of greater importance in predicting men's occupational consideration.

Two recent studies have expanded the scope of the study of gender differences in occupational self-efficacy. Matsui and Onglatco (1991), studying female Japanese clerical workers, found correlations between gender-role variables, assessed by the Bem Sex Role Inventory (BSRI; Bem, 1981), and self-efficacy for work tasks. Specifically, instrumentality (reflecting masculine gender-role orientation) was positively correlated with self-efficacy for work tasks across all occupational fields, whereas expressiveness (reflecting feminine gender-role orientation) was significantly correlated with self-efficacy only for feminine sex-typed work tasks (e.g., artistic, social, clerical). Stickel and Bonett (1991) compared college students' occupational self-efficacy to students' confidence in their ability to handle the demands of traditional or nontraditional occupations in conjunction with home/family demands (labeled *relational* self-efficacy). Women expressed stronger traditional than nontraditional occupational self-efficacy, and women also indicated stronger self-efficacy than men for combining traditional occupations with home/family demands. Interestingly, no significant gender differences emerged for self-efficacy for combining nontraditional careers and home/family demands. That is, men expressed similar relational self-efficacy estimates across traditional and nontraditional careers, whereas women reported higher relational self-efficacy for traditional careers.

CULTURE AND OCCUPATIONAL SELF-EFFICACY

A number of studies have included ethnically diverse samples (e.g., Bores-Rangel et al., 1990; Church et al., 1992; Post-Kammer & Smith, 1985, 1986; Williams & Leonard, 1988). As a group, these investigations generally support the applicability of career self-efficacy theory to high school and college-level students of color. For example, Church et al. (1992) reported similar results for Mexican-American and Native American high school equivalency students' career self-efficacy across varying levels of acculturation. However, only five studies have specifically examined racial/ethnic differences in the occupational self-efficacy of American racial/ethnic minority students (Hackett, Betz, Casas, & Rocha-Singh, 1992; Lauver & Jones, 1991; Noble, Hackett, & Chen, 1992; Post, Stewart, & Smith, 1991; Rotberg, Brown, & Ware, 1987). Four of these studies are addressed in this section; the fifth (Hackett et al., 1992) is discussed in the section describing research on the links between self-efficacy and academic achievement.

Rotberg et al. (1987) explored the relationships among occupational self-efficacy, vocational interests, gender, ethnicity, and socioeconomic status (SES) in a sample of community-college students. Their career self-efficacy instrument included gender-neutral occupations and an equal number of occupations at different levels (e.g., professional vs. skilled). The findings of Rotberg et al. partially replicated the results of previous studies, in that occupational self-efficacy was predictive of range of occupations considered, and occupational self-efficacy and interests were correlated. Gender, ethnicity, and SES were not predictive of the range of occupations considered. Gender-role, as measured by the BSRI (Bem, 1981), was predictive of occupational self-efficacy, but not predictive of the range of occupational alternatives considered.

Post et al. (1991) explored the math/science self-efficacy of male and female African–American first-year college students. They found that both occupational self-efficacy and interests were predictive of the math/science occupations considered by African–American men, but only interests entered as significant predictors of the math/science occupational consideration for African–American women. For nonmath/science occupations, interests were predictive for both women and men. However, for all students, occupational self-efficacy was significantly predictive of interest in math/science occupations (accounting for 39% of the variance in interests), indicating the possibility of an indirect effect of self-efficacy, through interests, on the range of alternatives considered by these students.

Lauver and Jones (1991) investigated racial/ethnic and gender differences in the occupational self-efficacy of ninth- and eleventh-grade rural high school students. Native American students expressed lower confidence in their abilities than Anglo or Hispanic students. Occupational self-efficacy was a significant predictor of occupational consideration for all students, but the patterns of significance differed somewhat by ethnicity. In addition to self-efficacy, gender was predictive of consideration of female-dominated occupations for Hispanic and Anglo students, but not for Native American students, whereas gender was predictive of the consideration of male-dominated occupations only for Anglo students. Overall, the occupational self-efficacy of the girls in this sample was quite high; in fact, girls' self-efficacy was higher than boys' for five of nine male-dominated occupations.

Noble et al. (1992) examined the occupational and academic self-efficacy of a diverse sample of ninth- and tenth-grade rural students, who were very similar to the students in the Lauver & Jones (1991) study. Contrary to the Post-Kammer & Smith (1985) results, Noble et al. found significant gender differences on occupational self-efficacy for more than half of the occupations sampled. Ethnic differences on occupational self-efficacy were virtually nonexistent; however, consistent differences by ethnicity for academic self-efficacy (i.e., self-efficacy for academic course work in high school) were found. Theses were due primarily to the lower academic self-efficacy expectations of Native American students, as in the Lauver & Jones study. Multiple regression analyses revealed that interests and occupational self-efficacy were significantly predictive of the range of traditional and nontraditional careers students have considered. While ethnicity, gender, grade point average (an ability index), academic self-efficacy, and outcome expectations were all included in these regression equations, none contributed significantly to the prediction of career consideration. Academic self-efficacy and outcome expectations did, however, contribute to the prediction of several education-related outcomes, for example, the likelihood of student's graduating from high school and going on to college.

The career self-efficacy literature has taken an international turn in recent years. Matsui, Ikeda, and Ohnishi (1989) studied the occupational self-efficacy of Japanese college students and reported results very similar to those of Betz and Hackett (1981). Women reported higher self-efficacy than men for traditionally female-dominated occupations and lower self-efficacy than men for nontraditional occupations (based on Japanese census data on percentages of women and men in various occupations). Matsui et al. (1989) also reported finding relationships between occupational self-efficacy and gender-related variables, such as perceptions of same-sex role models, personal gender-role stereotypes, and gender-related occupational stereotypes. Their findings are supportive of the hypothesis that gender-role socialization is influential in producing gender differences in career self-efficacy, and also suggest, along with the results of several other studies reported herein, that career self-efficacy may be applicable cross-culturally. Matsui and Tsukamoto (1991) compared self-efficacy for discrete work activities to occupational self-efficacy with a sample of Japanese undergraduates. They found self-efficacy for work activities to be predictive of general occupational self-efficacy, providing some evidence for the validity of occupational self-efficacy measures employing occupational titles. Matsui and Tsukamoto (1991) also found gender differences in self-efficacy for work activities. However, these gender differences appeared in only two of six occupational fields: men reported higher self-efficacy for mechanical activities, whereas women expressed stronger self-efficacy for artistic work activities.

Two British studies employed approaches for assessing occupational self-efficacy that differed from the Betz & Hackett (1981) procedures. Wheeler (1983) used two methods of measuring self-efficacy, operationalizing the construct as "perceived ability match" and "ease of success" for 17 occupations. Wheeler's deviation from Bandura's (1977) definition of the self-efficacy construct causes some problems in interpreting his results. Nonetheless, Wheeler did find gender differences in occupational self-efficacy; these gender differences were directly related to the percentages of men and women in each occupation. That is, men expressed higher occupational self-efficacy for 8 of 13 male-dominated jobs, whereas women expressed higher self-efficacy for 2 of 3 female-dominated jobs.

Clement (1987) employed descriptions of 20 occupations, 10 nontraditional and 10 traditional occupations for women, and assessed university student's self-efficacy for the job duties of the described occupations. Ratings of interest in and consideration of the occupations were also obtained. Clement's data revealed gender differences in occupational self-efficacy, but regression analyses indicated that for men, self-efficacy was a significant predictor for only 1 occupation, whereas interests were predictive for 16. For women, occupational self-efficacy was predictive of occupational consideration for 5 occupations, but interests were predictive for 19.

Clement concluded that Hackett and Betz's (1981) hypotheses regarding the importance of self-efficacy in predicting career choices were untenable. However, her sample was relatively homogeneous. Furthermore, separate regression analyses were conducted for each occupation, a procedure that is quite different from the grouping of occupations strategies (e.g., male-dominated or female-dominated) used in all other research on occupational self-efficacy. The procedural and sampling differences in Clement's investigation cast some doubt on the generalizability and validity of her results; nevertheless, her anomalous findings warrant further exploration.

OCCUPATIONAL SELF-EFFICACY AND VOCATIONAL INTERESTS

Because of the consistent findings of correlations between occupational self-efficacy and vocational interests, and the results from some studies indicating that interests may be a stronger predictor than self-efficacy of occupational consideration (e.g., Clement, 1987), questions have arisen as to whether the two constructs are interchangeable. Therefore, a number of researchers have attempted to grapple directly with the nature and extent of the self-efficacy/interest correspondence and the predictive utility of self-efficacy and interests. The Lapan, Boggs, and Morrill (1989) analyses revealed gender differences in two career fields typically non-traditional for women, that is, "Realistic" (mechanical, technical, outdoor occupations) and "Investigative" (scientific, medical, etc.). Lapan et al. demonstrated that, for first-year college students, interest in these two nontraditional occupational areas was strongly related to occupational self-efficacy. Furthermore, their path analysis supported a causal model containing occupational self-efficacy as a mediator of past performance accomplishments (e.g., years of high school math courses and mathematics scores on the ACT) in predicting occupational interests.

Lent, Larkin, and Brown (1989) found significant but moderate correlations between scientific/technical inventoried interests and self-efficacy for engineering and scientific occupations. Lent et al. (1989) also reported evidence for some unique contributions of both variables to the prediction of career-related behavior. Conversely, Lapan and Jingeleski (1992) argued that career self-efficacy, vocational interests, and expectations for occupational attainment (i.e., expectations about the occupation students felt they were likely to actually enter) are different manifestations of a single construct. In their study of the vocational aspirations of eighth graders, a principal components analysis of self-efficacy, interests, and expectations for occupational attainment scores indicated that one factor accounted for the majority of the variance across the three measures.

OCCUPATIONAL SELF-EFFICACY AND OTHER VARIABLES

Investigators have also explored the relationship of other career-relevant variables to occupational self-efficacy. Hannah and Kahn (1989) examined the influence of gender and SES on occupational self-efficacy, and on the level and field of occupations considered by 12th grade students. No gender differences in overall occupational self-efficacy were reported, but both males and females indicated stronger perceived efficacy for gender-stereotypical occupations. SES was also correlated with self-efficacy; low SES students reported weaker efficacy expectations than higher SES students.

Bores-Rangel et al. (1990) assessed the occupational self-efficacy of economically disadvantaged students studying for high school equivalency diplomas. Their sample was primarily composed of Hispanic students, at least some of whom were bilingual. Bores-Rangel et al. found relationships between self-efficacy, interests, and consideration of occupational activities and educational programs. They also reported inter-relationships between incentives and self-efficacy.

Numerous investigations have examined career self-efficacy in non-student populations. The most interesting of these is the Matsui and Onglatco (1992a) investigation of the relationships between career self-efficacy and occupational stress and strain. Their findings suggest that occupational self-efficacy (self-efficacy for work tasks) modified the relationship between occupational stress and perceived strain experienced by female Japanese clerical workers. Long (1989) found relationships between general self-efficacy and gender-role orientation (measured by the BSRI) with a sample of employed women, and several studies have been conducted on the career self-efficacy of university faculty members (Landino & Owens, 1988; Schoen & Winocur, 1988). And, of course, many other studies in the vocational literature have examined the role of self-efficacy mechanisms in the performance of adult workers.

SELF-EFFICACY AND COLLEGE MAJOR CHOICES

Some researchers have focused on the choice of immediate concern and relevance to college students, namely, choice of academic major. Because of the continuing problem of underrepresentation of women in scientific and technical career fields, Betz and Hackett (1983) examined the role of gender, past performance accomplishments, and math self-efficacy, in the selection of math-related college majors. They hypothesized that women's lower overall math self-efficacy might explain gender differences in academic-choice behavior, which might be an intermediate determinant of gender differences in the choices of math/scientific careers. Betz and Hackett developed a measure of mathematics self-efficacy with regard to three mathematical domains—everyday math tasks, math/science-related college courses, and math problems—to investigate their research questions. Gender differences in math self-efficacy in favor of men were reported, and these differences in math self-efficacy were found to predict gender differences in math-relatedness of college major choices.

Hackett (1985) followed up this line of research using a path analysis procedure to ascertain the possible causal ordering of predictors of math-related college major choices. Her data fit a self-efficacy model wherein gender influenced selection of high school math courses, which in turn influenced math achievement and math self-efficacy; math self-efficacy was then found to be the immediate predictor of choice of math/science college majors. Hackett and Betz (1989) reported further evidence that math self-efficacy is of greater importance than ability or part experience in predicting career-related choice behavior. They did not, however, find evidence that women's lower math self-efficacy expectations were *unrealistically* low. Efficacy ratings on the math problems subscale of the math self-efficacy measure, and performance on a parallel math problems test were highly correlated, indicating correspondence between confidence in math ability and actual math performance for college men and women.

Studies clarifying some of the relationships between self-efficacy and achievement have appeared in the educational literature (Schunk, Chap. 10, this volume). For example, Norwich (1987) found that previous math performance was more predictive of subsequent performance than math self-efficacy when tasks were familiar to students. Cooper and Robinson (1991) found significant but weak relationships between math self-efficacy and math performance and significant, moderate correlations between career self-efficacy and mathematics self-efficacy. Research has also moved into other areas relevant to the selection of scientific technical careers (Miura, 1987). For example, Hill, Smith, and Mann's (1987) results suggest that gender differences in computer-related self-efficacy are related to gender differences in enrollment in computer courses.

SELF-EFFICACY AND ACADEMIC ACHIEVEMENT AND PERSISTENCE

The studies previously reviewed in this chapter investigated general hypotheses about gender differences in self-efficacy and career-related choices. Another line of research has examined connections between self-efficacy and academic achievement and persistence in college. Lent,

Brown, and Larkin (1984; 1986) investigated the relationship between scientific/technical self-efficacy and achievement and persistence in scientific/technical college majors. Lent et al. (1984) assessed occupational self-efficacy for scientific/technical careers, employing a measure based on Betz and Hackett's (1981) assessment procedure, but using scientific/technical occupational titles. With their sample of college students who had declared engineering majors, Lent et al. (1984) found that students with higher levels of scientific/technical self-efficacy achieved higher grades and persisted longer in their declared majors. Although scientific/technical self-efficacy was related to mathematics aptitude and high school achievement, no gender differences in self-efficacy were found.

Lent et al. (1986) partially replicated and extended their 1984 study. First, they added another measure of self-efficacy, self-efficacy for "Academic Milestones," referring to confidence in one's ability to negotiate major hurdles in an engineering program. Discriminant validity was reported for the self-efficacy measures; the occupational and academic milestones self-efficacy measures were not correlated with self-esteem and career indecision. Lent et al. (1986) then explored the relationship of engineering and academic milestones self-efficacy and scientific/technical interests to academic achievement, persistence, and extent of consideration of scientific/technical occupations. The two self-efficacy scales were moderately correlated and differentially predictive. Occupational self-efficacy for engineering careers was significantly correlated with scientific/technical interests, but academic milestones self-efficacy was not. Academic milestones self-efficacy, on the other hand, was correlated with high school performance. Both self-efficacy measures were significantly predictive of consideration of scientific/technical occupations, but self-efficacy for academic milestones was somewhat more predictive of academic achievement and persistence in college. No gender differences were observed; Lent et al. (1986) attributed this to the homogeneity of their sample (i.e., students who had already declared an engineering major).

Hackett et al. (1992) partially replicated and extended the Lent et al. (1986) study, reporting similar results with an ethnically diverse sample. Some racial/ethnic differences and gender by ethnicity interactions were found, but neither gender nor ethnicity alone was a significant predictor of the academic achievement of engineering majors. Multiple regression analyses predicting college achievement indicated that academic self-efficacy and past performance were the strongest predictors; some additional predictive utility was obtained by the inclusion of measures of perceived faculty support, faculty discouragement, vocational interests, and measures of interpersonal support and perceived strain. Outcome expectations were also assessed in this study; self-efficacy and outcome

expectations were positively but only modestly related, and outcome expectations did not add to the prediction of academic achievement in
college. Finally, ethnicity was found to be predictive of occupational and
academic self-efficacy; Anglo students tended to express higher levels of
career self-efficacy than did Mexican–American students.

An investigation revealing the complexity of the self-efficacy–
achievement relationship was conducted by Brown, Lent, and Larkin
(1989). Their data revealed that academic and occupational self-efficacy
expectations were differentially predictive of the academic achievement
and persistence of college students. Academic milestones self-efficacy was
strongly predictive of grade point average and persistence, regardless of
aptitude. However, occupational self-efficacy moderated the relationship
between aptitude and academic achievement and persistence; occupational self-efficacy was not as strong a predictor of the achievement and
persistence of high-ability students, but did have a facilitative effect on
students of more moderate aptitude levels.

Lent, Lopez, and Bieschke (1993) explored a more complex social
cognitive model predicting important career-related behaviors by examining the role of math self-efficacy, math ACT scores, outcome expectations,
and math-course interests in predicting intentions to take math/science
courses, actual course selection, and grades in math/science courses. Math
self-efficacy mediated the influence of past performance on interests. The
influence of self-efficacy on intentions to take math courses was mediated
by interests, and both past math achievement and math self-efficacy predicted math performance (grades in a subsequent math course). Both self-
efficacy and outcome expectations predicted interest and enrollment in
math courses. Interestingly, past performance had both a direct and an
indirect influence, through self-efficacy, on grades. Overall, the Lent et al.
(1993) results are supportive of a more complete social cognitive model,
incorporating outcome expectations in interaction with self-efficacy in
prediction equations.

In a meta-analysis of investigations of self-efficacy/academic outcome relationships, Multon, Brown, and Lent (1991) reported evidence that
self-efficacy perceptions are significant predictors of performance and
persistence across a wide range of situations, and across studies using
various methods. And finally, Lent, Brown, and Larkin (1987) compared a
self-efficacy model with two alternative theoretical models predicting career and academic behavior. Results of regression analyses were supportive of the self-efficacy model. Self-efficacy was found to be more predictive
than interests of academic achievement and persistence, whereas both
interests and self-efficacy were significantly predictive of range of career
options. An interest congruence model, based on the Holland (1985)

person–environment (P–E) fit theory, was most predictive of career indecision. The Lent et al. (1987) results, in combination with the other studies reviewed thus far, strongly suggest that although perceived career efficacy is important in predicting career and academic choice and persistence, occupational self-efficacy may not be as useful in the prediction of other career-related behaviors (e.g., indecision and exploratory behavior). This actually is in keeping with the situation-specific nature of the self-efficacy construct. If self-efficacy is defined as judgments of one's capabilities with regard to specific tasks, problems, or activities, then assessments of efficacy judgments for occupations should be predictive of the *content* of choices, but would not be expected to predict career choice *process* variables (Lent & Hackett, 1987). In the next section, investigations of career self-efficacy related to the process of career development are reviewed.

SELF-EFFICACY AND CAREER DECISION-MAKING PROCESSES

Career decision making and career indecision have received a great deal of attention in the career literature over the years (Hackett et al., 1991). Several behavioral components of effective career decision making have been identified, including (a) goal selection, (b) obtaining relevant and accurate occupational information, (c) problem-solving capabilities, (d) planning skills, and (e) realistic self-appraisal skills (Crites, 1981). Taylor and Betz (1983) developed the Career Decision-Making Self-efficacy (CDMSE) scale to assess perceptions of efficacy with regard to these five dimensions of career decision making. A major assumption guiding their research was that effective career decision making involves not only the development of skills, but also confidence in one's decision-making abilities along these specific behavioral dimensions. Taylor and Betz (1983) hypothesized that low decision-making self-efficacy could impede exploratory behavior and the development of decision-making skills, and thus may be predictive of career indecision. Their findings supported the usefulness of the CDMSE scale in predicting career indecision, especially the aspects of indecision relating to lack of structure and lack of confidence in career decisions. Taylor and Betz did not find gender differences in CDMSE scores. Although their scale was designed to assess five aspects of the career decision-making process, their data supported the existence of one generalized factor, reflecting lack of confidence in career decision-making abilities. A construct validity study by Robbins (1985) further underscored the usefulness of employing the CDMSE scale as a generalized measure of self-efficacy for career decision making, and provided additional evidence for the relationship of CDMSE to career indecision.

Taylor and Popma (1990) extended this research by investigating the interrelationships between CDMSE scale scores and career indecision, occupational self-efficacy, career salience, and locus of control. Scores on the CDMSE scale were found to be unrelated to career salience; no gender differences on CDMSE were found, and CDMSE scale scores were only moderately related to occupational self-efficacy. However, Taylor and Popma's results were also supportive of the utility of CDMSE scale in predicting career indecision; of the variables examined, only CDMSE was significantly (and negatively) predictive of career indecision.

Several other studies have utilized the CDMSE scale. Matsui & Onglatco (1992b) reported evidence that CDMSE scores were positively correlated with gender-role (i.e., instrumentality as measured by the BSRI), and inversely related to career-choice anxiety. Furthermore, results from a path analysis with a sample of Japanese high school students suggested that CDMSE may partially mediate the influence of past academic achievement and instrumentality on career-choice anxiety and motivation to pursue a university education. Arnold and Bye (1989) reported a weak but significant relationship between gender and CDMSE scores, and a strong positive correlation between instrumentality scores on the BSRI and higher levels of self-efficacy for career decision making. Small but significant correlations between expressiveness scores on the BSRI and CDMSE scores were also found, suggesting that more flexible self-perceptions of gender roles can facilitate stronger self-efficacy for career decision making. Results by Nevill and Schlecker (1988) indicated that women with higher CDMSE and assertiveness scores displayed greater willingness than women who scored lower on these measures to engage in nontraditional career activities.

In a study illuminating important cognitive processes influencing the use of efficacy information, Nevill, Neimeyer, Probert, and Fukuyama (1986) found relationships between college students' vocational schemas, that is, cognitive information-processing capabilities, and CDMSE. Higher scores on the CDMSE scale were found to correspond to higher levels of cognitive integration for students whose cognitive processing was more differentiated. That is, when students' thinking is more complex, higher levels of CDMSE are associated with enhanced ability to integrate divergent information. Nevill et al.'s research suggests future avenues of inquiry relating self-efficacy research to more complex conceptualizations of self-perceptions.

Blustein (1989) investigated CDMSE in the prediction of career exploratory behavior, one component of career decision making. Higher scores on Taylor and Betz's CDMSE scale were found to be significantly related to greater exploratory behavior, and were a much stronger predictor of career exploration than age, gender, or goal-directedness. Niles and Sowa (1992) found career beliefs, personality hardiness, and general self-efficacy to be predictive of the CDMSE scores of college students. And Fukuyama, Probert, Neimeyer, Nevill, and Metzler (1988) examined the impact of a computerized, self-directed career-guidance program on CDMSE. Students receiving the computer-administered intervention reported enhanced CDMSE and reduced career indecisiveness. Although causal connections between these two variables were not examined directly, this intervention study at least confirms that strengthening CDMSE is associated with enhanced career decidedness.

Two studies contain indirect implications for the link between self-efficacy and career decision making. O'Hare and her colleagues (O'Hare & Beutell, 1987; O'Hare & Tamburri, 1986) found that self-efficacy for coping with career decision-making tasks moderated the relationship between anxiety and career decision making. Higher levels of self-efficacy for coping with career decision making were predictive of lower anxiety and higher levels of decisiveness (O'Hare & Tamburri, 1986); men reported higher levels of confidence in their ability to cope with career decision making than women (O'Hare & Beutell, 1987). These results must be viewed tentatively, however, in that self-efficacy for coping with career decision making was not measured in a manner consistent with Bandura's (1977) theory.

A number of investigations have focused on the contributions of self-efficacy theory to understanding career-development processes over the life span. Stumpf, Brief, and Hartman (1987), for example, found that self-efficacy for job-interview skills mediated the effects of past-performance experiences in job interviews on interview anxiety and performance. Betz and Hackett (1987) explored perceived efficacy with respect to agentic (or instrumental) behaviors facilitating career development. They found no gender differences in career self-efficacy, and only modest correlations between self-efficacy for career development tasks and actual behavioral performance. They also reported that pretest self-efficacy assessment positively influenced subsequent performance, probably by providing students with information about effective performance strategies. Finally, researchers have begun to examine career-adjustment processes later in life, such as the transition from work to retirement. Fretz, Kluge, Ossana, Jones, and Merikangas (1989), for example, found that higher levels of self-efficacy for adjusting successfully to retirement were correlated with lower levels of preretirement worry.

SOURCES OF CAREER SELF-EFFICACY

One of the benefits to counselors of the career self-efficacy construct is that it suggests ways in which unrealistic or detrimental self-perceptions may be modified, through the four sources of efficacy information. Results of the research cited thus far provide correlational evidence of the connection between objectively measured past performance accomplishments, anxiety, and career self-efficacy (e.g., Hackett, 1985). However, the direct causal relationships among performance, anxiety, and career self-efficacy have received less attention, and only recently have researchers begun testing Bandura's (1977) theoretical propositions about all of the possible sources of career self-efficacy information. We next address the studies examining the development and modification of career-related efficacy expectations.

Sources of Efficacy Information

T. Matsui, K. Matsui, and Ohnishi (1990) investigated students' perceptions about sources of efficacy information. They reported that three of the four sources of efficacy information were predictive of math self-efficacy, and that all three—performance accomplishments (high school math grades), modeling (seeing similar others perform math), and arousal (lower math anxiety)—were interrelated. The amount of variance accounted for was modest, suggesting that other factors are operative in influencing perceived efficacy for mathematics. Gender differences in favor of men were found in math self-efficacy, although the overall magnitude of these differences was small with this sample of Japanese college students. No gender differences were reported for the sources of efficacy information. Matsui et al. (1990) argued that few gender differences were found, due to the fact that students in their study had already passed through a selection process based partially on mathematics competence, and therefore might be expected to have similar math backgrounds and experiences, and therefore to perform similarly in the math domain.

Lent, Lopez, and Bieschke (1991) likewise explored sources of efficacy information and their relationships to gender, interest in taking math courses, and math self-efficacy. For the entire college student sample, gender and past performance accomplishments were the strongest predictors of math self-efficacy. The Lent et al. findings are congruent with Bandura's (1986) hypotheses that performance accomplishments have the most powerful influence on perceived efficacy. On the other hand, their results revealed that perceptions of past performance and scores on an objective measure of math achievement (math ACT scores) were not highly correlated, indicating that perceptions are not determined only by past performance. Results of regression analyses predicting interests and career choices supported a social cognitive model wherein past achievement influences self-efficacy, which in turn enhances interests, which is the strongest immediate predictor of choice. Lent et al. (1991) also found that outcome expectations mediated the relationship between self-efficacy and choices. Math self-efficacy was much more predictive of math/science career choices for students with strong positive outcome expectations about taking math/science courses, compared to students with weaker outcome expectancies. In an investigation with high school students, Lopez and Lent (1992) reported similar results for sources of math self-efficacy. One major difference was reported: Emotional arousal also contributed significantly to the prediction of math self-efficacy.

CAUSAL INFLUENCES OF PERFORMANCE ON SELF-EFFICACY

Several experimental analogue studies have been conducted to explore the causal links between performance and career-related self-efficacy, and between self-efficacy and interests. Hackett and Campbell (1987) examined the effects of success and failure experiences on task self-efficacy and task interest, and found that for a gender-neutral task, performance influences both self-efficacy and task interest, albeit to different degrees. Campbell and Hackett (1986) found a similar pattern of results using a gender-stereotypical task. In both studies, task success (i.e., successful completion of math or verbal problems) produced enhanced task self-efficacy and, to a lesser extent, increased task interest, whereas task failure resulted in lowered self-efficacy and task interest. Gender differences were found on the gender-stereotypical (math) task, but not on the gender neutral (verbal) task, and gender differences in attributional patterns were reported in both studies. Their results suggest that college women tend to ascribe task success externally (e.g., to luck) and task failure internally (e.g., to lack of ability), whereas college men may exhibit the opposite attributional pattern, with successful performance attributed to ability (internal attribution) and unsuccessful performance attributed to task difficulty (external attribution). In both studies, women were more strongly and negatively affected by task failure than men.

Hackett, Betz, O'Halloran, and Romac (1990) partially replicated and extended this line of research with similar results. Their study included both math and verbal tasks, and specifically examined the generalizability of the effects of performance on academic self-efficacy and self-perceptions of ability. Their findings demonstrated that task performance in one domain generalizes to some extent to self-efficacy in unrelated domains, but not to overall academic self-efficacy. Hackett et al. also provided evidence that task performance affects self-efficacy more strongly than task interest, suggesting that self-efficacy may be more sensitive to performance experiences than interests. While general career self-efficacy was not influenced by task performance, global self-perceptions of ability were affected in the expected directions. Hackett et al. speculated that the use of measures of academic and career self-efficacy that were not perceived by students to be closely related to the tasks performed might have resulted in the absence of relationships between task self-efficacy and the general career self-efficacy measures.

Finally, Zilber (1988) examined the hypothesis that attributions may mediate the effects of task performance on self-efficacy. Her findings revealed that attributions do, in fact, influence reactions to task performance, that task self-efficacy and self-enhancing attributions are correlated and that both seem to be necessary in predicting reactions to success or failure experiences. Her findings suggest that attributional patterns may mediate the effects of task performance on career self-efficacy. Much work remains to be done to integrate the attributional and self-efficacy frameworks, but such research may yield substantial payoffs in enhancing understanding of the role of self-perceptions in educational achievement and career development. This type of experimental research on the connections between performance and self-efficacy has appeared more frequently in the organizational behavior literature on worker performance (e.g., Locke, Frederick, Lee, & Bobko, 1984; Pond & Hay, 1989) than in career self-efficacy literature.

SUMMARY OF RESEARCH FINDINGS

We can draw several conclusions from the empirical investigations of career self-efficacy. First, we summarize the status of research on career self-efficacy, then examine the major methodological and conceptual issues, and finally identify possible future research directions.

CAREER SELF-EFFICACY, CAREER CHOICE, AND ACHIEVEMENT

Occupational self-efficacy is clearly predictive of occupational and college-major choice (Betz & Hackett, 1981, 1983), and is also predictive of academic achievement and persistence, albeit to a lesser degree. For achievement and persistence, assessment of self-efficacy with respect to more academically relevant variables, such as math or academic milestones self-efficacy, yields more predictive utility (e.g., Betz & Hackett, 1983; Lent et al., 1986; Schunk, Chap. 10, this volume). Occupational self-efficacy is not predictive of important components of career decision making, but self-efficacy assessments that are directly relevant to decision-making processes, such as self-efficacy for career decision making, *are* helpful in understanding potential problems in career development, such as indecision (Taylor & Betz, 1983; Taylor & Popma, 1990). Overall, it appears that career self-efficacy, variously defined, is predictive of a wide range of choice behaviors, as well as academic achievement and persistence in career-related pursuits.

SOURCES OF CAREER SELF-EFFICACY

Self-efficacy judgments are clearly mediators of past experience in the prediction of educational and occupational choices. Past performance accomplishments are strongly related to the development of strong career self-efficacy expectations, and occupational self-efficacy is a powerful predictor of choice behavior (Hackett & Lent, 1992). In predicting distant versus more immediate future behavior, and in predicting complex choice behavior, career self-efficacy is probably a better predictor than past achievement, in that career self-efficacy not only encompasses information about past performance, but also contains affective and motivational information. However, past performance alone may be a stronger predictor than self-efficacy of future performance when performance and self-efficacy are assessed in temporal proximity, or when students are very familiar with tasks (e.g., Hackett & Betz, 1989; Norwich, 1987). Bandura (1986) has stated that increased information about the tasks to be performed, as through repeated exposure, can enhance the realism of efficacy judgements.

Important work has been done to identify variables that moderate the self-efficacy/achievement correspondence. For example, development of strong self-efficacy expectations is more important for students of moderate ability levels than for higher ability students (Brown et al., 1989). Attributions also appear to moderate the effects of past performance on self-efficacy (Hackett et al., 1990). That is, given the same performance history, individuals who express self-enhancing attributions about their performance tend to express higher levels of self-efficacy (Zilber, 1988).

Finally, research on the other sources of career self-efficacy information has yielded mixed results. Results from some studies suggest that successful performance accomplishments are not only vital to the development of a strong sense of personal effectiveness, but that the other three sources of career self-efficacy (vicarious learning, physiological arousal, and verbal persuasion) contribute very little to the prediction of career self-efficacy over and above the effects of past performance (Lent et al., 1991). Other research provides evidence for a stronger effect of alternate sources of efficacy information on career self-efficacy (Lopez & Lent, 1992; Matsui et al., 1990; Stumpf et al., 1987). Career-related modeling, encouragement, and lowered anxiety and arousal may facilitate performance attempts in occupationally related areas, after which performance becomes the most powerful source of efficacy information (Lent & Hackett, 1991).

SELF-EFFICACY AND INTERESTS

Occupational self-efficacy is also related to other important predictors of career choice, in particular, vocational interests (Lapan et al., 1989). Much more work needs to be done in teasing out the self-efficacy/interest interrelationships. However, it seems now that the data are supportive of a social cognitive model wherein past experience influences both the development of interests and self-efficacy, but that vocational interests are not likely to develop in areas in which self-efficacy expectations are weak (e.g., Lent et al., 1987, 1991). Career self-efficacy and interests are moderately related and may be jointly predictive of career choice and development (Hackett & Lent, 1992). Specifically, Lent et al. (1991; Lent, Lopez, & Bieschke, 1993) suggest that past achievement influences interests through career self-efficacy, and that career self-efficacy affects future performance and choice directly, as well as indirectly, through interests.

GENDER, ETHNICITY, AND CAREER SELF-EFFICACY

Although gender differences in career self-efficacy are related to gender differences in career-related choice and achievement, in career self-efficacy they are not pervasive. Rather, gender differences in academic and career self-efficacy seem to be associated with perceptions of gender-relatedness of tasks, activities or occupations (e.g., Betz & Hackett, 1983; Hackett et al., 1990; Wheeler, 1983), and are more likely to appear in heterogeneous samples (e.g., Betz & Hackett, 1981; Lauver & Jones, 1991). The more gender-stereotypical an activity or occupation is perceived, the more likely it is that gender differences in self-efficacy will appear (Hackett et al., 1990). Furthermore, women seem to be more likely to modify their efficacy expectations in response to the gender-stereotypicality of a domain than men. For example, several studies have reported that men's career self-efficacy is similar across occupations, whereas women modify their efficacy expectations upward when anticipating performance in feminine gender-typed domains, and downward with respect to masculine gender-typed domains (Betz & Hackett, 1981; Bridges, 1988; Matsui et al., 1989). The studies on gender-role and career self-efficacy support the Hackett and Betz (1981) contention that gender differences in self-efficacy are related to the different socialization experiences of women and men (Hackett, 1985; Long, 1989; Matsui et al., 1989). Furthermore, some investigations of younger students have revealed fewer gender differences in occupational self-efficacy than have been revealed in research with college students (e.g., Post-Kammer & Smith, 1985), whereas other researchers have reported pervasive gender differences in younger students (e.g., Noble et al., 1992). So little research has been conducted on career self-efficacy in young populations that any strong conclusions about developmental processes and gender differences are premature.

Investigations of career self-efficacy in Britain and Japan suggest that career self-efficacy has international applicability (e.g., Clement, 1987; Matsui et al., 1989, 1990). The research conducted in this country with ethnic/minority populations likewise suggests that the findings from research on career self-efficacy are relevant cross-culturally (e.g., Hackett et al., 1992; Noble et al., 1992; Post et al., 1991). Nevertheless, some ethnic differences have been reported, and the topic requires more attention (e.g., Hackett et al., 1992; Noble et al., 1992).

IMPLICATIONS FOR FUTURE RESEARCH

In previous reviews of the career self-efficacy literature (Betz & Hackett, 1986; Lent & Hackett, 1987), major methodological problems and limitations of the research have been identified, including (a) lack of attention to the psychometric properties of career self-efficacy measures; (b) lack of research on ethnicity and career self-efficacy; (c) lack of attention to the career self-efficacy of younger children; (d) too much focus on gender differences and too few explorations of gender as a mediating variable; and (e) little attention to career self-efficacy in career and work adjustment. In addition to focusing on the limitations of the career self-efficacy literature, reviewers have outlined needed future directions, such as examinations of self-efficacy and key person variables relevant to career development (e.g., performance attributions; behavioral intentions; and other cognitive processes, such as cognitive complexity); investigations of the interactions between self-efficacy and important environmental variables, such as SES, social support, and barriers to career development; empirical tests of the causal elements of the career self-efficacy model, including theory comparisons; and research studies focused on career self-efficacy interventions (Betz & Hackett, 1986; Hackett & Lent, 1992; Lent & Hackett, 1987). Many of these issues have received some empirical attention in the last several years. There has been an increase in the number of studies that have included ethnically diverse and younger samples. The focus of career self-efficacy research has at least moved beyond career-choice issues *per se* to include investigations of the sources of efficacy information (e.g., Lent et al., 1993) and some of the dynamics of the career development process (e.g., Taylor & Popma, 1990). Increasing attention has been paid to the interactions of career self-efficacy and other key variables, such as interests (Lent et al.,1991; 1993), attributions (e.g., Zilber, 1988), cognitive complexity (e.g., Nevill et al., 1986), coping (e.g., O'Hare & Tamburri, 1986), and occupational stress and strain (Matsui & Onglatco, 1992a). Career self-efficacy and situational variables, such as SES (Rotberg et al., 1987) and social support (Hackett et al., 1992; Lauver & Jones, 1991), have been explored. And investigations examining the causal elements of the self-efficacy model (e.g., Lent et al., 1993), including comparisons between rival explanatory models (e.g., Lent et al., 1987; Siegal, Galassi, & Ware, 1985), have begun to appear more frequently. Despite this progress, further research is needed on each of the concerns and directions outlined above. In the following sections, we address a few of the most salient issues and pressing concerns facing career self-efficacy researchers today.

DEFINITIONAL AND MEASUREMENT PROBLEMS

One of the most vexing problems plaguing researchers on career self-efficacy has been operationalizing and measuring the construct. First, several studies have appeared in which self-efficacy has been operationalized in ways incompatible with Bandura's (1977) definition of the construct (Stumpf et al., 1987; Wheeler, 1983). For example, Wheeler (1983) measured occupational self-efficacy in terms of "Perceived Ability Match" and "Ease of Success" of various occupations; these approaches do not adequately capture the cognitive appraisal of future performance in Bandura's definition of self-efficacy. The measures employed in the studies by O'Hare and her colleagues (O'Hare & Beutell, 1987; O'Hare & Tamburri, 1986) are subject to similar criticisms. O'Hare and Tamburri (1986) adapted a work-coping scale to measure self-efficacy for coping with career decision making. Their procedure required respondents to rate the frequency with which they engaged in various behaviors; thus, cognitive appraisals of future performance, or self-efficacy, were not actually assessed, despite the self-efficacy label. The extent to which such work can be considered a true contribution to career self-efficacy literature is highly questionable.

Second, a number of authors have attempted to improve on Betz and Hackett's (1981) original assessment procedure, for example, by providing job descriptions along with occupational titles (Clement, 1987), assessing self-efficacy for specific work tasks (Matsui & Tsukamoto, 1991; Rooney & Osipow, 1992), attempting to balance the level of traditional and nontraditional occupations, or offering gender-neutral occupational options (Rotberg et al., 1987). Although some of the alternate approaches to assessing career self-efficacy may serve to advance the knowledge base, research attention has not yet focused on the differences between, relationships among, or even potential advantages across, the various measuring devices. Studies utilizing job descriptions (e.g., Clement, 1987; Rotberg et al., 1987; Stickel & Bonett, 1991), for example, may be assessing something altogether different from studies examining reactions to job titles. The provision of information about occupations listed on an occupational self-efficacy measure may be considered an intervention; that is, providing occupational information should enhance student's decision-making processes, thus altering career self-efficacy estimates. Furthermore, even studies that have used Betz and Hackett's (1981) procedures have often drawn on different listings of occupational titles (e.g., Branch & Lichtenberg, 1988). These variations in procedures make it quite difficult to compare results across studies.

Many of the published studies on career self-efficacy have reported adequate internal consistency reliabilities for the self-efficacy measures, but information on test–retest reliability is scanty (Hackett & Lent, 1992). Rarer still are studies reporting on the construct validity and other psychometric properties of career self-efficacy measures (examples of exceptions include Lent et al., 1986; Robbins, 1985; Stickel & Bonett, 1991; Taylor & Popma, 1990). More attention to the conceptual and measurement issues underlying career self-efficacy is crucial to advancing the research base. Therefore, the recent appearance of psychometric studies of career self-efficacy instruments is a welcome trend (Bonnett & Stickel, 1992; Rooney & Osipow, 1992). Rooney & Osipow's (1992) Task Specific Occupational Self-Efficacy Scale (TSOSS) seems to have the most potential for advancing the literature. Arguing that confidence in one's abilities to perform the *tasks* required for success in various occupational endeavors allows for a more precise estimate of occupational self-efficacy, they have developed an instrument that has broad potential applicability, and have provided impressive reliability and validity data for the TSOSS. Interestingly, their analyses of correlations between self-efficacy for occupational tasks and self-efficacy for corresponding occupations indicate considerable variability in the degree of relationship between task and general occupational self-efficacy estimates. The variations in degree of correspondence may reflect the fact that college students estimate career self-efficacy holistically, not necessarily in terms of task clusters. Students also tend to express fairly high levels of task self-efficacy on this scale; the wording of items may need some modification to elicit a broader range of efficacy estimates. Nevertheless, the TSOSS offers considerable advantages over currently available measures and also has potential as an intervention to bolster career self-efficacy. Matsui and Tsukamoto (1991) adopted a similar approach, measuring career self-efficacy with regard to work tasks, albeit without Rooney and Osipow's (1992) attention to psychometric adequacy. However, both efforts may result in instruments that may be used across research topics. For example, the TSOSS could be used along with study-specific career self-efficacy measures to assess generalizability across investigations.

Sampling Issues

Nature of the Sample

As reflected in the foregoing review of the empirical literature, sampling issues have created interpretational dilemmas. For example, Clement (1987) argued that career self-efficacy is not a viable construct, basing her argument on her failure to find gender differences and her finding that interests were the only significant predictor of occupational consideration. Yet, over half of her sample had already declared a major in psychology; students who have already narrowed their career choice are unlikely to display the same range of occupational consideration as a more heterogeneous college sample, as demonstrated in several other studies reporting gender differences (e.g., Betz & Hackett, 1981, 1983; Branch & Lichtenberg, 1987). Lent et al. (1984, 1986) also failed to find gender differences in their studies of engineering majors, but speculated that the homogeneous nature of the ample would dictate similar self-estimates of ability for men and women. Do the studies failing to find gender differences in career self-efficacy reflect a robust phenomenon as claimed by Clement (1987), or do they reflect the homogeneous nature of the samples under investigation, as hypothesized by Lent et al. (1986)? The latter explanation is most likely, but direct empirical tests are necessary to resolve the debate. Generally, researchers must consider the nature of their sample carefully when crafting their hypotheses.

Another example of sampling that produces interpretational difficulties is evident in Post-Kammer and Smith's (1985) investigation. They found few gender differences in eighth and ninth graders, drawing on the age differences between their sample and that of Betz and Hackett (1981) to explain the discrepancies in results. Yet, major differences between the samples in SES and ability could also have accounted for the results. Post-Kammer and Smith's sample was drawn from a private school for academically above-average students, who were probably quite different on several dimensions from the Betz and Hackett (1981) sample, drawn from introductory courses at a large state university with very low admission criteria. It might be expected, therefore, that girls and boys in the Post-Kammer and Smith (1985) high-ability sample would have similar efficacy expectations due to comparable ability and experiences. The hypothesis that sampling differences have caused the differential findings in the extent of gender differences in career self-efficacy was strengthened by the results from the Noble et al. (1992) investigation of a heterogeneous group of eighth and ninth graders.

Racial/Ethnic Diversity

Studies exploring cultural dynamics in career self-efficacy are not only rare, but also often simply examine racial/ethnic differences, rather than the effects of culture on career self-efficacy and career development. While it is mildly interesting to describe cultural differences, it is more important to explore the reasons for any existing ethnic differences, to examine similarities across racial/ethnic groups, and to study within-group variability. In addition to expanding the ethnic diversity of the samples in career self-efficacy research, ethnicity needs to be incorporated into more complex models of occupational choice in order to examine the interactions between past performance, other-person variables, self-efficacy, and environmental factors, such as social support and barriers (e.g., Hackett et al., 1992). In addition, acculturation and ethnic-identity development may need to be explored in order to explore any possible cultural influences on career self-efficacy (e.g., Church et al., 1992).

CAUSAL INVESTIGATIONS

One of the major advantages of the career self-efficacy approach to career development is that the theory offers specific guidance in designing career interventions. Yet, to date, very few investigations have focused on intervention issues. Research investigating causal links among performance, self-efficacy, and interests, along with studies investigating sources of career self-efficacy information, suggest intervention possibilities, but only one published study has examined counseling interventions designed to enhance career self-efficacy (Fukuyama et al., 1988). This is obviously an area in which research is sorely needed. Several researchers have devoted attention to the implications of self-efficacy theory for practice; their ideas may be useful guides for research efforts (e.g., Borders & Archadel, 1987; Goldfried & Robins, 1982; Lent & Hackett, 1991).

Also needed are causal modeling approaches to correlational data. A common research strategy in the career self-efficacy research has been to examine the complex relationships among variables via multiple regression analyses. Yet, often the research questions in these studies employing regression procedures to predict academic achievement and career and major choice would have been more satisfactorily addressed by path analysis, or even structural equation-modeling procedures (e.g., Hackett, et al., 1992; Lent et al., 1991). Inadequate sample size has been one barrier to the use of causal modeling procedures. The increasing use of causal modeling to test the hypothesized relationships among past performance, sources of efficacy information, career self-efficacy, outcome expectations, interests, and choice and achievement behavior is likely as the career self-efficacy research literature matures.

THEORY COMPARISONS

In addition to intervention studies, theory comparisons provide strong tests of the utility of self-efficacy theory in understanding career development and, as stated above, have begun to appear with increasing frequency. For example, Siegal et al. (1985) found a self-efficacy model superior to a math anxiety-aptitude model in explaining math achievement, and Smith, Arnkoff, and Wright (1990) reported evidence for a social cognitive model of test anxiety. Critically needed, however, are tests of a more complete social cognitive model (e.g., for example via the causal modeling procedures previously mentioned). Most of what has appeared in the career self-efficacy literature has included only a limited range of variables (e.g., Hackett, 1985), and studies have rarely included all of the major elements of the self-efficacy model (e.g., outcome expectations). The efforts of Lent et al. (1993) and Hackett et al. (1992) are isolated examples of movement toward increasing theoretical complexity.

An important step needed to advance the career self-efficacy literature is the formulation of an explicit set of theoretical propositions derived from social cognitive theory (Hackett & Lent, 1992). Such a theoretical statement must certainly include the major cognitive and affective elements of social cognitive theory. It should also include hypotheses about the interrelationships of career self-efficacy and other key person and environmental variables, such as vocational interests and work values, attributions, SES, gender, ethnicity, cognitive information-processing mechanisms, social support, opportunities and barriers, and other factors known to be important in career development. The career self-efficacy literature has now matured to the point at which more complex investigations of relevant phenomena require theoretical guidance of a type that is not now readily available, but rather must be culled piecemeal from the literature. The field of career development has traditionally suffered from a paucity of theory-based research (Hackett et al., 1991). Initially, career self-efficacy research was clearly conceptually based, but theory-building efforts have not kept pace with the advances in knowledge about career self-efficacy, self-efficacy theory, and research in general, or social cognitive theory. At least one such integrative theory-building attempt has begun (Lent, Brown, & Hackett, 1992). This and other theory-building efforts will undoubtedly stimulate renewed vigor and increased sophistication in the career self-efficacy research literature.

ACKNOWLEDGMENT: The authors would like to express their appreciation to Bob Lent, for his valuable insights on career self-efficacy theory and research.

REFERENCES

Arnold, J., & Bye, H. (1989). Sex and sex role self-concept as correlates of career decision making self-efficacy. *British Journal of Guidance and Counselling, 17*, 201–206.

Bandura, A. (1977). Self-efficacy: Toward a unifying theory of behavioral change. *Psychological Review, 84*, 191–214.

Bandura, A. (1986). *Social foundations of thought and action: A social cognitive theory.* Englewood Cliffs, NJ: Prentice-Hall.

Barling, J., & Beattie, R. (1983). Self-efficacy beliefs and sales performance. *Journal of Organizational Behavior Management, 5*, 41–51.

Bem, S. L. (1981). *Bem sex role inventory: Professional manual.* Palo Alto, CA: Consulting Psychologists Press.

Betz, N. E., & Fitzgerald, L. F. (1987). *The career psychology of women.* San Diego, CA: Academic Press.

Betz, N. E., & Hackett, G. (1981). The relationship of career-related self-efficacy expectations to perceived career options in college women and men. *Journal of Counseling Psychology, 28*, 399–410.

Betz, N. E., & Hackett, G. (1983). The relationship of mathematics self-efficacy expectations to the selection of science-based college majors. *Journal of Vocational Behavior, 23*, 329–345.

Betz, N. E., & Hackett, G. (1986). Applications of self-efficacy theory to understanding career choice behavior. *Journal of Social and Clinical Psychology, 4*, 279–289.

Betz, N. E., & Hackett, G. (1987). The concept of agency in educational and career development. *Journal of Counseling Psychology, 34*, 299–308.

Blustein, D. L. (1989). The role of goal instability and career self-efficacy in the career exploration process. *Journal of Vocational Behavior, 35*, 194–203.

Bonett, R. M., & Stickel, S. A. (1992). A psychometric analysis of the Career Attitude Scale. *Measurement and Evaluation in Counseling and Development, 25*, 14.

Borders, L. D., & Archadel, K. A. (1987). Self-beliefs and career counseling. *Journal of Career Development, 14,* 69–79.

Bores-Rangel, E., Church, T. A., Szendre, D., & Reeves, C. (1990). Self-efficacy in relation to occupational consideration and academic performance in high school equivalency students. *Journal of Counseling Psychology, 37,* 407–418.

Branch, L. E., & Lichtenberg, J. W. (1987, August). *Self-efficacy and career choice.* Paper presented at the Annual Meeting of the American Psychological Association, New York, NY.

Bridges, J. S. (1988). Sex differences in occupational performance expectations. *Psychology of Women Quarterly, 12,* 75–90.

Brown, S. D., Lent, R. W., & Larkin, K. C. (1989). Self-efficacy as a moderator of scholastic aptitude–academic performance relationships. *Journal of Vocational Behavior, 35,* 64–75.

Campbell, N. K., & Hackett, G. (1986). The effects of mathematics task performance on math self-efficacy and task interest. *Journal of Vocational Behavior, 28,* 149–162.

Church, A. T., Teresa, J. S., Rosebrook, R., & Szendre, D. (1992). Self-efficacy for careers and occupational consideration in minority high school equivalency students. *Journal of Counseling Psychology, 39,* 498–508.

Clement, S. (1987). The self-efficacy expectations and occupational preferences of females and males. *Journal of Occupational Psychology, 60,* 257–265.

Cooper, S. E., & Robinson, D. A. G. (1991). The relationship of mathematics self-efficacy beliefs to mathematics anxiety and performance. *Measurement and Evaluation in Counseling and Development, 24,* 4–11.

Crites, J. O. (1981). *Career counseling: Methods, models and materials.* New York: McGraw-Hill.

Dawis, R., & Lofquist, L. (1984). *A psychological theory of work adjustment.* Minneapolis: University of Minnesota Press.

Fretz, B. R., Kluge, N. A., Ossana, S. M., & Merikangas, M. W. (1989). Intervention targets for reducing preretirement anxiety and depression. *Journal of Counseling Psychology, 36,* 301–307.

Fukuyama, M. A., Probert, B. S., Neimeyer, G. J., Nevill, D. D., & Metzler, A. E. (1988). Effects of DISCOVER on career self-efficacy and decision making of undergraduates. *Career Development Quarterly, 37,* 56–62.

Goldfried, M. R., & Robins, C. (1982). On the facilitation of self-efficacy. *Cognitive Therapy and Research, 6,* 361–380.

Hackett, G. (1985). The role of mathematics self-efficacy in the choice of math-related majors of college women and men: A path analysis. *Journal of Counseling Psychology, 32,* 47–56.

Hackett, G., & Betz, N. E. (1981). A self-efficacy approach to the career development of women. *Journal of Vocational Behavior, 18,* 326–329.

Hackett, G., & Betz, N. E. (1989). An exploration of the mathematics self-efficacy/mathematics performance correspondence. *Journal for Research in Mathematics Education, 20,* 261–273.

Hackett, G., Betz, N. E., Casas, J. M., & Rocha-Singh, I. (1992). Gender, ethnicity, and social cognitive factors predicting the academic achievement of students in engineering. *Journal of Counseling Psychology, 39,* 527–538.

Hackett, G., Betz, N. E., O'Halloran, M. S., & Romac, D. S. (1990). Effects of verbal and mathematics task performance on task and career self-efficacy and interest. *Journal of Counseling Psychology, 37,* 169–177.

Hackett, G., & Campbell, N. K. (1987). Task self-efficacy and task interest as a function of performance on a gender-neutral task. *Journal of Vocational Behavior, 30,* 203–215.

Hackett, G., & Lent, R. W. (1992). Theoretical advances and current inquiry in career psychology. In S. D. Brown & R. W. Lent (Eds.), *Handbook of Counseling Psychology* (2nd ed., pp. 419–452). New York: Wiley.

Hackett, G., Lent, R. W., & Greenhaus, J. H. (1991). Advances in vocational theory and research: A 20-year retrospective. *Journal of Vocational Behavior, 38*, 3–38.

Hannah, J. S., & Kahn, S. E. (1989). The relationship of socioeconomic status and gender to the occupational choices of grade 12 students. *Journal of Vocational Behavior, 34*, 161–178.

Hill, T., Smith, N. D., & Mann, M. F. (1987). Role of efficacy expectations in predicting the decision to use advanced technologies: The case of computers. *Journal of Applied Psychology, 72*, 307–313.

Holland, J. L. (1985). *Making vocational choices* (2nd ed.). Englewood Cliffs, NJ: Prentice-Hall.

Krumboltz, J. D., Mitchell, A. M., & Jones, G. B. (1976). A social learning theory of career selection. *The Counseling Psychologist, 6*, 71–81.

Landino, R. A., & Owen, S. V. (1988). Self-efficacy in university faculty. *Journal of Vocational Behavior, 33*, 1–14.

Lapan, R. T., Boggs, K. R., & Morrill, W. H. (1989). Self-efficacy as a mediator of investigative and realistic general occupational themes on the Strong–Campbell Interest Inventory. *Journal of Counseling Psychology, 36*, 176–182.

Lapan, R. T., & Jingeleski, J. (1992). Circumscribing vocational aspirations in junior high school. *Journal of Counseling Psychology, 39*, 81–90.

Lauver, P. J., & Jones, R. M. (1991). Factors associated with perceived career options in American Indian, White, and Hispanic rural high school students. *Journal of Counseling Psychology, 38*, 159–166.

Layton, P. L. (1984). *Self-efficacy, locus of control, career salience, and women's career choice.* Unpublished doctoral dissertation, University of Minnesota, Minneapolis.

Lent, R. W., Brown, S. D., & Hackett, G. (1992). *Toward a unified social cognitive theory of career/academic interest, choice, and performance.* Manuscript submitted for publication.

Lent, R. W., Brown, S. D., & Larkin, K. C. (1984). Relation of self-efficacy expectations to academic achievement and persistence. *Journal of Counseling Psychology, 31*, 356–362.

Lent, R. W., Brown, S. D., and Larkin, K. C. (1986). Self-efficacy in the prediction of academic performance and perceived career options. *Journal of Counseling Psychology, 33*, 165–169.

Lent, R. W., Brown, S. D., & Larkin, K. C. (1987). Comparison of three theoretically derived variables in predicting career and academic behavior: Self-efficacy, interest congruence, and consequence thinking. *Journal of Counseling Psychology, 34*, 293–298.

Lent, R. W., & Hackett, G. (1987). Career self-efficacy: Empirical status and future directions [Monograph]. *Journal of Vocational Behavior, 30*, 347–382.

Lent, R. W., & Hackett, G. (1991, August). *Translating self-efficacy theory into practice.* Paper presented at the Annual Meeting of the American Psychological Association, San Francisco, CA.

Lent, R. W., Larkin, K. C., & Brown, S. D. (1989). Relation of self-efficacy to inventoried vocational interests. *Journal of Vocational Behavior, 34*, 279–288.

Lent, R. W., Lopez,, F. G., & Bieschke, K. J. (1991). Mathematics self-efficacy: Sources and relation to science-based career choice. *Journal of Counseling Psychology, 38*, 424–430.

Lent, R. W., Lopez, F. G., & Bieschke, K. J. (1993). Predicting mathematics-related choice and success behaviors: Test of an expanded social cognitive model. *Journal of Vocational Behavior, 42*, 223–236.

Levi, L. (1990). Occupational stress: Spice of life or kiss of death? *American Psychologist, 45*, 1142–1145.

Locke, E. A., Frederick, E., Lee, C., & Bobko, P. (1984). Effect of self-efficacy, goals, and task strategies on task performance. *Journal of Applied Psychology, 69*, 241–251.

Long, B. C. (1989). Sex-role orientation, coping strategies, and self-efficacy of women in traditional and nontraditional occupations. *Psychology of Women Quarterly, 13*, 307–324.

Lopez, F. G., & Lent, R. W. (1992). Sources of mathematics self-efficacy in high school students. *Career Development Quarterly, 41*, 3–12.

Matsui, T., Ikeda, H., & Ohnishi, R. (1989). Relations of sex-typed socializations to career self-efficacy expectations of college students. *Journal of Vocational Behavior, 35*, 1–16.

Matsui, T., Matsui, K., & Ohnishi, R. (1990). Mechanisms underlying math self-efficacy learning of college students. *Journal of Vocational Behavior, 37*, 225–238.

Matsui, T., & Onglatco, M. L. (1991). Instrumentality, expressiveness, and self-efficacy in career activities among Japanese working women. *Journal of Vocational Behavior, 39*, 241–250.

Matsui, T., & Onglatco, M. L. (1992a). Career self-efficacy as a moderator of the relation between occupational stress and strain. *Journal of Vocational Behavior, 41*, 79–88.

Matsui, T., & Onglatco, M. L. (1992b). Career orientedness of motivation to enter the university among Japanese high school girls. *Journal of Vocational Behavior, 40*, 351–363.

Matsui, T., & Tsukamoto, S. (1991). Relation between career self-efficacy measures based on occupational titles and Holland codes and model environments: A methodological contribution. *Journal of Vocational Behavior, 38*, 78–91.

Miura, I. T. (1987). The relationship of computer self-efficacy expectations to computer interest and course enrollment in college. *Sex Roles, 16*, 303–311.

Multon, K. D., Brown, S. D., & Lent, R. W. (1991). Relation of self-efficacy beliefs to academic outcomes: A meta-analytic investigation. *Journal of Counseling Psychology, 38*, 30–38.

Nevill, D. D., Neimeyer, G. J., Probert, B., & Fukuyama, M. (1986). Cognitive structures in vocational information processing and decision making. *Journal of Vocational Behavior, 28*, 110–122.

Nevill, D. D., & Schlecker, D. I. (1988). The relation of self-efficacy and assertiveness to willingness to engage in traditional/nontraditional career activities. *Psychology of Women Quarterly, 12*, 91–98.

Niles, S. G., & Sowa, C. J. (1992). Mapping the nomological network of career self-efficacy. *Career Development Quarterly, 41*, 13–21.

Noble, A. J., Hackett, G., & Chen, E. C. (1992, April). *Relations of career and academic self-efficacy to the career aspirations and academic achievement of ninth and tenth grade at risk students.* Paper presented at the annual meeting of the American Educational Research Association, San Francisco, CA.

Norwich, B. (1987). Self-efficacy and mathematics achievement: A study of their relation. *Journal of Educational Psychology, 79*, 384–387.

O'Hare, M. M., & Beutell, N. J. (1987). Sex differences in coping with career decision making. *Journal of Vocational Behavior, 31*, 174–181.

O'Hare, M. M., & Tamburri, E. (1986). Coping as a moderator of the relation between anxiety and career decision making. *Journal of Counseling Psychology, 33*, 255–264.

Osipow, S. H. (1986). Career issues through the life span. In M. S. Pallak & R. O. Perloff (Eds.), *Psychology and work: Productivity, change, and employment* (pp. 141–168). Washington, DC: American Psychological Association.

Pond, S. B., & Hay, M. S. (1989). The impact of task preview information as a function of recipient self-efficacy. *Journal of Vocational Behavior, 35*, 17–29.

Post, P., Stewart, M. A., & Smith, P. L. (1991). Self-efficacy, interest, and consideration of math/science and non-math/science occupations among college freshmen. *Journal of Vocational Behavior, 38*, 179–186.

Post-Kammer, P., & Smith, P. L. (1985). Sex differences in career self-efficacy, consideration, and interests of eighth and ninth graders. *Journal of Counseling Psychology, 32*, 551–559.

Post-Kammer, P., & Smith, P. L. (1986). Sex differences in math and science career self-efficacy among disadvantaged students. *Journal of Vocational Behavior, 29,* 89–101.

Robbins, S. B. (1985). Validity estimates for the Career Decision-Making Self-efficacy Scale. *Measurement and Evaluation in Counseling and Development, 18,* 64–71.

Rooney, R., & Osipow, S. H. (1992). Task-specific occupational self-efficacy scale: The development and validation of a prototype. *Journal of Vocational Behavior, 40,* 14–32.

Rotberg, H. L., Brown, D., & Ware, W. B. (1987). Career self-efficacy expectations and perceived range of career options in community college students. *Journal of Counseling Psychology, 34,* 164–170.

Rounds, J. B., & Tracey, T. J. (1990). From trait-and-factor to person-environment fit counseling: Theory and process. In W. B. Walsh & S. H. Osipow (Eds.), *Career counseling* (pp. 1–44). Hillsdale, NJ: Erlbaum.

Schoen, L. G., & Winocur, S. (1988). An investigation of the self-efficacy of male and female academics. *Journal of Vocational Behavior, 32,* 307–320.

Siegal, R. G., Galassi, J. P., & Ware, W. B. (1985). A comparison of two models for predicting mathematics performance: Social learning versus math aptitude-anxiety. *Journal of Counseling Psychology, 32,* 531–538.

Smith, R. J., Arnkoff, D. B., & Wright, T. L. (1990). Test anxiety and academic competence: A comparison of alternative models. *Journal of Counseling Psychology, 37,* 313–321.

Stickel, S. A., & Bonett, R. M. (1991). Gender differences in career self-efficacy: Combining a career with some and family. *Journal of College Student Development, 32,* 297–301.

Stumpf, S. A., Brief, A. P., & Hartman, K. (1987). Self-efficacy expectations and coping with career-related events. *Journal of Vocational Behavior, 31,* 91–108.

Super, D. E. (1990). A life-span, life-space approach to career development.In D. Brown, L. Brooks, and Associates, *Career choice and development* (pp. 197–261). San Francisco, CA: Jossey-Bass.

Taylor, K. M., & Betz, N. E. (1983). Applications of self-efficacy theory to the understanding and treatment of career indecision. *Journal of Vocational Behavior, 22,* 63–81.

Taylor, K. M., & Popma, J. (1990). An examination of the relationships among career decision-making self-efficacy, career salience, locus of control, and vocational indecision. *Journal of Vocational Behavior, 37,* 17–31.

Wheeler, K. G. (1983). Comparisons of self-efficacy and expectancy models of occupational preferences for college males and females. *Journal of Occupational Psychology, 56,* 73–78.

Williams, T. M., & Leonard, M. M. (1988). Graduating black undergraduates: The step beyond retention. *Journal of College Student Development, 29,* 69–75.

Zilber, S. M. (1988, August). *The effects of attributional styles, sex, and task performance on task and career self-efficacy expectations.* Paper presented at the meeting of the American Psychological Association, Atlanta, GA.

CHAPTER 10

SELF-EFFICACY AND EDUCATION AND INSTRUCTION

DALE H. SCHUNK

Current theoretical accounts of learning and instruction postulate that students are active seekers and processors of information (Pintrich, Cross, Kozma, & McKeachie, 1986; Shuell, 1986). Research indicates that students' cognitions influence the instigation, direction, strength, and persistence of their achievement behaviors (Schunk, 1989b; Weinstein, 1989; Zimmerman, 1990).

This chapter reviews the role of one type of personal cognition: *self-efficacy*, defined as "people's judgments of their capabilities to organize and execute courses of action required to attain designated types of performances" (Bandura, 1986, p. 391). Since Bandura's (1977) original paper, self-efficacy theory has been applied in educational settings to various grade levels (e.g., elementary, secondary, postsecondary), content domains (reading, writing, mathematics), and student ability levels (average, gifted, remedial). Researchers have examined how personal and environmental (instructional, social) factors affect self-efficacy and how self-efficacy influences learning, motivation, and achievement (Schunk, 1989a). This research has helped clarify and extend the role of self-efficacy as a mecha-

DALE H. SCHUNK • Department of Educational Studies, Purdue University, West Lafayette, Indiana 47907.

Self-Efficacy, Adaptation, and Adjustment: Theory, Research, and Application, edited by James E. Maddux. Plenum Press, New York, 1995.

nism underlying behavioral change, maintenance, and generalization. Although most educational self-efficacy research has focused on students, researchers increasingly are exploring the role of teachers' efficacy (Ashton & Webb, 1986).

The chapter initially provides an overview of self-efficacy theory as it pertains to education. Self-efficacy research is discussed here that is relevant to student learning, motivation, and achievement, along with some substantive issues. The chapter concludes with suggestions for future research.

SELF-EFFICACY THEORY

Bandura (1977) hypothesized that self-efficacy affects choice of activities, effort, and persistence. Compared with students who doubt their learning capabilities, those with high self-efficacy for accomplishing a task participate more readily, work harder, and persist longer when they encounter difficulties.

Learners acquire information to appraise self-efficacy from their performance accomplishments, vicarious (observational) experiences, forms of persuasion, and physiological reactions. Students' own performances offer them reliable guides for assessing their self-efficacy. Successes raise self-efficacy and failures lower it, but once a strong sense of self-efficacy is developed, a failure may not have much impact (Bandura, 1986).

Learners also acquire self-efficacy information from knowledge of others through classroom social comparisons. Similar others offer the best basis for comparison. Students who observe similar peers perform a task are apt to believe that they, too, are capable of accomplishing it. Information acquired vicariously typically has a weaker effect on self-efficacy than performance-based information; the former effect easily can be negated by subsequent failures.

Students often receive persuasive information from teachers and parents that they are capable of performing a task (e.g., "You can do this"). Positive feedback enhances self-efficacy, but this increase will be temporary if subsequent efforts turn out poorly. Students also acquire efficacy information from physiological reactions (e.g., heart rate, sweating). Symptoms signaling anxiety might be interpreted to mean that one lacks skills.

Information acquired from these sources does not automatically influence self-efficacy; rather, it is cognitively appraised (Bandura, 1986). In appraising efficacy, learners weigh and combine their perceptions of their ability, the difficulty of the task, the amount of effort expended, the amount of external assistance received, the number and pattern of successes and failures, the perceived similarity to models, and persuader credibility (Schunk, 1989b).

Self-efficacy is not the only influence in educational settings. Achievement behavior also depends on knowledge and skills, outcome expectations, and the perceived value of outcomes (Schunk, 1989b). High self-efficacy does not produce competent performances when requisite knowledge and skills are lacking. Outcome expectations, or beliefs concerning the probable outcomes of actions, are important because students strive for positive outcomes. Perceived value of outcomes refers to how much learners desire certain outcomes relative to others. Learners are motivated to act in ways that they believe will result in outcomes they value.

Bandura and his colleagues have applied self-efficacy theory to therapeutic contexts to help explain behavioral change in feared situations (Bandura, 1977, 1986). This research (e.g., with snake phobics) investigated behaviors that participants knew how to perform but typically did not because of anxiety, low self-efficacy, and negative outcome expectations ("If I get near the snake, it will bite me"). Some school activities involve performance of previously learned skills, but much time is spent acquiring new knowledge, skills, and strategies. At the start of a learning activity, students differ in their self-efficacy for acquiring the new material as a result of prior experiences and aptitudes (abilities, attitudes). As students work on the task, personal factors (e.g., goal setting, information processing) and situational factors (e.g., rewards, teachers' feedback) provide cues that signal how well they are learning and which they use to assess self-efficacy for further learning. Motivation is enhanced when students perceive they are making progress. Higher motivation and self-efficacy promote task engagement and skill acquisition (Schunk, 1989a).

The following sections summarize research illustrating the role of self-efficacy in education. The first section (Factors Affecting Self-efficacy) discusses research on the effects of goal setting, information processing, models, feedback, and rewards, on self-efficacy for learning and performing skills. The second section (Predictive Utility of Self-Efficacy) reports on studies examining the relation of self-efficacy to achievement outcomes. This review is not comprehensive or exhaustive. It focuses on cognitive skills, although self-efficacy research has been conducted with other types of skills (e.g., social, motor). Within the domain of cognitive skills, a representative sample of studies is reviewed; to conserve space, methodological details have been omitted. For additional reviews, interested readers should consult other sources (Bandura, 1986; Hackett & Betz, Chap. 9, this volume; Locke & Latham, 1990; Schunk, 1989a).

FACTORS AFFECTING SELF-EFFICACY

GOAL SETTING

Goal setting is hypothesized to be an important cognitive process affecting achievement outcomes (Bandura, 1988; Locke & Latham, 1990; Schunk, 1989b). Students who set or are given a goal may experience a sense of self-efficacy for attaining it and make a commitment to attempt it. They engage in activities that they believe will produce goal attainment: attending to instruction, rehearsing information to be remembered, expending effort and persisting. Self-efficacy is substantiated as learners observe goal progress, which conveys to them that they are becoming skillful (Elliott & Dweck, 1988). Providing students with feedback on goal progress also raises self-efficacy (Schunk & Swartz, 1992a, 1992b). Heightened self-efficacy sustains motivation and promotes learning.

The benefits of goals depend on proximity, specificity, and difficulty (Bandura, 1986, 1988; Locke & Latham, 1990). Proximal (close-at-hand) goals enhance performance better than distant goals, because students can judge progress toward the former easier than toward the latter. It also is easier to judge progress toward goals incorporating specific performance standards than toward general goals (e.g., "Do your best"). Pursuing easier goals may be effective during initial skill acquisition, but difficult goals are more beneficial as skills develop, because they offer more information about capabilities.

Effects of goal setting on self-efficacy have been obtained in several studies. Bandura and Schunk (1981) found that during subtraction instruction, providing children with a proximal goal heightened self-efficacy, as well as motivation (rate of problem solving) and skill acquisition, more than did giving them a distant goal or a general goal. The distant goal resulted in no benefits compared with the general goal. During a long-division instruction program, Schunk (1983b) showed that giving children specific performance goals enhanced self-efficacy more than providing no explicit goals.

Allowing students to set goals may enhance goal commitment. Schunk (1985) found that self-set goals also promote self-efficacy. Sixth-grade learning-disabled students received subtraction instruction. Children either set their own performance goals, had goals assigned by the experimenter, or did not set or receive goals. Self-set goals led to the highest self-efficacy and skill.

One problem with goal-setting research is that it has focused on such outcomes as quantity of work or amount of time spent. These *product* goals concern what students should know or accomplish as a result of learning. In contrast, *process* goals involve techniques and strategies students use to promote learning (Weinstein & Mayer, 1986). A process goal might be to learn to use a *learning strategy*, or systematic plan for improving information processing and task performance. Research in various domains has shown that students taught strategies typically improve their skills (Borkowski, 1985) and that use of effective strategies correlates positively with self-efficacy (Pintrich & De Groot, 1990; Zimmerman & Martinez-Pons, 1990).

Process goals may enhance self-efficacy and achievement more than product goals, because providing students with a process goal highlights strategy use as a means to improve skills. Students may experience a sense of self-efficacy for attaining the goal (learning the strategy), which is substantiated as they work at the task. Learners who believe they are learning a useful strategy feel efficacious and motivated to apply the strategy, which increase skills and transfer (Schunk, 1989a). In contrast, providing students with a product goal may not convey that the strategy is important. Learners who believe that a strategy does not contribute much do not employ it systematically or feel confident about learning (Borkowski, 1985).

Research testing these ideas has yielded mixed results. Schunk and Rice (1989) taught remedial readers a comprehension strategy to find main ideas. Children received a product goal of answering questions, a process goal of learning to use the strategy, or a general goal of working productively. The process and product goals enhanced comprehension skill and self-efficacy for finding main ideas more than did the general goal, but the former two conditions did not differ. A follow-up study found that a process goal plus feedback on progress in using the strategy led to higher self-efficacy and skill than the process and product goal conditions (Schunk & Rice, 1991). Such strategy feedback, which conveys that the strategy is effective and that children can continue to improve their skills by applying it, may be especially important with remedial students, who might not be able to determine on their own the benefits of using the strategy. In support of this point, during writing strategy instruction with average and gifted children, Schunk and Swartz (1992a, 1992b) found that process goals plus progress feedback promoted self-efficacy, achievement, strategy use, and transfer (maintenance, generalization) of achievement outcomes more than did product and general goals; however, on most measures the process goal and process goal plus progress feedback conditions did not differ. Further research is needed to clarify how process goals affect achievement outcomes.

Another problem is that most goal-setting research is of short duration. This type of research can study basic processes, but it does not fully capture the nature of learning and motivation in education. Many academic goals are long term: earning a college degree, completing a science-fair project, raising one's grade point average. We need educational research that explores goal setting over lengthy time periods (see Hackett & Betz, Chap. 9, this volume, for a discussion of career self-efficacy). Schunk and Swartz (1992a, 1992b) obtained evidence for maintenance of self-efficacy, skills, and strategy use, over a 6-week period, but research is needed over longer periods. Morgan (1985) did not assess self-efficacy, but found that proximal goals raised academic performance and intrinsic interest among college students over an academic year, which suggests that goal proximity may influence self-regulatory processes associated with studying over time. Longitudinal studies could determine the nature of this influence and whether self-efficacy is strengthened as students progress toward long-term goals.

INFORMATION PROCESSING

Researchers have investigated how the demands of cognitively processing academic material influences self-efficacy. Students who believe they will experience great difficulty comprehending material are apt to have low self-efficacy for learning it, whereas those who feel capable of handling the information-processing demands should feel efficacious (Schunk, 1989b). Higher self-efficacy leads students to perform those activities that they believe will produce learning. As students work on tasks, they derive information about how well they are learning. The perception that they are comprehending material enhances self-efficacy and motivation. The perception of little progress may not lower self-efficacy and motivation if students believe they can perform better by using a better strategy.

Salomon (1984) found that mental effort relates to self-efficacy. Children judged their efficacy for learning from television or from written text; they watched a televised film or read the comparable text, judged the amount of mental effort necessary to learn, and were tested on the content. Students judged that mental effort was greater for text and demonstrated higher achievement scores from reading text. For reading text, self-efficacy correlated positively with mental effort and achievement; for TV, it correlated negatively. Students who observed TV felt more efficacious about learning, but expended less effort and achieved at a lower level.

Among college students, Meier, McCarthy, and Schmeck (1984) demonstrated that self-efficacy for writing relates to cognitive processing dimensions. Students wrote essays at the beginning and end of a semester; at the start of the course, they also judged self-efficacy for accomplishing writing objectives. Self-efficacy accurately predicted end-of-semester writing performance. Information-processing indices relating to self-efficacy were synthesis-analysis (searching for meaning by categorizing ideas and comparing and contrasting categories) and elaborative processing (personalizing and concretizing by relating ideas to personal experiences; see Hackett & Betz, Chap. 9, this volume, for more discussion of self-efficacy among college students).

Self-efficacy correlates positively with motivation to employ learning strategies. Pintrich and De Groot (1990) had seventh graders judge self-efficacy and use of various strategies, including effort management and persistence. Self-efficacy correlated positively with reported strategy use. Zimmerman and Martinez-Pons (1990) had students in grades 5, 8, and 11, judge use of various learning strategies that included motivational components, as well as self-efficacy for performing mathematical and verbal tasks. Self-efficacy was positively correlated with reported strategy use across domains.

Instructional studies support the idea that teaching students to use strategies raises self-efficacy and achievement. Schunk and Gunn (1985) taught children to use a long-division strategy. As part of the instruction, children observed an adult emphasize the importance of either strategy use or positive achievement beliefs (effort, efficacy); some students received both forms of information. Although stressing the importance of strategy use enhanced motivation and skills, emphasizing both strategy use and positive beliefs led to the highest self-efficacy.

Graham and Harris (1989b) taught learning-disabled students a strategy for writing essays. Strategy instruction improved students' essay quality. Gains were maintained up to 12 weeks following training, and skills and strategy use were generalized to writing stories. In a similar study, learning-disabled children received strategy instruction on writing stories (Graham & Harris, 1989a). Training improved the children's use of story grammar elements. Gains were maintained after 2 weeks, and outcomes were generalized to the resource room. In both studies, strategy instruction raised self-efficacy for writing essays and stories.

One means of teaching strategies involves having students verbalize aloud the component steps while applying them (Schunk, 1989b). *Strategy verbalization* can facilitate learning because it directs students' attention to important task features, assists strategy encoding and retention, and helps students work systematically (Harris, 1982). By highlighting a strategy that improves performance, verbalization also conveys to students the fact that they have control over learning, and perceived control over outcomes can enhance self-efficacy (Schunk, 1989b).

To determine the effects of strategy verbalization, Schunk and Rice (1984) gave listening-comprehension instruction to children with low language skills. Students either verbalized strategic steps prior to applying them to questions, or received strategy instruction but did not verbalize steps. Strategy verbalization promoted self-efficacy across grades (2, 3, 4) and comprehension among third and fourth graders but not among second graders. Perhaps the demands of verbalization, along with those of the comprehension task, were too complex for the youngest students. These children may have focused on the comprehension task, which interfered with strategy encoding and retention. In a follow-up study (Schunk & Rice, 1985), fourth and fifth graders with reading comprehension deficiencies received instruction and practice. Verbalization of a reading comprehension strategy led to higher self-efficacy and comprehension across grades.

Schunk and Cox (1986) found that having students with learning disabilities verbalize a subtraction strategy while applying it raised self-efficacy, skill acquisition, and motivation. The greatest benefits were obtained when students verbalized throughout the instructional program. Students who were told to stop overtly verbalizing midway through the program apparently failed to internalize the strategy and discontinued its use. Having students fade verbalizations to a covert (silent) level may help them self-regulate their performances. Graham and Harris (1989a, 1989b) encouraged students to fade strategic statements during training.

Future research might investigate the relation of changes in information processing (including strategy use), self-efficacy, motivation, and learning, as students work on tasks. Researchers in such domains as writing and mathematics often have students verbalize aloud as they work on tasks to determine differences between more- and less-skilled students, and how processing changes as skills develop (Romberg & Carpenter, 1986; Scardamalia & Bereiter, 1986). In addition to these *think-aloud* protocols over extended periods, researchers also could periodically assess changes in self-efficacy and skills.

MODELS

Students acquire much self-efficacy information vicariously from peers and teachers. Modeled displays can convey to observers that they are capable and can motivate them to attempt the task; observed failures may lower students' self-efficacy and dissuade them from working. Vicarious effects may be negated by subsequent personal experiences. A vicarious increase in self-efficacy may be short-lived if observers subsequently perform poorly (Schunk, 1989a).

Research demonstrates the benefits of models on self-efficacy, motivation, and achievement. Zimmerman and Ringle (1981) had children observe a model unsuccessfully attempt to solve a puzzle for a long or short time and verbalize statements of confidence or pessimism, after which children attempted the puzzle themselves. Observing a low-persistence but confident model raised the children's self-efficacy; observing a pessimistic model persist for a long time lowered the children's self-efficacy. Relich, Debus, and Walker (1986) found that exposing low-achieving children to models explaining mathematical division and providing children with attributional feedback stressing ability and effort had a positive effect on self-efficacy.

Brown and Inouye (1978) investigated students' perceived similarity in competence to models. College students judged self-efficacy for solving anagrams and attempted to solve them, after which they were told that they performed better than, or the same, as a model. They then observed a model fail, judged self-efficacy, and attempted the anagrams again. Telling students that they were more competent than the model led to higher self-efficacy and persistence than telling them they were equal to the model in competence.

Schunk and Hanson (1985) compared peer mastery and coping models with adult–teacher models and no models. Peer *mastery models* solved subtraction with regrouping problems correctly and verbalized statements reflecting high self-efficacy and ability, low task difficulty, and positive attitudes. Peer *coping models* initially made errors and verbalized negative statements, but then verbalized coping statements (e.g., "I need to pay attention to what I'm doing") and eventually verbalized and performed as well as mastery models.

Peer models increased self-efficacy and skill better than the teacher model or no model; teacher-model children outperformed no-model students. Schunk and Hanson had hypothesized that their low-achieving subjects might perceive themselves as more similar to coping models, but there were no differences in outcomes between the mastery- and coping-model conditions. Although subjects' prior successes involved problems without regrouping, they might have recalled those successes and believed that if the models could learn, they could too.

A follow-up study (Schunk, Hanson, & Cox, 1987) used a task (fractions) on which children had experienced few successes. This study also tested the idea that multiple models are better than a single model, because multiple models increase the likelihood that students will view themselves as similar to at least one model (Schunk, 1989a). The results showed that multiple models—coping or mastery—promoted outcomes as well as a single coping model and better than a single mastery model. Children who observed single models judged themselves more similar in competence to coping than to mastery models. Benefits of multiple models were not due to perceived similarity in competence.

These results help clarify the operation of modeling in educational settings, but more information is needed on the role of perceived similarity to models. The Schunk et al. (1987) study suggests that similarity may be important when students have few cues to assess efficacy. Students learn from many models, including teachers dissimilar in age, competence, and other characteristics. They also weigh and combine sources of efficacy information from diverse sources: They may observe peers succeeding and receiving positive feedback from teachers (e.g., "You can do this") but experience difficulties when they attempt to perform the task. Research should explore the conditions under which similarity is important.

FEEDBACK

Theory and research support the idea that feedback can affect self-efficacy in important ways. *Attributional feedback* links students' successes and failures with one or more *attributions*, or perceived causes of outcomes (Schunk, 1989a). Attributional feedback is a persuasive source of self-efficacy information (see Maddux, this volume). Linking success with effort supports students' perceptions of their progress, sustains motivation, and increases self-efficacy (Schunk, 1989b). The timing of feedback also is important. Early successes signal high learning ability; ability feedback for early successes can enhance self-efficacy for learning. Effort feedback for early successes should be credible with students who have to work hard to succeed.

Research supports these ideas. Schunk (1982) found that linking children's prior achievements with effort (e.g., "You've been working hard") led to higher self-efficacy, motivation, and skill, compared with emphasizing the future benefits of effort ("You need to work hard"). In the Schunk and Cox (1986) study, students received effort feedback during the first half of the instructional program, effort feedback during the second half, or no effort feedback. Each type of feedback promoted self-efficacy, motivation, and skill better than no feedback; first-half feedback increased effort attributions and motivation during the first half of the program. Given students' learning disabilities, effort feedback for early or later successes likely seemed credible because students had to work to succeed. Students may have interpreted the feedback as indicating that they were becoming skillful and capable of further learning.

Working with average students, Schunk (1983a) showed that ability feedback for successes ("You're good at this") enhanced self-efficacy and skill better than effort feedback or ability- plus-effort feedback. Although these three conditions raised children's motivation equally well, ability-plus-effort subjects judged effort expenditure greater than did ability-only students. Ability-plus-effort subjects may have discounted ability information in favor of effort attribution.

The preceding results suggest a need to explore how students interpret attributional feedback at different stages of skill development. Effort feedback may be credible early in learning, when students have to work to succeed. As skills develop, students should succeed with less effort; thus, ability feedback may become more credible. Effort feedback might even lower self-efficacy, because as students become skillful, attributing their successes to their efforts might leave them wondering why they still have to work hard to succeed. Research that periodically assessed students' self-efficacy, skills, and interpretations of feedback, could determine which feedback sequences best promote achievement outcomes.

Another persuasive source of self-efficacy information is feedback concerning students' competencies. Telling students they are capable of performing in a given way can enhance their self-efficacy and lead to greater motivation and skill acquisition. During a long-division instructional program, Schunk (1983c) gave children either easy or difficult goals; within each goal condition children received persuasive feedback ("You can work 25 problems") or social comparative feedback, indicating the level of performance attained by similar students (which matched the persuasive feedback). Persuasive feedback increased self-efficacy; feedback plus difficult goals led to the highest skill.

Performance feedback, indicating that students are making progress in learning, should raise self-efficacy, motivation, and achievement, especially when students cannot reliably determine progress on their own. Schunk (1983d) found that self-monitoring of subtraction progress provided reliable performance feedback and promoted self-efficacy and achievement. At the end of each instructional session, children either recorded the number of pages completed (self-monitoring) or had the number recorded for them (external monitoring); no-monitoring children neither recorded pages nor had them recorded by others. Self- and external monitoring promoted self-efficacy and skill better than no monitoring. The former conditions did not differ, which suggests that the key variable was monitoring rather than its agent. In the absence of monitoring, children may have been uncertain of how well they were learning.

Strategy feedback is hypothesized to enhance self-efficacy because it conveys to students that the strategy is effective, that they are making progress in learning, and that they are capable of further skill improvement. Research needs to determine the mechanism whereby such feedback enhances achievement outcomes. Studies (Schunk & Rice, 1991; Schunk & Swartz, 1992a, 1992b) suggest that enhanced self-efficacy produced by the feedback may be partly responsible.

REWARDS

According to Bandura (1986), rewards are informative and motivating. As students work on tasks, they learn which actions result in positive outcomes (successes, teacher praise, high grades). Such information guides future actions. Anticipation of desirable outcomes motivates students to persist. Rewards enhance self-efficacy when they are linked with students' accomplishments and convey to students that they have made progress in learning. Receipt of the reward also symbolizes progress. In contrast, rewards offered for task participation do not convey progress information.

Research supports these ideas. During mathematics instruction (Schunk, 1983e), children were told either that they would earn points for each problem solved and could exchange points for prizes (performance-contingent rewards) or that they would receive prizes for participating (task-contingent rewards). Performance-contingent rewards enhanced motivation, self-efficacy, and skill; offering rewards for participation led to no benefits. Schunk (1984) found that performance-contingent rewards and proximal goals raised children's motivation equally well during division instruction, and that combining rewards with goals led to the highest self-efficacy and learning. These results suggest that rewards-plus-goals provided clear information to children about their learning progress.

Much has been written about the deleterious effect on students' intrinsic interest of offering them rewards for performing tasks they enjoy (Lepper, 1983). Less has been written about ways to help students develop interest. The development of interest may depend, in part, on an enhanced a sense of competence for the activity. In support of this point, Bandura and Schunk (1981) found that proximal goals promoted children's self-efficacy and intrinsic interest. Research might test the idea that performance-contingent rewards raise interest through their effects on children's perceptions of learning progress and self-efficacy. Given the prevalence of rewards in education, this research would have important implications for classroom practice.

PREDICTIVE UTILITY OF SELF-EFFICACY

CORRELATION/REGRESSION ANALYSES

Self-efficacy research has examined the relation of self-efficacy to such educational outcomes as motivation, persistence, and achievement (see also Hackett and Betz, Chap. 9, this volume). Significant and positive correlations have been obtained (range of $r = .38-.42$) between self-efficacy for learning (assessed prior to instruction) and subsequent task motivation (Schunk & Hanson, 1985; Schunk et al., 1987). Self-efficacy for learning judgments also correlate positively with posttest self-efficacy and skill (range of $r = .46-.90$; Schunk, 1989a). Studies in different domains have yielded significant and positive correlations between posttest self-efficacy and skill (range of $r = .27-.84$); Schunk, 1989a).

Multiple regression has been used to determine the percentage of variability in skillful performance accounted for by self-efficacy. In the Schunk (1982) study, posttest self-efficacy and rate of problem solving during instruction (an index of motivation) accounted for significant increments in posttest skill variability. Schunk and Swartz (1992a) found that posttest self-efficacy was the strongest predictor of children's writing skills. Among college students, McCarthy, Meier, and Rinderer (1985) found that self-efficacy for successfully performing various writing skills was the strongest predictor of subsequent writing performance.

Collins (1982) demonstrated that self-efficacy predicts motivation and achievement across levels of student ability. Children identified as high, average, or low in mathematical ability were classified as high or low in self-efficacy for solving word problems. Students were given problems to solve (some were unsolvable) and could rework any they missed. Low- and average-ability students with high self-efficacy worked longer on unsolvable problems than low self-efficacy students. Regardless of ability, students with higher self-efficacy reworked more problems than students with lower self-efficacy.

The predictive utility of self-efficacy cross domains was demonstrated by Shell, Murphy, and Bruning (1989). College students completed measures of self-efficacy, outcome expectations, and skill for reading and writing tasks. Regression analyses showed that self-efficacy and outcome expectancies predicted reading achievement, with self-efficacy being the stronger predictor; only self-efficacy accounted for a significant proportion of variance in writing achievement.

Conversely, Norwich (1987) found that self-efficacy did not contribute to the prediction of mathematical performance beyond the effects of mathematical self-concept and prior performance. Children judged self-efficacy for solving a particular type of mathematics problem and then attempted to solve two problems. Given the evidence showing self-efficacy to be a significant predictor, it seems possible that the limited sample of self-efficacy tasks in this study restricted the variability of self-efficacy and its potential prediction.

CAUSAL MODELS

Several self-efficacy studies have tested causal models (see also Hackett & Betz, Chap. 9, this volume). Schunk (1981) employed path analysis to reproduce the correlation matrix comprising long-division instructional treatment, self-efficacy, persistence, and skill. The most parsimonious model showed a direct effect of treatment on skill and an indirect effect through persistence and self-efficacy, an indirect effect of treatment on persistence through self-efficacy, and a direct effect of self-efficacy on skill and persistence. Schunk and Gunn (1986) used path analysis to examine the effects on changes in children's division skill due to use of strategies, attributions, and self-efficacy. The largest direct influence on skill was due to use of effective strategies; skill also was heavily influenced by self-efficacy. The strongest influence on self-efficacy was ability attributions for success, which suggests that instructional variables may affect self-efficacy in part through the intervening influence of attributions. In the Relich et al. (1986) study, self-efficacy exerted a direct effect on division skill, and instructional treatment had both a direct and an indirect effect on skill through self-efficacy.

Schack (1989) used path analysis with gifted children to test the causes and consequences of self-efficacy. Variables measured were grade level, gender, years in the gifted program, previous independent projects, and self-efficacy for working on independent investigations, which was assessed before and after a minicourse on research methodology (a type of independent investigation) and at the end of the school year. End-of-year self-efficacy was strongly influenced by previous participation in independent investigations and by self-efficacy assessed after the minicourse. The latter measure also predicted subsequent participation in independent investigations.

Locke, Frederick, Lee, and Bobko (1984) investigated goal difficulty during brainstorming by college students as they gave uses for objects.

Students set or were assigned goals. Self-efficacy for moderate to difficult goals predicted students' performances. Self-efficacy and goal commitment related positively among subjects who set their goals. Path analysis showed that self-efficacy exerted a direct effect on goal choice and that subsequent performance was affected by self-efficacy, goals, prior performance, and strategies used.

FUTURE DIRECTIONS

The preceding review makes it clear that self-efficacy theory is useful for explaining many aspects of student achievement. At the same time, researchers have only begun to explore the antecedents and consequences of self-efficacy in education. The remainder of this chapter provides a suggested agenda for future research.

MOTIVATIONAL INDICES

Future research needs to investigate various indices of academic motivation to determine their relation to self-efficacy. This thrust derives from Bandura's (1986) point that self-efficacy influences choice of activities, effort, and persistence. These effects are seen most clearly in contexts in which behavior reflects performance of previously learned skills (e.g., engaging in feared activities). In educational settings, the influence of self-efficacy on these motivational indices is complex. Choice of activities may not be a good index, because students usually do not choose to participate in learning activities (Brophy, 1983). Choice represents a narrow motivational outcome and is most meaningful under a limited set of conditions (e.g., activities during free time).

There also are problems with persistence. Clinical research shows that in feared situations, phobic individuals judge their self-efficacy to be low and do not persist at threatening activities (Bandura, 1986). Persistence tends to increase as self-efficacy develops. In learning situations, students persist, in part, because teachers keep them working. Self-efficacy is a poor predictor of persistence when students do not have the choice to work on a task. Educational research has yielded inconsistent findings on the relation of self-efficacy to persistence (Schunk, 1989a). As skills develop, higher self-efficacy may not always lead to greater persistence. Self-efficacy could relate negatively, rather than positively, to persistence, because students with higher self-efficacy are likely to be skillful and not have to persist as long to correctly answer questions, solve problems, or write sentences.

Cognitive effort may be a better index of academic motivation (Corno

& Mandinach, 1983). Much student time during instruction is spent attempting to understand content (Peterson, Swing, Braverman, & Buss, 1982). We might expect that students with higher self-efficacy for learning would attend to instruction, rehearse information to be remembered, organize information and make it meaningful, monitor level of understanding, and cue memory for task-relevant knowledge. In turn, these actions should produce better learning.

Other potential indices of motivation may be selection and use of effective learning strategies (Borkowski, Johnston, & Reid, 1987). Researchers investigating motivational influences on learning strategies have shown that students with high self-efficacy are likely to use effective learning strategies (Pintrich & De Groot, 1990; Schunk & Swartz, 1992a, 1992b; Zimmerman & Martinez-Pons, 1990). Future research should examine in depth the link between self-efficacy and strategies, especially by determining students' actual strategy use as they acquire skills.

TRANSFER

There is an urgent need for research on maintenance and generalization of self-efficacy and achievement outcomes. The study of transfer in educational domains typically has been confined to maintenance over brief periods and to generalization across variations in content (e.g., reading passages, arithmetic problems). Graham and Harris (1989a, 1989b) and Schunk and Swartz (1992a, 1992b) found that changes in self-efficacy, skill, and strategy use, brought about by educational interventions, maintained themselves for up to 12 weeks and generalized to other tasks. Despite these positive findings, these studies did not determine the extent to which self-efficacy contributed to transfer of skill and strategy use. Researchers need to explore the predicted causal links between self-efficacy and maintenance and generalization of skills and strategies.

A related question concerns the generality of self-efficacy itself. *Self-efficacy* is usually defined as perceived capabilities within specific domains (Bandura, 1986; Schunk, 1989a). Although most investigators have not investigated whether self-efficacy generalizes beyond specific domains, there is some evidence for a generalized sense of self-efficacy (Smith, 1989).

We might expect some generality of self-efficacy from one educational domain to another, but research is needed in this area. In new learning situations, students' aptitudes and prior experiences affect their initial self-efficacy for learning (Schunk, 1989b). Students with high mathematical ability, who generally perform well in mathematics, should have higher self-efficacy for learning new content than students with lower ability, who have had learning difficulties. Self-efficacy might transfer to the extent that the new domain builds on prior skills; for example, self-efficacy for subtracting and for multiplying should transfer to the learning of division. There even could be transfer across dissimilar domains to the extent that students believe the two domains share skills. Thus, students who believe that writing term papers and preparing science-fair projects involve plans and organization, and who feel efficacious about planning and organizing term papers, may have high self-efficacy for performing well on their first science-fair project.

CONCEPTIONS OF ABILITY

An important new area of research concerns the relation of self-efficacy to *conceptions of ability*, or beliefs about the nature of ability and the role it plays in achievement (Dweck & Leggett, 1988; Nicholls, 1983). Students with an entity (fixed) view of ability conceive it as a global and stable trait. Learning is possible to the limit set by ability. Students attempt to gain positive judgments of their competence from others and avoid negative judgments. Those with self-doubts work lackadaisically and expend little effort on difficult tasks. Learners who believe they are capable select tasks at which they can succeed, persist longer, and expend effort. In contrast, students with an incremental perspective of ability view it as comprising skills and increasing with experience. Ability is roughly synonymous with learning. Regardless of whether students view their ability as high or low, they adopt a goal of increasing their competence and they persist and expend effort because they believe effort enhances ability.

Wood and Bandura (1989) found that ability conceptions influence goal setting, self-efficacy, and self-regulation. Subjects with an incremental view of ability maintained high self-efficacy, set challenging goals, applied rules efficiently, and performed better; subjects holding an entity belief showed a decline in self-efficacy. Elliott and Dweck (1988) showed that children who were given a goal of learning chose challenging tasks and persisted in applying effective strategies, regardless of whether they viewed their ability as high or low. Children given a goal of displaying competence (performance goal), who perceived ability as high, persisted in using effective task strategies; those who perceived ability as low were less likely to use strategies. Research is needed on the operation of conceptions of ability in educational settings as students are acquiring new skills. Such research would promote our understanding of how self-efficacy relates to other types of achievement beliefs.

CLASSROOM GOALS

A related line of research is examining relations among types of classroom goals, perceived competence (self-efficacy), motivation, and achievement. Researchers are increasingly finding that students adopt classroom goals that may not reflect those of the teacher (Wentzel, 1992). Meece, Blumenfeld, and Hoyle (1988) assessed goals, perceived competence, motivation, and cognitive engagement. Goals were task mastery (understanding material), ego/social (pleasing others), and work-avoidant (minimizing effort). Active cognitive engagement referred to self-regulatory activities (review material not understood, make material meaningful); superficial engagement comprised strategies to complete work with minimal effort (copy answers, skip hard material). Students with task-mastery goals reported more active cognitive engagement; those with high motivation to learn placed greater emphasis on learning goals. Perceived competence related positively to motivation and task-mastery goals.

Schunk and Swartz (1992b) found that providing children with a goal of learning to use a writing strategy and with feedback on their progress increased task orientation (desire to independently master and understand academic work) and decreased ego orientation (desire to perform well to please the teacher and avoid trouble). Self-efficacy correlated positively with task orientation and negatively with ego orientation. Future research might investigate whether changes in achievement brought about by modifying students' goal orientation are mediated by the effects of goal orientations on self-efficacy.

TEACHING EFFICACY

Self-efficacy is applicable to teachers as well as students. Ashton and Webb (1986) define *teaching efficacy* as personal beliefs about capabilities to help students learn. They postulate that self-efficacy should influence teachers' activities, efforts, and persistence. Teachers with low self-efficacy may avoid planning activities that they believe exceed their capabilities, may not persist with students having difficulties, may expend little effort to find materials, and may not reteach content in ways students might better understand. Teachers with higher self-efficacy might develop challenging activities, help students succeed, and persevere with students who have trouble learning. These motivational effects enhance student learning and substantiate teachers' self-efficacy by conveying they can help students learn.

Correlational data show that self-efficacy is related to teaching behaviors. Ashton and Webb (1986) found that teachers with higher self-efficacy were likely to have a positive classroom environment (e.g., less student anxiety and teacher criticism), support students' ideas, and meet the needs of all students. High teaching self-efficacy was positively associated with use of praise, individual attention to students, checking on students' progress in learning, and their mathematical and language achievement. Woolfolk and Hoy (1990) had prospective teachers judge self-efficacy, bureaucratic orientation (e.g., extent of rule conformity and organizational loyalty), pupil control ideology (custodial vs. humanistic), and motivational style (one that encourages student autonomy and responsibility). Two efficacy dimensions were distinguished. Teaching efficacy assessed whether teachers believed that students' motivation and performance derived mostly from home. Personal efficacy gauged whether teachers felt that with effort they could affect unmotivated students. The two efficacy measures were uncorrelated; teaching efficacy related negatively to pupil control and bureaucratic orientation.

Experimental studies are needed in which variations in teachers' self-efficacy brought about by interventions are systematically related to changes in teaching behaviors and then to student performance. Research also should explore the reciprocal relation between teacher efficacy and teacher–student interactions. When introducing content, teachers might convey that all students can learn or that some may have difficulty (Brophy, 1983). While presenting content, teachers may link new material to what students know or they may attempt little integration. These differences ought to affect students' self-efficacy and motivation. In turn, how students react to teachers should influence teachers' self-efficacy. Students who respond enthusiastically may enhance teachers' self-efficacy and motivate them to plan strong lessons. When classes seem baffled or unenthusiastic, teachers may begin to question their teaching competence and wonder whether additional effort will produce better results.

RESEARCH METHODS

The proliferation of self-efficacy research in the past 15 years has added to our understanding of the construct, but it also has resulted in a multitude of measures. Following Bandura's original lead, most researchers have developed self-efficacy measures appropriate for the domain being studied. At a minimum, researchers should report reliability data in research reports (Hackett & Betz, Chap. 9, this volume). It is useful to include self-efficacy instruments as appendixes to articles (Pintrich & De Groot, 1990).

Self-efficacy researchers typically have employed quantitative methods using between-conditions comparisons in short-term studies. There is a need for longitudinal studies and alternative forms of data collection (e.g., case studies, oral histories). Although such studies might include fewer subjects, they would yield rich data sources. Self-efficacy assessments might be similarly broadened from reliance on numerical scales to include qualitative indexes. Subjects could describe how confident they feel about performing tasks in different situations, and statements could be scored for strength and generality of self-efficacy. A scoring procedure might be devised, analogous to that used with the CAVE (content analysis of verbatim explanations) technique (Seligman, 1991). This technique, which has been employed to score individuals' verbal and written statements for attributional style, assigns a numerical score to statements based on how permanent, pervasive, and personal they are.

Much research has related self-efficacy to such measures as students' self-reports of intentions to engage in activities and use of learning strategies. This type of research has advantages and typically yields valid data (Assor & Connell, 1992), but it does not take into account the intricacies of classroom teaching and learning. There is a need for classroom research with teachers teaching academic content. This type of research will provide invaluable information on the role of self-efficacy in education.

ACKNOWLEDGMENTS: The author's research described in this chapter was supported by grants from the National Science Foundation, the National Institute of Mental Health, the Spencer Foundation, the University of North Carolina at Chapel Hill, and the University of Houston. I wish to thank James E. Maddux for his helpful comments on an earlier version of this chapter.

REFERENCES

Ashton, P. T., & Webb, R. B. (1986). *Making a difference: Teachers' sense of efficacy and student achievement*. New York: Longman.

Assor, A., & Connell, J. P. (1992). The validity of students' self-reports as measures of performance affecting self-appraisals. In D. H. Schunk & J. L. Meece (Eds.), *Student perceptions in the classroom* (pp. 25–47). Hillsdale, NJ: Erlbaum.

Bandura, A. (1977). Self-efficacy: Toward a unifying theory of behavioral change. *Psychological Review, 84*, 191–215.

Bandura, A. (1986). *Social foundations of thought and action: A social cognitive theory*. Englewood Cliffs, NJ: Prentice-Hall.

Bandura, A. (1988). Self-regulation of motivation and action through goal systems. In V. Hamilton, G. H. Bower, & N. H. Frijda (Eds.), *Cognitive perspectives on emotion and motivation* (pp. 37–61). Dordrecht, The Netherlands: Kluwer.

Bandura, A., & Schunk, D. H. (1981). Cultivating competence, self-efficacy, and intrinsic interest through proximal self-motivation. *Journal of Personality and Social Psychology, 41*, 586–598.

Borkowski, J. G. (1985). Signs of intelligence: Strategy generalization and metacognition. In S. Yussen (Ed.), *The growth of reflection in children* (pp. 105–144). New York: Academic Press.

Borkowski, J. G., Johnston, M. B., & Reid, M. K. (1987). Metacognition, motivation, and controlled performance. In S. J. Ceci (Ed.), *Handbook of cognitive, social, and neuropsychological aspects of learning disabilities* (Vol. 2, pp.147–173). Hillsdale, NJ: Erlbaum.

Brophy, J. (1983). Conceptualizing student motivation. *Educational Psychologist, 18*, 200–215.

Brown, I., Jr., & Inouye, D. K. (1978). Learned helplessness through modeling: The role of perceived similarity in competence. *Journal of Personality and Social Psychology, 36*, 900–908.

Collins, J. (1982, March). *Self-efficacy and ability in achievement behavior.* Paper presented at the meeting at the American Educational Research Association, New York, NY.

Corno, L., & Mandinach, E. B. (1983). The role of cognitive engagement in classroom learning and motivation. *Educational Psychologist, 18*, 88–108.

Dweck, C. S., & Leggett, E. L. (1988). A social cognitive approach to motivation and personality. *Psychological Review, 95*, 256–273.

Elliott, E.S., & Dweck, C. S. (1988). Goals: An approach to motivation and achievement. *Journal of Personality and Social Psychology, 54*, 5–12.

Graham, S., & Harris, K. R. (1989a). Components analysis of cognitive strategy instruction: Effects on learning disabled students' compositions and self-efficacy. *Journal of Educational Psychology, 81*, 353–361.

Graham, S., & Harris, K. R. (1989b). Improving learning disabled students' skills at composing essays: Self-instructional strategy training. *Exceptional Children, 56*, 210–214.

Harris, K. R. (1982). Cognitive-behavior modification: Application with exceptional children. *Focus on Exceptional Children, 15*, 1–16.

Lepper, M. R. (1983). Extrinsic reward and intrinsic motivation: Implications for the classroom. In J. M. Levine & M. C. Wang (Eds.), *Teacher and student perceptions: Implications for learning* (pp. 281–317). Hillsdale, NJ: Erlbaum.

Locke, E. A., Frederick, E., Lee, C., & Bobko, P. (1984). Effect of self-efficacy, goals, and task strategies on task performance. *Journal of Applied Psychology, 69*, 241–251.

Locke, E. A., & Latham, G. P. (1990). *A theory of goal setting and task performance.* Englewood Cliffs, NJ: Prentice-Hall.

McCarthy, P., Meier, S., & Rinderer, R. (1985). Self-efficacy and writing: A different view of self-evaluation. *College Composition and Communication, 36*, 465–471.

Meece, J. L., Blumenfeld, P. C., & Hoyle, R. H. (1988). Students' goal orientations and cognitive engagement in classroom activities. *Journal of Educational Psychology, 80*, 514–523.

Meier, S., McCarthy, P. R., & Schmeck, R. R. (1984). Validity of self-efficacy as a predictor of writing performance. *Cognitive Therapy and Research, 8*, 107–120.

Morgan, M. (1985). Self-monitoring of attained subgoals in private study. *Journal of Educational Psychology, 77*, 623–630.

Nicholls, J. G. (1983). Conceptions of ability and achievement motivation: A theory and its implications for education. In S. G. Paris, G. M. Olson, & H. W. Stevenson (Eds.), *Learning and motivation in the classroom* (pp. 211–237). Hillsdale, NJ: Erlbaum.

Norwich, B. (1987). Self-efficacy and mathematics achievement: A study of their relation. *Journal of Educational Psychology, 79*, 384–387.

Peterson, P. L., Swing, S. R., Braverman, M. T., & Buss, R. (1982). Students' aptitudes and their reports of cognitive processes during direct instruction. *Journal of Educational Psychology, 74*, 535–547.

Pintrich, P. R., Cross, D. R., Kozma, R. B., & McKeachie, W. J. (1986). Instructional psychology. *Annual Review of Psychology, 37*, 611–651.

Pintrich, P. R., & De Groot, E. V. (1990). Motivational and self-regulated learning components of classroom academic performance. *Journal of Educational Psychology, 82*, 33–40.

Relich, J. D., Debus, R. L., & Walker, R. (1986). The mediating role of attribution and self-efficacy variables for treatment effects on achievement outcomes. *Contemporary Educational Psychology, 11,* 195–216.

Romberg, T. A., & Carpenter, T. P. (1986). Research on teaching and learning mathematics: Two disciplines of scientific inquiry. In M. C. Wittrock (Ed.), *Handbook of research on teaching* (3rd ed., pp. 850–873). New York: Macmillan.

Salomon, G. (1984). Television is "easy" and print is "tough": The differential investment of mental effort in learning as a function of perceptions and attributions. *Journal of Educational Psychology, 76,* 647–658.

Scardamalia, M., & Bereiter, C. (1986). Research on written composition. In M. C. Wittrock (Ed.), *Handbook of research on teaching* (3rd ed., pp. 778–803). New York: Macmillan.

Schack, G. D. (1989). Self-efficacy as a mediator in the creative productivity of gifted children. *Journal for the Education of the Gifted, 12,* 231–249.

Schunk, D. H. (1981). Modeling and attributional effects on children's achievement: A self-efficacy analysis. *Journal of Educational Psychology, 73,* 93–105.

Schunk, D. H. (1982). Effects of effort-attributional feedback on children's perceived self-efficacy and achievement. *Journal of Educational Psychology, 74,* 548–556.

Schunk, D. H. (1983a). Ability versus effort attributional feedback: Differential effects on self-efficacy and achievement. *Journal of Educational Psychology, 75,* 848–856.

Schunk, D. H. (1983b). Developing children's self-efficacy and skills: The roles of social comparative information and goal setting. *Contemporary Educational Psychology, 8,* 76–86.

Schunk, D. H. (1983c). Goal difficulty and attainment information: Effects on children's achievement behaviors. *Human Learning, 2,* 107–117.

Schunk, D. H. (1983d). Progress self-monitoring: Effects on children's self-efficacy and achievement. *Journal of Experimental Education, 51,* 89–93.

Schunk, D. H. (1983e). Reward contingencies and the development of children's skills and self-efficacy. *Journal of Educational Psychology, 75,* 511–518.

Schunk, D. H. (1984). Enhancing self-efficacy and achievement through rewards and goals: Motivational and informational effects. *Journal of Educational Research, 78,* 29–34.

Schunk, D. H. (1985). Participation in goal setting: Effects on self-efficacy and skills of learning disabled children. *Journal of Special Education, 19,* 307–317.

Schunk, D. H. (1989a). Self-efficacy and achievement behaviors. *Educational Psychology Review, 1,* 173–208.

Schunk, D. H. (1989b). Self-efficacy and cognitive skill learning. In C. Ames & R. Ames (Eds.), *Research on motivation in education: Vol. 3: Goals and cognitions* (pp. 13–44). San Diego: Academic Press.

Schunk, D. H., & Cox, P. D. (1986). Strategy training and attributional feedback with learning disabled students. *Journal of Educational Psychology, 78,* 201–209.

Schunk, D. H., & Gunn, T. P. (1985). Modeled importance of task strategies and achievement beliefs: Effects on self-efficacy and skill development. *Journal of Early Adolescence, 5,* 247–258.

Schunk, D. H., & Gunn, T. P. (1986). Self-efficacy and skill development: Influence of task strategies and attributions. *Journal of Educational Research, 79,* 238–244.

Schunk, D. H., & Hanson, A. R. (1985). Peer models: Influence on children's self-efficacy and achievement. *Journal of Educational Psychology, 77,* 313–322.

Schunk, D. H., Hanson, A. R., & Cox, P. D. (1987). Peer-model attributes and children's achievement behaviors. *Journal of Educational Psychology, 79,* 54–61.

Schunk, D. H., & Rice, J. M. (1984). Strategy self-verbalization during remedial listening comprehension instruction. *Journal of Experimental Education, 53,* 49–54.

Schunk, D. H., & Rice, J. M. (1985). Verbalization of comprehension strategies: Effects on children's achievement outcomes. *Human Learning, 4,* 1–10.

Schunk, D. H., & Rice, J. M. (1989). Learning goals and children's reading comprehension. *Journal of Reading Behavior, 21,* 279–293.

Schunk, D. H., & Rice, J. M. (1991). Learning goals and progress feedback during reading comprehension instruction. *Journal of Reading Behavior, 23,* 351–364.

Schunk, D. H., & Swartz, C. W. (1992a). *Goals and progress feedback: Effects on self-efficacy and writing achievement.* Unpublished manuscript, University of North Carolina, Chapel Hill.

Schunk, D. H., & Swartz, C. W. (1992b). *Writing strategy instruction with gifted students: Effects of goals and feedback on self-efficacy and skills.* Unpublished manuscript, University of North Carolina, Chapel Hill.

Seligman, M. E. P. (1991). *Learned optimism.* New York: Knopf.

Shell, D. F., Murphy, C. C., & Bruning, R. H. (1989). Self-efficacy and outcome expectancy mechanisms in reading and writing achievement. *Journal of Educational Psychology, 81,* 91–100.

Shuell, T. J. (1986). Cognitive conceptions of learning. *Review of Educational Research, 56,* 411–436.

Smith, R. E. (1989). Effects of coping skills training on generalized self-efficacy and locus of control. *Journal of Personality and Social Psychology, 56,* 228–233.

Weinstein, C. E., & Mayer, R. E. (1986). The teaching of learning strategies. In M. C. Wittrock (Ed.), *Handbook of research on teaching* (3rd ed., pp. 315–327). New York: Macmillan.

Weinstein, R. S. (1989). Perceptions of classroom processes and student motivation: Children's views of self-fulfilling prophecies. In C. Ames & R. Ames (Eds.), *Research on motivation in education: Vol. 3: Goals and cognitions* (pp. 187–221). San Diego: Academic Press.

Wentzel, K. R. (1992). Motivation and achievement in adolescence: A multiple goals perspective. In D. H. Schunk & J. L. Meece (Eds.), *Student perceptions in the classroom* (pp. 287–306). Hillsdale, NJ: Erlbaum.

Wood, R., & Bandura, A. (1989). Impact of conceptions of ability on self-regulatory mechanisms and complex decision making. *Journal of Personality and Social Psychology, 56,* 407–415.

Woolfolk, A. E., & Hoy, W. K. (1990). Prospective teachers' sense of efficacy and beliefs about control. *Journal of Educational Psychology, 82,* 81–91.

Zimmerman, B. J. (1990). Self-regulating academic learning and achievement: The emergence of a social cognitive perspective. *Educational Psychology Review, 2,* 173–201.

Zimmerman, B. J., & Martinez-Pons, M. (1990). Student differences in self-regulated learning: Relating grade, sex, and giftedness to self-efficacy and strategy use. *Journal of Educational Psychology, 82,* 51–59.

Zimmerman, B. J., & Ringle, J. (1981). Effects of model persistence and statements of confidence on children's self-efficacy and problem solving. *Journal of Educational Psychology, 73,* 485–493.

CHAPTER 11

COLLECTIVE EFFICACY

STEPHEN J. ZACCARO, VIRGINIA BLAIR, CHRISTOPHER PETERSON, and MICHELLE ZAZANIS

One's perceptions or beliefs about expected competency in an achievement domain are a critical determinant of motivation and performance. Constructs that incorporate such beliefs and have been tied to successful performance include effectance motivation (White, 1959), personal causation (DeCharms, 1968), locus of control (Rotter, 1966), intrinsic motivation (Deci, 1975), explanatory style (Peterson & Seligman, 1984), personal control (Greenberger & Strasser, 1986), and self-efficacy (Bandura, 1977, 1982, 1986). A common component across these constructs is a self-perceived performance mastery that governs choices within an achievement domain and "encourages intellectual, emotional, behavioral, and physiological vigor in the face of challenge" (Peterson & Stunkard, 1989, p. 820).

Conceptual and empirical studies of perceived mastery and competence have focused almost exclusively on the individual (Peterson & Stunkard, 1989), yet most individual behavior occurs in a manner that is decidedly influenced by social factors. Such influence reflects multiple levels of interdependence. At a minimum, individuals often require resources and support from their surrounding social environment, even if there is little or no coaction or interaction with other individuals. At a

STEPHEN J. ZACCARO, VIRGINIA BLAIR, and MICHELLE ZAZANIS • George Mason University, Department of Psychology, Fairfax, Virginia 22030. CHRISTOPHER PETERSON • University of Michigan, Department of Psychology, Ann Arbor, Michigan 48109.

Self-Efficacy, Adaptation, and Adjustment: Theory, Research, and Application, edited by James E. Maddux. Plenum Press, New York, 1995.

higher level of interdependence, individuals may coact to produce an aggregated product. While there may be little interaction, characteristics of the aggregate (e.g., group size, reward systems) may still influence its members' beliefs about personal mastery and hence the nature of their performance (e.g., Latane, Williams, & Harkins, 1979). Finally, at the most complex level of interdependence, individuals often behave in complete concert with others. Such behavior typically has the characteristics of integration, coordination, and synchronization. Individual actions are fully dependent upon the actions of others to produce a collective outcome. Indeed, such actions often cannot be distinguished from one another; only the collective or aggregated product is identifiable.

A full understanding of how perceived competence contributes to individual action requires recognition of its social component. Several studies have examined self-efficacy and personal control within groups and organizations. The samples for these studies included students in a simulated organization (Bandura & Jourden, 1991; Bandura & Wood, 1989; Wood & Bandura, 1989; Wood, Bandura, & Bailey, 1990), insurance agents and clerks (Barling & Beattie, 1983; Greenberger, Strasser, Cummings, & Dunham, 1989), university faculty (Taylor, Locke, Lee, & Gist, 1984), and nursing service personnel (Greenberger et al., 1989). In these studies, the key variables were typically individual perceptions of personal competence and were often significantly associated with motivation and performance. Nonetheless, in several of these settings, individual actions still required some intervention in the form of resource allocation, information exchange, or modeled behavior by elements of the embedding social context. That is, an individual's responses were not entirely independent of other responses in the social environment. This suggests that the performance of individuals in these studies may be partially explained not only by self-efficacious beliefs, but also by perceptions of their collective competence.

In acknowledgement of this point, Bandura (1986) suggested that people have "a sense of collective efficacy that they can solve their problems and improve their lives through concerted effort" (p. 449). He extended collective efficacy to refer to social aggregations, ranging from groups to nations and cultures. Thus, individuals may believe their embedding social environments as well as themselves to be efficacious or helpless with respect to specific situational demands. As with self-efficacy, such beliefs in turn influence an individual's choices, motivation, actions, and performance within the collective (Bandura, 1986). Furthermore, the aggregation of these individual reactions will dictate the nature of the collective response.

Several researchers have argued for additional investigations of collective efficacy (e.g., Bandura, 1986; Gist, 1987); unfortunately, their calls have been relatively unheeded. Some studies have tied collective efficacy or similar constructs to group cohesion and performance (Spink, 1990b, Zaccaro, Peterson, Blair, & Gilbert, 1990; Zander, 1971). Others have linked it to prior group performance (Mesch, Farh, & Podsakoff, 1989; Zaccaro et al., 1990) and to subsequent group goal setting (Weldon & Weingart, 1993). Nonetheless, there has been little development of collective efficacy, either as a theoretical construct, or in terms of its measurement. This lack of attention and understanding is attributable to problems in initial conceptions of collective efficacy and its treatment as a mere extension of self-efficacy theory to larger aggregations. For example, while it is generally accepted that collective efficacy refers to people's beliefs about the collective as a whole, it has not been clear that these beliefs are *shared*, and therefore may represent a group-level rather than an individual-level phenomenon. Whether collective efficacy represents independent member beliefs or a shared sense of competence has significant conceptual and methodological implications.

If collective efficacy is conceptualized as a group-level phenomenon, then attention must be focused on how individual perceptions of collective competence are aggregated in a conceptually appropriate manner (Shamir, 1990). Furthermore, the variability in members' efficacious beliefs regarding the group is as meaningful as the central tendency in those beliefs. Groups in which there is complete agreement among members on the degree of group competence may be more cohesive than groups in which members disagree about group capabilities, particularly if the group is perceived as quite strong. Likewise, differences in perceptions of collective efficacy may be linked to role differentiation within the group as members who believe the group is strong assume more central group roles. Unfortunately, the few studies that have examined collective efficacy or related constructs have not attended to these conceptual implications.

The purpose of this chapter is to examine these issues more closely by providing a conceptual definition of *collective efficacy*. Prior research usually has treated collective efficacy as a straightforward extension of self-efficacy from individuals to groups, organizations, and other aggregations. Whereas self-efficacy theory contributes significantly to an understanding of collective efficacy, the elaboration of self-perceptions to the collective requires a number of modifications. This chapter elucidates a conceptual approach to collective efficacy, incorporating those factors that change or emerge as the unit of perception moves from the individual to the collective. The corresponding measurement implications of this conceptual approach are also examined. Furthermore, the antecedents and consequences of collective efficacy are defined; some of these are in common with those of self-efficacy, whereas others are unique to perceptions and beliefs about the collective. This chapter concludes with some implications regarding collective efficacy for group and organizational dynamics.

DEFINITION AND MEASUREMENT
OF COLLECTIVE EFFICACY

In previous studies, collective efficacy has been defined in a variety of ways. Bandura (1986) referred to it as people's "perceptions of the groups' efficacy to effect change" (p. 451). Shea and Guzzo (1987) described a very similar construct, called *group potency*, as "the collective belief of a group that it can be effective" (p. 335). Mesch et al. (1989) operationalized *collective efficacy* as group members' perceptions of what performance level the group could attain and the certainty they felt in reaching that level. Shamir (1990) defined *collective efficacy* as "the perceived probability that collective effort will result in collective accomplishments" (p. 316). Finally, Weldon and Weingart (1993) specified it as "an individual's judgment of how well the group can execute actions required to perform the task" (p. 11).

These definitions have in common a judgment by group members of the overall ability of the collective to act effectively. In this sense, *collective efficacy* has been defined as a direct extension of self-efficacy to a unit larger than the individual. Indeed, empirical studies that have measured collective efficacy adopted the measurement procedures recommended for self-efficacy (Mesch et al., 1989; Spink, 1990b). However, most of these definitions do not consider those factors that are unique to perceptions of the collective. For example, in the aforementioned definitions, there is considerable ambiguity as to whether such perceptions of competence represent part of the collective's shared belief structure, merely reflect individual-level beliefs, or are some combination of both. Shea and Guzzo's (1987) notion of group potency refers clearly to a collective belief, whereas Weldon and Weingart (1988, 1993) describe an individual's judgment of the group. The other definitions specify individual-level beliefs, but imply some level of aggregated responses. However, as noted by Gist (1987) and Shamir (1990), there remains significant confusion as to how this aggregation is to occur.

Moving conceptually from the individual to the group also means that a definition of collective efficacy must acknowledge the notion of collective coordination and the integration of individual contributions to collective effort. The importance of this element can be seen in alternate approaches to operationalizing collective efficacy. In one instance, collective efficacy can be measured as the mere sum of an individual's judgments of every other group member's abilities and resources regarding the task confronting the group. Although this approach may provide some information regarding collective competence, it misses the key elements of interaction, coordination, and integration. Indeed, many definitions of group action and performance emphasize precisely these elements (e.g., Fleishman & Zaccaro, 1992). Thus, a more useful approach to defining collective efficacy is to consider *both* judgments of members' abilities *and* perceptions of how well group members work together in achieving collective outcomes.

DEFINING COLLECTIVE EFFICACY

Accordingly, we suggest that collective efficacy represents *a sense of collective competence shared among individuals when allocating, coordinating, and integrating their resources in a successful concerted response to specific situational demands.* The "collective" can be any aggregation larger than the individual, from dyads to nations. This definition has several key elements. These include (a) collective efficacy as shared beliefs, (b) perceptions of competence in a collective's coordination activities, (c) consideration of other members' resources, and (d) the situational and behavioral, or task specificity of collective efficacy.

Collective Efficacy as Shared Beliefs

The definition of *collective efficacy* offered here refers to a belief or perception regarding aggregate capabilities that is shared by members of the collective (Zaccaro, Blair, Peterson, & Gilbert, 1992). "Shared beliefs" mean that there is a significant degree of interdependence among member judgments. That is, perceptions of collective competence are influenced not only by actual conditions within the group, but also, to a large extent, on how *other* group members perceive and convey their interpretations of these conditions. This suggests that collective efficacy may have both individual and group-level components (Kenny & La Voie, 1985). If there is little or no variability among group members regarding collective competence, and this homogeneity cannot be attributed to factors external to the group (e.g., easy group task, overwhelming environmental stressors), then these efficacious beliefs are to be considered group-level phenomena. However, if there is considerable heterogeneity or variability in individual perceptions of the group, then a significant amount of variance in collective efficacy is defined by individual-level processes. Furthermore, the antecedents and consequences of collective efficacy may differ at the collective versus the individual unit of conceptual analysis.

The emphasis on collective efficacy as a shared belief means that such judgments become part of the group's normative belief structure, or the group culture. Levine and Moreland (1991) defined two perspectives regarding group culture. The first is culture as "a set of *thoughts* that are shared among group members" (p. 258). These thoughts include knowledge about the unique nature of the group, its past history, present state, and future plans, the norms and climate of the group, and its relationship to the external environment. Levine and Moreland also included knowledge about the quality and effectiveness of the group in its culture. Thus, collective efficacy helps define the group for its members.

Levine and Moreland's second perspective on group culture emphasizes "a set of *customs* that embody the thoughts that group members share" (p. 258). These customs are behavioral expressions that take the form of routines, verbal accounts of group events, jargon, rituals, and symbols. This suggests a critical point about collective efficacy as a shared belief, that it significantly affects the way group members define and interpret their collective experiences. Group tasks and situations may be approached through a series of rituals and routines that reflect a high (or low) sense of collective competence. Furthermore, how group members explain group events reflects this sense of competence and indeed can strongly determine how the group reacts to similar situations in the future. For example, members of professional sport teams with strong collective efficacy may explain a particular loss by attributing it to factors that are specific to that contest only, and believe that those factors will not recur (cf. Zaccaro, Peterson, & Walker, 1987). Alternatively, each win is interpreted as indicative of the group's stable characteristics, as further evidence of the group's collective competence; thus there is a stronger expectation that group success will continue. Finally, collective efficacy becomes embodied in the symbols and language of the group. Highly efficacious groups may adopt representations (e.g., names, mascots, animal symbols) that reflect their sense of strength. Also, this sense of strength becomes embodied in the group's communications, both internally and externally. These representations are manifestations of collective efficacy that help define the group culture and serve critical recruitment and socialization functions (Levine & Moreland, 1991; Moreland & Levine, 1982, 1989). Potential members are made aware of the group's strength and the corresponding expectations that accompany admission to the group. New members are put through rituals and processes that convey the collective sense of group excellence, the norms that are tied to this sense, and their own responsibilities in contributing to and maintaining that collective competence. In this way, new group members quickly acquire perceptions of collective efficacy, despite their lack of extensive involvement in group affairs and their relative unawareness of the group's history.

Perceived Competence in Group Coordination

A second key element of the definition of *collective efficacy* is its emphasis on group coordination capabilities. In a taxonomic classification of group performance, Fleishman and Zaccaro (1992) delineated several functions that formed the basis of successful collective action. These functions include information exchange regarding member resources, the team task and environmental characteristics, resource distribution and task assignments, timing and activity pacing, response coordination, motivational enhancement, and monitoring and adjustment of task and group activities. Problem identification, strategy development, and solution generation are additional coordination functions (Hackman & Morris, 1975; Levine & Moreland, 1990). The degree to which a group can successfully implement the full range of these functions determines to a large extent the degree of group success. Member beliefs about a group's collective efficacy necessarily include perceptions of how well the group members can accomplish each of the aforementioned coordination activities. This highlights a critical difference between self-efficacy and its collective counterpart. *Self-efficacy* reflects beliefs about how well individuals can marshal their knowledge, skills and abilities to accomplish a particular task. *Collective efficacy* refers to a group member's beliefs not only about how well each and every other group member can marshal individual resources to accomplish the group task, but also how well group members can coordinate and combine their resources. In a group that has moderate levels of knowledge, skills, and abilities among its members, but great coordinative capabilities, members may perceive greater collective efficacy than members of a group with significantly greater resources, but less ability to integrate and coordinate these resources.

The inclusion of perceived coordination capabilities in the conceptual definition of *collective efficacy* assumes that all collective tasks require a significant degree of coordination and integration. Yet, several classifications of group tasks emphasize a category of situations seemingly characterized by a lack of member interdependence. For example, Steiner (1972) defined *additive tasks* as those tasks on which group performance is a mere summative function of individual efforts and resources. Likewise, Shaw (1963, 1981) defined *group tasks* in terms of "the degree to which integrated action of group members is required to complete the task" (1981, p. 364). One end of this dimension is anchored by full coordination and synchronization of actions, whereas the other end defines tasks that "could be completed by each group member working independently and at his or her own speed" (p. 364). Even on such tasks, however, *independence of action* does not mean that individual group members are not influenced in some manner by the activities of other group members. Such members may be affected by the speed and intensity of their peer's actions. Furthermore, they may alter the strength and nature of their own responses in accordance with earlier group activities, even when these responses are not dependent upon such activities for timing and coordination. For example, *team performance* in a wrestling tournament is typically defined as the sum of individual wins and losses. All matches are apparently independent of one another. However, members of a high-performing wrestling team may alter their own match strategy to compensate for the outcomes of earlier matches and their team's standing at the time of their own contest. A less-than-expected standing may result in a riskier strategy to accumulate more points, whereas a higher standing may call for a more conservative strategy. Although members' activities in this situation are presumed to be independent by conventional group-task taxonomies, choices regarding the character of those activities may still be contingent on other members' responses. Therefore, measures of collective efficacy in such situations require some acknowledgment even of this degree of coordination (Kane, Marks, Zaccaro, & Blair, 1993). Indeed, this prescription applies to the measurement of collective efficacy in any collective endeavor.

Perception of Collective Resources

The preceding arguments emphasized perceptions of the group's ability to allocate and integrate individual members' resources. Key elements of these perceptions are an individual member's judgments of (a) the resources retained by other group members and, perhaps more important, (b) the willingness of the other group members to contribute their knowledge, skills, and abilities to collective effort. Several studies have documented the "sucker effect" (Jackson & Harkins, 1985; Kerr, 1983; Kerr & Bruun, 1983; Shepperd, 1993) as a source of low team motivation. This effect emerges from the perception that other group members are taking advantage of one's own efforts; that is, others in the group are not seen as contributing an equal effort to the collective endeavor. The consequence is a perception of lower group efficacy and therefore a lessening of one's own motivation to work on behalf of the group.

A second consideration regarding perceptions of collective resources is the composition of the group. For some resources, homogeneity of resources and capabilities across group members may be more critical for group success than a more variable mix of resources. For example, on a physical team task, the combination of resources that should yield the highest perceptions of collective efficacy are high physical strength and endurance in all group members (Widmeyer, 1990). Researchers have delineated several skills, abilities, and traits for which homogeneity across group members is likely to contribute to maximum group success in sport teams (see Widmeyer, 1990, for a review). Accordingly, for these resources, collective efficacy is determined both by their level and their degree of invariance across group members. However, for other task-related resources, member heterogeneity will contribute to high collective efficacy. To the degree that the group task is fairly complex and its accomplishment requires a variety of different skills, heterogeneous groups are more likely to contain these skills than homogeneous groups, and therefore are likely to be more successful (Hoffman & Maier, 1961; Laughlin, Branch, & Johnson, 1969; Shaw, 1981; Steiner, 1972; Widmeyer, 1990). Furthermore, groups with a compatible mix of characteristics may be more effective on some tasks than groups with a diverse but incompatible set of attributes (Reddy & Byrnes, 1972; Schutz, 1955, 1958; Widmeyer, 1990). These distinctions illustrate the complexity of collective-efficacy judgments. When members determine their group's competence relative to particular tasks and situational demands, they must not only inventory the amount of knowledge, skills, and abilities residing in the group, but also judge whether the best or most appropriate mix of resources (i.e., homogeneous, heterogeneous, compatible) exists among group members. Complicating these judgments further is the fact that the best mix of resources is likely to vary from task to task (Steiner, 1972).

Situational Specificity of Collective Efficacy

The final element in the definition of *collective efficacy* is the specificity of judgments regarding group capabilities. In studying self-efficacy, Bandura (1977; 1986) prescribed a microanalytic strategy that emphasizes perceived competence in a specific or single performance domain that may or may not generalize to other domains. Individuals join in collective action to accomplish goals that cannot be attained by themselves working alone (Katz & Kahn, 1978; Skinner, 1953). Accordingly, beliefs about collective efficacy include the aggregated ability to achieve the purpose or goal for which the group was formed. A softball team forms perceptions of its collective competence to play softball; a band develops judgments about its musical competence (typically, in a narrow domain of music forms); and a therapy group may focus on the collective's skill in reducing individual anxiety.

Many groups, however, are formed around a very broad set of goals and are therefore confronted with a variety of tasks and performance situations related to these goals. For example, organizations and many work groups develop with a goal of achieving success (e.g., making a profit) in a dynamic and complex environment (Katz & Kahn, 1978). Schein (1985) argued that such groups and organizations develop, as part of their culture, shared views of how well their entity relates to the surrounding environment. Such beliefs are invariably more general than the efficacious beliefs prescribed by Bandura. Indeed, organizational researchers have identified other psychological concepts that reflect perceptions of collective competence, share many of the properties of collective efficacy, but operate at a much more general level (e.g., *collective control*, Zaccaro et al., 1990; *group potency*, Shea & Guzzo, 1987). These constructs refer to members' perceptions that their group can successfully resolve *any* task or demand it may confront. Such beliefs may influence group risk taking and group persistence in novel situations significantly more than specifically targeted competence beliefs.

THE MEASUREMENT OF COLLECTIVE EFFICACY

Bandura (1977, 1986) prescribed that self-efficacy be measured along the dimensions of magnitude, strength, and generality (see also, Maddux, Chap. 1 this volume). The same prescription is applicable to collective efficacy, with the significant modification that the focus be on the collective as a whole. The definition of collective efficacy emphasizes the group's capability in coordinating individual resources to achieve collective success. Accordingly, measures of collective efficacy should assess the respondents' perceptions of how well the group can work together in successful accomplishment. *Magnitude* refers to the perceived level of performance the group can attain by working together. *Strength* refers to the amount of confidence members have in their coordination skill and the achievement of a particular performance standard. *Generality* refers to perceptions of these coordination skills that are generalized across group tasks.

Because *collective efficacy* refers to a shared sense of competence, the method of aggregation becomes critical. *Shared beliefs* mean that statistically there should be a significant degree of response nonindependence among group members. Specifically, this suggests a lesser degree of variability within groups than between groups when all other differentiating factors are controlled (Florin, Giamartino, Kenny, & Wandersman, 1990; Kenny, 1985; Kenny & La Voie, 1985). Such patterns of response invariance across group members may be assessed by computing intraclass correlations. Kenny and La Voie (1985) indicated that these correlations assess the percentage of variance in the measure that is at the group level. A large positive intraclass correlation indicates that the variance in the measure is mostly at the group level (p. 344). To the degree that measures of group members' collective efficacy evidence significant group-level variance, subsequent statistical analysis must use group-level scores. These scores are likely to be the mean perceptions of the magnitude, strength, and generality of collective efficacy across group members.

Typically, measures of group variability regarding collective efficacy demonstrate moderate amounts of group variance, suggesting both individual and group-level effects. Kenny and his colleagues described the separation and analysis of such effects (Florin et al., 1990; Kenny & La Voie, 1985; Kenny & Stigler, 1983). The demonstration of significant variance in efficacy beliefs among group members has great theoretical import. Such variability may explain the emergence of a strong and hierarchical group structure, in which the magnitude and strength of members' collective efficacy determines their role within the group. Alternatively, strong group cohesion may require low variability among members regarding perceived group competence. Groups will not remain harmonious if some members perceive their group to be strong and others perceive it to be weak. These possible consequences of variability in collective efficacy require its analysis at multiple levels.

ANTECEDENTS AND CONSEQUENCES OF COLLECTIVE EFFICACY

Perceptions of self-competence have significant psychological and emotional implications for subsequent individual action (Maddux & Lewis, Chap. 2, this volume; Peterson & Stunkard, 1989). High perceived competence leads to more vigorous responses, even when an individual is confronted with difficult obstacles and initial failure. Perceptions of incompetence result in behavioral withdrawal and helplessness, even when the holder of such perceptions is faced with relatively easy task demands (Peterson & Stunkard, 1989; Seligman, 1975). Collective efficacy has similar consequences. Furthermore, collective efficacy is determined in part by events and experiences similar to those that determine self-efficacy (see Maddux, Chap. 1, this volume). However, qualities of the collective as a whole add a number of other variables to those associated with self-efficacy. The following sections describe the causal determinants and effects that are common to both self- and collective efficacy, as well as those variables that are unique to perceptions and beliefs about collective competence.

ANTECEDENTS OF COLLECTIVE EFFICACY

Perceptions of collective efficacy emerge from two sets of experiences by the individual group member. One is the quality of prior events experienced either directly or vicariously and shared by other group members; the other is the nature of social processes and influences operating within the collective.

Prior Performance

Regarding self-efficacy, Bandura (1982, 1986) defined personally experienced performance as *enactive attainment* and performances experienced vicariously as *modeling influences*. He regarded enactive attainment as the strongest determinant of self-efficacy. Likewise, Guzzo (1986) argued that prior performance was a significant antecedent of felt confidence in a group's performance capabilities. A few studies have provided empirical support for this assertion. Simkin, Lederer, and Seligman (1983) investigated an analogue of learned helplessness at the group level by having members of dyads experience either noncontingent failure or noncontingent success in turning off an aversive noise. A third group did not have any performance experiences. Relative to the control group, successful dyads performed better at a coordinated escape from aversive noise, whereas failing dyads did worse. Although these experimenters did not measure perceptions of group capabilities, they suggested that individuals in the failure condition developed expectations from their experiences that further concerted action would be ineffective (p. 621). Hodges and Carron (1992) reported that experimental groups experiencing failure in competition with a confederate group indeed indicated lower collective efficacy on successive performance trials. In the more natural setting of a wrestling team tournament, Kane et al. (1993) found that a team's record in the previous two seasons was related to individual wrestler's perceptions of collective efficacy at the beginning of camp. Also, team camp performance was related to generalized collective efficacy (or collective control; cf. Zaccaro et al., 1992). Taken together, these studies indicate an important link between prior group performance and collective efficacy.

Other researchers have noted that the *pattern* of prior performance determines the strength and nature of its association with collective efficacy. Specifically, group members need to share a significant number of performance experiences in order to develop a coherent and consistent sense of collective. Indeed, Felts, Bandura, Albrecht, and Corcoran (cited in Spink, 1990a) reported that the collective efficacy of hockey teams at the beginning of a season appeared no different than the sum of the self-efficacies of individual team members. The results of a second study, however, showed that over the length of a season, collective efficacy became more clearly differentiated from aggregated individual efficacies (Felts, Corcoran, & Lirigg, cited in Spink, 1990a).

Also, prior performance patterns must be fairly consistent. A steady pattern of success (or failure) is more likely to result in attributions of high (or low) ability and corresponding beliefs about future competence than a performance pattern of mixed success and failure. Support for this is provided by Zaccaro et al. (1992), who found that perceptions of high or low collective control were stronger after consistent patterns of success or failure than inconsistent performance patterns. Mesch et al. (1989) showed that a single instance of failure may actually boost collective efficacy. Nadler (1979) argued that group performance feedback can have cuing effects in which groups adjust their performance strategy in accordance with information gained from failure. The result can be a boost in perceived collective competence regarding the next performance task. Mesch et al. (1989) found that, indeed, groups that failed on a word-recognition task reported more strategy development, higher group goals, and higher magnitudes and strength of collective efficacy than groups that experienced success. However, although these data are suggestive, stable perceptions of collective efficacy most likely necessitate a greater number and variety of group performance experiences.

Groups can develop a sense of collective competence vicariously by observing the experiences of other similar groups in similar performance domains. Model groups provide important cues about appropriate response patterns in specific performance domains (Bandura, 1977, 1986). Furthermore, such groups may provide social-comparison information that informs members of similarly situated groups of their own expected capabilities (Bandura, 1986). However, as with self-efficacy, enactive attainment or direct experiences in the performance domain is likely to be a more potent source of perceived collective competence than vicarious experience.

Leadership Processes and Collective Dynamics

Weldon and Weingart (1988, 1993) argued that leadership behaviors within the group are an important determinant of collective efficacy. One such behavior is verbal persuasion of subordinates. Several theories and models of leadership emphasize that effective leaders encourage their subordinates and, through persuasion and exhortation, enhance their perceptions of their capabilities (Bass, 1985). Furthermore, many critical leadership functions are directed at fusing a capable team from disparate individuals and, perhaps more important, building perceptions among individual members of their combined and collective abilities (Fleishman et al., 1991). Leadership actions that persuade and develop subordinate competency beliefs may be as critical a determinant of collective efficacy as the group's prior performance experiences, if not more so. Sport team coaches spend much of their time developing new skills in team members and exhorting them on game day. These acts can indeed be the strongest influences on a team's sense of efficacy.

Leaders also contribute more directly to collective efficacy by specifically enhancing group functioning. The path–goal theory of leadership (Evans, 1970, 1974; Fulk & Wendler, 1982; House, 1971; House & Dressler, 1974; House & Mitchell, 1974; Stinson & Johnson, 1975) argues that the role of leaders is to facilitate the group's progress toward its goals. House and Mitchell (1974) defined the following four sets of leadership styles that can promote such progress (see also Yukl, 1989, p. 100):

1. Supportive leadership, or establishing a cohesive, friendly, and supportive workgroup environment
2. Directive leadership, or clarifying subordinate role requirements and expectations, establishing work rules, and planning work procedures
3. Participative leadership, or consulting with subordinates on critical group decisions
4. Achievement oriented leadership, or establishing difficult group goals, high performance standards, and an orientation toward excellence within the group.

Depending upon situational contingencies, each of these styles can enhance group functioning and capabilities. To the degree that leaders display these styles, subordinates should feel a stronger sense of collective efficacy. Support for this was found in a study of multiple kinds of groups and organizations by Gilbert, Zaccaro, Zazanis, and DeMiranda (1992). They collected measures of perceived collective competence and subordinate reports of their leader's initiating structure, consideration, integration, and production-emphasis behaviors. They found that collective control was significantly correlated with the frequency of these leadership styles. Future research should focus on longitudinal patterns in order to determine the specific roles leadership actions have in the development of collective efficacy.

Effective leadership processes, as well as other cues about the group's processes and communication dynamics, contribute to an overall sense of smooth collective functioning. When individuals in groups synchronize their actions extremely well, it creates a sense of flow and efficiency that contributes to positive beliefs about the group's coordination capabilities. Indeed, in such conditions, group members begin to act and react to *anticipated* actions by other group members. Group members receive process feedback that contributes to a heightened sense of collective efficacy.

Two group factors that contribute to perceptions of effective group process are group size and group cohesion. Members of smaller groups are generally better able to coordinate their activities than their counterparts in larger groups. As group size increases, individual members participate less, exhibit greater disagreements and dissension, and are absent more often (Bales, Strodtbeck, Mill, & Roseborough, 1951; Gibb, 1951; Indik, 1965; Shaw, 1981). As these factors occur, the group's sense of collective efficacy would be expected to decline, accompanied by decreases in individual contributions to the group. Studies of *social loafing* demonstrate that as group size increases, individual effort and performance declines (Latane et al., 1979; Sanna, 1992; Williams & Karau, 1991; Zaccaro, 1984). These findings can perhaps be attributed in part to a lowered sense of collective efficacy felt by group members as group size increases and coordination is perceived to be more difficult.

Alternatively, a larger group can mean that more resources are available to the group (Milliken & Vollrath, 1991). The greater the number of different resources groups can apply to a task, the stronger is the probability of success. In such circumstances, then, group size may be positively associated with members' perceptions of collective efficacy.

Group cohesion, defined as the degree or strength of adherence to the group existing among its members (Carron, 1982; Cartwright, 1968), is a second process determinant that can, in turn, enhance collective efficacy. As cohesion increases, the group as a whole gains more influence over individual members, and there is greater acceptance of group norms, assigned roles, and performance standards (Cartwright, 1968; Festinger, 1950; Forsyth, 1990). Furthermore, the group more strongly resists forces toward disruption (Carron, 1982; Gross & Martin, 1953). Each of these changes associated with group cohesion enhances the performance capabilities of the group; hence, members of highly cohesive groups should perceive their groups to be highly efficacious. In a study of cohesion and collective efficacy, Spink (1990b) reported that among volleyball teams, high and low efficacy teams differed on two dimensions of group cohesion, individual attraction to the group task, and the group's degree of social harmony. These findings support group cohesiveness as another possible determinant of collective efficacy, through its effects on group processes. It should be noted, however, that group cohesion can also be a result of collective efficacy (Zaccaro et al., 1992), a point that is examined in the next section.

CONSEQUENCES OF COLLECTIVE EFFICACY

The importance of self-efficacy beliefs for behavior is that such beliefs promote greater motivation, perseverance, persistence, and response vigor (Bandura, 1977, 1982, 1986; Peterson & Stunkard, 1989). Self-efficacy has also been linked to the establishment of more rigorous performance goals and, in turn, more planning, strategy development, and higher performance (Earley & Lituchy, 1991; Eden, 1988; Locke, Frederick, Lee, & Bobko, 1984; Locke & Latham, 1990; see also Maddux, Chap. 1, this volume). Similar influences are proposed as consequences of perceived collective efficacy.

Goals and Subsequent Performance

As members feel more confident of their group's coordinative capabilities in particular performance domains, they will be more motivated to work on behalf of the group, to persist in the face of experienced collective difficulties and obstacles, and to be willing to accept more difficult challenges for the group. Groups will also set more difficult goals and be more committed to these goals (Mesch et al., 1989; Weldon & Weingart, 1988, 1993). Consequently, highly efficacious groups should perform better than groups having low collective efficacy.

A small number of empirical studies have provided support for these assertions. Zaccaro et al. (1992) found that perceptions of collective competence were correlated with the amount of individual effort planned on a subsequent idea-generation task in laboratory groups. Mesch et al. reported extremely high correlations between collective efficacy in laboratory groups and levels of established group goals. Kane et al. (1993) found that perceived collective competence was associated with team goals in a wrestling tournament, team goals for the following season, and with team performance standards, norms, and expectations. Taken together, these studies demonstrate support for the influence of collective efficacy on individual- and team-performance processes.

These and other studies have also demonstrated strong associations between perceptions of collective competence and subsequent team performance (cf. Spink, 1990a). Zaccaro et al. (1992) found that collective control in laboratory groups was correlated with the quantity of ideas generated on a brainstorming task. Mesch et al. (1989) also found significant correlations between collective efficacy and subsequent performance on a word-association task. Hodges and Carron (1992) reported that, after failing on a muscular-endurance task, groups high in collective efficacy improved their subsequent performance, while low collective-efficacy groups exhibited lower performance. Similar associations between collective efficacy and performance have been reported in several studies on sport teams (work by Feltz and her colleagues, cited in Spink, 1990a, 1990b). These findings suggest that the consequences of collective efficacy are similar to those of individual self-efficacy. It should be noted, however, that most of these studies report only zero-order correlations, with the attendant possibility of spurious effects. Also, few if any studies have included perceived collective competence in analysis of mediational models, as has been the case with self-efficacy (e.g., Earley & Lituchy, 1991; Locke et al., 1984). These tests are required because collective efficacy is proposed as mediating the effects of several variables on group goal setting and motivation (cf. Weldon & Weingart, 1988, 1993).

Group Cohesion

Another consequence of collective efficacy is group cohesion. Perceptions of strong group competence should be associated with increases in the desirability of group, and therefore in group cohesiveness (Kane et al., 1993; Spink, 1990b). Also, several studies have shown that successful performance significantly increases subsequent group cohesion (Bakeman & Helmreich, 1975; Farris & Lim, 1969; Staw, 1984). This effect has been explained mostly by arguing that group cohesion is an attribution made to the group because of its prior performance (Bakeman & Helmreich, 1975; Staw, 1984). Zaccaro et al. (1992) suggested instead that the effects of prior performance on subsequent group cohesion were mediated entirely by perceptions of collective efficacy that were also enhanced by successful group outcomes. They reported results from an exploratory mediational analysis that supported this interpretation.

Zaccaro et al. (1992) demonstrated that group cohesion may be a consequence of collective efficacy. However, group cohesion may also be a causal antecedent of collective efficacy (cf. Spink, 1990a). Understanding the precise associations between these two variables may require a differentiation among forms of cohesion as either antecedents or consequences of perceived efficacy. Carron (1982) distinguished between *individual-level cohesion*, or the individual's desire for membership in the group, and *group-level cohesion*, or the group's resistance to disruption. Individual-level cohesion may be a predictor of collective efficacy, whereas the group's ability to withstand disruptive influences may be a consequence of perceived collective competence. Research should be directed toward examining these and other possible linkages between collective efficacy and group cohesion.

SUMMARY AND IMPLICATIONS

A sense of efficacy is an important determinant of people's actions in social performance domains (Bandura, 1986). Yet, little follow-up work has been reported on perceptions of collective efficacy. Most of the empirical studies that have appeared do not adhere to a systematic theoretical framework. Most studies merely extend principles about self-efficacy, including its measurement and associated outcomes, to the level of the collective. While these principles surely underlie a theoretical framework about collective efficacy, what is also needed is an understanding of the differences that emerge as the focus changes from the individual to the aggregate. Specifically, a conception of collective efficacy must incorporate the notion of necessary coordination and cooperation that is inherent in groups and organizations. Likewise, the measurement of this conception must incorporate the shared nature of personal beliefs in a group or an organization.

In this chapter, collective efficacy was defined as *a sense of collective competence shared among individuals when allocating, coordinating, and integrating their resources in a successful concerted response to specific situational demands.* This definition sets as a critical aspect of collective efficacy members' perceptions of how well they coordinate their individual resources in a collective endeavor. Thus, the emphasis is clearly on perceived coordination capabilities. This quality has important methodological implications that need additional attention. Specifically, the measurement of team coordination capabilities in terms of magnitude and strength require further specification. Also, it is not yet clear what is the most appropriate way to aggregate individual perceptions of the collective (Gist, 1987). This chapter also offers a number of antecedents and consequences—some correspondent to self-efficacy, others clearly unique to properties of the collective— that will hopefully galvanize subsequent research in this area.

A number of implications and questions emerge from the notions about collective efficacy described in this chapter and from those offered by others (Bandura, 1986; Gist, 1987; Spink, 1990a). One such question concerns the relationship between collective efficacy and self-efficacy within the group (cf. Spink, 1990a). Self-efficacy within the group has two foci. One is how competent individuals feel about their own skills relative to the group task. Incongruence between perceptions of self-efficacy and collective efficacy can produce interesting group dynamics. Imagine individuals who believe their group to be largely ineffective in meeting its purpose, but their own capabilities to be quite good. These individuals will react quite differently within the group from those who believe their group to be quite capable, but perceive themselves to be inadequate. Such incongruence may affect attributions of responsibility for collective outcomes (cf. Schlenker, 1975; Schlenker & Miller, 1977; Zaccaro et al., 1987), as well as subsequent reward allocations, communication dynamics, and role differentiation within the group. Furthermore, to the degree that membership in the collective is critical to one's self-esteem and social identity (Tajfel & Turner, 1986; Turner & Oakes, 1989), mismatches between self-efficacy and collective efficacy can have critical implications for personal affect and mental health.

A second focus of self-efficacy within the group is the individuals' perceptions of their ability to contribute to the group's coordination requirements. Note that this does not refer to collective success *per se*, or even to an individual's sense of mastery regarding the specific group task. Instead, this perceived competence refers to expected success in working well with others. It emphasizes social abilities and skills (Fleishman & Reilly, 1991), rather than more direct task abilities. These perceptions can influence how strongly one works on behalf of the group, the strength of one's desire to remain with the group, and the degree to which one seeks a more central role within the group.

Collective efficacy can be used as an explanatory mechanism for several phenomena related to group and organizational dynamics. For example, Peterson and Stunkard (1989) suggested that low motivation among members of groups within bureaucracies may result from their feeling a lack of connection between their own efforts and collective production. Low collective efficacy within members of groups and organizations therefore has implications for organizational commitment (Mowday, 1978, 1979), organizational citizenship behaviors (Organ, 1977, 1988), and other work motivation processes (Gist, 1987; Shamir, 1990).

Peterson and Stunkard (1989) also suggested that perceived collective competence explains why some health-promotion staffs are more successful in their efforts at community interventions than others. They argued that when such health personnel have high collective efficacy, they are more successful in galvanizing community support and better able to handle the various obstacles that are typical of most community health interventions. The same observations generalize to any organization, whether industrial, military, social, or voluntary in nature. High levels of collective efficacy should facilitate a team or organization's responses to environmental stress. Collective efficacy promotes persistence and perseverance in the face of significant demands. Thus, efficacious groups should succeed more readily under stressful circumstances than groups of lower efficacy. Likewise, collective efficacy may also be linked to greater readiness for group risk taking. Strong faith in the likely success of collective action appears to be a critical determinant for the eventual success of entrepreneurial work teams (Larson & LaFasto, 1989; Whetten, 1987).

This chapter has referred almost exclusively to groups and organizations when describing collective efficacy. This concept has been applied, however, to communities, societies, cultures, and nations (e.g., Bandura,

1986). A critical question in these applications, however, is how beliefs about efficacy change as the focus becomes more encompassing. This chapter describes changes that emerge as one moves from the individual to a relatively small collective. What other changes occur as the collective becomes larger, broader, and hence qualitatively different? How do the relationships between personal and collective efficacy change in such settings? The answers to these questions have important implications for understanding, assessing, and ultimately generating collective efficacy and successful social change in these larger aggregations.

REFERENCES

Bakeman, R., & Helmreich, R. (1975). Cohesiveness and performance: Covariation and causality in an underseas environment. *Journal of Experimental Social Psychology, 11,* 478–489.

Bales, R. F., Strodtbeck, F. L., Mills, T., & Roseborough, M.E. (1951). Channels of communication in small groups. *American Social Review, 16,* 461–468.

Bandura, A. (1977). Self-efficacy: Toward a unifying theory of behavioral change. *Psychological Review, 84,* 191–215.

Bandura, A. (1982). Self-efficacy mechanism in human agency. *American Psychologist, 37,* 122–147.

Bandura, A. (1986). *Social Foundations of thought and action: A social cognitive theory.* Englewood Cliffs, NJ: Prentice-Hall.

Bandura, A., & Jourden, F. J. (1991). Self-regulatory mechanisms governing the impact of social comparison on complex decision making. *Journal of Personality and Social Psychology, 60*(6), 941–951.

Bandura A., & Wood, R. (1989). Effect of perceived controllability and performance standards on self-regulation of complex decision making. *Journal of Personality and Social Psychology, 36,* 805–814.

Barling, J., & Beattie, R. (1983). Self-efficacy beliefs and sales performance. *Journal of Organizational Behavior Management, 5,* 41–51.

Bass, B. M. (1985). *Leadership and performance beyond expectations.* New York: Free Press.

Carron, A. V. (1982). Cohesiveness in sport groups: Interpretations and considerations. *Journal of Sport Psychology, 4,* 123–138.

Cartwright, D. (1968). The nature of group cohesiveness. In D. Cartwright & A. Zander (Eds.), *Group dynamics: Research and theory* (3rd ed., pp 91–109). New York: Harper & Row.

DeCharms, R. (1968). *Personal causation.* New York: Academic Press.

Deci, E. L. (1975). *Intrinsic motivation.* New York: Plenum Press.

Earley, P. C., & Lituchy, T. B. (1991). Delineating goal and efficacy effects: A test of three models. *Journal of Applied Psychology, 76,* 81–98.

Eden, D. (1988). Pygmalion, goal setting, and expectancy: Compatible ways to boost productivity. *Academy of Management Review, 13,* 639–652.

Evans, M. G. (1970). The effects of supervisory behavior on the path–goal relationship. *Organizational Behavior and Human Performance, 5,* 277–298.

Evans, M. G. (1974). Extensions of a path–goal theory of motivation. *Journal of Applied Psychology, 59,* 172–178.

Farris, G. F., & Lim, F. G. (1969). Effects of performance on leadership, cohesiveness, influence, satisfaction, and subsequent performance. *Journal of Applied Psychology, 53,* 490–497.

Festinger, L. (1950). Informal social communication. *Psychological Review, 57,* 271–282.

Fleishman, E. A., Mumford, M., Zaccaro, S. J., Levin, K. Y., Korotkin, A. L., & Hein, M. B. (1991). Taxonomic efforts in the description of leader behavior: A synthesis and functional interpretation. *Leadership Quarterly, 2,* 245–287.

Fleishman, E. A., & Reilly, M. (1991). Human Abilities: Their definition, measurement, and job task requirements. Palo Alto, CA: Consulting Psychologists Press.

Fleishman, E. A., & Zaccaro, S. J. (1992). Toward a taxonomy of team performance functions. In R. W. Swezey & E. Salas (Eds.), *Teams: Their training and performance* (pp. 31–56). Norwood, NJ: Ablex.

Florin, P., Giamartino, G. A., Kenny, D. A., & Wandersman, A. (1990). Levels of analysis and effects: Clarifying group influence and climate by separating individual and group effects. *Journal of Applied Social Psychology, 20,* 881–900.

Forsyth, D. (1990). *Group dynamics.* Pacific Grove, CA: Brooks/Cole.

Fulk, J., & Wendler, E. R. (1982). Dimensionality of leader–subordinate interactions: A path–goal investigation. *Organizational Behavior and Human Performance, 30,* 241–264.

Gibb, C. A. (1951). An experimental approach to the study of leadership. *Occupational Psychology, 25,* 233–248.

Gilbert, J., Zaccaro, S. J., Zazanis, M., & De Miranda, G. (1992, August). *Different forms of cohesiveness as substitutes for leadership.* Paper presented at the annual meeting of the American Psychological Association, Washington, DC.

Gist, M. E. (1987). Self-efficacy: Implications for organizational behavior and human resource management. *Academy of Management Review, 12,* 472–485.

Greenberger, D. B., & Strasser, S. (1986). Development and application of a model of personal control in organizations. *Academy of Management Review, 11,* 164–177.

Greenberger, D. B., Strasser, S., Cummings, L. L., & Dunham, R. B. (1989). The impact of personal control on performance and satisfaction. *Organizational Behavior and Human Decision Processes, 43,* 29–51.

Greenberger, D. B., Strasser, S., & Lee, S. (1988). Personal control as a mediator between perceptions of supervisory behaviors and employee reactions. *Academy of Management Journal, 31,* 405–417.

Gross, N., & Martin, W. E. (1953). On group cohesiveness. *American Journal of Sociology, 57,* 546–564.

Guzzo, R. A. (1986). Group decision making and group effectiveness in organizations. In P. Goodman & Associates (Eds.), *Designing effective work groups* (pp. 34–71). San Francisco, CA: Jossey-Bass.

Hackman, J. R., & Morris, C. G. (1975). Group tasks, group interaction processes, and group performance effectiveness: A review and proposed integration. In L. Berkowitz (Ed.), *Advances in experimental social psychology,* (Vol. 8). New York: Academic Press.

Hodges, L., & Carron, A. V. (1992). Collective efficacy and group performance *International Journal of Sport Psychology, 23,* 48–59.

Hoffman, L. R., & Maier, N. R. F. (1961). Quality and acceptance of problem solutions by members of homogeneous and heterogeneous groups. *Journal of Abnormal and Social Psychology, 62,* 401–407.

House, R. J. (1971). A path–goal theory of leader effectiveness. *Administrative Science Quarterly, 16,* 321–339.

House, R. J., & Dressler, G. (1974). The path–goal theory of leadership: some *post hoc* and *a priori* tests. In J. G. Hunt & L. L. Larson (Eds.), *Contingency approaches to leadership* (pp. 29–55). Carbondale: Southern Illinois University Press.

House, R. J., & Mitchell, T. R. (1974). Path–goal theory of leadership. *Journal of Contemporary Business, 3,* 81–97.

Indik, B. P. (1965). Organization size and member participation: Some empirical tests of alternative explanations. *Human Relations, 18,* 339–350.

Jackson, J. M., & Harkins, S. G. (1985). Equity in effort: An explanation of the social loafing effect. *Journal of Personality and Social Psychology, 49,* 1199– 1206.

Kane, T. D., Marks, M. A., Zaccaro, S. J., & Blair, V. W. (1993, March). *The moderating effects of attributional style on goal theory processes.* Paper presented at the annual meeting of the Society for Industrial Organizational Psychology, San Francisco, CA.

Katz, D., & Kahn, R. L. (1978). *The social psychology of organizations,* (2nd ed.) New York: Wiley.

Kenny, D. A. (1985). The generalized group effect model. In J. Nesselroade & A. Von Eye (Eds.), *Individual development and social change* (pp. 343–351). New York: Academic Press.

Kenny, D. A., & La Voie, L. (1985). Separating individual and group effects. *Journal of Personality and Social Psychology, 48,* 339–348.

Kenny, D. A., & Stigler, J. (1983). Program Level: A Fortran program for group–individual analysis. *Behavior Research Methods and Instrumentation,* 606.

Kerr, N. L. (1983). Motivation losses in small groups: A social dilemma analysis *Journal of Personality and Social Psychology, 45,* 819–828.

Kerr, N. L., & Bruun, S. E. (1983). Dispensability of member effort and group motivational losses: Free-rider effects. *Journal of Personality and Social Psychology, 44,* 78–94.

Larson, C. E., & LaFasto, F. M. J. (1989). *Teamwork: What Must Go Right/What Can Go Wrong.* Newbury Park, CA: Sage.

Latane, B., Williams, K., & Harkins, S. (1979). Many hands make light the work: The causes and consequences of social loafing. *Journal of Personality and Social Psychology, 37,* 822–832.

Laughlin, P., Branch, L., & Johnson, H. (1969). Individual versus triadic performance on unidimensional complementary tasks as a function of initial ability level. *Journal of Personality and Social Psychology, 12,* 144–150.

Levine, J. M., & Moreland, R. L. (1990). Progress in small group research. *American Review of Psychology, 41,* 585–614.

Levine, J. M., & Moreland, R. L. (1991). Culture and socialization in work groups. In L. B. Resnick, J. M. Levine, & S. D. Teasley (Eds.), *Perspectives on socially shared cognition.* Washington, DC: American Psychological Association.

Locke, E. A., Frederick, E., Lee, C., & Bobko, P. (1984). Effect of self-efficacy, goals, and task strategies on task performance. *Journal of Applied Psychology, 69,* 241–251.

Locke, E. A., & Latham, G. P. (1990). *A theory of goal setting and task performance.* Englewood Cliffs, NJ: Prentice-Hall.

Mesch, D. J., Farh, J., & Podsakoff, P. M. (1989, August). *Effects of feedback sign on group goal setting, strategies, and performance: An empirical examination of some control theory hypotheses.* Paper presented to the Organizational Behavior Division at the annual meeting of the Academy of Management, Washington, DC.

Milliken, F. J., & Vollrath, D. A. (1991). Strategic decision-making tasks and group effectiveness: Insights from theory and research on small group performance. *Human Relations, 44,* 1229–1253.

Moreland, R. L., & Levine, J. M. (1982). Socialization in small groups: Temporal changes in individual–group relations. In L. Berkowitz (Ed.), *Advances in experimental social psychology.* (Vol. 15, pp. 137–192). New York: Academic Press.

Moreland, R. L., & Levine, J. M. (1989). Newcomers and oldtimers in small groups. In P. Paulus (Ed.), *Psychology of group influence* (2nd ed., pp. 143–186). Hillsdale, NJ: Erlbaum.

Mowday, R. T. (1978). The exercise of upward influence in organizations *Administrative Science Quarterly, 23,* 137–156.

Mowday, R. T. (1979). Leader characteristics, self-confidence, and methods of upward influence in organizational decision situations. *Academy of Management Journal, 22*, 709–725.

Nadler, D. A. (1979). The effects of feedback on task–group behavior: A review of the experimental research. *Organizational Behavior and Human Performance, 23*, 309–338.

Organ, D. W. (1977). A reappraisal and reinterpretation of the satisfaction-causes performance hypothesis. *Academy of Management Review, 2*, 46–53.

Organ, D. W. (1988). *Organizational citizenship behavior: The good soldier syndrome.* Lexington, MA: Heath.

Peterson, D., & Seligman, M. E. P. (1984). Causal explanations as a risk factor for depression: Theory and evidence. *Psychological Review, 91*, 347–374.

Peterson, C., & Stunkard, A. (1989). Personal control and health promotion. *Social Science Medicine, 26*, 819–828.

Reddy, W. B., & Byrnes, A. (1972). The effects of interpersonal group composition on the problem-solving behavior of middle managers. *Journal of Applied Psychology, 56*, 516–517.

Rotter, J. B. (1966). Generalized expectancies for internal versus external control of reinforcement. *Psychological Monographs, 80*, 1–28.

Sanna, L. J. (1992). Self-efficacy theory: Implications for social facilitation and social loafing. *Journal of Personality and Social Psychology, 62(3)*, 774–786.

Schein, E. H. (1985). *Organizational culture and leadership: A dynamic view.* San Francisco: Jossey-Bass.

Schlenker, B. R. (1975). Group members' attributions of responsibility for prior group performance. *Representative Research in Social Psychology, 6*, 96–108.

Schlenker, B. R., & Miller, R. S. (1977). Group cohesiveness as a determinant of egocentric perceptions in cooperative groups. *Human Relations, 11*, 1039–1055.

Schutz, W. C. (1955). What makes groups productive? *Human Relations, 8*, 465–499.

Schutz, W. C. (1958). *FIRO: A three-dimensional theory of interpersonal behavior.* New York: Holt, Rinehart & Winston.

Seligman, M. E. P. (1975). *Helplessness: On depression, development, and death.* San Francisco: Freeman.

Shamir, B. (1990). Calculations, values, and identities: The sources of collectivistic work motivation. *Human Relations, 43*, 313–332.

Shaw, M. E. (1963). Scaling group tasks: A method for dimensional analysis. *JSAS Catalog of Selected Documents in Psychology, 3*, 8.

Shaw, M. E. (1981). *Group dynamics: The psychology of small group behavior* (3rd ed.) New York: McGraw-Hill.

Shea, G. P., & Guzzo, R. A. (1987). Groups as human resources. In K. Rowland & G. Ferris (Eds.), *Research in personnel and human resources management*, (Vol. 5, pp. 323–356). Greenwich, CT: JAI Press.

Shepperd, J. A. (1993). Productivity loss in performance groups: A motivation analysis. *Psychological Bulletin, 113*, 67–81.

Simkin, D. K., Lederer, J. P., & Seligman, M. E. P. (1983). Learned helplessness in groups *Behavior Research and Therapy, 21*, 613–622.

Skinner, B. F. (1953). *Science and human behavior.* New York: The Free Press.

Spink, K. S. (1990a). Collective efficacy in the sport setting. *International Journal of Sport Psychology, 21*, 380–395.

Spink, K. S. (1990b). Group cohesion and collective efficacy of volleyball teams. *Journal of Sport and Exercise Psychology, 12*, 301–311.

Steiner, I. (1972). *Group process and productivity.* New York: Academic Press.

Staw, B. M. (1984). Organizational behavior: A review and reformulation of the field's outcome variables. *Annual Review of Psychology, 35,* 627–666.

Stinson, J. E., & Johnson, T. W. (1975). The path–goal theory of leadership: A partial test and suggested refinement. *Academy of Management Journal, 18,* 242–252.

Tajfel, H., & Turner, J. C. (1986). The social identity theory of intergroup behavior. In S. Worchel & W. G. Austin (Eds.), *Psychology of intergroup relations,* (2nd ed., pp. 7–24). Chicago: Nelson-Hall.

Taylor, M. S., Locke, E. A., Lee, C., & Gist, M. E. (1984). Type A behavior and faculty research productivity: What are the mechanisms? *Organizational Behavior and Human Performance, 34,* 402–418.

Turner, J. C., & Oakes, P. J. (1989). Self-categorization theory and social influence. In P. B. Paulus (Ed.), *Psychology of group influence* (2nd ed., pp. 233–275). Hillsdale, NJ: Erlbaum.

Weldon, E., & Weingart, L. R. (1988, August). *A theory of group goals and group performance.* Paper presented at the annual meeting of the Academy of Management, New Orleans, LA.

Weldon, E., & Weingart, L. R. (1993). Group goals and group performance. *British Journal of Social Psychology, 32*(4), 307–334.

Whetten, D. A. (1987). Organizational growth and decline processes. *American Review of Sociology, 13,* 335–358.

White, R. E. (1959). Motivation reconsidered: The concept of competence *Psychological Review, 66,* 247–333.

Widmeyer, W. N. (1990). Group composition in sport. *International Journal of Sport Psychology, 21,* 264–285.

Williams, K. D., & Karau, S. J. (1991). Social loafing and social compensation: The effects of expectations of co-worker performance. *Journal of Personality and Social Psychology, 61,* 570–581.

Wood, R., & Bandura, A. (1989). Impact of conceptions of ability on self-regulatory mechanisms and complex decision making. *Journal of Personality and Social Psychology, 56,* 407–415.

Wood, R., Bandura, A,. & Bailey, T. (1990). Mechanisms governing organizational performance in complex decision-making environments. *Organizational Behavior and Human Decision Making Processes, 46,* 181–201.

Yukl, G. A. (1989). *Leadership in organizations* (2nd ed.). Englewood Cliffs, NJ: Prentice-Hall.

Zaccaro, S. J. (1984). Social loafing: The role of task attractiveness. *Personality and Social Psychology Bulletin, 10,* 99–106.

Zaccaro, S. J., Blair, V., Peterson, C., & Gilbert, J. A. (1992). *Collective control: Causes and consequences of group members' beliefs about group competence* Manuscript submitted for publication.

Zaccaro, S. J., & McCoy, M. C. (1988). The effects of task and interpersonal cohesiveness on performance of a disjunctive group task. *Journal of Applied Social Psychology, 18,* 837–851.

Zaccaro, S. J., Peterson, C., Blair, V. W., & Gilbert, J. (1990, August). *Some antecedents and consequences of collective control.* Paper presented at the annual meeting of the American Psychological Association, Boston, MA.

Zaccaro, S. J., Peterson, C., & Walker, S. (1987). Self-serving attributions for individual and group performance. *Social Psychology Quarterly, 50,* 257–263.

Zander, A. (1971). *Motives and goals in groups.* New York: Academic Press.

PART V

COMMENTARY

CHAPTER 12

SELF-EFFICACY AND OUTCOME EXPECTANCIES
A CONCLUDING COMMENTARY

IRVING KIRSCH

Paraphrasing Ebbinghaus's comment about psychology, self-efficacy has a short history, but a long past. Self-efficacy is a judgment about personal capabilities that is intimately tied to expectancies about the outcome of contemplated actions. Expectancy has been explored extensively by many psychological theorists and researchers (e.g., Atkinson, 1957; Edwards, 1954; Lewin, 1936; Rotter, 1954; Tolman, 1955; Vroom, 1964) and has led to many important applications. The term *expectancy* was used in a very broad sense, however. Expectancies derived from self-efficacy judgments were not distinguished from those derived from beliefs about contingencies in the social environment. Thus, drawing a theoretical distinction between these constructs was an important theoretical contribution (Bandura, 1977a). At the same time, because many early measures of "expectancy" were indistinguishable from contemporary measures of self-efficacy, careful reading of the earlier literature reveals many important facts about self-efficacy. For example, studies conducted prior to 1970 reveal that (1) the debilitating effect of failure on self-efficacy is greater than the facilitating effect of success, (2) spaced practice weakens the effect of the most recently

---

IRVING KIRSCH • Department of Psychology, University of Connecticut, Storrs, Connecticut 06269.

Self-Efficacy, Adaptation, and Adjustment: Theory, Research, and Application, edited by James E. Maddux. Plenum Press, New York, 1995.

experienced performance feedback on self-efficacy and strengthens that of prior feedback, (3) induced changes in self-efficacy for a particular task generalize to other tasks, and (4) self-efficacy is correlated across dissimilar tasks. (See Kirsch, 1986, for a detailed review of these and other findings from early research on self-efficacy.)

The data reviewed in the chapters of this book substantiate the fact that self-efficacy is a useful and important construct capable of predicting behavior in clinical, academic, and employment settings, among others. That self-efficacy affects behavior substantially is unquestionable. However, a theory is more than a listing of variables that affect behavior. We also want to understand the ways in which these variables are related to each other and the mechanisms by which they impact behavior. With respect to self-efficacy, an important task is to understand its relation to outcome expectancies.

SUBTYPES OF OUTCOME EXPECTANCY AND THEIR RELATION TO SELF-EFFICACY

An outcome expectancy is a person's subjective probability that a particular behavior, if performed in some particular situation, will lead to some particular outcome (cf. Rotter, 1954). This definition seems straightforward enough, but, in fact, it is ambiguous. The ambiguity in traditional definitions of outcome expectancy is revealed in the following sets of statements:

> Outcome and efficacy expectations are differentiated, because individuals can believe that a particular course of action will produce certain outcomes, but if they entertain serious doubts about whether they can perform the necessary activities such information does not influence their behavior. (Bandura, 1977a, p. 193)
> There are countless activities that people believe will bring admiration, fame, and fortune, but they do not pursue them because they believe they do not have what is takes to succeed. A low sense of efficacy nullifies the motivating potential of alluring outcome expectations. (Bandura, 1992, p. 123)

> For most activities, outcomes are determined by level of competence. Hence, the types of outcomes people anticipate depend largely on how well they believe they will be able to perform in given situations. . . . People's beliefs about their efficacy largely determine the outcomes they expect their efforts to produce. Hence, if you know their perceived self-efficacy, you mostly know the types of anticipated outcomes on which they are acting. (Bandura, 1992, p. 123)

From the first set of statements, we can surmise the following defini-tion of the term *outcome expectancy*: An outcome expectancy is a subjective probability that a particular behavior, *if performed by someone at a given level of competence*, will be followed by a particular outcome. Based on the second set of statements, however, we would surmise the following defini-tion: An outcome expectancy is a person's subjective probability that *his or her performance* of a behavior will be followed by a particular outcome.

That these are different constructs can be shown by examining their relations to self-efficacy. Indeed, revealing this ambiguity in the definition of *outcome expectancy* is one of the contributions of self-efficacy theory. Before proceeding further, however, it will be helpful to provide explicit labels for the two distinguishable constructs ambiguously denoted by the term *outcome expectancy*. This distinction is not new (see Kirsch, 1985; Maddux, Chap. 1, this volume) and various labels have been proposed. It has been proposed that the term *outcome expectancy* be restricted to one or another of these meanings. This is problematic, however, because it is inconsistent with previous usage and is bound to engender greater confu-sion. At this point, I recommend recognizing both constructs as subtypes of outcome expectancy. The following labels are consistent with the way terms have been used in the literature: Let us refer to an outcome expec-tancy of the first type as a *means–ends belief* and to an outcome expectancy of the second type as a *personal outcome expectancy*. A means–ends belief is a person's subjective probability that a successfully executed behavior will be followed by a particular outcome. A personal outcome expectancy is a subjective probability that the person's own behavior would be followed by a particular outcome. For example, the belief that playing basketball exceptionally well brings fame and fortune is a means–ends belief, whereas a person's expectancy of achieving fame and fortune by playing basketball is a personal outcome expectancy.

The distinction between means–ends beliefs and personal outcome expectancies is critical to answering the question "What is the relationship between self-efficacy and outcome expectancy?" The answer depends on the type of outcome expectancy to which one is referring.

Self-efficacy and means–ends beliefs are conceptually independent constructs. This is not to say that they are unrelated empirically. The belief that important outcomes are contingent on a behavior might lead some individuals to optimistically overestimate (or pessimistically underesti-mate) their ability to perform it. Similarly, low self-efficacy might lead one to defensively underestimate the likelihood or value of an outcome ("Who wants to go to a crummy old graduate school anyway?"). But effects of this sort are likely to be relatively weak. More importantly, there is no *logically necessary* connection between self-efficacy and this type of outcome expec-

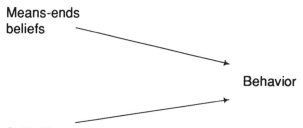

FIGURE 1. Means–ends beliefs and self-efficacy as determinants of achievement behavior.

tancy. Following Bandura (1977a), the relationship between self-efficacy and means–ends beliefs as determinants of behavior is diagrammed in Figure 1.

In contrast, there is a causal relationship between self-efficacy and personal outcome expectancies (Bandura, 1992; Kirsch, 1985b). Self-efficacy is one important determinant of personal outcome expectancies; means–ends beliefs are another. As illustrated in Figure 2, the effects of self-efficacy and means–ends beliefs on behavior are mediated by personal outcome expectancies, which illustrates the following propositions (adapted from Bandura, 1977a, p. 193; 1992, p. 123):

> People can believe that a particular course of action, if performed effectively, will produce certain outcomes. These are their pertinent means–ends beliefs. However, if they entertain serious doubts about whether they can perform the necessary activities (i.e., if they have low self-efficacy for the required task), such information will not influence their behavior. This is because the types of outcomes people anticipate (their personal outcome expectancies) depend not only on their means–

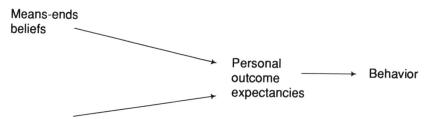

FIGURE 2. Personal outcome expectancies as mediators of the effects of means–ends beliefs and self-efficacy on achievement behavior.

ends beliefs, but also on how well they believe they will be able to perform in given situations (i.e., their perceived self-efficacy). Their decision to engage in some particular behavior ultimately depends on their belief that *their* behavior in that situation will produce particular outcomes and also on the value they attach to those anticipated outcomes (cf. Rotter, 1954).

TASK LOCUS OF CONTROL AS A MODERATOR VARIABLE

Behavior is most directly determined by personal outcome expectancies and values. Examining the relationship between self-efficacy and means–ends beliefs does not mean establishing which variable is the better predictor of behavior. In fact, the only accurate answer to this question is "It depends!" The relative importance of self-efficacy and means–ends beliefs in predicting behavior depends on many things, including the thoroughness with which self-efficacy and outcome expectancies have been evaluated. The full range of potentially relevant self-efficacy and outcome expectancies in a particular situation is rarely (if ever) assessed in a single study. Most important, the relative contributions of self-efficacy and outcome expectancies depend on the nature of the situation and the type of behavior upon which the outcomes depend.

Consider the following behaviors: entering a raffle or sweepstakes, buying theft insurance, using a condom, voting for a particular candidate, buying a certain product, going to a movie or concert, swallowing a pill and so on. The salient outcomes of these and many other important behaviors do not depend much on quality of performance. Were one to risk the mirth of subjects by assessing self-efficacy for these behaviors (e.g., "How likely it is that you would be able to vote for candidate X"), one would not be likely to find much variation in subjects' responses. Hence, almost all of the variance in behavior (e.g., whether candidate X was voted for) would be accounted for by means–ends beliefs.

Now consider these behaviors: taking a test, pursuing a particular course of study in school, performing job functions, playing a competitive game, such as tennis or chess, and so on. Because the outcomes of these behaviors are largely determined by ability, the outcomes one expects might be almost entirely determined by self-efficacy, and measuring both self-efficacy and personal outcome expectancy would be redundant. There may be little variation in means–ends beliefs in these situations, so it is not likely to be a very important predictor variable.

Finally, consider such behaviors as beginning a business, playing poker, and investing in the stock market. The consequences of these behaviors are only partly dependent on skill. They are also dependent on luck and other factors that are beyond personal control, such as changes in the economy and fluctuations in the stock market. In these cases, neither self-efficacy alone nor means–ends beliefs alone are sufficient to account for variability in expected outcomes, and hence in behavior.

The dimension on which I have sorted these behaviors may be recognized as related to the construct of locus of control (Rotter, 1966). Because of the success of the Internal-External (I-E) scale at predicting behavior (albeit weakly) across a wide variety of situations, locus of control is most frequently thought of as a generalized expectancy. But the initial studies in which the construct was developed were more concerned with locus of control for particular tasks in specific situations than with generalized expectancies. The outcomes of some behaviors are governed primarily by chance or other external factors, whereas the outcomes of other behaviors are governed primarily by skill and effort. As a consequence, expected outcomes may be perceived as dependent primarily on skill or primarily on chance.

Task locus of control can be defined as the degree to which the outcome of a particular behavior in a specific situation is perceived as dependent on skill. Rotter and his colleagues (Holden & Rotter, 1962; James & Rotter, 1958; Rotter, Liverant, & Crowne, 1961) demonstrated that the familiar effect of intermittent reinforcement on resistance to extinction holds only when outcomes are perceived as governed by chance. When outcomes were perceived as dependent on ability, continuous reinforcement produced greater resistance to extinction. The reasons for these results are not difficult to fathom. Imagine the difference between always doing well on math exams and sometimes doing well on them. Always doing well on a skilled task leads people to have high levels of confidence in their ability at that task and, therefore, to be more persistent in the face of adversity. In other words, consistently positive performance feedback produces high levels of self-efficacy that are relatively stable and resistant to change. Now imagine the difference between operating a soda machine that always delivers its product and operating one that often returns one's coins, so that one may have to insert the coin two or three times before finally getting the desired product. Intermittent reinforcement of this sort would make it take longer for an individual to realize that the machine is empty. In other words, self-efficacy judgments (and the outcome expectancies they produce) based on consistent performance feedback are likely to be more stable and resistant to change than judgments based on inconsistent feedback. Conversely, means–ends beliefs (and the outcome expectancies they produce) are likely to be more stable when based on the experience of inconsistent consequences.

In summary, the relative impact of means–ends beliefs and self-efficacy beliefs in determining personal outcome expectancies and behavior depends on the perceived locus of control of the particular task. Note that it does not depend on the person's generalized expectancy as measured by instruments like the I-E scale, except to the degree that this generalized expectancy contributes to the person's perception of the factors controlling the outcome of the behavior. Self-efficacy determines expectancies for outcomes that are perceived as contingent on skill; mean–ends beliefs determine them for outcomes that are not perceived as skill-dependent.

It is also important to note that locus of control, whether considered in relation to a particular task or as a generalized expectancy, represents a continuum, rather than a dichotomy. Although some outcomes are almost completely independent of actual or perceived competence, few outcomes are entirely dependent on skill. Various external factors can play a role in the outcomes of such skilled behaviors as taking a test or playing a competitive game. For that reason, the perceived ratio of internal (i.e., skill) to external determinants of an expected outcome will determine the relative influence of means–ends and self-efficacy beliefs on consequent outcome expectancy. For example, a student's grade on an upcoming test might be seen by the student as depending partly on the instructor's grading practices and, therefore, only partly on the student's ability. If a particular instructor is perceived to grade capriciously, the influence of self-efficacy on expected grade is likely to be weak. Thus, task locus of control moderates the relation of these variables to expected outcomes and to behavior.

SUBTYPES OF SELF-EFFICACY

Having considered subtypes of outcome expectancy, it is now necessary to consider subtypes of self-efficacy. Early measures of self-efficacy were exclusively concerned with perceived ability to accomplish the target behavior (e.g., approaching a feared stimulus or abstaining from an addictive behavior). The development of measures of coping self-efficacy, as described by Williams (Chap. 3, this volume) with respect to anxiety, and by DiClemente, Fairhurst, and Piotrowski (Chap. 4, this volume) with respect to addictive behaviors, represents an important enrichment of self-efficacy research. Coping self-efficacy refers to beliefs about one's ability use various coping strategies to "prevent, control, or cope with a potential difficulty" (Williams, Chap. 3, this volume). Examples of coping self-efficacy are the belief that one can control aversive thoughts (Williams) and that one can be assertive (DiClemente et al.)* Besides validating the hypothesized relationship between coping efficacy and behavior, the conceptual relationship between these different types of self-efficacy needs to elucidated. How are coping and task self-efficacy related? How are they related to the various forms of outcome expectancy (means–ends beliefs and personal outcome expectations)? How do these variables interact to produce behavior?

It is notable that measures of coping efficacy have been developed only for phobic and addictive behaviors, but not for academic or job-related behaviors. As noted by Maddux (Chap. 1, this volume), self-efficacy for approaching a feared stimulus, for tolerating pain, for refraining from smoking, or for limiting one's caloric intake is different from self-efficacy for performing academic tasks or job requirements. Unlike the performance of academic or employment tasks, these tasks produce highly aversive immediate consequences (e.g., panic, pain, withdrawal symptoms, and hunger) that can be ended by terminating the behavior. The inhibition of performance of these tasks may not be due to a skill deficit, at least not to any lack of the cognitive or motor abilities required to perform the task. Instead, failures to approach a feared stimulus or to abstain from smoking may be associated with low self-efficacy for coping with the expected aversive consequences of the behavior.

If the failure to approach a feared stimulus, voluntarily tolerate a painful stimulus, or refrain from lighting a cigarette is not due to lack of the ability to do these things, why do people indicate a perceived lack of ability on self-efficacy questionnaires? Elsewhere, I have attributed this to a linguistic habit of saying "can't" under certain circumstances, when one literally means "won't" (Kirsch, 1982). When you ask people if they could do something that violates their moral standards or that would result in extremely aversive consequences, they are likely to interpret the work "could" figuratively rather than literally.

Contrary to Williams's (Chap. 3, this volume) implication, this does not imply a linguistic abnormality. Instead, it is almost universal. Consider your answers to the following questions: Could you eat a live worm? Could you laugh out loud during the middle of a funeral? Could you kill a baby kitten? I assume that you would answer at least some of these questions negatively. Why? Do you lack the conviction that you can successfully execute these behaviors (Bandura, 1977a)? Do you lack the "capa-

---

*Williams uses the term *coping self-efficacy* to refer to traditional scales measuring self-efficacy for approaching a feared stimulus. Because these scales ask people to rate ability to execute the targeted behavioral task, rather than their ability to cope, it is more accurate to refer to the construct they measure as *task self-efficacy*.

bility to organize and execute" these actions (Bandura, 1986, p. 391)? Perhaps you lack the "capabilities to exercise control" over these events (Bandura, 1989, p. 1175). I expect that none of these reasons explain your low self-efficacy ratings. More likely, you are "unable" to do these things because doing so would evoke extreme disgust, embarrassment, guilt, or shame. Clearly, when you say you cannot do these things, you mean something different than when you say you cannot solve a difficult calculus problem, lift a 300-pound weight, or successfully execute the job requirements of an astronaut. One of the recurring themes in this book is that there are different kinds of outcome expectations. The difference between self-efficacy for killing a kitten and lifting a weight demonstrates that there are different kinds of self-efficacy expectations as well.*

There are considerable data indicating that self-efficacy for the performance of highly aversive tasks are indications of willingness or behavioral intention, rather than genuine judgments of ability. Recall that in achievement situations, personal outcome expectancies are largely dependent on self-efficacy judgments (Bandura, 1992). For highly aversive tasks, the relationship between outcome expectancy and task self-efficacy is precisely the reverse. Both real and hypothetical incentives have been shown to affect efficacy ratings for approaching a feared stimulus, tolerating pain, and refraining from smoking, but not efficacy ratings for nonaversive achievement tasks (Baker & Kirsch, 1991; Corcoran & Rutledge, 1989; Kirsch, 1982; Schoenberger, Kirsch, & Rosengard, 1991).†

Of course, this does not mean that phobics, addicts, or subjects in a pain experiment are lacking in will or simply do not want to behave properly (see Williams, Chap. 3, this volume). What it does mean is that the experience of panic is so intense and aversive for some people that they are willing to endure exceptionally high costs to avoid or end it. Similarly, addicts generate a variety of rationalizations (e.g., "Just one can't make a difference") to avoid or end withdrawal symptoms. Indeed, when the value (positive or negative) and likelihood of immediately anticipated outcomes are sufficiently extreme, it is not unusual for us to experience our

---

*In some situations self-efficacy for lifting a weight may be very much like self-efficacy for killing a kitten, or approaching a phobic stimulus. When cardiac patients report that they cannot lift heavy objects, they are not judging their strength (Ewart, Chap. 7, this volume). Instead, they are expressing their belief that doing so would endanger their lives. It is not the nature of the behavior that determines one's interpretation of a self-efficacy question, but rather the perception of extreme consequences.
†Williams's objection (Chap. 3, this volume) to my 1982 study, on the grounds that subjects were not genuinely neurotic, seems strange, given the continuity between "normal" and "abnormal" behavior that is assumed in social cognitive theory (see Maddux & Lewis, Chap. 2, this volume).

voluntary behavior as beyond our control. This does not, however, negate the fact the behavior actually is voluntary and is governed by outcome expectancies and values in the same way as other behaviors. Whereas task self-efficacy for aversive tasks is equivalent to *intention* (as the term is defined in reasoned action theory; Ajzen & Fishbein, 1980), coping self-efficacy is not. Furthermore, self-efficacy theory has always stressed coping self-efficacy in certain domains (Bandura, 1986), despite the unfortunate, almost exclusive reliance on measures of task efficacy. Phobic anxiety and avoidance should be related to people's beliefs in their ability to control the scary thoughts that the phobic situation engenders. Coping efficacy should affect the outcomes that one expects to experience (e.g., fear or relief of emotional distress), which should in turn affect task self-efficacy.

THE IMPORTANCE OF SUBJECTIVE RESPONSES

"Being anxious means primarily feeling anxious. The essence and *sine qua non* of anxiety is the subjective feeling of fear" (Williams, Chap. 3, this volume). When phobic persons enter treatment, their goal is not just to overcome their phobic avoidance; they also want to overcome their phobic anxiety. Few phobic clients would be satisfied with the ability to perform feared tasks, while remaining extremely frightened. Converting agoraphobia into a panic disorder without agoraphobia is not their goal. In fact, avoidance is not a central component of some anxiety disorders. Similarly, reducing the experience of pain is at least as important a goal as helping a person to tolerate it longer, and increasing the activity level of a depressed person is subsidiary to enhancing the person's mood. While behavioral goals are paramount in treating addictive behaviors, subjective experiences (e.g., withdrawal symptoms) may play a central role in maintaining the maladaptive behavior.

Although self-efficacy is an excellent predictor of behavior, it does not fare quite as well in predicting subjective responses (see Williams, Chap. 3, this volume). The prediction of subjective responses is better accomplished by response expectancies (Kirsch, 1985a, 1990). *Response expectancy* and *stimulus expectancy* are subcategories of *outcome expectancy*. Stimulus expectancies are beliefs about the occurrence of external events, such as grades, prizes, recognition, and financial rewards. Responses expectancies are anticipations of one's own subjective reactions. These include anxiety expectancy, pain expectancy, expected panic, expectations about the course of one's depressed mood, the anticipation of withdrawal symptoms, expected craving, and so forth. Because they are a type of outcome expectancy, response expectancy is a determinant of intentional behavior; subjective reactions such as pain and fear are among the outcomes people consider in choosing a course of action. However, response expectancies have a property that they do not share with stimulus expectancies: As amply demonstrated by the literature on placebos, response expectancies tend to be self-confirming. Among the responses that can be changed by the manipulation of response expectancies are pain, anxiety, depression, alertness, tension, sexual arousal, and alcohol craving and consumption (reviewed in Kirsch, 1990). Physiological effects of modified response expectancies include changes in pulse rate, blood pressure, penile tumescence, endorphin release, skin conditions (i.e., contact dermatitis and warts), gastric function, and possibly malignancies (Kirsch, 1990).

Williams (Chap. 3, this volume) is unclear about "how the anticipation of anxiety or of panic could cause one to become anxious or panicky." If pain expectancies affect pain (Baker & Kirsch, 1991), expectancies about depression affect depression (Kirsch, Mearns, & Catanzaro, 1990), and expected mirth produces experienced mirth (Wilson, Lisle, Kraft, & Wetzel, 1989), why is it so difficult to believe that expected anxiety might drive the experience of anxiety? In fact, the causal effects of anxiety expectancy seem particularly easy to fathom. Fear is produced by the anticipation of aversive outcomes. For many people, the experience of fear or panic is extremely aversive. Therefore, one would expect them to be frightened by the expectancy that they are about to experience this dreaded feeling.

More important, the data clearly indicate that expected anxiety or panic affects the experience of anxiety or panic. As shown by Williams in Chapter 3, anxiety expectancy is as highly correlated with self-reported fear as self-efficacy is with approach behavior. Furthermore, the association of anxiety expectancy with reported fear remains significant and substantial even when self-efficacy, danger expectancy, and initial fear levels are statistically controlled (Schoenberger et al., 1991). Moreover, fear can be substantially altered by expectancy manipulations (Kirsch & Henry, 1977; Kirsch, Tennen, Wickless, Saccone, & Cody, 1983; Mavissakalian, 1987; Southworth & Kirsch, 1988).

Self-efficacy theory and response expectancy theory are not antithetical. They are both part of the broad network of social cognitive theory that has evolved from the conceptual foundations established by the social learning theories of Bandura (1977b), Mischel (1973), and Rotter (1954). In fact, self-efficacy and response expectancy are complementary constructs, especially in dealing with behaviors that are associated with highly aversive subjective outcomes (e.g., phobia, depression, pain, and addictions). Figure 3 depicts the conceptual relationship between response expectancies, stimulus outcome expectancies (e.g., incentives), coping self-efficacy

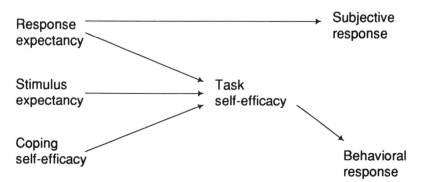

FIGURE 3. An integrative model of the relationship of expectancy variables to subjective and behavioral responses.

(i.e., perceived ability to execute coping strategies, such as thought control), task self-efficacy (e.g., self-efficacy for approaching a phobic stimulus, tolerating pain, or abstaining from addictive behaviors), subjective responses (e.g., anxiety, depression, pain, craving, etc.), and behavior. Initial data strongly support much of this model (e.g., Baker & Kirsch, 1991; Schoenberger et al., 1991).*

FUZZY BOUNDARIES AND CONCEPTUAL OVERLAP— A FINAL CAUTIONARY NOTE

In many of the chapters in this book (including this one), considerable emphasis has been placed on precise delineation of theoretical constructs. Self-efficacy should be distinguished from outcome expectancy; outcome expectancy should be distinguished from outcome value, and so forth. Furthermore, the various subtypes of outcome and self-efficacy expectancies need to be distinguished, because they function differently as causes of behavior. Mislabeling of measuring instruments in this area of research is not uncommon, and it typically leads to erroneous conclusions. If and

---

*Williams (Chap. 3, this volume) is mistaken when he attributes to me the view that "self-efficacy predicts behavior only because self-efficacy is correlated with anticipated anxiety." The causal model that I proposed (Kirsch, 1990) is similar to the one presented here, in that it hypothesizes a direct path between self-efficacy and behavior and views anxiety expectancy as only one cause of self-efficacy for approaching a phobic stimulus. As Williams correctly notes, the data "make clear that self-efficacy . . . cannot easily be dismissed as a mere inert by-product of anticipated fear." The data are equally clear that anxiety expectancy cannot be dismissed as a mere by-product of self-efficacy.

when meta-analyses are conducted in this area, the problem is likely to be compounded. Unless meta-analytic researchers take extreme care in evaluating the operations by which constructs have been measured, rather than simply relying on the names that have been given to them, apples will be mixed with oranges and compared to oranges mixed with pears.

Despite this admonition, a certain amount of conceptual overlap may be unavoidable. Perhaps it is due to the vagaries of language or the complexity of human cognition, but the boundaries of these adjacent constructs are fuzzy. Consider some examples.

O'Leary and Brown (Chap. 8, this volume) describe a study in which self-efficacy for pain reduction was assessed (Bandura, O'Leary, Taylor, Gauthier, & Gossard, 1987). I have referred to a study in which pain expectancy was assessed (Baker & Kirsch, 1991). Is there much difference between believing that one can reduce one's pain by using a coping strategy and believing that one's pain will, in fact, be lower when one uses that strategy? In many instances, measures of these constructs will be virtually identical, as will the data they produce. Yet, one is a self-efficacy judgment and the other is a response expectancy, which is a type of outcome expectancy. Similar overlap would occur between measures of self-efficacy for controlling one's mood and measures of affective response expectancy.

Does this mean that self-efficacy and response expectancy are indistinguishable? Certainly not! Anxiety expectancy is not the same thing as the belief that one can approach a feared stimulus. Despite the high negative correlation (between .65 and .90) between the two constructs, it is possible to have high levels of both approach self-efficacy and anxiety expectancy, in which case one is likely to approach the feared stimulus, but feel terrified while so doing (see Williams, Chap. 3, this volume). Nevertheless, there are situations in which particular measures of self-efficacy overlap with measures of response expectancy. In these circumstances, the use of both measures is redundant, and the choice of which to use is arbitrary.

A similar overlap can exist between some measures of self-efficacy ("How confident are you that you can solve most of the math problems on this page?") and measures of corresponding stimulus outcome expectancies ("How likely is it that you will receive a passing grade on this math exam?"). When outcomes are largely dependent on skill, differences between self-efficacy and personal outcome expectancy may be little more than semantics. Nevertheless, the differentiation between the two constructs is useful, because self-efficacy is only one of the determinants of personal outcome expectancies, and in some cases the two constructs will not be related. For example, the expectancy that one will win the toss of a coin is not likely to be related to one's self-efficacy for tossing the coin.

In summary, the various expectancy constructs are overlapping sets and can be represented by a Venn diagram in which the circle representing each construct overlaps with at least some of the other circles. This does not necessarily indicate a shortcoming of social cognitive theory. As Kihlstrom (1985, p. 405) notes, "natural categories are best regarded as fuzzy sets whose instances are related by family resemblance." Although fuzziness of the boundaries of expectancy subtypes may be unavoidable, it makes theory development difficult and hazardous. It is probably at least partially responsible for some of the acrimony that has plagued discourse about self-efficacy. The difficult task ahead of us is to combine tolerant, collaborative theory integration with critical (but not antagonistic) scholarly evaluation.

REFERENCES

Ajzen, I., & Fishbein, M. (1980). *Understanding attitudes and predicting social behavior*. Englewood Cliffs, NJ: Prentice-Hall.
Atkinson, J. W. (1957). Motivational determinants of risk-taking behavior. *Psychological Review, 46*, 359–372.
Baker, S., & Kirsch, I. (1991). Cognitive mediators of pain perception and tolerance. *Journal of Personality and Social Psychology, 61*, 504–510.
Bandura, A. (1977a). Self-efficacy: Toward a unifying theory of behavioral change. *Psychological Review, 84*, 191–215.
Bandura, A. (1977b). *Social learning theory*. Englewood Cliffs, NJ: Prentice-Hall.
Bandura, A. (1986). *Social foundations of thought and action: A social cognitive theory*. Englewood Cliffs, NJ: Prentice-Hall.
Bandura, A. (1989). Human agency in social cognitive theory. *American Psychologist, 44*, 1175–1184.
Bandura, A. (1992). On rectifying the comparative anatomy of perceived control: Comments on "Cognates of Personal Control." *Applied and Preventive Psychology, 1*, 121–126.
Bandura, A., O'Leary, A., Taylor, C. B., Gauthier, J., & Gossard, D. (1987). Perceived self-efficacy and pain control: Opioid and nonopioid mechanisms. *Journal of Personality and Social Psychology, 53*, 563–571.
Corcoran, K. J., & Rutledge, M. W. (1989). Efficacy expectation changes as a function of hypothetical incentives in smokers. *Psychology of Addictive Behaviors, 3*, 22–29.
Edwards, W. (1954). The theory of decision making. *Psychological Bulletin, 51*, 380–417.
Holden, K. B., & Rotter, J. B. (1962). A nonverbal measure of extinction in skill and chance situations. *Journal of Experimental Psychology, 63*, 163–169.
James, W. H., & Rotter, J. B. (1958). Partial and 100 percent reinforcement under chance and skill conditions. *Journal of Experimental Psychology, 55*, 397–403.
Kihlstrom, J. F. (1985). Hypnosis. *Annual Review of Psychology, 36*, 385–418.
Kirsch, I. (1982). Efficacy expectations or response predictions: The meaning of efficacy ratings as a function of task characteristics. *Journal of Personality and Social Psychology, 42*, 132–136.
Kirsch, I. (1985a). Response expectancy as a determinant of experience and behavior. *American Psychologist, 40*, 1189–1202.

Kirsch, I. (1985b). Self-efficacy and expectancy: Old wine with new labels. *Journal of Personality and Social Psychology, 49,* 824–830.

Kirsch, I. (1986). Early research on self-efficacy: What we already know without knowing we knew. *Journal of Social and Clinical Psychology, 4,* 339–358.

Kirsch, I. (1990). *Changing expectations: A key to effective psychotherapy.* Pacific Grove, CA: Brooks/Cole.

Kirsch, I., & Henry, D. (1977). Extinction vs. credibility in the desensitization of speech anxiety. *Journal of Consulting and Clinical Psychology, 45,* 1052–1059.

Kirsch, I., Mearns, J., & Catanzaro, J. (1990). Mood-regulation expectancies as determinants of depression in college students. *Journal of Counseling Psychology, 37,* 306–312.

Kirsch, I., Tennen, H., Wickless, C., Saccone, A. J., & Cody, S. (1983). The role of expectancy in fear reduction. *Behavior Therapy, 14,* 520–533.

Lewin, K. (1936). *Principles of topological psychology.* New York: McGraw-Hill.

Mavissakalian, M. (1987). The placebo effect in agoraphobia. *Journal of Nervous and Mental Disease, 175,* 95–99.

Mischel, W. (1973). Toward a cognitive social reconceptualization of personality. *Psychological Review, 80,* 252–283.

Rotter, J. B. (1954). *Social learning and clinical psychology.* Englewood Cliffs, NJ: Prentice-Hall.

Rotter, J. B. (1966). Generalized expectancies for internal versus external control of reinforcement. *Psychological Monographs, 80* (1, Whole No. 609).

Rotter, J. B., Liverant, S., & Crowne, D. P. (1961). The growth and extinction of expectancies in chance controlled and skilled tasks. *Journal of Psychology, 52,* 161–177.

Schoenberger, N., Kirsch, I., & Rosengard, C. (1991). Cognitive theories of human fear: An empirically derived integration. *Anxiety Research, 4,* 1–13.

Southworth, S., & Kirsch, I. (1988). The role of expectancy in exposure-generated fear reduction in agoraphobia. *Behaviour Research and Therapy, 26,* 113–120.

Tolman, E. C. (1955). Principles of performance. *Psychological Review, 62,* 315–326.

Vroom, V. H. (1964). *Work and motivation.* New York: Wiley.

Wilson, T. D., Lisle, D. J., Kraft, D., & Wetzel, C. G. (1989). Preferences as expectation-driven inferences: Effects of affective expectations on affective experience. *Journal of Personality and Social Psychology, 56,* 519–530.

CHAPTER 13

ON RECTIFYING
CONCEPTUAL ECUMENISM

Albert Bandura

This brief commentary is testimony to Maddux's resilient sense of efficacy. Because of a burdensome load of commitments, I repeatedly thwarted his requests to prepare a commentary for this edited volume. An editor of lesser efficacy would have long accepted the futility of further enlistment efforts. However, as the clinching efficacious act, Maddux sent me the complete manuscript with the implication that his failed attempts called into question a central tenet of self-efficacy theory, namely, that an unshakable sense of efficacy enables one to find a way to succeed in the face of seemingly insurmountable obstacles. Reading the concluding commentary with its serious misconceptions about the nature of human efficacy created an additional self-persuasive influence to put pen to paper. Because of time constraints I will confine my remarks mainly to Kirsch's concluding commentary.

Kirsch begins his commentary with the view that variations in beliefs about the contingent relation between performance and outcomes represent fundamentally different types of outcome expectancies. The belief

Some of the material presented in this commentary is drawn from the forthcoming book, *Self-Efficacy: The Exercise of Control*. New York: Freeman.

ALBERT BANDURA • Department of Psychology, Stanford University, Stanford, California 94305.

Self-Efficacy, Adaptation, and Adjustment: Theory, Research, and Application, edited by James E. Maddux. Plenum Press, New York, 1995.

that outcomes are contingent on certain performances is presumed to be a *means-end belief* at the general level, but a *personal outcome expectancy* at the personal level. These two sets of expectations are said to represent different "constructs." In point of fact, the structure of the assumed contingency between performance and outcome is the same in both instances. Consider, for purposes of illustration, the outcome expected to result from academic performances. If attaining a superior level of academic performance qualifies students for distinguished social recognition and scholarships, the belief about the means for securing those outcomes is the same for oneself as for one's academic peers. In contending that expected outcomes for oneself and for others represent different constructs, Kirsch seems to be confusing expected outcome contingencies with belief about whether one can produce the performances required to gain the outcomes. A student performing mediocrely would not expect to be showered with academic commendations and scholarships. But the same applies to other students as well. Nor would peers who perform mediocrely expect to be showered with academic honors and the valued coin of the academic realm. Stellar grades by self will bring expected honors; stellar grades by others will bring expected honors. In short, the performers differ but the performance–outcome contingency is identical.

The outcomes that result from a given performance may, of course, vary depending on the age, gender, race, social status or other attributes. In such instances, individuals expect the same performances to produce different outcomes for themselves and for dissimilar others. An example would be women receiving lower pay than men for performing the same occupational role equally well. However, this variation simply reflects different expected payment values within the same basic contingency operating between occupational performance and paychecks, not different constructs as Kirsch contends. In situations where individuals expect to be punished for actions that others are rewarded for, the difference is one of contingency, not of construct. The construct of conditional relation between action and outcome applies equally to self and to others.

It only creates needless conceptual confusion to treat expected performance–outcome contingencies as representing dissimilar constructs bearing different names when the performer is oneself or others. Readers are informed in italicized emphasis that there is no *"logically necessary"* relation between beliefs about the contingencies operating for oneself and for others. Why would anyone ever expect them to be logically related? That is not the way societies structure their contingency systems. When women were disfranchised, the differential performance outcomes a woman expected in many areas of life for herself and for men was dictated not by logical necessity, but by prejudicially structured contingencies. Nor was racial segregation, which prescribed differential outcome contingencies in education, public accommodation, employment and interpersonal relationships, logically ordained.

There is no fixed relation between efficacy beliefs and outcome expectations. Self-efficacy theory distinguishes degrees of controllability by personal means, which affects the extent to which self-efficacy beliefs shape outcome expectancies and how much outcomes expectations add incrementally to prediction of performance (Bandura, 1986). In activities where outcomes are highly contingent on quality of performance, efficacy beliefs account for most of the variance in expected outcomes. For example, marathon runners who are fully assured in their capabilities to attain a victorious performance will expect their efforts to produce prize money and social recognition, whereas those who concede they lack the capabilities to outrun their competitors will not expect to be showered with money and media attention. Thus, when variations in perceived self-efficacy are partialed out, the outcomes expected for one's performances are redundant and add little or not predictive increment. Redundancy of predictors should not be misinterpreted as indifference to outcomes. Students may value academic awards highly, but their perceived scholastic efficacy determines whether or not they expect to get them.

Efficacy beliefs subsume only part of the variance in expected outcomes when outcomes are not completely controlled by quality of performance. And finally, expected outcomes are independent of self-efficacy beliefs if contingencies are restrictively structured so that no level of competence can produce desired outcomes. During the era when professional sports were racially segregated, minority athletes, however talented, could not gain the lucrative rewards offered by professional athletic franchises. It is a mundane observation that not all outcomes are personally controllable. No one studies the exercise of human efficacy to control the local rainfall, for example, unless one seeks to explain people's resort to proxy control expressed in ceremonial rituals to influence the rain gods to deliver desired droplets. Social cognitive theory not only acknowledges degrees of personal controllability but specifies the way in which different patterns of efficacy beliefs and outcomes expectations produce distinctive motivational, affective, and behavioral effects (Bandura, 1982).

While on the topic of outcome expectations, I should like to comment on the conceptual and empirical separateness of efficacy beliefs and performance outcome expectations because the issue needs to be more clearly framed than it is in the introductory chapter. The cognitive regulation of human functioning involves two control belief systems operating in concert (Figure 1). The first, concerns beliefs in one's capabilities to attain given levels of performance. The second concerns the outcomes expected

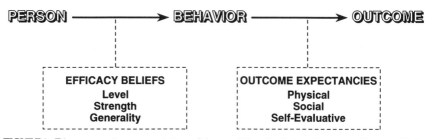

FIGURE 1. Diagrammatic representation of the conditional relations between efficacy beliefs and outcome expectancies. In given domains of functioning, efficacy beliefs vary in level, strength and generality. The outcomes that flow from a given course of behavior can take the form of positive or negative physical, social, and self-evaluative effects.

to flow from those performances. Outcome expectations can take three major forms (Bandura, 1986). One class of outcomes includes the pleasant and aversive physical effects of the behavior. Human behavior is partly regulated by the social reactions it evokes. The positive and negative reactions of others constitute the second major class of outcomes. People do not behave like weathervanes, constantly shifting to whatever social influences happen to impinge upon them at the moment. They adopt personal standards, and regulate their behavior by their self-sanctions. They do things that give them self-satisfaction and self-worth, and refrain from behaving in ways that breed self-dissatisfaction. This third major class of outcomes concerns the positive and negative self-evaluative reactions to one's behavior. Evaluative self-reaction is one of the more influential regulators of human behavior, but the most neglected in most analyses of personal change.

Some confusion has been introduced in the literature because performance attainments are often misconstrued as outcomes. A performance is an accomplishment; an outcome is something that flows as a result of an activity. For example, in the achievement domain, the letter grades of A, B, C, D, and F are markers of different levels of performance attainments not outcomes. Performance grade levels do not foretell particular outcomes. Performances at the A level may bring self-satisfaction and social approval in circles that value academic achievement, but social censure in subgroups of peers who devalue academic achievement and are quick to ridicule, harass and, ostracize academic achievers (Ogbu, 1990; Solomon, 1992). In the health domain, the markers of difficult levels of attainment may be the amount of change achieved in weight, exercise, smoking or nutritional habits. The outcomes of changes in health habits include the positive and negative physical, social and self-evaluative consequences produced by those attainments.

Those who misconstrue a marker of a performance as an outcome of itself launch themselves on an endless performance regress. An *A* level academic performance becomes an "outcome" of a certain level of study behavior but then the study behavior itself becomes an "outcome" of something else the student did to bring it about and so it goes on endlessly with each attainment being an "outcome" of its precursor which then becomes an "outcome" of its precursor! Construing a given marker of weight as an outcome similarly inaugurates one on an endless regressive series. People do not struggle to shed pounds just to shed pounds. They do so for the resulting outcomes that include physical health benefits, social benefits and self-evaluative benefits. If weight loss had no physical effects whatsoever, others couldn't care less whether individuals are svelte or plump and their weight had no bearing on their self-satisfaction, people would not go around starving themselves endlessly solely for pound losses (the alleged outcome). The weight-reduction and diet industries would promptly go out of business. This is the conceptual muddle created by misinterpreting an attainment marker as an outcome of its inceptive self. If researchers choose to construe a performance marker as an outcome, it is their conceptual and methodological problem to defend. A view of outcomes that self-efficacy theory categorically rejects should not be foisted on it and then portrayed as its problem in separating performances from outcomes.

In social cognitive theory, efficacy beliefs operate as one of many determinants that regulate human motivation, affect and action (Bandura, 1986). Research aimed at maximizing the amount of variance explained in human functioning should, therefore, include the full set of determinants in the causal structure posited by the theory rather than only the self-efficacy component. The recent years have witnessed a proliferation of mini-models designed to explain human functioning in given domains. The conceptual models devised to explain health behavior, which are summarized by Maddux, Brawley and Boykin (Chap. 6, this volume), is a good case in point. The particular factors singled out in the various conceptual schemes overlap with subsets of determinants encompassed by social cognitive theory. Table 1 presents the main determinants in social cognitive theory and their kindred conceptual brethren in different models of health behavior.

If people lack awareness of how their lifestyle habits affect their health they have little reason to put themselves through the misery of changing bad health habits they enjoy. The various conceptual models presuppose adequate knowledge of health risks and usually find it to be high. *Knowledge* creates the precondition for change, but additional self influences are needed to overcome the impediments to adopting new lifestyle habits.

TABLE 1. Summary of the Main Sociocognitive Determinants
and Their Areas of Overlap in Different Conceptual Models of Health Behavior

Theories	Self-Efficacy	Outcome Expectations			Goals		Impediments	
		Physical	Social	Self-Evaluative	Proximal	Distal	Personal and Situational	Health System
Social cognitive theory	✓	✓	✓	✓	✓	✓	✓	✓
Health belief model		✓	✓				✓	✓
Theory of reasoned action		✓	✓		✓			
Theory of planned action	✓	✓	✓		✓			
Protective motivation theory	✓	✓						

Psychosocial Determinants of Health Behavior

Beliefs of *personal efficacy* occupy a pivotal regulative role in the socio-cognitive causal structure because they not only operate in their own right but act upon other classes of determinants (Bandura, in press). Efficacy beliefs facilitate acquisition of knowledge structures on which skills are founded. Such beliefs also regulate motivation by shaping aspirations, strength of commitment to them, and the outcomes expected for one's efforts. Moreover, the self-assurance with which people approach and manage difficult tasks determines whether they make good or poor use of their capabilities. Insidious self-doubts can easily overrule the best of skills. Most conceptual models of health behavior now include a perceived efficacy determinant (Ajzen, 1985; Maddux & Rogers, 1983; Schwarzer, 1992).

In addition to the regulative function of self-efficacy beliefs, *outcome expectations* concerning the effects produced by different health habits contribute to health behavior. As already noted, these outcome expectations take the form of detrimental or beneficial physical effects, favorable or adverse social consequences, and positive or negative self-reactions. Most of the factors in the various conceptual models correspond to one or more of these different types of outcome expectations. The perceived severity of, and susceptibility to, health impairment in the health belief model represents the detrimental side of expected physical outcomes (Becker, 1974; Rosenstock, 1974). The perceived benefits of preventive action correspond to positive outcome expectations. Rogers' (1983) model of protective motivation includes the threat component of perceived severity and susceptibility, but adds the efficacy determinant.

In the theories of reasoned action (Ajzen & Fishbein, 1980) and planned behavior (Ajzen, 1985), the intention to engage in a behavior is governed by attitudes toward the behavior and by subjective norms. The labels differ but these two sets of determinants correspond, in their operationalization, to different classes of outcome expectations. Attitude is measured in terms of perceived outcomes and the value placed on those outcomes. Norms are measured by perceived social pressures by significant others and one's motivation to comply with their expectations. Norms correspond to expectations of social outcomes for a given behavior. In social cognitive theory, normative influences regulate actions through two regulatory mechanisms. These include social sanctions and self sanctions. Norms influence behavior anticipatorily by the social consequences they provide. Behavior that fulfills social norms gains positive social reactions; behavior that violates social norms brings social censure. In addition, social norms convey behavioral standards. Adoption of modeled standards creates a self-regulatory system that operates through internalized self sanctions. In the case of self sanctions, which are not explicitly included in the theories of reasoned or planned action, people regulate their behavior anticipatorily through self-evaluative reactions.

In sociocognitive theory, *cognized goals* rooted in a value system provide further self incentives and guides to health behavior. Goals may be distal ones that serve an orienting function or specific proximal ones that regulate effort and guide action in the here and now. Intentions are essentially equivalent to proximal goals. There is little, if any, difference between, I aim to, and I intend to, perform an activity. Goals are an interlinked facet of a motivational mechanism that operates through self-monitoring, aspirational standards and affective self-reaction rather than simply being a disjoined predictor. In causal structures, efficacy beliefs affect goal setting and whether substandard performances spark greater effort or are demoralizing. But goals make independent contribution to performance (Wood & Bandura, 1989; Zimmerman & Bandura, 1994; Zimmerman, Bandura, & Martinez-Pons, 1992).

Personal change would be trivially easy if there were no *impediments* or barriers to surmount. Hence, perceived barriers are an important factor in the health belief model (Becker, 1990; Rosenstock, 1974), and elaborated versions of it (Schwarzer, 1992). Social cognitive theory distinguishes between different types of barriers. Some of the barriers are conditions that impede performance of the health behavior itself. These types of impediments form an integral part of self-efficacy assessment as gradations of challenges to successful performance. The regulation of health behavior is not solely an intrapsychic matter. Some of the barriers to healthful living reside in health systems rather than in personal or situational impediments. Unavailability of health resources presents a second class of barriers to healthful behavior that is rooted in how health services are socially and economically structured.

We are now in the era of cafeteria-style theorizing in which constructs are plucked from divergent theories and strung together in various combinations as alternative conceptual schemes. The development of a comprehensive theory of human behavior should focus on broad integrative constructs. The cafeteria style of theorizing multiplies predictors unnecessarily in several ways. Similar factors, but bearing different names, are often included in the same composite model as though they were separate classes of determinants. This creates needless redundancy among predictors. Moreover, facets of a higher-order construct are sometimes treated as entirely different types of determinants as when attitudes, normative influences and outcome expectations are included in a conglomerate model as different constructs when, operationally, they simply represent different types of outcome expectations. Following the timeless dictum that the more the better, some researchers overload their conceptual model with a host of factors that contribute trivially to health habits. All too often, the eclectic additive approach gets passed off as integrative theorizing presumably combining the best of different approaches. Scientific progress is better achieved by encompassing more fully the determinants within an integrated theory than by creating conglomerate models with constructs picked from divergent theories with the attendant problems of redundancy, fractionation and theoretical disconnectedness.

Some researchers have tested whether factors included in alternative conceptions of health behavior add incremental prediction over and above a subset of sociocognitive determinants. In several of these studies the sociocognitive determinants included efficacy beliefs, expected health benefits, and satisfaction or dissatisfaction with the changes achieved in health habits (Dzewaltowski, 1989, Dzewaltowski, Noble, & Shaw, 1990). Both efficacy beliefs and affective self-reactions to personal progress contributed to adherence to healthful behavior. Attitudes and perceived social pressure similarly accounted for healthful behavior, but they did not improve prediction when added to the subset of sociocognitive determinants.

Most of the models of health behavior are concerned mainly with predicting health habits but offer little guidance on how to change them. In addition to providing a unified conceptual framework, social cognitive theory imbeds the sociocognitive determinants in a large body of knowledge that specifies their origins, the processes through which they produce their effects, and how to modify them to enhance human health (Bandura, 1986, in press).

The exercise of personal agency through efficacy belief involves the self-regulation of cognitive, motivational, affective and motoric contributors to psychosocial functioning. A large body of research documents the intricate way in which beliefs of personal efficacy regulate these contributors to human adaptation and change (Bandura, 1992, in press).

The recent years have witnessed major changes in the conception of human ability (Bandura, 1990; Sternberg & Kolligan, 1990). An ability is not a fixed property that one does or does not have within one's behavioral repertoire. Rather it involves a generative capability in which cognitive, social, motivational and behavioral skills must be organized and effectively orchestrated to serve diverse purposes. There is a marked difference between possessing knowledge and skills and being able to use them well under difficult circumstances. Hence, people with the same skills may perform poorly, adequately, or outstandingly depending on fluctuations in their judgments of personal efficacy and the cognitive and motivation processes they activate.

Perceived self-efficacy is concerned with belief in one's agentive capabilities, but the events over which personal influence is exercised varies. It may entail control over one's own motivation, thought processes, affective states, actions, or environmental events, depending on what individuals seek to manage. Kirsch's reasoning about the contribution of personal efficacy to human functioning relies on a trivialized view of the self-management of life events. He argues that in the case of academic and occupational functioning there is skill variability so that efficacy belief is an influential contributor. However, in other areas of functioning he detaches an elementary motor act from the larger activity of managing life events, reports that there is no skill variation in the elemental act, and then concludes that beliefs of personal efficacy do not account for variations in functioning.

This conceptual detachment (Kirsch, 1982) was first applied to the efficacy of snake phobics to manage interactions with snakes, which are known to become resistantly hyperactive when people start reaching for them and squeezing them. Kirsch argued that all phobics possess the necessary motoric responses in their behavioral repertoire. Since the ambulatory and grasping responses verify full capability to manage hyperactive snakes, he reasoned, people's beliefs in their efficacy are presumably unrelated to their reptilian venturesomeness. Surviving herpetologists, who rightly value the skills needed to control the behavior of reptiles, including unfriendly venomous ones, would be much amused by the view that an ambulatory and motoric grasping capability fully equips individuals to manage transactions with shifty reptiles. The powerful treatments that rapidly wipe out phobic dysfunction build a strong sense of coping efficacy by equipping phobics with strategies for controlling reptiles (Bandura, 1988). Their motoric grasping capability may be uniformly high before and after treatment, but their snake management efficacy is markedly enhanced by treatment. The stronger the perceived self-efficacy to manage different intensities of interaction with the phobic object the higher the performance attainments. In the present commentary, Kirsch detaches elementary motoric acts from complex adaptations in other areas of functioning and then argues, as in the grasping act, that everyone possesses the capability in their behavioral repertoire. I shall comment briefly on these various conceptual ectomies.

In the alleged ecumenical spirit, Kirsch claims that assessment of perceived efficacy for self-management of health-related behavior, such as "using a condom" or "swallowing a pill" will "risk the mirth of subjects." It is not the mirth of subjects, but the trifleness of Kirsch's conception of self-regulation of health habits that is the problem requiring correction. Let us consider first the use of condoms as a safeguard against sexually transmitted diseases, especially infection with the AIDS virus. Self-protection against HIV infection requires social and self-regulative skills and a strong sense of personal efficacy to use them effectively and consistently in managing sexual relationships. Self-efficacy scales assess, not the isolated act of donning a condom, but perceived self-regulatory efficacy to surmount the numerous interpersonal impediments to condom use. The items include perceived capability to negotiate regular condom use and to resist pressure for unsafe sex from monogamous or casual partners, when intoxicated or high on drugs, when strongly attracted to the partner, when caught up in an arousing intimacy without a condom and, if all else fails, to exercise control by refusing to engage in unprotected sexual activity with a partner who continues to reject condom use.

A growing body of research corroborates that a high sense of self-regulatory efficacy is accompanied by self-protective intentions and sexual practices (Bandura, 1993). Moreover, interventions grounded in self-efficacy theory equip participants with the skills and sense of personal efficacy to protect themselves against this deadliest of viruses through regular condom use (Jemmott & Jemmott, 1992; Jemmott, Jemmott, & Fong, 1992; Jemmott, Jemmott, Spears, Hewitt, & Cruz-Collins, 1991). In Kirsch's simplistic analysis, everyone knows how to don a condom so there is not issue of personal efficacy. This trifling conception is essentially a penisectomy in which the fervent organ is severed from the interpersonal dynamics that determine if it gets sheathed or not. The knowledge and interventions stemming from thoughtful research conducted within the self-efficacy framework stand in stark contrast to Kirsch's cavalier attitude that efforts to assess perceived self-efficacy for condom use would constitute a mirthful exercise.

Self-regulation of health habits is not achieved through an act of will as Kirsch would lead one to believe. It involves enlistment of complex skills in monitoring one's behavior and its determinants, regulating one's motivation by effective use of self incentives, making decisions that do not eventuate in risky predicaments, enlisting cognitive aids to bolster self-regulating efforts and selecting and structuring environments conducive to healthful practices (Bandura, 1988, in press). These various subfunctions have to be orchestrated in concert to manage ever-changing situations.

Perceived self-regulatory efficacy operates similarly in the regulation of other health habits. Efficacy beliefs are not assessed at the trivialized level conceived by Kirsch, such as swallowing a pill. Efficacy beliefs must be measured against gradations of challenges or impediments to successful performance. Development of appropriate self-efficacy scales requires extensive conceptual and exploratory inquiry to identify the major impediments to the adoption and maintenance of health-promoting habits. Individuals judge their efficacy to surmount the different sets of impediments. For example, in assessing people's perceived self-efficacy to adhere to exercise habits, they are not asked whether they can walk briskly but whether they can get themselves to stick to their walking routine when they are tired, depressed, under pressure from work, have more interesting things to do, face foul weather, and the like. Adherence to medication regimens is a serious problem in medical treatments. Some people can get themselves to surmount the impediments, others cannot. Contrary to Kirsch's simplistic view, the issue of personal efficacy is not whether people believe they can swallow a pill, but whether they believe they have the efficacy to get themselves to take their pills regularly as prescribed, whatever forms the dissuading conditions might take. A substantial body of evidence in the health domain is consistent in showing that self-regulatory efficacy contributes importantly to adherence to health-promoting regimens (Bandura, in press).

Kirsch's discussion of subtypes of self-efficacy is simply a continuation of the detachment of elemental acts from complex adaptations. For example, we are told that, since everyone is able to refrain from lighting a cigarette, people's beliefs in their efficacy to exercise control over smoking behavior have no bearing on success rates in smoking cessation. Readers are presented a vacuous depiction of self-regulation as cigarette lighting rather than a thoughtful analysis of how people's beliefs in their self-regulatory capabilities affect their struggle to free themselves of their addictions. Informative studies are being conducted into the influential role of perceived self-regulatory efficacy in the self-management of addictive substances. Overcoming dependence on nicotine by breaking the smoking habit is but one example. These programs of research assess perceived self-efficacy to resist pressures to smoke across a variety of instigative conditions that strain the exercise of personal control (DiClemente, Fairhurst, & Piotrowski, 1995; Marlatt, Baer, & Quigley, 1995). They include social inducements to smoke, negative mood states, interpersonal conflicts and engagement in a host of positive activities in settings where smoking was deeply imbedded and thus keep activating urges to smoke. Efficacy beliefs predict initiation of habit change, maintenance of smoking cessation, vulnerability to relapse, and recovery from lapses. Self-efficacy research has also contributed new insights into the self-regulation of alcohol and drug dependence.

Kirsch is of the view that, for "aversive" tasks, self-efficacy is equivalent to willingness or intentions as defined by Ajzen and Fishbein. The belief that one can manage effectively certain life events (*self-efficacy*) differs conceptually from whether one intends to do so (*intention*). If one firmly believes that it is not within one's power to do something it is self-contradictory to intend to do it. In drawing perfunctorily on the work on intention, Kirsch is in for a major surprise because both Ajzen and Fishbein regard efficacy beliefs and intentions as different factors. Indeed, Ajzen

(1985) has expanded the theory of reasoned action by adding an efficacy factor called perceived behavioral control. It is ironic that Kirsch invokes Ajzen in the rechristening of self-efficacy as intention in aversive activities because Ajzen posits that it is precisely on difficult and aversive tasks that people need the staying power of efficacy belief to succeed.

The conceptual separation of efficacy belief and intention is fully corroborated empirically. Regardless of whether the activity is "aversive" or not, efficacy beliefs affect performance both directly and by influencing intentions (de Vries & Backbier, 1994; deVries, Dykstra, & Kuhlman, 1988; Dzewaltowski, 1989; Dzewaltowski, Noble, & Shaw, 1990; Kok, deVries, Mudde, & Stretcher, 1991; Schwarzer & Fuchs, 1995). The results of numerous studies similarly show that perceived behavioral control affects behavior both directly and through its impact on intention (Ajzen & Madden, 1986). In the introductory chapter to this volume, Maddux uncritically accepts Kirsch's claim that efficacy is intention in situations including potentially aversive elements, apparently unaware of the growing body of empirical evidence that disputes this very view. We shall return later to the basis on which this erroneous claim was originally founded.

As the above studies demonstrate, perceived self-efficacy is an important determinant of "willingness" or intention. The activities of everyday life are strewn with frustrating, boring, stressful and painful elements. This is part and parcel of daily living. Even simple reflection would reveal that most pursuits come with a goodly load of aversiveness that people override to attain what they desire. If they curtailed their activities because of aversive aspects they would lead massively constricted lives. It is people's beliefs in their efficacy to succeed that promotes willingness to undertake aversive pursuits and enables them to sustain the necessary effort in the face of innumerable difficulties and to put up with a lot of aversiveness. Those who distrust their capabilities to manage environmental demands quickly convince themselves of the futility of effort. Kirsch's commentary is heavily focused on the supposedly behavior paralyzing effects of aversiveness generated by "response expectancies." For example, anticipation of aversive withdrawal symptoms is said to keep people hooked on addictive substances. Refraining from smoking is cited as one such aversive nemesis. Such psychopathology theorizing has grave explanatory problems. There is the theoretical embarrassment of 40 million people with a history of nicotine dependence who have quit smoking on their own without any professional help! This massive rate of success has created a lot of aversiveness for the tobacco industry. The task for Kirsch to explain is not the allegedly self-fulfilling nature of aversive response expectancies but why 40 million puffers were not deterred from quitting their nicotine fixes by response expectancies of aversive withdrawal symptoms. It is better to have a theory that can explain adaptational successes as well as dysfunctions and that provides explicit strategies on how to promote success.

To return to our smokers, they see little point to even trying if they believe they do not have what it takes to quit the habit. If they make an attempt they give up easily in the absence of quick results or setbacks. Those who have a high sense of efficacy accept temporary aversiveness as part of the price of mastering a habit that is injurious to their health. Longitudinal studies of heavy smokers who have tried to stop smoking on their own confirm that successful quitters had a stronger sense of self-regulatory efficacy at the outset than the relapsers and continuous smokers (Carey & Carey, 1993). Those who believe they can mount the effort needed to override their discomfort and cravings break their smoking habit. Neither demographic factors, length of smoking history, number of past attempts to break the smoking habit, length of prior abstinence, nor degree of physical dependence on nicotine differentiate relapsers from abstainers, whereas perceived self-regulatory efficacy does (Barrios, 1985; Haaga, 1989; Killen, Maccoby, & Taylor, 1984; Yates & Thain, 1985). Godding and Glasgow (1985) compared the relative predictiveness of perceived self-efficacy and outcome expectations encompassing a wide array of positive and negative outcomes representing Kirsch's "stimulus expectancies" and "response expectancies." Perceived self-efficacy was a strong predictor of smoking behavior. Outcome expectancies did not correlate significantly with any aspect of smoking behavior.

The same is true for the aversive condition of alcoholism. Efficacy beliefs predict maintenance of sobriety, outcome expectations do not (Solomon & Annis, 1990). Such studies provide further testimony that if people believe they can succeed in mastering dependence on addictive substance they are willing to put up with a lot of misery. These findings on addictive behavior and agoraphobic dysfunctions to be reviewed next, lend little support for Kirsch's preoccupation with expected aversiveness as the prime ruler of human behavior. When outcome expectations emerge as independent predictors, they contribute much less to variance in drinking behavior than do efficacy beliefs (Young, Oei, & Crook, 1991). The same relative predictiveness of efficacy beliefs and expectations of aversive outcomes is corroborated in activities that contribute to acute and chronic clinical pain (Lackner, Carosella, & Feuerstein, in press; Williams & Kinney, 1991). Expectations of pain intensity and catastrophizing harm are largely products of perceived efficacy and, therefore, do not contribute independently to prediction of pain-inducing behavior when the influence of efficacy beliefs is factored out.

In his comments on Ewart's research on the role of perceived self-efficacy in postcoronary functioning, Kirsch disembodies presumed consequences from the efficacy beliefs that spawn them. Patients who believe they have robust cardiac capabilities judge themselves efficacious to resume a physically active lifestyle and thereby strengthen their cardiovascular functioning (Taylor, Bandura, Ewart, Miller, & DeBusk, 1985). In contrast, those who believe their cardiac capabilities have been seriously impaired judge themselves incapable of strenuous activity and can easily scare themselves by their perceived vulnerability.

At an earlier time, Kirsch (1982) rechristened efficacy beliefs as anticipated fear and argued that it was anticipated fear not people's beliefs in their efficacy that regulates phobic and avoidant behavior. Over the years numerous studies using diverse methodologies tested whether fear, either anticipated or experienced, regulates avoidant behavior. The results are remarkably consistent in showing that fear or anxiety does not control avoidant or phobic behavior (Bandura, 1986; Bolles, 1975; Leitenberg, Agras, Butz, & Wincze, 1971; Orenstein & Carr, 1975; Rescorla & Solomon, 1967; Schroeder & Rich, 1976).

The interesting question is why the belief that anticipatory anxiety controls avoidant behavior has remained so firmly entrenched in clinical thinking despite evidence to the contrary from severe phobic dysfunctions that the anxiety control theory is designed to explain. A good place to look for the answer is in the force of confirmatory biases in judgments of causality (Nisbett & Ross, 1980). Confirming instances, in which anxiety and avoidance occur jointly, remain highly salient in people's minds, whereas nonconfirming instances, in which anxiety and approach behavior occur together, or avoidance occurs without anxiety is less memorable. It is not that the nonconfirming instances are any less prevalent. Quite the contrary. People regularly perform activities despite high anxiety. Thus, for example, actors strut on stage even though intensely anxious while waiting to go on, athletes engage in competitive athletic activities despite a high level of precompetition anxiety, and students take intimidating examinations although beset by aversive anticipatory anxiety. Similarly, people regularly take self-protective action without having to wait for anticipatory anxiety to impel them to action. They strap on seat belts to prevent injury, disinfect things to protect against infections, and disconnect electrical appliances before repairing them without having to conjure up anticipatory images of self-execution or an anxious state before they can take action. These different types of disconfirming occurrences tend to be ignored in judging the relation between anxiety and avoidance.

Williams (1992) has analyzed numerous data sets from studies in which perceived self-efficacy, anticipated anxiety and phobic behavior were measured. Perceived self-efficacy accounts for variation in phobic behavior when anticipated anxiety is partialed out, whereas the relationship between anticipated anxiety and phobic behavior essentially disappears when the influence of perceived self-efficacy is controlled. In short, people will pursue meaningful but aversive activities they believe they can master regardless of how much distress they will have to endure in the process.

Popular explanations for why agoraphobics constrict their lives is that they fear they will become anxious, overcome by a panic attack, or catastrophic consequences will befall them. The findings show that neither anticipated anxiety, anticipated panic, nor perceived danger predict agoraphobic behavior after controlling for the influence of efficacy beliefs. In contrast, efficacy beliefs are highly predictive of agoraphobic behavior when variations in anticipated panic, anticipated anxiety, and perceived danger are controlled (Williams, Kinney, & Falbo, 1989). Researchers who are correlating anxiety with phobic behavior without including perceived self-efficacy in the causal analysis are providing not only incomplete but misleading accounts of phobic dysfunction. Given the substantial body of consistent evidence for the predictive power of efficacy beliefs, they should be regularly included in tests of causal models of phobic dysfunctions and their treatment. Studies of other threatening activities similarly demonstrate that perceived self-efficacy accounts for variation in performance, whereas level of anxiety has little or no effect (McAuley, 1985; Meece, Wigfield, & Eccles, 1990; Ozer & Bandura, 1990; Pajares & Miller, 1994; Siegel, Galassi, & Ware, 1985). Kirsch continues to portray anticipatory anxiety (i.e., response expectancy) as a major determinant of avoidant action but, surprisingly, makes no mention of this large body of disconfirming evidence.

Perceived self-efficacy plays an influential role in the regulation of affective states. It does so through beliefs concerning personal control of *action, thought,* and *affect*. Let us consider first the action-oriented approach. Beliefs that one can exercise behavioral control influence how potential threats are perceived and cognitively processed. If people believe they can manage threats they do not conjure up calamities and frighten themselves. But if they believe they cannot control potential threats they dwell on their coping deficiencies, view many aspects of their environment as fraught with danger and experience high anxiety. Through inefficacious thinking they distress themselves and constrain and impair their functioning. In experiments in which people are given a behavioral means for controlling painful stimuli but do not use it, simply the self-knowledge that one can exercise control should one choose to do so reduces anxiety arousal (Geer, Davison, & Gatchel, 1970; Glass, Singer, Leonard, Krantz, & Cummings, 1973).

The power of belief in behavior control to transform, cognitively, threatening situations into safe ones and thereby ameliorate anxiety is graphically illustrated in a study of agoraphobics by Sanderson, Rapee and Barlow (1989). Inhaling carbon dioxide usually provokes panic attacks in agoraphobics. Agoraphobics received the same amount of carbon dioxide but under different beliefs of control. One group could do nothing to control the amount of carbon dioxide they received. A second group was led to believe they could regulate the amount of carbon dioxide they received by turning a dial. In fact, the dial had no effect on the flow of carbon dioxide. Agoraphobics who believed they were exercising behavioral control showed no rise in anxiety and rarely experienced panic attacks or catastrophic thoughts (Figure 2). In contrast, those who knew they could not exercise any control experienced mounting anxiety. They had a high rate of panic attacks and catastrophic thoughts about dying, going crazy and losing control.

The impact of perceived behavioral control on anxiety arousal does not operate solely through its effects on attentional and construal processes. Efficacy beliefs alter anxiety also by supporting efficacious courses of action that actually change threatening environments into safer ones (Bandura, in press). The transformation of environments reflects a proactive rather than simply a reactive mode of adaptation.

The thought-oriented approach to the regulation of affective states centers on perceived cognitive capabilities to control perturbing, intrusive trains of thought. Efficacy in thought control is measured by the ease with which disturbing cognitions can be dismissed from consciousness or reconstrued in ways that make them less distressful. The ability to exercise control over one's thoughts has been shown to be an important factor in the regulation of cognitively-generated emotional states. It is not the sheer frequency of disturbing cognitions but the perceived inability to turn them off that is the major source of distress. Aversive cognitions are unrelated to anxiety when the influence of perceived thought control efficacy is controlled, whereas thought control efficacy is strongly related to anxiety arousal when frequency of aversive cognitions is controlled (Kent & Gibbons, 1987).

Anxiety and phobic behavior are controlled by both coping efficacy and thought control efficacy. This is shown in a study designed to help women to deal with the pervasive social threat of sexual violence (Ozer & Bandura, 1990). The lives of many women are distressed and constricted by a low sense of efficacy to cope with the threat of sexual assault. To increase their self-protective efficacy, women participated in a mastery modeling program. They were taught how to defend themselves against unarmed assailants by disabling them with a powerful strike to vital areas of the body. They mastered the self-defense skills in repeated simulated assaults by assailants wearing heavily padded gear. The women practiced

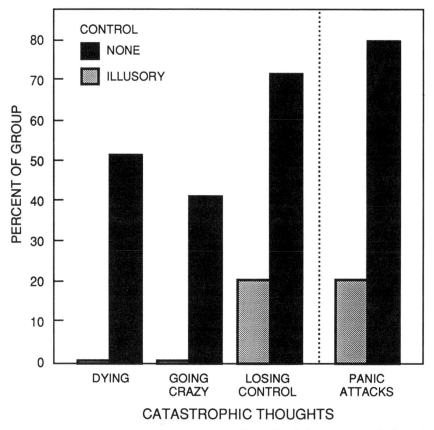

CATASTROPHIC THOUGHTS

FIGURE 2. Rate of panic attacks, catastrophic thoughts and level of anxiety arousal exhibited by agoraphobics under illusory control or no control over threatening physical events (Sanderson, Rapee, & Barlow, 1989).

how to disable their assailants when ambushed frontally, from the back and when pinned down in the dark.

Mastery modeling raised their perceived behavioral efficacy to protect themselves and to control distressing intrusive thoughts. As a result, they suffered less anxiety and lived freer and more active lives. Figure 3 presents the path analysis of the causal structure. Perceived self-efficacy influences behavior through two pathways. In one path of influence, perceived behavioral efficacy reduces perceived vulnerability and increases ability to distinguish between safe and risky situations. These changes reduce avoidant behavior and increase participant behavior. In the second path of influence, cognitive control efficacy reduces ruminative

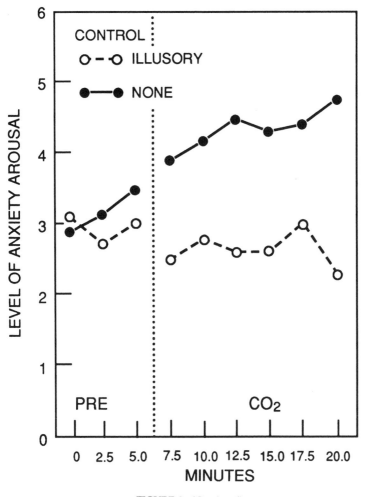

FIGURE 2. (*Continued*)

aversive thoughts, anxiety arousal and avoidant behavior. A strong sense of behavioral efficacy that one can exercise control over social threats makes it easier to dismiss frightening thoughts that intrude on one's consciousness.

Anxiety management through efficacy beliefs in one's behavioral capabilities and thought control serve mainly to prevent stressful activation. The affect-oriented approach is concerned with perceived efficacy to ameliorate stress and anxiety once it is aroused. This is achieved by

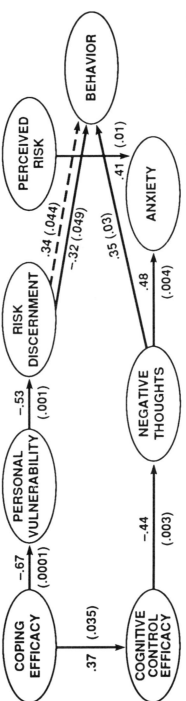

FIGURE 3. Path analysis of the causal structure of coping behavior regarding interpersonal threats. The numbers on the paths of influence are the significant standardized path coefficients; the numbers in parentheses are the significance levels. The solid line to behavior represents avoidant behavior, the hatch line represents participant behavior (Ozer & Bandura, 1990).

positive reappraisal of stressors, relaxation, calming self-talk, shifting attention from stressors to soothers and seeking social support. Arch (1992a,b) has given special attention to perceived self-efficacy to regulate affective states in aversive situations. She examined the independent contribution of different forms of perceived efficacy to willingness to present a talk to a large unfamiliar audience and to field questions. Each of the three facets of perceived self-efficacy—action efficacy to fulfill stressful performance demands, thought control efficacy to rid oneself of apprehensive thoughts, and affect regulation efficacy to alleviate emotional distress accompanying performance—predicts anxious expectations and willingness to undertake the activity. Perceived behavioral efficacy and affective control efficacy predict willingness to subject oneself to stressful speechmaking, whereas anxious expectations do not when variations in self-efficacy are controlled.

The initial investigations into the contribution of efficacy beliefs to anxiety centered solely on behavioral control efficacy. Subsequent research verified that thought control efficacy further improves prediction of anxiety arousal (Ozer & Bandura, 1990). Extension of self-efficacy theory to the regulation of affective states demonstrated that affective control efficacy accounts for additional variance in anxiety. Thus, the results taken as a whole reveal that the more facets of self-efficacy that are considered the stronger the prediction of anxiety arousal.

According to Kirsch, expected anxiety creates anxiety. In the studies offered in support of this view, phobics are asked if they expect to be anxious and are then asked how anxious they are as they perform the task. This methodology comes dangerously close to a reliability check. Will you be anxious? Are you anxious? To ask essentially the same question on two occasions with the identical self-report method includes a high degree of common method bias that can produce artifactually inflated relationships. Williams (1995) raises questions about how anxiety expectancy breeds anxiety. Kirsch responds to Williams' query by providing examples (i.e., *"expected mirth produces experienced mirth"*) rather than specifying the governing mechanism. Oh, that it were that simple. If people could make themselves joyous simply by "mirthful expectation" the populous would be deliriously happy. The merchants of Prozac would find themselves most unmirthful. In point of fact, mirthful expectation is dashed by unmirthful reality so often that people adopt superstitious protective rituals. They superstitiously scale down mirthful expectations as if this cognitive maneuver will forestall disappointing happenings.

Explanation by description is hardly satisfying, especially considering that in most situations involving elements of threat performers typically experience high expected anxiety but are surprised by their lower level of anxiousness as they perform the activity. Indeed, it is so common that it has become a dictum that the anticipation is worse than the actuality. Telch and Rachman (1994) devote an entire issue of a journal to research demonstrating that, regardless of whether the participants are agoraphobics, claustrophobics, snake phobics, panic patients or social phobics, their anticipated fear commonly exceeds the fear they experience in actuality. Thus, the anxiety expectancy notion explains more than is observed. Given the typically diminished carryover from anticipation to actuality, the explanatory problem for Kirsch is why expected anxiety often fails to "*drive the experience of anxiety*" to the level his scheme would lead one to expect. To advance understanding of the determinants of anxiety arousal, investigators would do well to adopt a conceptual scheme that offers a more substantial theoretical gruel.

Kirsch (1982) conducted a study of pretend performances to distinguish between belief of personal efficacy and willingness or intention rooted in expected discomfort. Students who said they feared snakes were offered escalating imaginary incentives to hold a snake and to toss a wad of paper into a wastepaper basket at varying distances. These tasks were selected on the grounds that paper throwing involves skill but, since ambulatory and grasping responses already reside in the behavioral repertoire, snake handling involves only intention. More snake handlers persuaded themselves they could handle a snake as the imaginary incentives were raised to a million dollars, saving another's life, or sparing one's own life. Many of the paper tossers also persuaded themselves that they could marshall sufficient dexterity to hit a wastepaper basket for a cool million or to save their lives, but fewer of them believed they could do it at 50 feet (24%) than at a shorter distance (46%). Since snake handlers were somewhat more persuadable than paper tossers that they could fulfill the pretend performance demands, Kirsch concluded that reptilian venturesome reflects intention.

Holding aside for the time being the value of data about imaginary attainments for issues clarified by data of actual attainments, task comparisons are a tricky business. The tasks must be equated on all dimensions except the one to which the attribution will be made. Adopting Kirsch's ectomized view of ability, both tossing responses and handling responses are firmly ensconced in subjects' behavioral repertoires. To continue with Kirsch's line of reasoning, since everyone knows how to toss a wad of paper, it involves no skill variation. The ease with which performance demands can be fulfilled by tossing responses and handling responses depends, of course, on the stringency of the accuracy requirements. Kirsch fails to recognize that he has performed a confounded make-believe study in which the aversiveness of the activity is confounded with differential accuracy demands. To spare their lives his undergraduates had to hit a distant tiny target, whereas they could secure their survival simply by handling a snake, however awkwardly or poorly they did it. The beauty of the make-believe methodology is that it can be easily calibrated to produce any result one desires. For example, by enlarging the target area for paper tossing and adding a tough accuracy requirement for snake handling (i.e., hold the struggling beast for a lengthy period without it moving in the slightest) one could demonstrate that undergraduates are more easily persuaded they can fulfill performance demands for paper tossing than for reptile handling.

The preceding comments are not meant to encourage the start up of a cottage industry of make-believe experimentation. That efficacy belief and intention represent different factors has been established conceptually and verified empirically in rigorous studies of people struggling to exercise some control over their well-being without requiring trivial pretend studies. The empirical evidence bearing on this issue was cited earlier.

It should be noted in passing that the rationale guiding the above study rests on the erroneous premise that perceived capability is a fixed entity in a behavioral repertoire and, therefore, should not be changeable by social influence. According to this line of reasoning, the offer of money should not alter the ambulatory and grasping responses ensconced in the repertoire. Hence, the reasoning goes, if one can strengthen people's beliefs in their efficacy by the prospect of escalated benefits, such evidence challenges the status of self-efficacy measures in phobic domains of functioning. In point of fact, personal efficacy is a changeable belief system not an immutable entity firmly moored to a fixed faculty of the organism. People alter judgments of their efficacy on the basis of direct mastery experiences; social comparison with the performances of others; inferences from bodily states; and varied forms of social persuasion, including bogus normative comparisons, arbitrary evaluative feedback and monetary lures (Bandura, 1986). This discussion has descended to the trivial level of paper wads not because they have much to do with self-efficacy theory, but because Kirsch cites these studies as providing evidence that judgments of efficacy on aversive tasks reflect intention rather than perceived capability.

Inspired by Kirsch's ectomized view of ability, Corcoran and Rutledge (1989) extended the make-believe methodology to show that college smokers were more persuadable by hefty imaginary payments that they could quit smoking than shoot a basketball through a hoop at a hopelessly distant location. The authors concluded that efficacy probes assess skill in basketball and only will in control of nicotine dependence. The claim that management of substance abuse is a matter of will rather than skill will come as a great surprise to therapists and substance abusers alike. To achieve success with addictive disorders substance abusers have to devote laborious hours to mastering self-management skills that enable them to exercise control over addictive substances, prevent relapses and regain control after setbacks and to create life satisfactions that compete with substance abuse (Annis & Davis, 1989; Gossop, Green, Phillips, & Bradly, 1990; Marlatt & Gordon, 1980; Miller & Baca, 1983). I have commented elsewhere (Bandura, 1991), on Corcoran's irredeemingly simplistic view that skill training does not teach anything new but only increases the frequency of responses. Pity those indefatigable violinists, pianists, neurosurgeons, tennis players, managers, professors and their graduate students who learned nothing new from their extended labors, beyond boosting their response rates.

The make-believe undertaking by Corcoran and Rutledge merely demonstrates that it is tough to raise beliefs of personal efficacy by social persuasion alone when performance demands are set at an incredibly high level. Both shooting basketballs through hoops and self-management of addictive substances involve skills, but the latter relies on self-regulatory skills, the former on motor skills. It is not as though simply deciding to cease addictive behavior promptly eliminates it without the individual repeatedly mobilizing self-regulative efforts and strategies to bring it about and to continue to override instigations to resume use of the substance. Success in difficult endeavors is not the product of a will but the result of concerted self-regulative influence.

Kirsch mistakenly believes he scores points in asserting that there is no exercise of personal efficacy in getting oneself to eat a worm. There most certainly is! People will neither attempt this gustatory feat nor pull it off successfully unless they believe they have the efficacy to override any feelings of revulsion. In acting on their efficacy belief they have to muster whatever motivational and cognitive strategies they have at their disposal that help them to succeed. This may require enlisting energizing self incentives, transforming cognitively the creepy crawler into something more relishable, or resorting to a dissociative cognitive strategy in which wormy thoughts are supplanted by competing positive thoughts that keep the creepy crawler out of consciousness as it is being ground down. Kirsch acknowledges that perceived self-efficacy to manage aversiveness fosters performance but, surprisingly, is unaware that this same self-regulatory capability applies equally to the consumption of the sacrificial worm in the interest of scientific advancement. In this wormy example, Kirsch reveals both his exceedingly narrow view of efficacious agency and his contradictoriness on issues of personal efficacy.

The items in self-efficacy scales carefully avoid technical jargon, which only creates needless ambiguities. For example, in measuring the perceived efficacy of snake phobics to cope with snakes they judge the strength of their belief that they can catch a snake that is loose in the room and hold it for a designated period. To do so, they have to chase a shifty reptile as it slithers away, catch it in a way that enables them to exercise full control over it as it struggles to escape and continue to hold it while it flails about. It calls for a lot of versatile coping to fulfill these performance demands. Coping is conventionally defined as managing problem situations. However, because the items neither use the technical term "coping," nor focus on anxiety reduction, Kirsch is displeased with the use of the term coping self-efficacy.

Kirsch uses this same line of reasoning to rechristen the efficacy scales used by Williams to measure the perceived efficacy of agoraphobics to deal with performance demands in different domains of functioning. These include navigating automobiles through progressively more taxing traffic and road conditions, climbing to greater heights, shopping in increasingly crowded settings and the like. Kirsch questions the appropriateness of Williams' use of the term coping self-efficacy and suggests that it be renamed task self-efficacy. The recommended relabeling is based on a psychopathology view of coping that is narrowly limited to managing aversive experiences during adaptation. There is much more to coping than ministering aversiveness. It includes decision making, enlisting self motivators and other supportive resources, selecting and testing strategies, restructuring environments and many other regulatory skills. It is for individuals to decide whether they can manage given environmental demands with whatever resources they believe they have at their command without assessors prescribing in the test items particular strategies for each adaptational attainment.

The present postscript addressed a number of misconceptions of self-efficacy theory in Kirsch's commentary. But one can point to some encouraging changes in his views over time. Self-efficacy is no longer being misconstrued as anxiety or as influencing avoidant behavior only indirectly through anxiety. Perceived self-regulatory efficacy, which affects self-motivation, thinking processes, affective well-being and attainments, is now recognized as an influential contributor to the quality of human functioning, albeit still narrowly confined to the self-management of aversiveness. The empirical evidence that perceived self-efficacy is not willingness or intention, whether the activities involve potentially aversive elements or not, has yet to be acknowledged. It is time to jettison the trifling conception of human efficacy as isolated motor acts detached from agentive adaptational events. This ecumenical route will save a lot of printer's ink and stately trees.

REFERENCES

Ajzen, I. (1985). From intentions to actions: A theory of planned behavior. In J. Kuhl & J. Beckman (Eds.), *Action-control: From cognition to behavior* (pp. 11–39). Heidelberg: Springer.

Ajzen, I., & Fishbein, M. (1980). *Understanding attitudes and predicting social behavior*. Engle-wood Cliffs, NJ: Prentice-Hall.

Ajzen, I., & Madden, T. J. (1986). Prediction of goal-directed behavior: Attitudes, intentions, and perceived behavioral control. *Journal of Experimental Social Psychology, 22*, 453–474.

Annis, H. M., & Davis, C. S. (1989). Relapse prevention. In R. K. Hester & W. R. Miller (Eds.), *Handbook of alcoholism treatment approaches* (pp. 170–182). New York: Pergamon Press.

Arch, E. C. (1992a). Affective control efficacy as a factor in willingness to participate in a public performance situation. *Psychological reports, 71*, 1247–1250.

Arch, E. C. (1992b). Sex differences in the effect of self-efficacy on willingness to participate in a performance situation. *Psychological Reports, 70*, 3–9.

Bandura, A. (1982). Self-efficacy mechanism in human agency. *American Psychologist, 37*, 122–147.

Bandura, A. (1986). *Social foundations of thought and action: A social cognitive theory*. Englewood Cliffs, NJ: Prentice-Hall.

Bandura, A. (1988). Perceived self-efficacy: Exercise of control through self-belief. In J. P. Dauwalder, M. Perrez, & V. Hobi (Eds.), *Annual series of European research in behavior therapy* (Vol. 2, pp. 27–59). Lisse (NL): Swets & Zeitlinger.

Bandura, A. (1990). Reflections on nonability determinants of competence. In R. J. Sternberg & J. Kolligian, Jr. (Eds.), *Competence considered* (pp. 315–362). New Haven, CT: Yale University Press.

Bandura, A. (1991). Human agency: The rhetoric and the reality. *American Psychologist, 46*, 157–162.

Bandura, A. (1992). Exercise of personal agency through the self-efficacy mechanism. In R. Schwarzer (Ed.), *Self-efficacy: Thought control of action* (pp. 3–38). Washington, D.C.: Hemisphere.

Bandura, A. (1993). Social cognitive theory and exercise of control over HIV infection. In R. J. DiClemente & J. L. Peterson (Eds.), *Preventing AIDS: Theories and methods of behavioral interventions* (pp. 25–59). New York: Plenum.

Bandura, A. (in press). *Self-efficacy: The exercise of control*. New York: Freeman.

Barrios, F. X. (1985). A comparison of global and specific estimates of self-control. *Cognitive Therapy and Research, 9*, 455–469.

Becker, M. H. (Ed.) (1974). The health belief model and personal health behavior. *Health Education Monographs, 2*, 324–473.

Becker, M. H. (1990). Theoretical models of adherence and strategies for improving adher-ence. In S. A. Schumaker, E. B. Schron, & J. K. Ockene (Eds.), *The handbook of health behavior change* (pp. 5–43). New York: Springer.

Bolles, R. C. (1975). *Learning theory*. New York: Holt, Rinehart, & Winston.

Carey, K. B., & Carey, M. P. (1993). Changes in self-efficacy resulting from unaided attempts to quit smoking. *Psychology of Addictive Behaviors, 7*, 219– 224.

Corcoran, K. J., & Rutledge, M. W. (1989). Efficacy expectation changes as a function of hypothetical incentives in smokers. *Psychology of Addictive Behaviors, 3*, 22–29.

deVries, H., & Backbier, M. P. H. (1994). Self-efficacy as an important determinant of quitting among pregnant women who smoke: The ∅-pattern. *Preventive Medicine, 23*, 167–174.

deVries, H., Dijkstra, M., & Kuhlman, P. (1988). Self-efficacy: The third factor besides attitude and subjective norm as a predictor of behavioral intentions. *Health Education Research, 3*, 273–282.

DiClemente, C. C., Fairhurst, S. K., & Piotrowski, N. A. (1995). The role of self-efficacy in addictive behaviors. In J. E. Maddux (Ed.), *Self-efficacy, adaptation and adjustment: Theory, research and application*. New York: Plenum.

Dzewaltowski, D. A. (1989). Towards a model of exercise motivation. *Journal of Sport and Exercise Psychology, 11*, 251–269.

Dzewaltowski, D. A., Noble, J. M., & Shaw, J. M. (1990). Physical activity participation: Social cognitive theory versus the theories of reasoned action and planned behavior. *Journal of Sport and Exercise Psychology, 12,* 388–405.

Geer, J. H., Davidson, G. C., & Gatchel, R. I. (1970). Reduction of stress in humans through nonveridical perceived control of aversive stimulation. *Journal of Personality and Social Psychology, 16,* 731–738.

Glass, D. C., Singer, J. E., Leonard, H. S., Krantz, D., & Cummings, H. (1973). Perceived control of aversive stimulation and the reduction of stress responses. *Journal of Personality, 41,* 577–595.

Godding, P. R., & Glasgow, R. E. (1985). Self-efficacy and outcome expectations as predictors of controlled smoking status. *Cognitive Therapy and Research, 9,* 583–590.

Gossop, M., Green, L., Phillips, G., & Bradley, B. (1990). Factors predicting outcome among opiate addicts after treatment. *British Journal of Clinical Psychology, 29,* 209–216.

Haaga, D. A. F. (1989). Articulated thoughts and endorsement procedures for cognitive assessment in the prediction of smoking relapse. *Psychological Assessment, 1,* 112–117.

Jemmott, L. S., & Jemmott, J. B., III (1992). Increasing condom-use intentions among sexually active black adolescent women. *Nursing Research, 41,* 273–278.

Jemmott, J. B., III, Jemmott, L. S., & Fong, G. T. (1992). Reductions in HIV risk-associated sexual behaviors among black male adolescents: Effects of an AIDS prevention intervention. *American Journal of Public Health, 82,* 372–377.

Jemmott, J. B., III, Jemmott, L. S., Spears, H., Hewitt, N., & Cruz-Collins, M. (1991). Self-efficacy, hedonistic expectancies, and condom-use intentions among inner-city black adolescent women: A social cognitive approach to AIDS risk behavior. *Journal of Adolescent Health, 13,* 512–519.

Kent, G., & Gibbons, R. (1987). Self-efficacy and the control of anxious cognitions. *Journal of Behavior Therapy and Experimental Psychiatry, 18,* 33–40.

Killen, J. D., Maccoby, N., & Taylor, C. B. (1984). Nicotine gum and self-regulation training in smoking relapse prevention. *Behavior Therapy, 15,* 234–248.

Kirsch, I. (1982). Efficacy expectations as response predictors: The meaning of efficacy ratings as a function of task characteristics. *Journal of Personality and Social Psychology, 42,* 132–136.

Kok, G., deVries, H., Mudde, A. N., & Strecher, V. J. (1991). Planned health education and the role of self-efficacy: Dutch research. *Health Education Research, 6,* 231–238.

Lackner, J. M., Carosella, A. M., & Feuerstein, M. (in press). Pain expectancies, pain, and functional self-efficacy expectancies as determinants of disability in chronic low back patients. *Journal of Consulting and Counseling Psychology.*

Leitenberg, H., Agras, W. S., Butz, R., & Wincze, J. (1971). Relationship between heart rate and behavioral change during treatment of phobias. *Journal of Abnormal Psychology, 78,* 59–68.

Maddux, J. E., Rogers, R. W. (1983). Protection motivation and self-efficacy: A revised theory of fear appeals and attitude change. *Journal of Experimental Social Psychology, 19,* 469–479.

Marlatt, G. A., Baer, J. S., & Quigley, L. A. (1995). Self-efficacy and addictive behavior. In A. Bandura (Ed.), *Self-efficacy in changing societies* (pp. 288–314). New York: Cambridge University Press.

Marlatt, G. A., & Gordon, J. R. (1980). Determinants of relapse: Implications for the maintenance of behavior change. In P. O. Davidson & S. M. Davidson (Eds.), *Behavioral medicine: Changing health lifestyles* (pp. 410–452). New York: Brunner/Mazel.

McAuley, E. (1985). Modeling and self-efficacy: A test of Bandura's model. *Journal of Sport Psychology, 7,* 283–295.

Meece, J. L., Wigfield, A., & Eccles, J. S. (1990). Predators of math anxiety and its influence on young adolescents' course enrollment intentions and performance in mathematics. *Journal of Educational Psychology, 82,* 60–70.

Miller, W. R., & Baca, L. M. (1983). Two-year follow-up of bibliotherapy and therapist-directed controlled drinking training for problem drinkers. *Behavior Therapy, 14,* 441–448.

Nisbett, R., & Ross, L. (1980). *Human inference: Strategies and shortcomings of social judgment.* Englewood Cliffs, NJ: Prentice-Hall.

Ogbu, J. U. (1990). Cultural model, identity, and literacy. In J. W. Stigler, R. A. Shweder, & G. H. Herdt (Eds.), *Cultural psychology: Essays on comparative human development* (pp. 520–541). Cambridge, England: Cambridge University Press.

Orenstein, H., & Carr, J. (1975). Implosion therapy by tape-recording. *Behaviour Research and Therapy, 13,* 177–182.

Ozer, E. M., & Bandura, A. (1990). Mechanisms governing empowerment effects: A self-efficacy analysis. *Journal of Personality and Social Psychology, 58,* 472–486.

Pajares, F., & Miller, M. D. (1994). Role of self-efficacy and self-concept beliefs in mathematical problem solving: A path analysis. *Journal of Educational Psychology, 86,* 193–203.

Rescorla, R. A., & Solomon, R. L. (1967). Two-process learning theory: Relationships between Pavlovian conditioning and instrumental learning. *Psychological Review, 74,* 141–182.

Rogers, R. W. (1983). Cognitive and physiological processes in fear appeals and attitude change: A revised theory of protection motivation. In J. T. Cacioppo & R. E. Petty (Eds.), *Social Psychophysiology* (pp. 153–176). New York: Guilford.

Rosenstock, I. M. (1974). The health belief model and preventive health behavior. *Health Education Monographs, 2,* 354–386.

Sanderson, W. C., Rapee, R. M., & Barlow, D. H. (1989). The influence of an illusion of control on panic attacks induced via inhalation of 5.5% carbon dioxide-enriched air. *Archives of General Psychiatry, 46,* 157–162.

Schroeder, H. E., & Rich, A. R. (1976). The process of fear reduction through systematic desensitization. *Journal of Consulting and Clinical Psychology, 44,* 191–199.

Schwarzer, R. (1992). Self-efficacy in the adoption and maintenance of health behaviors: Theoretical approaches and a new model. In R. Schwarzer (Ed.), *Self-efficacy: Thought control of action* (pp. 217–243). Washington, D.C.: Hemisphere.

Schwarzer, R., & Fuchs, R. (1995). Self-efficacy and health. In A. Bandura (Ed.), *Self-efficacy in changing societies* (pp. 259–288). New York: Cambridge University Press.

Siegel, R. G., Galassi, J. P., & Ware, W. B. (1985). A comparison of two models for predicting mathematics performance: Social learning versus math aptitude-anxiety. *Journal of Counseling Psychology, 32,* 531–538.

Solomon, K. E., & Annis, H. M. (1990). Outcome and efficacy expectancy in the prediction of post-treatment drinking behaviour. *British Journal of Addiction, 85,* 659–666.

Solomon, R. P. (1992). *Black resistance in high school.* Albany, NY: State University of New York Press.

Sternberg, R. J., & Kolligian, J., Jr. (Eds.) (1990). *Competence considered.* New Haven, CT: Yale University Press.

Taylor, C. B., Bandura, A., Ewart, C. K., Miller, N. H., & DeBusk, R. F. (1985). Exercise testing to enhance wives' confidence in their husbands' cardiac capabilities soon after clinically uncomplicated acute myocardial infarction. *American Journal of Cardiology, 55,* 635–638.

Telch, M. J., & Rachman, S. (1994). The overprediction of fear. *Behaviour Research and Therapy, 32* (Whole No. 7).

Williams, S. L. (1992). Perceived self-efficacy and phobic disability. In R. Schwarzer (Ed.), *Self-efficacy: Thought control of action* (pp. 149–176). Washington, D.C.: Hemisphere.

Williams, S. L. (1995). Self-efficacy and anxiety and phobic disorders. In J. E. Maddux (Ed.), *Self-efficacy, adaptation and adjustment: Theory, research and application.* New York: Plenum.

Williams, S. L., & Kinney, P. J. (1991). Performance and nonperformance strategies for coping with acute pain: The role of perceived self-efficacy, expected outcomes, and attention. *Cognitive Therapy and Research, 15,* 1–19.

Williams, S. L., Kinney, P. J., & Falbo, J. (1989). Generalization of therapeutic changes in agoraphobia: The role of perceived self-efficacy. *Journal of Consulting and Clinical Psychology, 57,* 436–442.

Wood, R., & Bandura, A. (1989). Social cognitive theory of organizational management. *Academy of Management Review, 14,* 361–384.

Yates, A. J., & Thain, J. (1985). Self-efficacy as a predictor of relapse following voluntary cessation of smoking. *Addictive Behaviors, 10,* 291–298.

Young, R. McD., Oei, T. P. S., & Crook, G. M. (1991). Development of a drinking self-efficacy questionnaire. *Journal of Psychopathology and Behavioral Assessment, 13,* 1–15.

Zimmerman, B. J., & Bandura, A. (1994). Role of self-regulatory factors in the development of writing literacy. *American Educational Research Journal, 31,* 845–862.

Zimmerman, B. J., Bandura, A., & Martinez-Pons, M. (1992). Self-motivation for academic attainment: The role of self-efficacy beliefs and personal goal-setting. *American Educational Research Journal, 29,* 663–676.

CHAPTER 14

LOOKING FOR COMMON GROUND
A COMMENT ON KIRSCH AND BANDURA

JAMES E. MADDUX

To close this volume, I decided to use my "editor's prerogative" of getting in the last word by making a few remarks on the commentaries by Kirsch and Bandura. Because of space limitations, I will restrict my comments to four issues. Two are issues on which Kirsch and Bandura seem to disagree but on which common ground seems greater than at first glance. The first of these is Kirsch's distinction between two uses of the term "outcome expectancies"—means–end beliefs and personal outcome expectancies. The second concerns Kirsch's distinction between task–self efficacy and coping self-efficacy and the nonutility of assessing self-efficacy as the belief in one's ability to perform simple motor acts. As often happens in these kinds of exchanges, Kirsch and Bandura are in greater agreement on these issues than it would appear from reading their comments. The difficulty is a reflection of the complexity of what may seem to be simple conceptual issues. Two additional issues that I will address briefly are Kirsch's claims about response expectancies and Bandura's concept of

JAMES E. MADDUX • Department of Psychology, George Mason University, Fairfax, Virginia 22030.

Self-Efficacy, Adaptation, and Adjustment: Theory, Research, and Application, edited by James E. Maddux. Plenum Press, New York, 1995.

attainment markers and outcomes. Although I find myself in disagreement with each on various points, I am nonetheless very grateful to them
for taking the time to contribute their comments.

TYPES OF OUTCOME EXPECTANCY

Kirsch contends that research and theory on expectancies have employed two different constructs that have been called "outcome expectancies." According to Kirsch, some studies have assessed perceptions of the
conditional relation between an action and its outcome and called this an
outcome expectancy. Other studies have assessed the belief that one probably will or will not be able to attain a certain outcome—a belief that
includes the belief that a course of action will produce a certain outcome
and the person's belief that he/she can perform the course of action (i.e., a
self-efficacy belief)—and called *that* an outcome expectancy. He suggests
that we should not use the same term to refer to both types of measures.

Kirsch then suggests two terms for these two uses of the term outcome
expectancy. The first is a *means–end belief*, which Kirsch defines as "a
person's subjective probability that a successfully executed behavior will
be followed by a particular outcome" (Kirsch, Chap. 12, this volume). (This
concept and term have been used by other researchers, as noted in Chapter
1 of this volume). The second is a *personal outcome expectancy*, which he
defines as "a subjective probability that the person's *own behavior* would be
followed by a particular outcome" and as "their belief that *their* behavior
in that situation will produce particular outcomes" (Kirsch, this volume,
emphasis author's). He gives as an example of a means-end belief "the
belief that playing basketball exceptionally well brings fame and fortune"
(Kirsch, this volume), and as an example of a personal outcome expectancy "a person's expectancy of achieving fame and fortune by playing
basketball" (Kirsch, this volume). Kirsch also suggests (see his Figure 2)
that a personal outcome expectancy (my belief that I probably can or
cannot attain the outcome) is the result of means–end expectancy (my
belief that the behavior, if successfully executed, probably will or will not
produce the outcome) *and* a self-efficacy belief (my belief that I can perform the behavior at the necessary level of proficiency). For example, I
know that it is possible to make millions playing basketball extraordinarily
well (high means–end expectancy), but because I know I am a lousy
basketball player (low self-efficacy), I know that *I* cannot make millions
from playing basketball (low personal outcome expectancy).

Bandura challenges the viability of this distinction. He contends that
Kirsch's definitions of means–end expectancies and personal outcome

expectancies assume that "expected outcomes for oneself and for others represent different constructs" (Bandura, Chap. 13, this volume). According to Bandura, Kirsch is "confusing expected outcome contingencies with belief about whether one can produce the performances required to gain the outcomes" and does not believe that "the structure of assumed contingency between performance and outcome is the same" at the general level and the personal level (Bandura, this volume).

If one looks only at Kirsch's *definition* of personal outcome expectancy ("a subjective probability that *one's own* behavior would be followed by a particular outcome"), it could indeed be interpreted as Bandura interprets it—as suggesting that the relationship between *my own* behavior and specific outcomes differs from that of *other people* performing the same behavior at the same level of proficiency. The problem with one-sentence definitions of complex constructs is they are open to various interpretations. However, Kirsch's examples and his Figure 2 make it clear that he is *not* proposing that perceived performance–outcome contingencies (means–end expectancies) change when the performer is oneself as opposed to another person. He is proposing, instead, that personal outcome expectancies depend, in part, on perceived performance-outcome contingencies (means–end expectancies), which are beliefs that a particular behavior performed by *anyone* at a certain level of proficiency probably will or will not produce a particular outcome. This definition assumes that an expected performance–outcome contingency (means–end belief) is the same construct whether the performer is oneself or another person.

Bandura asserts that "in activities where outcomes are highly contingent on quality of performance, efficacy beliefs account for most of the variance in expected outcomes" (Bandura, this volume). This statement implies a definition of outcome expectancy that is consistent with Kirsch's definition of personal outcome expectancy but not with the definition of means–end beliefs. Thus, Bandura and Kirsch agree on the relationship between self-efficacy and Kirsch's personal outcome expectancy and Bandura's outcome expectancy. Their disagreement seems to concern the utility of the concept of means–end beliefs.

TYPES OF SELF-EFFICACY

The second issue on which Kirsch and Bandura seem to agree more than disagree is the distinction between task self-efficacy and coping self-efficacy and the non-utility of assessing self-efficacy as the belief that one can perform simple motor acts, that is, task self-efficacy. Kirsch defines *task self-efficacy* as "perceived ability to accomplish the target behavior"

(Kirsch, this volume) and *coping self-efficacy* as "beliefs about one's ability to prevent, control, or cope with potential difficulty" (Kirsch, this volume, adapted from Williams, this volume). This definition of task self-efficacy is very similar to Bandura's original definition of self-efficacy expectancy ("the conviction that one can successfully execute the *behavior* required to produce the outcomes") (Bandura, 1977, p. 193, emphasis added). The definition of coping self-efficacy is very similar to Bandura's more recent definition of self-efficacy as the "belief about whether one can produce the *performances* required to gain the outcomes" (Bandura, this volume, emphasis added), with a "performance" defined not as a behavior but as a "performance attainment" or a "marker of a performance" such as getting the letter grade A or losing weight. (One must "prevent, control, or cope with" a lot of difficulties—anxiety, fatigue, discouragement, social pressures—to get an A or lose weight. Also see discussion at end of this chapter.)

This distinction between task and coping self-efficacy is the basis for Kirsch's distinction between self-efficacy for "using a condom" or "swallowing a pill" and self-efficacy for "taking a test" or "playing a competitive game." He seems to be making the distinction that Bandura (this volume) makes between self-efficacy for performing an isolated, simple motor act (task self-efficacy, which Bandura views as trifling) and self-efficacy for managing various skills during the performance of complex tasks. Bandura interprets Kirsch as advocating asking subjects whether they can put on a condom and suggests that this is Kirsch's conception of self-efficacy for condom use. However, this does not seem to be Kirsch's position. Nor does Kirsch advocate this as the way we should assess "perceived efficacy for management of health-related behavior" (Bandura, this volume). Both Kirsch and Bandura see that sort of question as trifling. To the contrary, Kirsch (this volume) applauds the development of broader measures of self-efficacy (coping self-efficacy) that *explicitly* ask subjects about more than their ability to perform motor tasks (task self-efficacy).

In his examples, however, Kirsch is not as clear as he might have been. For example, Kirsch's phrase "using a condom" can be interpreted as either the simple motor act of "donning a condom" (as Bandura interprets it) or the complex self-regulatory skill of "surmount[ing] the numerous personal impediments to condom use" (Bandura, this volume). The former interpretation leads to assessing task self-efficacy, the latter to coping self-efficacy or self-regulatory efficacy. I think Kirsch means the former when he suggests that assessing self-efficacy for "using a condom" (task self-efficacy) would not be useful. Also, "swallowing a pill" can refer to either the isolated act of swallowing a pill or taking one's medication on a regular basis as prescribed. Again, I think Kirsch means the former when he suggests that assessing self-efficacy for simply "swallowing a pill" would not be useful.

For this reason, it seems that Kirsch and Bandura agree that "donning a condom" and "using condoms regularly during sexual activities" are not the same, and that "swallowing a pill" and "taking your pills regularly as prescribed" are not the same. They also agree that assessing self-efficacy for the isolated act of donning a condom or swallowing a pill (task self-efficacy) would be useless because such measures are not what self-efficacy should be about. I think Kirsch is in agreement with Bandura's statement that self-efficacy scales for condom use should assess "not the isolated act of donning a condom, but perceived self-regulatory efficacy to surmount the numerous interpersonal impediments to condom use" (Bandura, this volume) and that self-efficacy for taking medication should assess "not whether people believe they can swallow a pill, but whether they believe they have the efficacy to get themselves to take their pills as prescribed, whatever forms the dissuading conditions might take" (Bandura, this volume). Both of these latter statements are consistent with Kirsch's and Williams' definition of coping self-efficacy.

Along the same lines, I think Bandura and Kirsch agree that abstinence from smoking consists not of the self-regulation of the simple motor act of lighting a cigarette but of the complex task of managing "social inducements to smoke, negative mood states, interpersonal conflicts and engagement in a host of positive activities in settings [that] keep activating the urge to smoke" (Bandura, this volume). Contrary to what Bandura suggests, Kirsch does not state that "people's beliefs in their efficacy to exercise control over smoking behavior have no bearing on success rates in smoking cessation" (Bandura, this volume). Instead, Kirsch states that "failures . . . to abstain from smoking may be associated with *low self-efficacy for coping* with the aversive consequences of the behavior" (Kirsch, this volume, emphasis added).

By drawing a distinction between task self-efficacy and coping self-efficacy Kirsch *is* suggesting, as Bandura indicates, that "elemental acts" can be detached from "complex adaptations" and that self-efficacy for these elemental acts (task self-efficacy) can be assessed independently of self-efficacy for complex adaptations (coping self-efficacy or self-regulatory efficacy). Certainly we can question the practical utility of separating task self-efficacy from coping self-efficacy when assessing self-efficacy for smoking, condom use, and other behaviors and complex adaptations. Lighting (or not lighting) a cigarette is a simple motor act. Giving up cigarettes, however, is difficult—not because of the physical difficulty involved in lighting up or not lighting up but because of the difficulty encountered coping with the pressures and urges to smoke in various situations and the unpleasant consequences of nicotine withdrawal. Likewise, putting on a condom is easy, but remembering to do so in the heat of passion or daring to ask an amorous partner to do so is difficult. Thus, assessing *task* self-efficacy for smoking (e.g., not striking a match) or condom use (e.g., putting on a condom) may be pointless, but assessing coping self-efficacy is essential.

In most of daily life, in fact, coping self-efficacy is more crucial than task self- efficacy. Most of our valued life goals and successes do not require the performance of physically difficult tasks (e.g., lifting heavy objects, returning a 120 mph tennis serve). Instead, the major obstacles to success in our personal strivings are more similar to those involved in abstaining from smoking and using condoms regularly during sex— dealing with emotional and/or physical discomfort, coping with social disapproval, and so on. However, since complex tasks consist of elemental acts performed under specific circumstances, assessing self-efficacy for the specific "tasks" involved in some complex adaptations may be useful. For example, if I were Andre Agassi's tennis coach, I would be concerned not with his "self-efficacy for winning the U.S. Open," although "winning the U.S. Open" is a marker of performance attainment similar to getting the letter grade A or losing 20 pounds. I would be concerned, instead, with his self-efficacy for serving with speed and accuracy, returning his opponent's serve, hitting an overhead slam, returning a cross-court shot to his backhand, and so on. In a sense, I would be detaching elemental acts (a serve, a backhand return) from a complex adaptation (winning the U.S. Open or winning a specific game or match), but doing so seems useful in this case since coaches are concerned with teaching specific elemental skills and increasing self-efficacy for those skills (although certainly not only with elemental skills).

Kirsch's distinction between task self-efficacy and coping self-efficacy is also the basis for his discussion of the relationship between self-efficacy and intentions. Contrary to what Bandura states, Kirsch does not say that "self-efficacy is equivalent to willingness or intentions" (Bandura, this volume). Instead, Kirsch says that "*task* self-efficacy for *aversive tasks* is equivalent to intentions [but] *coping* self-efficacy is not" (Kirsch, this volume, emphasis added). Because coping self-efficacy is concerned with the complex self-regulation of skills and abilities in the face of challenge and difficulty, coping self-efficacy is essentially self-efficacy (or self-regulatory efficacy) as Bandura defines it. Thus, Kirsch and Bandura agree that self-efficacy for complex self-regulation and the ability to cope with difficult and shifting circumstances are *not* equivalent to intentions. I understand

Kirsch to say that if we ask people about their efficacy for performing *simple motor tasks* that may lead to aversive consequences, their answers will be based not on their assessment of their motoric skills (e.g., the ability to walk, in the case of approaching a snake; or the ability to utter the words "no thanks" when offered a cigarette) but on their assessment of their ability to deal with the potential aversive consequences (e.g., pain, discomfort, unpleasant thoughts and emotions). What Kirsch seems to be saying is that when people say they *cannot* refrain from lighting a cigarette, they did not mean that they do not possess the necessary motor skills, but that they expect to have difficulty dealing with the situational pressures and possible discomforts, which is what coping self-efficacy encompasses.

RESPONSE EXPECTANCIES AND ANXIETY

Kirsch suggests that response expectancies, particularly expected aversive affective reactions such as anxiety, are important in some kinds of behavior, as discussed above. In his criticism of Kirsch's discussion of response expectancies, Bandura states that Kirsch views "expected aversiveness as the prime ruler of human behavior" (Bandura, this volume). Kirsch's claim, however, is much more modest. He suggests, instead, that response expectancies such as expected anxiety are better predictors of subjective responses such as anxiety than is self-efficacy. He also states that "response expectancy is *a determinant* of intentional behavior" (Kirsch, this volume, emphasis added). Kirsch does not state that anxiety produces avoidant behavior. He states, instead, that expected or anticipated anxiety predicts anxiety. He cites research demonstrating that anxiety expectancy accounts for variance in self-reported anxiety when self-efficacy is partialed out and that the relationship between self-efficacy and anxiety disappears when the influence of anxiety expectancy is controlled. In his chapter in this volume, Williams agrees with Kirsch when he concludes, based on his own review of the research, that "anticipations of panic/anxiety are related to anxiety arousal independently of self-efficacy." Williams (this volume) also states that research on people with phobias has shown that "the correlations between anticipated anxiety and level of coping behavior were quite high, averaging about .70 across the various data sets, but these were consistently somewhat lower than the correlations between self-efficacy and behavior, which averaged about .80." Thus, research indicates that anxiety (response) expectancies are good predictors of phobic behavior, although not as good as self-efficacy. Thus, Bandura is right that self-efficacy is the best predictor of phobic behavior, and Kirsch is right that anxiety expectancies are the best predictors of anxiety and are also pretty good predictors of phobic behavior.

Finally, Kirsch does respond to Williams' (this volume) question about how anxiety expectancy generates anxiety. Kirsch states: "Fear is produced by the anticipation of aversive outcomes. For many people, the experience of fear or panic is extremely aversive. Therefore, one would expect them to be frightened by the expectancy that they are about to experience this dreaded feeling" (Kirsch, this volume).

OUTCOMES AND ATTAINMENT MARKERS

Although not discussed in Kirsch's commentary, I want to address Bandura's discussion of the distinction between an outcome and a marker of performance or attainment. Bandura states that getting the letter grade A is not an outcome but rather a marker of a performance or attainment from which outcomes flow. Although getting an A is indeed a marker of performance or attainment, it also can be viewed as an *outcome*—the outcome or consequence of the successful performance of many other behaviors (e.g., studying, taking tests, writing papers) and successful coping with many obstacles to executing these behaviors (e.g., anxiety, fatigue, discouragement, social pressures). Certainly, as Bandura indicates, wanted or unwanted outcomes may occur if one gets an A in a course; but those outcomes (e.g., social approval) may lead to other outcomes (e.g., a high-paying job), which may lead to other outcomes (e.g., a big house and a fancy car), ad infinitum. Viewing a good job as an outcome that results from getting good grades in college does not prevent us from viewing the good grades as an outcome of other behaviors. In fact, it is useful to do so. Students study hard for a test to get a good grade on that test, which is the most proximal outcome for which they are striving. The A in the course and the resulting social approval and high-paying job come later. Viewing any of these events as outcomes does not prevent us from viewing the other events as outcomes.

Another example may help. As Bandura states, "people do not struggle to shed pounds just to shed pounds" (Bandura, this volume); they do so to be healthier and look more attractive. Likewise, however, people do not count calories just to count calories; they do so to shed pounds; and they view shedding pounds as a possible outcome of counting calories. If people who are trying to lose weight did not believe that losing weight might be the outcome of counting calories and exercising, they would probably throw away their calorie charts and walking shoes. In working with a client who wants to lose 20 pounds, I would indeed focus on the benefits (outcomes) of losing 20 pounds (the marker of attainment). However, because I would want to motivate the client to perform specific weight-loss strategies, I would want him to view losing weight as the outcome of implementing those strategies. Outcomes occur at various levels, and some outcomes lead to other outcomes. Studying and attending class may lead to a college degree, which may lead to a higher income, which may lead to nice clothes and stereos.

Certainly, as Bandura indicates, the practice of seeing everything as an outcome of something else can be extended to the point of absurdity. For example, reading a page of print is the outcome of numerous eye movements, but I would not advocate assessing self-efficacy for "rapidly moving your eyes across a line of print" if I were assessing self-efficacy for study skills. Seeing an event such as getting an A or losing 20 pounds as both a marker of attainment or performance *and* as an outcome that results from certain behaviors and that leads to other outcomes is not inherently illogical or problematic. In fact, sometimes it is eminently practical.

INDEX